Sam Feinstein, Group ’55, and Midcentury Abstraction in Philadelphia

WoodmereArtMuseum

Woodmere is grateful to the Samuel L. Feinstein Trust and the Muriel and Mary Frances Kiley Foundation for their support of this exhibition and catalogue.

Woodmere Art Museum receives state arts funding support through a grant from the Pennsylvania Council on the Arts, a state agency funded by the Commonwealth of Pennsylvania and the National Endowment for the Arts, a federal agency.

Support provided in part by The Philadelphia Cultural Fund.

Front cover: Pieta I (detail of Fig. 6), 1956, by Sam Feinstein (Samuel L. Feinstein Trust)

ISBN Number: 978-1-888008-01-2

Photography by Jack Ramsdale unless otherwise noted. Catalogue designed by Barb Barnett and Kelly Edwards; edited by Gretchen Dykstra and Lucy Medrich.

EXHIBITIONS

Sam Feinstein: The Early Years

September 26, 2020–January 24, 2021
at Springside Chestnut Hill Academy

Group '55 and Midcentury Abstraction in Philadelphia

September 26, 2020–January 24, 2021
at Woodmere Art Museum

Sam Feinstein: Immersive Abstraction

July 24, 2020–January 24, 2021
at Woodmere Art Museum

CONTENTS

FOREWORD

WILLIAM R. VALERIO, PHD

The Patricia Van Burgh Allison Director and Chief Executive Officer

Sam Feinstein: The Early Years at Springside Chestnut Hill Academy (SCH), together with *Group '55 and Midcentury Abstraction in Philadelphia* and *Sam Feinstein: Immersive Abstraction* at Woodmere, showcase a unique shared history in Philadelphia's cultural and educational community: Feinstein and his wife Barbara Crawford were teachers at Springside Chestnut Hill Academy, and their impact on the life of the school is deep. As chronicled in these pages, many of their students entered into lifelong journeys in the arts as a result of their inspiration. They were also leading players in a movement that changed the art scene of Philadelphia more broadly. Feinstein was the leader of Group '55, an alliance of artists who, in the late 1950s, cracked the conservative shell of the city's art scene, opening many minds to the beauty and intellectual challenges of abstraction, which was then an avant-garde phenomenon in American art.

Unlike most of the Abstract Expressionists in New York, Feinstein, Crawford, and their many Philadelphia counterparts were educators and artists in equal measure: they not only taught at SCH and in our city's esteemed professional art schools and academies, but also organized public forums at the Free Library of Philadelphia, broadcasting their ideas and inspiring a public dialogue that would continue in the galleries where their exhibitions took place and on the pages of the newspapers that reviewed their work. Group '55 was interdisciplinary in its approach to abstraction as a language in arts, and the forums were well attended because they included the voices of painters alongside dancers, composers, and architects, embracing a wide array of interests and professions.

Together with my friend Stephen Druggan, head of school at SCH, and all my colleagues there and at Woodmere, I extend deepest gratitude to Patricia Stark Feinstein, Sam Feinstein's widow, who approached us with a vision of the shared opportunity associated with rediscovering Feinstein, Crawford, and Group '55 and partnering with us to tell a story about these artists. Thank you, Pat, for sharing your extraordinary archive of documents, forum transcripts, newspaper clippings, gallery ephemera, and other materials, and for the financial support that makes these exhibitions possible. Your essay, *Understanding Sam Feinstein*, offers a portrait of an artist devoted to sharing his creative passions in different ways at different phases of his life. We are grateful as well to Sascha Feinstein, the artist's son, for his contributions to this project and his essay, *My Father's Lasting Lessons on Art*, which is about art as a vital source of life-giving energy.

Special thanks also to Pia Druggan, Ellen Fishman, and Melissa Maddonni Haims at SCH, who organized the school's show and have been wonderful partners all along. We also extend our appreciation to Theodore Clattenberg, Thorpe Feidt, Binney Meigs, Lewis Tanner Moore, Bonnie Warwick, and John Wenzel, who shared their remembrances.

The three exhibitions also fill an important gap in the scholarship on modernism in Philadelphia. In the pages of this catalogue, guest curator Barbara A. Wolanin chronicles the story of Group '55

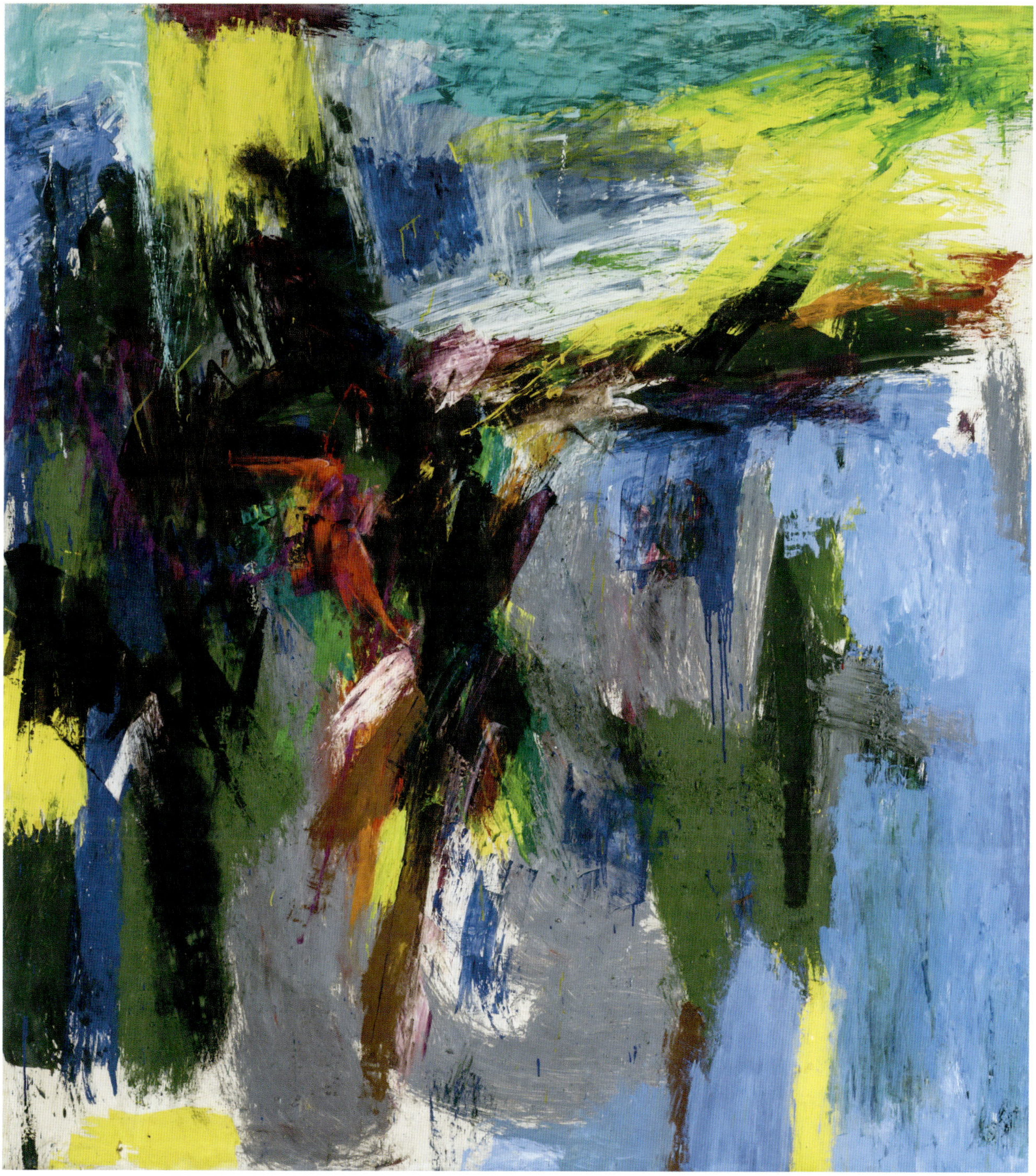

FIGURE 1. **Untitled**, 1959, by Sam Feinstein (Samuel L. Feinstein Trust)

FIGURE 2. **Untitled**, 1960, by Michael Ciliberti (Woodmere Art Museum: Gift of the artist, 2016) Photograph by Rick Echelmeyer

and the Philadelphia Abstract Artists (the offshoot group that included many of the same artists that continued into the 1960s) and writes compellingly about the major exhibitions, public forums, and critical reception that gave shape to the movement. In so doing, she demonstrates that the accomplishments of Feinstein and the artists of Group '55 represent a hitherto unexplored bridge between modernist practices in early twentieth-century Philadelphia and the art of today. More specifically, the artists of Group '55 drew strength from the legacy of the city's great modernist Arthur B. Carles, and followed his example and direct encouragement to embrace the teachings of German émigré and abstract painter Hans Hofmann, who, like Carles, was one of the century's great colorists. Feinstein was also a major champion of Hofmann. This mutual admiration and cross fertilization of ideas between artists represent a major current American art in general, and it continues to inspire painters today. With Wolanin's expertise in Carles, her scholarship on Quita Brodhead and Jane Piper (who were part of Group '55), and her ongoing interaction with the contemporary artists of Philadelphia, there could be no art historian better suited to conveying the importance of Group '55 to the cross-generational trajectory of the arts in Philadelphia and to the big picture of American art. We extend our deepest gratitude.

That this catalogue tells the story of Group '55 as an interdisciplinary movement is due to the contributions of three additional authors. Victoria Schuh, who writes about Malvena Taiz and modern dance in Philadelphia, was also involved in the research and organization of archival materials that made this exhibition possible. Thomas Patteson writes about composers Joseph Castaldo, Vincent Persichetti, and George Rochberg. Izzy Kornblatt writes about the participation in Group '55 of architect Louis Kahn, the most renowned figure in our story. Kornblatt's view of Kahn is that of a Philadelphian through and through, whose embrace of the visual arts was an essential component of his vision.

Many family members of artists and gallerists embraced this show and expressed confidence in the importance of the history we pieced together including, Safiya Carter, Lori Austin, Flora Becker, Virginia Mesibov, Sydney Milliken, Andrea Wagman-Christian, Mary Rood Hendler, and Victoria Angela. We thank them for their generous sharing of information, photographs, and recollections. Many have also donated important paintings to Woodmere, such that the story of Group '55 and its many voices are now embedded in the museum's collection: Reid and Dorothy Bechtle, Charlie Brodhead, Barbara Gillette Price, McCormick Gallery, Fredrica and Howard Wagman, Gregory and Candace Wilkin, Rosina Feldman, Harvey S. Shipley Miller, the Estate of Raymond Hendler, Berry Campbell, the Lachman Family, Ronald Rumford, Karen Segal, and Roslyn Silverman Hahn. We owe special thanks also to Peter Paone for sharing his account of Philadelphia's artistic climate in the 1950s, and to lenders to the exhibition: Elizabeth Osborne, Patrick Terenchin, Esther and Stephen Hrabrick, Andrea Herr-Turoff, Laurie Wagman, the Sanford Greenberg Estate, and the Estate of Mitchel G. Wagman. Special thanks to William Whitaker, curator and collections manager of the Architectural Archives at the University of Pennsylvania, for helping us imagine how best to represent Louis Kahn in our exhibition.

Finally, it is my privilege to know and to have visited the homes and studios of two artists who were part of Group '55. Margo Allman was a student of Feinstein and is a practicing artist today who recently exhibited her work at the Delaware Art Museum. The late Michael Ciliberti was a neighbor here in Chestnut Hill. A long-standing member of Woodmere and a wonderful artist, Ciliberti came to me early in the years of my directorship and shared his memories of Group '55, an exciting chapter in his career. To Valerie and Michael Ciliberti, thank you both for making me want to know more, and for preparing me to understand the significance of the project that is realized in this catalogue and exhibition. Woodmere's friend, the artist Bill Scott, deserves special recognition for being a sounding board in this undertaking and for his championing of so many of the artists who are part of this important history. We are also inspired by the work of Sid Sachs, chief curator and director of exhibitions at the Rosenwald-Wolf Gallery, University of the Arts, and his recent exhibition, *Invisible City: Philadelphia and the Vernacular Avant-garde*, which included Group '55. Woodmere's curatorial and education staff—Laura Heemer, Rachel Hruszkewycz, Amanda Monroe, Rick Ortwein, and Hildy Tow—executed every aspect of this exhibition and catalogue with the highest level of professionalism and care. Finally and once again, we all join in expressing immense gratitude to Patricia Stark Feinstein, whose passion permeates every aspect of the catalogue and exhibitions.

FOREWORD

STEPHEN DRUGGAN, EDD
Head of School, Springside Chestnut Hill Academy

If there is one constant that has united and inspired humanity throughout history and across cultures, it is art. As I have learned during my time at Springside Chestnut Hill Academy (SCH), our talented arts faculty stands on the shoulders of the greats who preceded them, in particular Sam Feinstein and Barbara Crawford.

Our special exhibition *Sam Feinstein: The Early Years* is a companion to Woodmere's *Group '55 and Midcentury Abstraction in Philadelphia* and *Sam Feinstein: Immersive Abstraction*. Sam was our art director and taught at Chestnut Hill Academy (then the boys school) from 1938 to 1942, after which Barbara took over his post. Our show traces Sam's journey toward Abstract Expressionism through his watercolors, oil paintings, and illustrations from the 1930s through the mid-1950s, along with a film he made about Hans Hofmann and a selection of works by Barbara.

The journey that led to this exhibition began in the fall of 2018, when Patricia Stark Feinstein, Sam's widow and head of the Samuel L. Feinstein Trust, approached the school and generously offered to loan us a number of canvases. Tasked with selecting that work, our curatorial team set off to meet Pat in New York, where she shared stories of Sam's career as an artist, his years teaching at our school, and his first marriage, to Barbara. On that fortuitous day, the Woodmere team was also present, and the idea for a joint exhibition was born.

After that meeting, the Feinstein Trust lent us three large, breathtaking canvases that currently adorn the walls of our McCausland Lower School. When one walks into the building's main entrance, *Starry Night* (1970s–80s) and *Opposing Elements* (1980s) capture the eye with their bright blues, reds, and yellows. Upstairs, in Doran Hall, one cannot help but be mesmerized by the explosion of colors and light coming from Sam's untitled painting of 1990–2002. Pat subsequently spent the day with our students and introduced them to these works, as well as

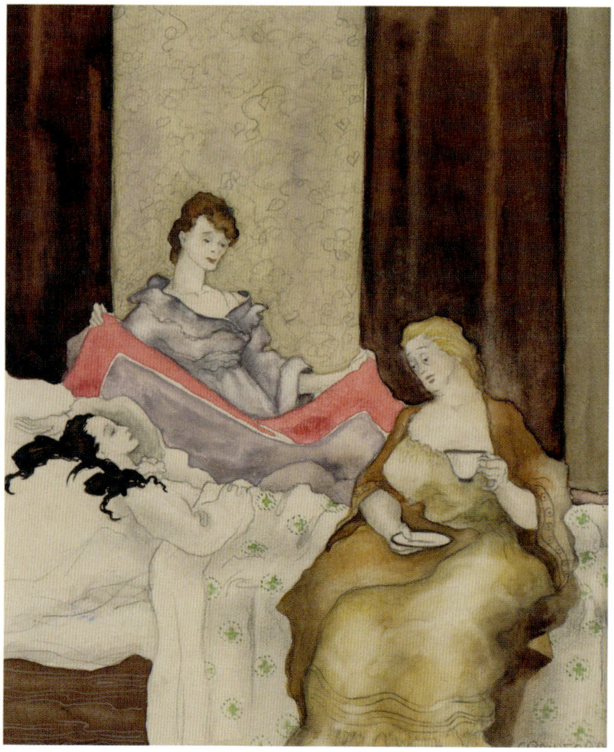

FIGURE 3. **Sleeping Beauty**, 1935, by Barbara Crawford (Springside Chestnut Hill Academy)

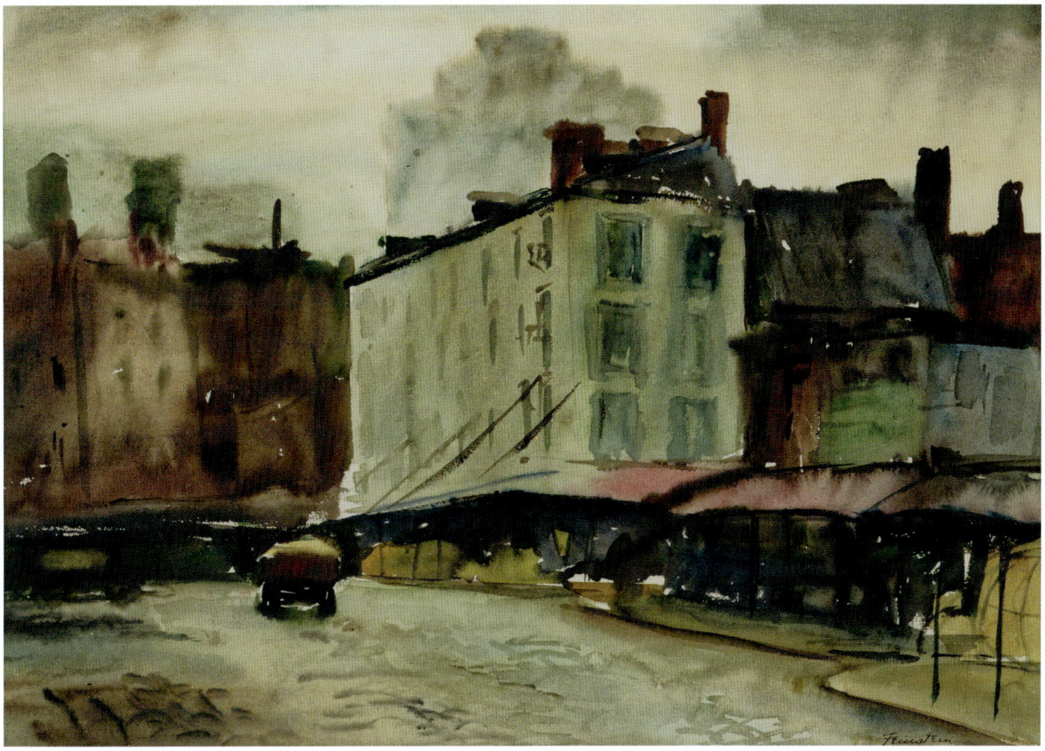

FIGURE 4. **Market AM**, 1930s, by Sam Feinstein (Samuel L. Feinstein Trust)

to some of Sam's earlier, figurative paintings. The students were energized by her stories about Sam and asked many perceptive questions, to which Pat responded with characteristic insight and grace.

When I became head of SCH, one of my first meetings was with Bill Valerio, Woodmere's director. That also happened to be the day that Germantown Avenue was closed so that Harry Bertoia's incredible sculpture *Free Interpretation of Plant Forms* could be moved onto Woodmere's grounds. It was at this meeting that I learned of the Museum's mission: to tell the story of Philadelphia's art and artists. We too treasure and believe in furthering the arts in Chestnut Hill and are fortunate to partner with the Museum for student visits and poetry slams. We extend our very special thanks to Bill and the entire Woodmere team for partnering with us on this important exhibition and catalogue.

This exhibition would not be possible without the generous support and mentorship of Pat and the Feinstein Trust. Pat shared a wealth of information, archival photographs, films, and research, and she guided us in choosing work and related ephemera for the exhibition. We are grateful to the Chestnut Hill Academy and Springside School alumni who shared their stories about Sam and Barbara with us: John Wenzel '41, Theodore Clattenberg '59, Thorpe Feidt '59, Bonnie Warwick '61, Lewis Tanner Moore '71, and Binney Meigs '72. And we extend our thanks to Sascha Feinstein, who generously contributed an essay on his father for this catalogue.

Thank you as well to SCH's wonderful team: Ellen Fishman, our director of the arts and new media, for spearheading this venture; Melissa Maddonni Haims, parent volunteer and our amazing curator; and my wife, Pia Druggan, art historian and assistant curator for this show.

Group '55 and Midcentury Abstraction in Philadelphia

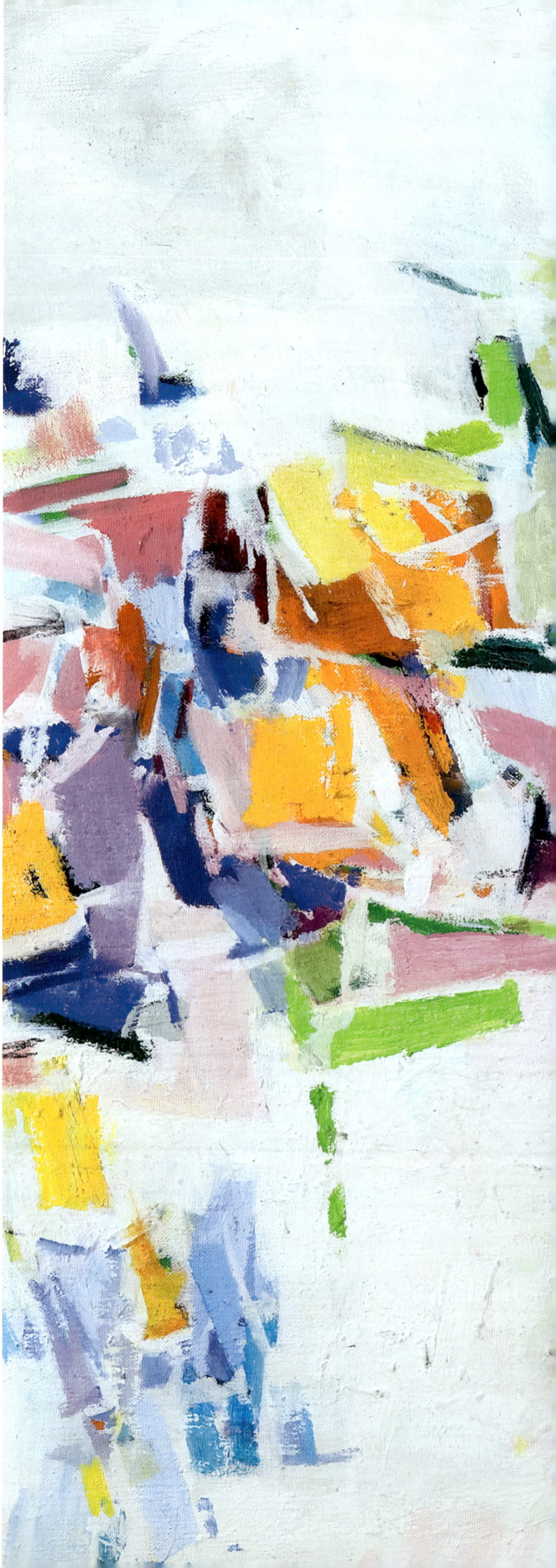

FIGURE 5. Trade Winds 2 (detail of Fig. 153), 1958, by Jane Piper (Woodmere Art Museum: Gift of Karen Segal, 2017) Photograph by Rick Echelmeyer

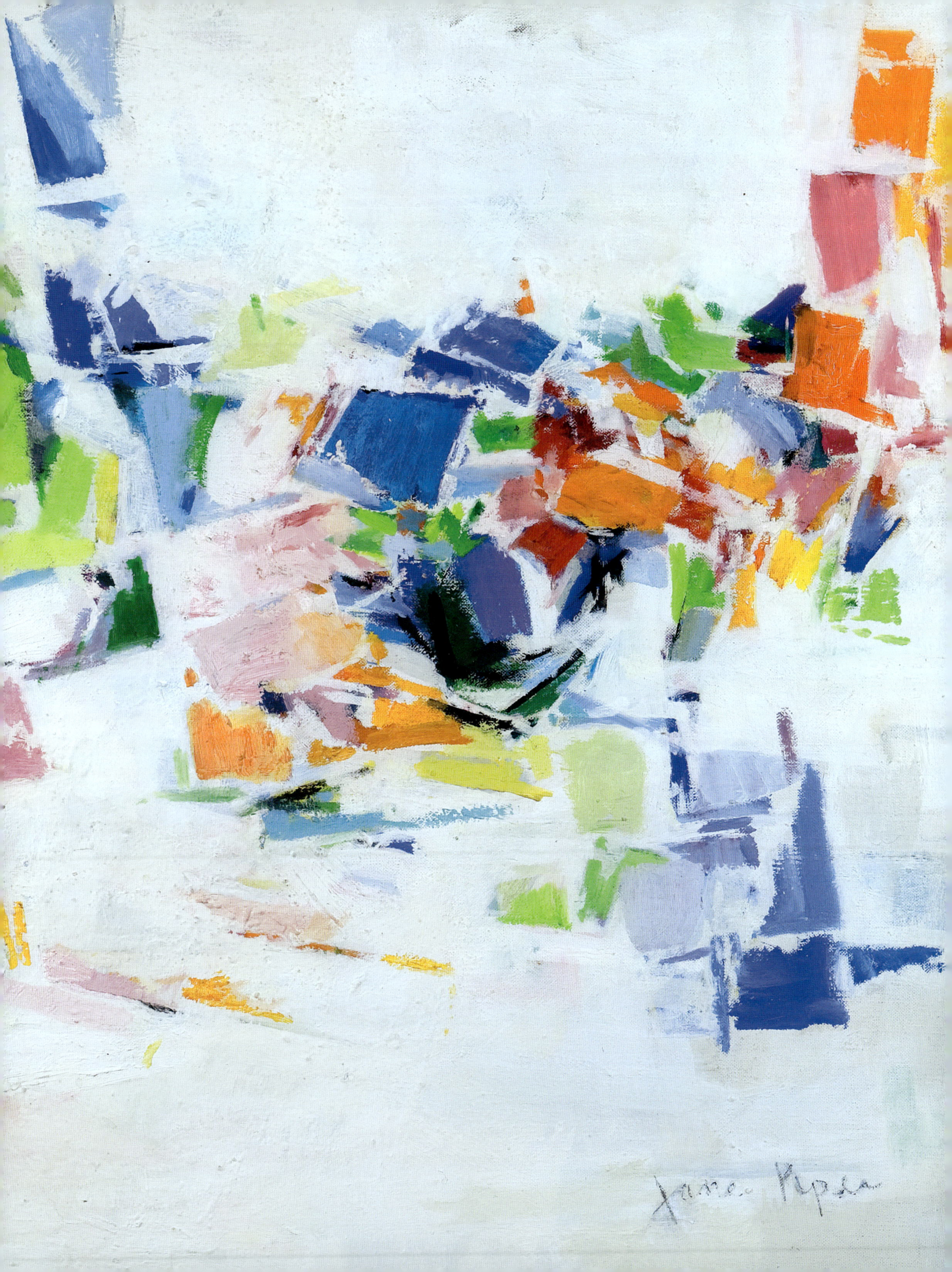
Jane Piper

ABSTRACT PAINTING IN PHILADELPHIA: GROUP '55 AND THE PHILADELPHIA ABSTRACT ARTISTS

BARBARA A. WOLANIN, PHD

The story of a passionate contingent of dedicated abstract painters who came together in staid 1950s Philadelphia to discuss the intellectual and philosophical basis for their art is being told in detail here for the first time. Excited about sharing their work and exploring connections among various forms of creative expression, these artists organized exhibitions and well-attended public forums. Although little known today, Group '55, organized and led by Sam Feinstein, and its offshoot, Philadelphia Abstract Artists, led by C. Ronald Bechtle, were memorable and life changing for the artists and provided thought-provoking encounters with the contemporary art for the many thousands of people who saw their shows and were in their audiences. Their interactions had a lasting impact on the Philadelphia art community as well as on their own art and teaching, on the work of future generations of Philadelphia artists, and on the cultural life of the city.

Feinstein played a pivotal role in this story. His own distinctive abstract painting evolved directly out of his close association with the pioneering Abstract Expressionists, especially Hans Hofmann. His dedication to teaching others equaled his commitment to his own art. His crusade as an educator comprised not only his own painting classes. It was expanded by his important voice as a writer for *Art Digest* and as a public speaker. His enormous ambition included educating the wider public about the significance of abstract painting and its place in the history of art. The strength of his convictions and the energy he put into leading Group '55 were admired, but they also sparked rebellion and led to the breaking apart of his original group.

The groups' activities remained vivid for the participants for the rest of their lives. Early member Michael Ciliberti, who was active in both groups and titled one of his paintings *Group '55* (fig. 8), conveyed his enthusiasm:

> Group '55 was the most exciting thing in my life. I was well aware of the Abstract Expressionists in New York, and to meet artists that were working in that same manner in Philadelphia was invigorating and stimulating for my own creative work. It also provided the opportunity to listen to creative people in other fields—musicians, architects, and philosophers whose thinking in many ways paralleled that of the abstract painters.[1]

Laurie Wagman, who accompanied her husband, Mitchel G. Wagman, to gatherings, recalls: "Group '55 and the Philadelphia Abstract Artists reflected the resilience and courage of unconventional thinkers. . . . At a time of societal conservatism, they shared a vision of complex connection that included the humanities, philosophical exploration, and art criticism. [They were trying to] communicate a new world."[2] Artist Ben Herr, a student at the time, remembered: "There was just this time when amazing things were happening—it was a ball. . . . You didn't know it at the time how special it was."[3]

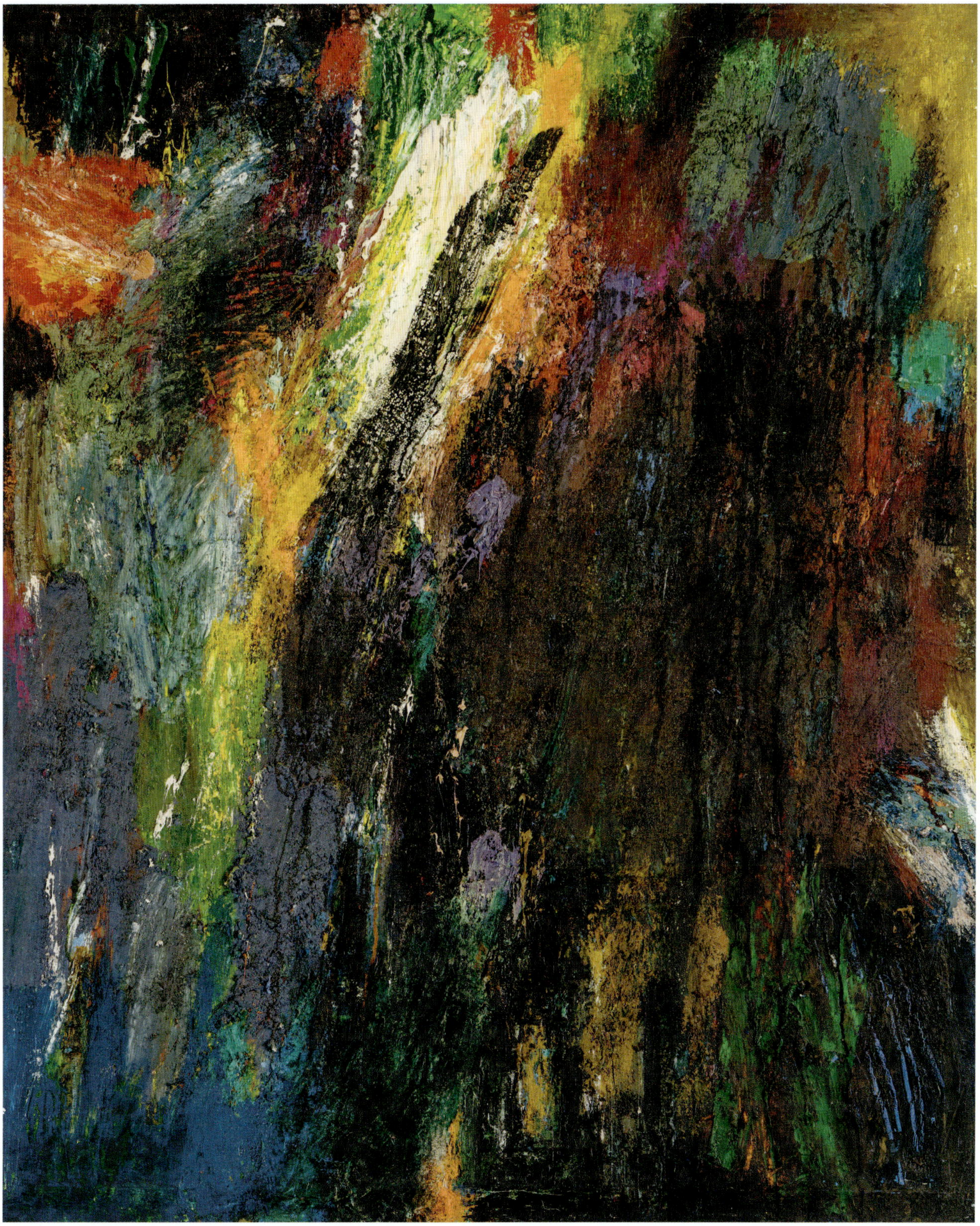

FIGURE 6. Pieta I, 1956, by Sam Feinstein (Samuel L. Feinstein Trust)

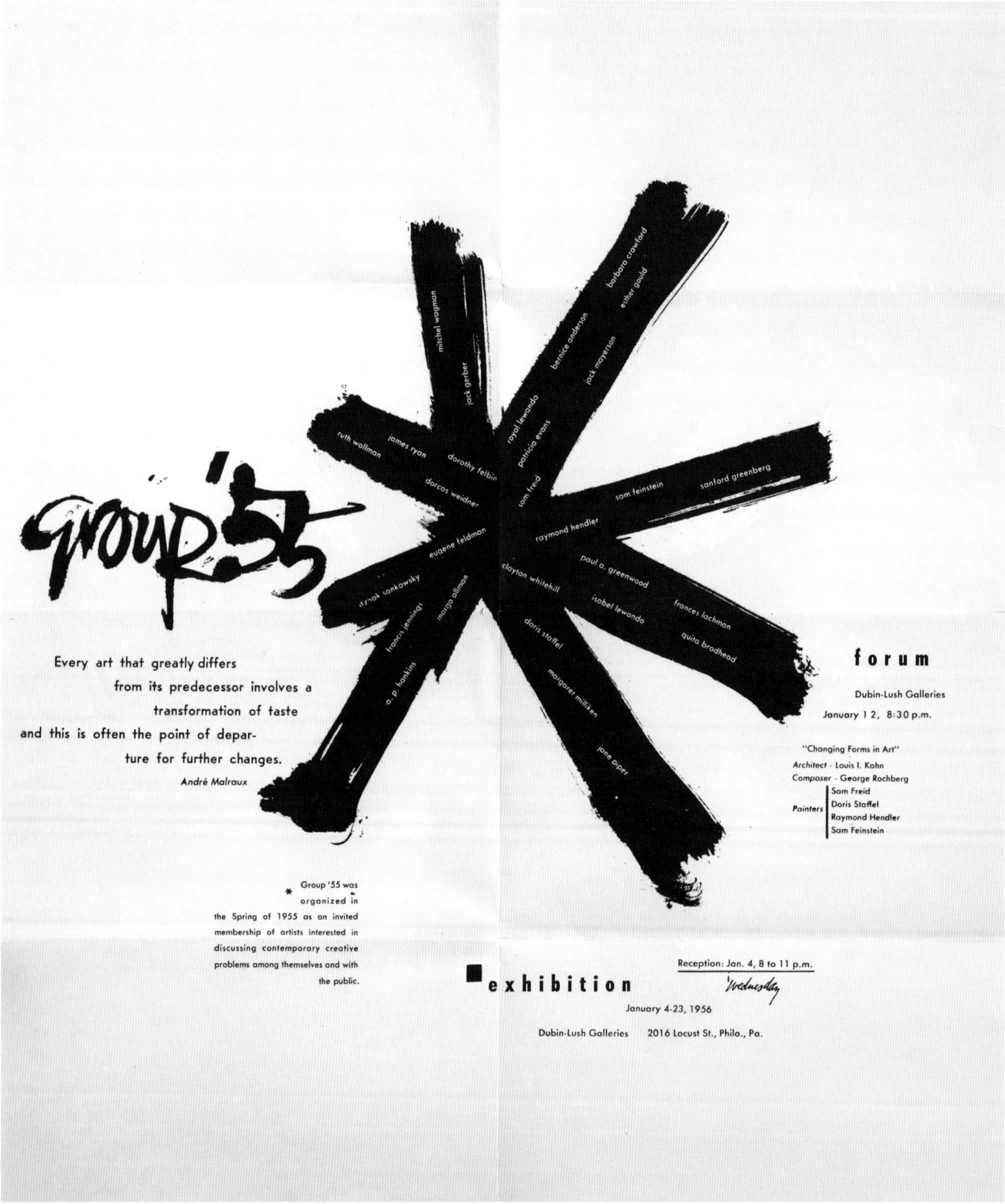

FIGURE 7. Poster announcing the first Group '55 exhibition and forum (Samuel L. Feinstein Trust)

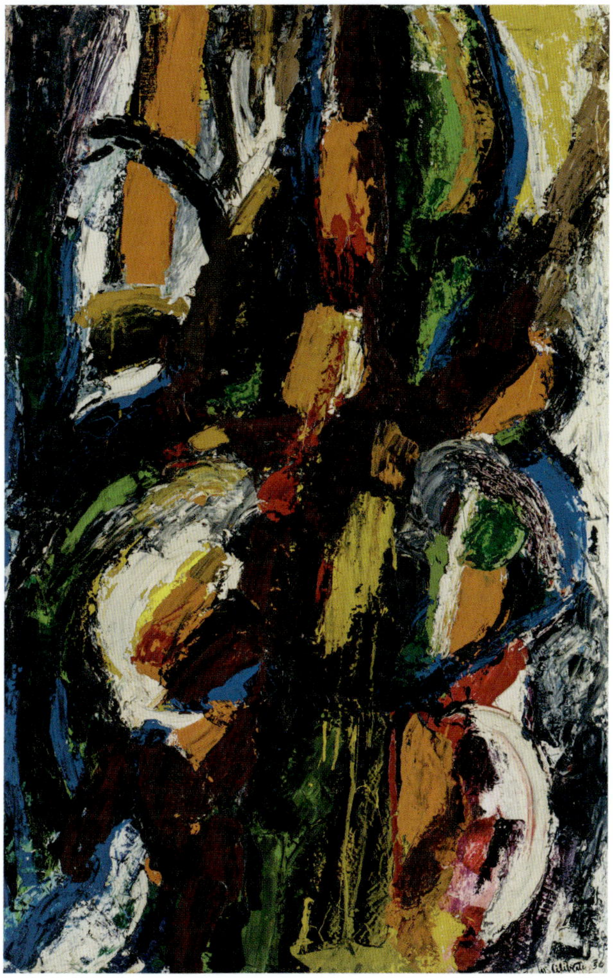

FIGURE 8. **Group '55**, c. 1956, by Michael Ciliberti (Courtesy of Valerie Ciliberti)

Members Quita Brodhead, Sanford Greenberg, Jane Piper, and Doris Staffel also spoke of Group '55 with pride and pleasure of having been part of the group. They were impressed by hearing prominent Philadelphia architect Louis Kahn, who asserted at one of the group's events:

> Beauty cannot be built into anything. It is something which grows out of acceptance, out of love, out of affinity, out of empathy, and out of all the things you speak about, that beauty must emerge [into] something which does warm you, that you feel toward it, learn from it, grow from it.[4]

Group '55 was launched with an invitation from Sam Feinstein to about fifteen of Philadelphia's abstract artists to gather at the Dubin Gallery in May 1955 and to "bring your ideas about aims, activities, and a name for the group."[5] At a follow-up meeting in September, the artists voted to call themselves simply "Group '55," in honor of the year they began.

A poster announcing the group's first exhibition and forum listed the names of members and described the purpose of the fledgling organization (fig. 7): "Group '55 was organized in the spring of 1955 as an invited membership of artists interested in discussing contemporary creative problems among themselves and with the public." Feinstein understood their efforts in the context of the history of art: "Although such discussions have usually centered around contemporary art, we are primarily interested in relating the art of the present to that of the past."[6] Feinstein drafted different versions of the mission statement; one read: "Group '55 is composed of artists united by their exploration of contemporary forms to express the spirit of our time." Members wanted to nurture a community of artists and thinkers, promoting the exchange of ideas. They believed that educating the public about abstract art was their civic responsibility. This foundational emphasis no doubt resonated with members who were teachers, but it was also part of Philadelphia's Quaker heritage and its tradition of working for the common good.

In January 1956, the energetic coterie of two dozen artists led by Feinstein was up and running, with a group exhibition at the Dubin-Lush Galleries (which had been recently incorporated at 2016 Locust Street in Philadelphia) and the first in a series of thought-provoking public forums and programs that brought abstract painters and representatives of other creative fields, such as architecture, dance, and music, together with laymen from a variety of professions. The goal was to explore parallels and connections between abstract painting and other fields to better understand its significance in the contemporary world. Under Feinstein's leadership, the group would organize a dozen exhibitions and an equal number of related programs over the next two and a half years. Differing opinions and personality conflicts within Group '55 ultimately led many members to split into a new group, Philadelphia Abstract Artists, led by Bechtle, which mounted seven exhibitions from 1957 to 1962, eventually including some additional artists in their shows. Through the 1960s some of these artists continued to exhibit and teach together, carrying on some of the ideas and ideals of Group '55. Fortunately, leaders of both groups recognized the importance of their work for posterity and carefully preserved the printed materials, meeting minutes, recordings, and correspondence that have made it possible to tell their story.[7]

Art of the Present: Abstract Expressionism

The Group '55 artists were exploring an abstract language for their painting and wanted their art to be better understood and appreciated. For them, representational art belonged to the past, although they appreciated the underlying visual elements—form, space, color—that made the work of past masters expressive and meaningful. They sometimes applied the term "Abstract Expressionism," embraced by the New York pioneers they admired, to their own work, but they more often used terms such as "representational" and "nonrepresentational" or "abstract art."

Like the artists of the New York School—Jackson Pollock, Willem de Kooning, and Mark Rothko, among others—members of Group '55 lived in the dynamic but turbulent and terrifying postwar period. Questioning the old gave rise to new forms of expression. The world was overshadowed by the horrors of World War II and the fear of annihilation by the atomic bomb, heightened by the Cold War. Liberal thinkers were seen as threatening and were being attacked. Artists feared being accused of Communist affiliations by the members of the House Un-American Activities Committee and then by Senator Joseph McCarthy. In a 1954 letter to the national art magazine *Art Digest*, for which Feinstein was writing, Carroll A. Osborne criticized the publication for its "left-wing odors, instilled in the paintings of 'abstract artists' who . . . make designs, smears, blotches and scribblings of the brush and pen; thereby calling it art and attempt to push onto the public the idea they are the last word in the art world."[8]

Artists took note of scientific advancements that were changing the concepts of matter and the universe, such as Albert Einstein's theories of space-time, the uncertainty principle, and quantum mechanics. Compelling microscopic and macroscopic images of the world were being made for the first time. These ideas permeated discussions among Philadelphia painters. As Staffel remembered:

> [We were] interested in both the conventional view of things and the ultimate view of things—so that we talked on basically two levels, and the group was composed of most of the people that we knew who were painting with concern for the essences of things rather than the

appearance of things. . . . The universe is made of, is composed of particles that are impermanent and that are always changing but that universe is changed by the viewer and it is trying to find for yourself a language in forms that expresses that excitement about the, you would almost say, the arriving, and the duration and the succession of a moment.[9]

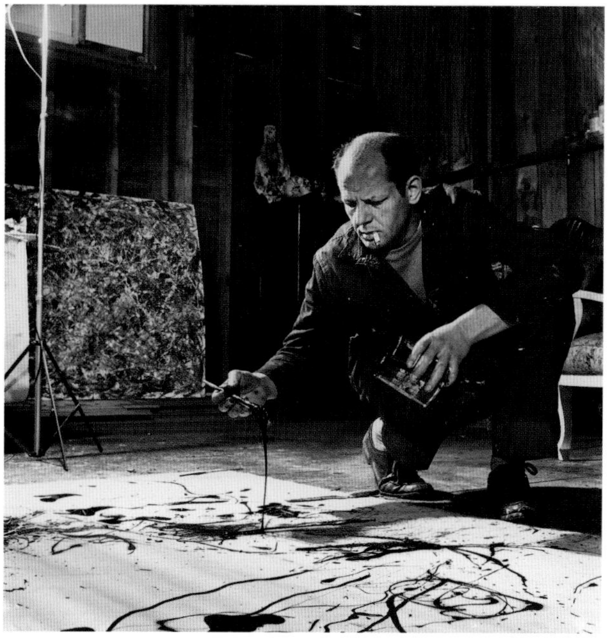

FIGURE 9. Jackson Pollock in his studio, April 1, 1949. Photograph by Martha Holmes. The LIFE Picture Collection via Getty Images

Group '55 painters believed strongly that abstract art was the art of their time. Pollock had broken from tradition with allover skeins of paint layered on canvases on the floor. He had his first solo exhibition in 1943; the following year, the Museum of Modern Art bought one of his works. And although the popular press initially made fun of his drip paintings, by 1949 *Life* magazine was posing the question, "Is he the greatest living painter in the United States?"[10] A few galleries were presenting solo shows for experimental artists, but it was not until Leo Castelli hung the now-famous *Ninth Street Show* in Greenwich Village in 1951, just four years before the Philadelphia group first met, that New York artists working independently exhibited together for the first time. Thomas Hess championed the new movement in *Art News*. Rival critics Harold Rosenberg and Clement Greenberg began focusing on the "new expressive abstraction." Rosenberg described the new work as "action painting" and the canvas as "an arena in which to act." Taking a formalist approach and tracing a line through the history of modern art, Greenberg focused on abstraction as being avant-garde, dismissing subject matter and stressing the importance of the flat picture plane. Both writers foresaw that New York would become the new international center of modern art. Both had learned from and admired Hofmann, who, since his arrival in the United States in 1932, had been the primary exponent of the artistic principles developed in Europe by Matisse, Picasso, Kandinsky, and others.[11]

Having studied with Hofmann in Provincetown and New York, Feinstein integrated the elder artist's concepts and insights with his own and produced a film that documents Hofmann's process and statements on painting. Beginning in 1953 as Philadelphia correspondent for *Art Digest*, Feinstein sympathetically reviewed many of the important New York artists and was part of the New York art scene, as he worked there as a freelance filmmaker during the week. By 1956, the so-called second generation of Abstract Expressionists were gaining attention in exhibitions like the Museum of Modern Art's *Twelve Americans*. Philadelphia artists often traveled to New York to catch the latest shows and meet the artists.

The New York avant-garde had been gathering over drinks at the Cedar Bar and had rented space nearby for their own Eighth Street Club, where they would talk, party, and gather on Friday nights to engage with speakers such as political theorist Hannah Arendt, scholar Joseph Campbell, composers John Cage and Virgil Thomson, philosophers, proponents of Zen Buddhism, and poets. The talks and panels were stimulating for the Philadelphia artists who attended, including Feinstein, Bechtle, Piper, Wagman, and Raymond Hendler.[12] Although the Club's panels undoubtedly inspired Group '55 forums, it is important to note that the Club's audience was limited to member artists, gallery owners, critics, and invited guests. In contrast, the ambitious goal of the Philadelphia group was to educate the public at large.

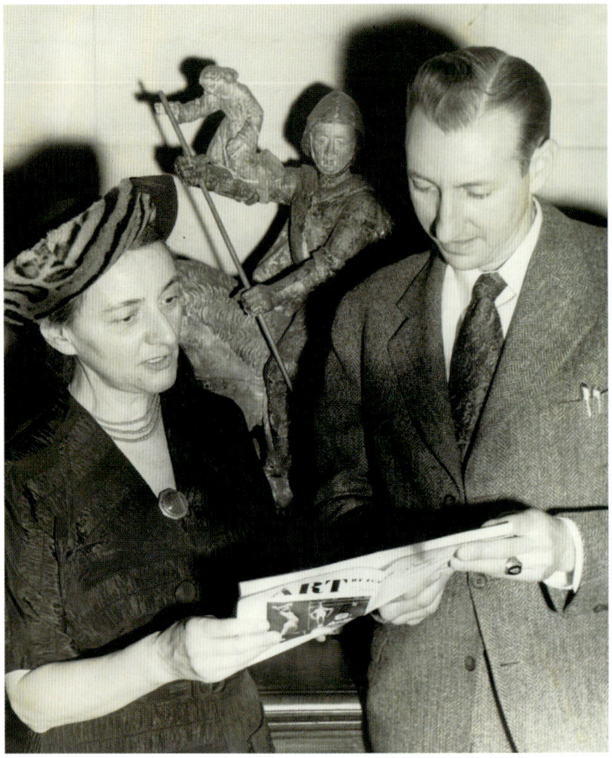

FIGURE 10. Washington County Museum of Fine Arts director Bruce Etchison and Philadelphia art critic Dorothy Grafly, juror for 1951 Cumberland Valley Artists Exhibition with the January 1950 issue of *Art in Focus*, 1951 (Archives, Washington County Museum of Fine Arts, Hagerstown, MD)

Even with the growing recognition of Abstract Expressionism by writers and museums, many critics and much of the public remained skeptical of paint freely brushed and dripped or pictures that did not represent familiar or recognizable subjects. Pollock was facetiously called "Jack the Dripper" by *Time* magazine at the time of his death, in 1956. Longtime New York art critic Emily Genauer wrote an article titled "Critic Deplores New Art of Nothingness" about how little meaning she found in the abstract work of Franz Kline and David Smith, which she saw as devoid of "symbolic, emotional, or formal significance."[13] As late as 1959, art critic John Canaday, in his first article for the *New York Times*, expressed his hatred of Abstract Expressionism and derided the artists painting in the style as "charlatans."[14] So it is perhaps unsurprising that there was resistance to abstract art in Philadelphia as well.

Often in Philadelphia newspaper reviews and forum discussions, the more general descriptive terms of "abstract," "nonobjective," "nonrepresentative," and even "nonfigurative" were used rather than "Abstract Expressionist." One wonders if perhaps Philadelphia artists were separating themselves from the wild often inebriated behavior and lifestyle of some of the New York artists.

The Sedate Philadelphia Art Scene

For years, the Philadelphia art world had been dominated by the academic and realist tradition grounded in the nineteenth century with Thomas Eakins and the curriculum of the Pennsylvania Academy of the Fine Arts (PAFA), the nation's first museum and art school. PAFA's collection and exhibitions tended to focus on historical and representational art.

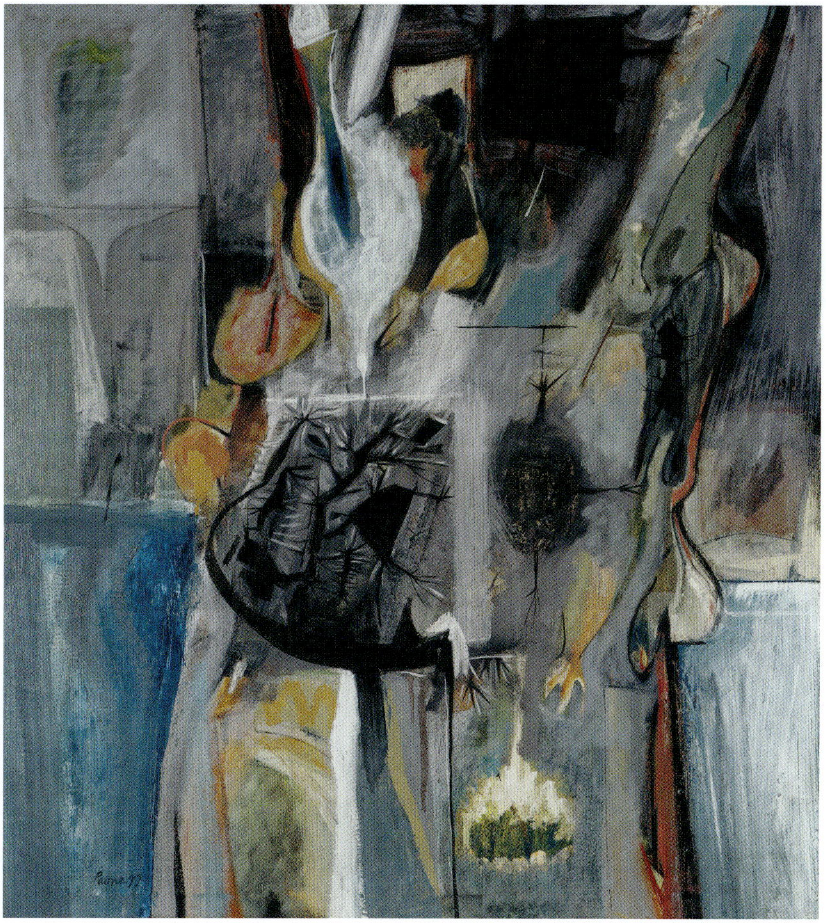

FIGURE 11. **Untitled**, 1957, by Peter Paone (Woodmere Art Museum: Museum purchase, 2019)

This view was echoed by art critic and writer Dorothy Grafly, a force in the Philadelphia art world, who preceded Feinstein as Philadelphia correspondent for *Art Digest* and kept readers abreast of gallery exhibitions and art events through her monthly subscription newsletter, *Art in Focus* (fig. 10). Her comments over the years would reveal her continuing skepticism about abstract art. In a 1955 exhibition review, she concluded, "The great vitality of semiabstract work in the show overshadows out-and-out abstraction which leaves one with a sense of unfulfillment, and a hint of emptiness behind color-space pyrotechnics."[15]

Her father, Charles Grafly, had taught sculpture at PAFA for decades. He had opposed the modernism espoused by some of his fellow instructors, especially Arthur B. Carles, who had participated in and defended the 1913 Armory Show.[16] The ongoing battle between the academics and the modernist teachers continued into the early 1920s. Carles taught the Saturday morning sketch class, encouraging students to follow their own styles and interests but sharing his love of color. He helped bring three exhibitions of modern art to PAFA, ending with one of the Barnes collection in 1923 that was lambasted for being "degenerate." Carles was fired from PAFA in 1925 but continued to teach privately. When he was incapacitated and stopped painting in 1941, his last works foretold the future of American painting. He was considered a "prophet" of Abstract Expressionism, admired by Hofmann.[17]

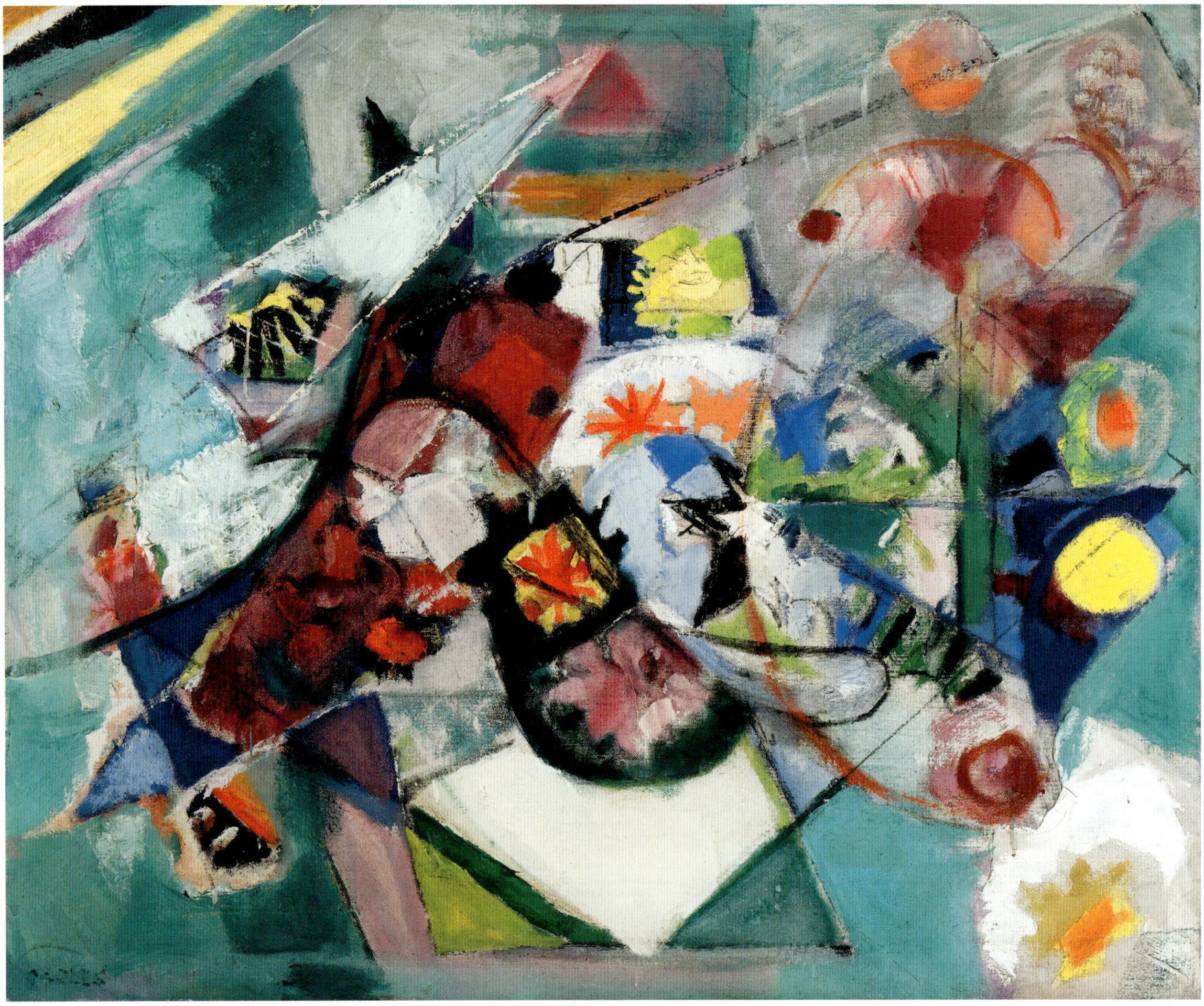

FIGURE 12. **Abstract Bouquet**, 1939, by Arthur B. Carles (Woodmere Art Museum: Partial museum purchase and partial gift of Fredrica and Howard Wagman, 2011) Photograph by Rick Echelmeyer

In 1953, Carles's memorial exhibition was cosponsored by the Philadelphia Museum of Art and held at PAFA. Seen and appreciated by many of the Group '55 painters, it was reviewed for *Art Digest* by Feinstein, who wrote with deep respect for Carles's mastery of color, which he was aiming for in his own work:

> Carles was more than a painter's painter—he was an artist's artist. His handling of pigment alone—the effective sensual harmony of surface—would assure the admiration and despair of the technique-minded. But beyond this is the symphonic color structure of his work. A good Carles (and there are many great ones in this show) has the supple rhythm of a symphony by Mozart. Its component hues are interwoven into a cadence of resonant color. Its forms seem always alert, as if impelled by some inner necessity into an elegant blossoming.[18]

A great Carles is the dynamic *Abstract Bouquet* (fig. 12), now in the collection of Woodmere Art Museum and included in this exhibition, would have been seen by Group '55 artists at the Philadelphia Museum of Art in 1955 and at PAFA in 1958.[19] According to artist Bill Scott, the painting was admired by Piper and Brodhead.

The battle that Carles and his allies fought was renewed in the 1950s. PAFA continued to be a bastion of the nineteenth-century academic tradition, with its annual exhibition juried by realists was just beginning to include abstract work. In contrast, the Philadelphia Museum School of Industrial Art (renamed the Philadelphia College of Art in 1964 and now merged into the University of the Arts) had been "taken over" by abstract artists, according to Peter Paone, then a student who was most interested in figurative art. Although he was experimenting with abstraction at the time, as seen in an untitled work that seems inspired by surrealist figurative imagery and abstract dreamscapes (fig. 11), he was dismayed that drawing classes were gone from the curriculum. Among those teaching abstract painting at the Museum School during this period were Carles's daughter, Mercedes Matter (who was commuting from New York); Piper (also a student of Carles); Staffel; Kline; and Melville Price, who had his students using house paints and four-inch brushes. Paone described a "war" going on in the art world.[20] Another painter who was a student at PAFA at the same time but who embraced abstract painting (fig. 155) was Ben Herr, who became Price's studio assistant in a building where Kline's studio was just a floor away. Herr's strokes of black and his daring inclusion of debris such as burlap in *Gettysburg* (fig. 14) evoke the burning and destruction of war.

A Handful of Brave Galleries

At this time Philadelphians could view or show abstract art in only a few venues. Some Philadelphia abstract artists took part in institutional group exhibitions, including the Friends' Central School annuals.[21] The Philadelphia Art Alliance, at 251 South 18th Street, was a pioneer in showing abstraction in 1949 and 1950, including work by future Group '55 member Bernice Anderson.[22] Advanced work could also be seen in the sixth-floor galleries at Gimbels department store, which had given Carles a solo exhibition as early as 1935.[23] Grafly and future Group '55 member Sam Freid were on the art committee that curated two exhibitions in 1953, including the *One World Art Exhibition*, which represented a wide range of styles.[24]

Among the first private galleries in Philadelphia to show abstract painting was the Dubin Gallery (later Dubin Galleries). Future host of Group '55 Henry P. (Hank) Dubin was one of the few gallery owners supporting abstract painters. At the time *Art in Focus* listed thirty-five or so galleries in the area, many showing antiques or European masters. At the end of 1953 Feinstein described the climate:

> Philadelphians cross Rittenhouse Square making the rounds of the galleries within its radius, and their autumn temper is an index to the coming season. No doubt the usual controversies will ensue over nonrepresentational art. There are many here who still believe that abstraction is the decay of art, and an increasing number who are searching for the penicillin in the mold. Philadelphians know that time will bring the answer.[25]

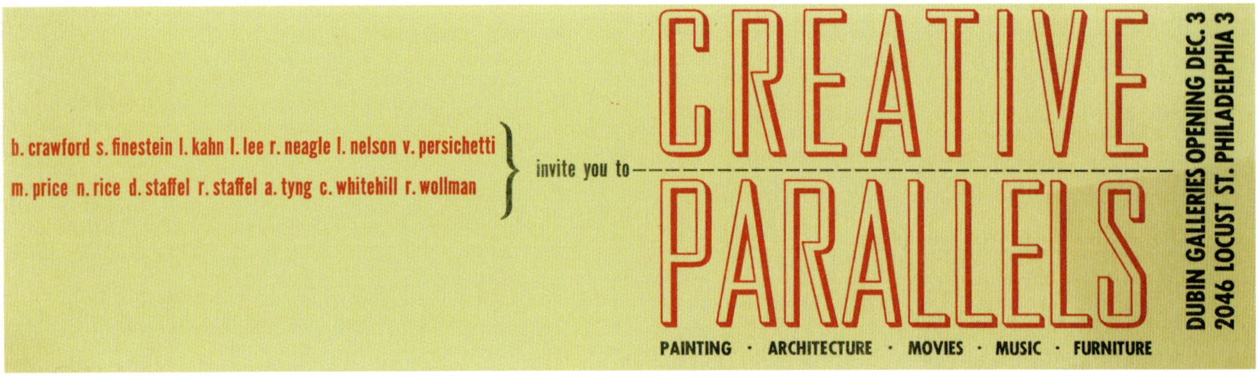

FIGURE 13. Invitation to *Creative Parallels* at the Dubin Galleries (Samuel L. Feinstein Trust)

Dubin was a key player in the story of Group '55. As early as 1949, he hung abstract watercolors by future Group '55 member Ruth Zion, then painting as Ruth Wollman, followed by a show of work by Freid and his wife, Hilda Berger Freid. In 1951, Dubin announced "Paintings by Ray Hendler (fresh from Paris). First one-man show in America," which was followed the next year by "First Philadelphia exhibition by Ken Noland, young Washington painter."[26] Dubin's first gallery was at 312 South 16th Street. In 1950, he moved to 2046 Locust Street, where he showed watercolors by Sam Freid and oils by Staffel.

An early exhibition at the Dubin Galleries in the spirit of later Group '55 forums was *Creative Parallels: Painting, Architecture, Movies, Music, Furniture* (fig. 13), in December 1952. It included paintings by Feinstein and his wife, Barbara Crawford, along with Staffel, Zion, and Clayton Whitehill. Their paintings were shown along with architectural photographs by Kahn, ceramics by Rudolf Staffel, works on paper by composer Vincent Persichetti and architect Anne Tyng, and film notes. Reviewer Gertrude Benson called the show "provocative . . . implying relationships between the arts," suggesting that "the differences between the arts are not as great as their basic unity."[27]

In 1953, Dubin moved to 2016 Locust Street, doing the renovations himself. Over the next year he mounted a show of Piper's paintings as well as an exhibition of drawings by Feinstein and oils by Crawford, perhaps the beginning of the strong connection between Dubin and Feinstein. Anne Lowenberg, then listed as director of the Dubin Galleries, was likely in charge of day-to-day operations, but what role she played in exhibitions is not known.[28] In August 1955, Dubin formed a corporation with another nearby gallery owner, Beryl Lush, to create the Dubin-Lush Galleries. Later that year Dubin-Lush exhibited future Group '55 members Sanford Greenberg, whose show sold out, and Eugene Feldman, in addition to Larry Day, who was then painting abstractly, as in *Various Asides* (fig. 19). Day was in the circle of the Group '55 artists but never became a member.

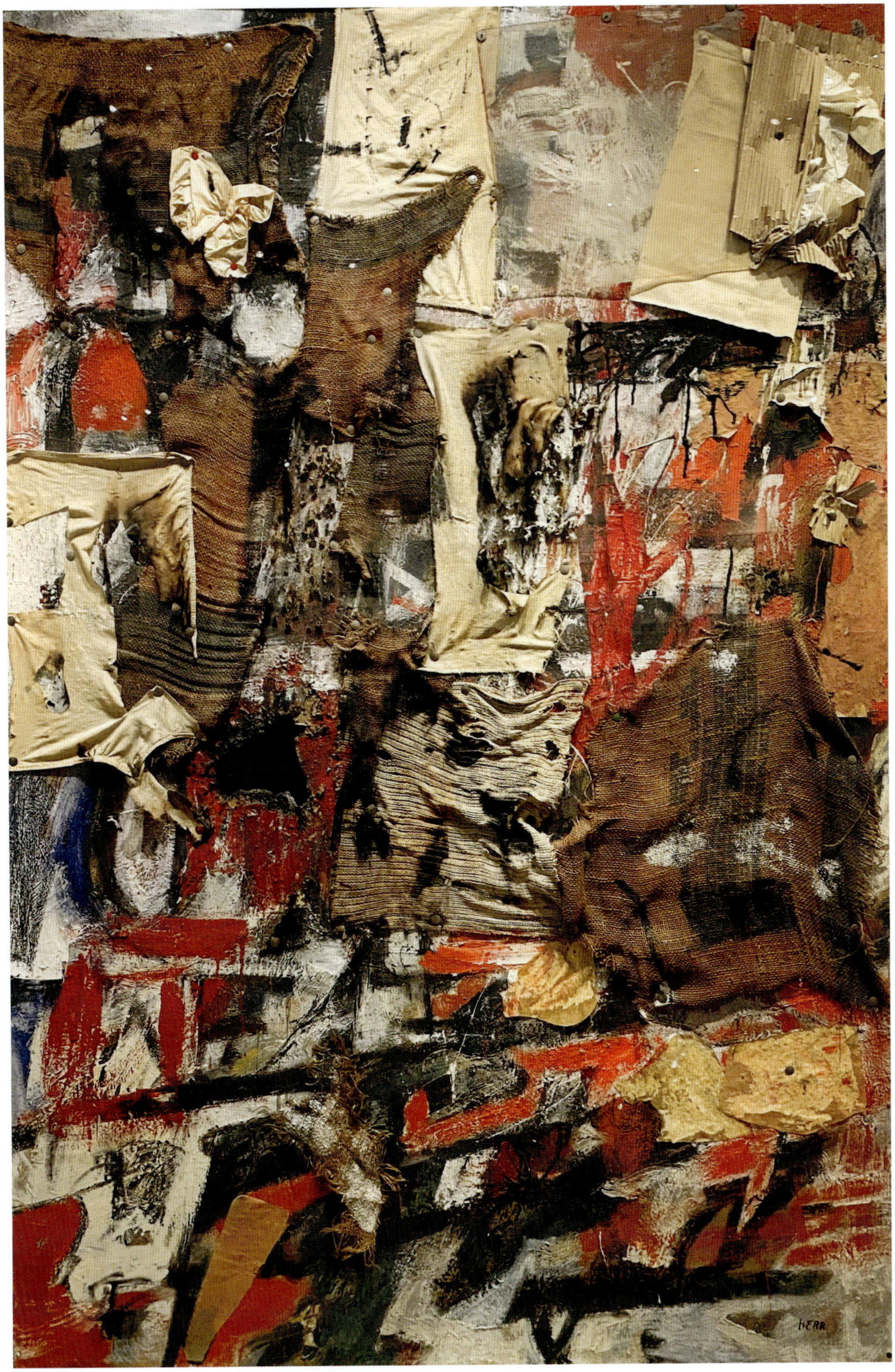

FIGURE 14. **Gettysburg**, 1955, by Ben Herr (Collection of Andrea Herr-Turoff)

Opening of *Abstract Expressionist-Impressionist Paintings by Artists Showing in New York Galleries* and *Work by Members of Group '55*, Dubin Galleries/Gallery '55, February 15, 1957. The shows included work by Sam Feinstein, Frances Lachman, and Margaret Milliken. (Courtesy of Sydney Milliken)

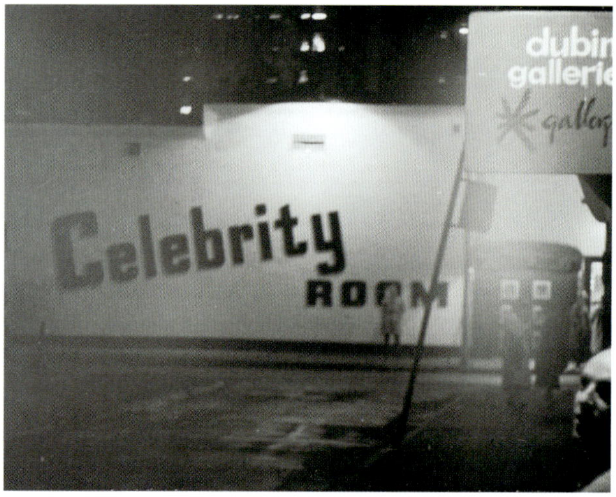

FIGURE 15. The only known image of the sign outside the Dubin Galleries/Gallery '55.

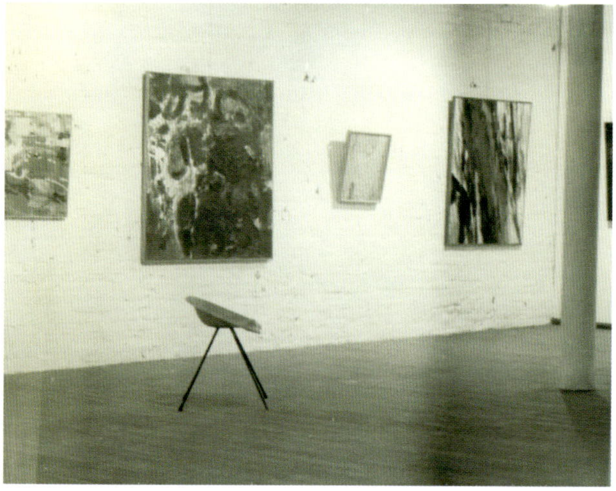

FIGURE 16. Installation view of *Abstract Expressionist-Impressionist Paintings by Artists Showing in New York Galleries.*

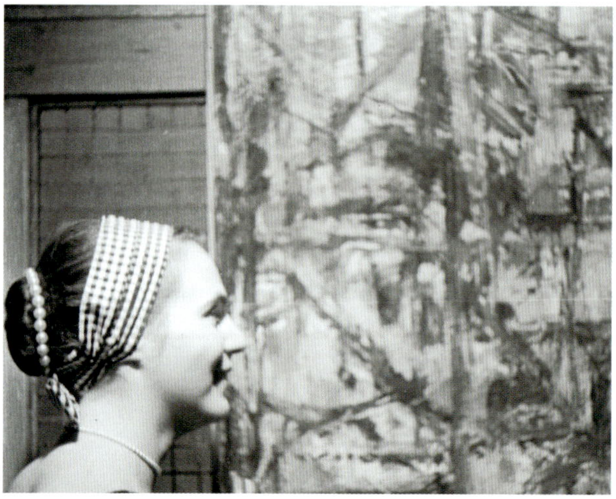

FIGURE 17. Unidentified woman at the gallery opening.

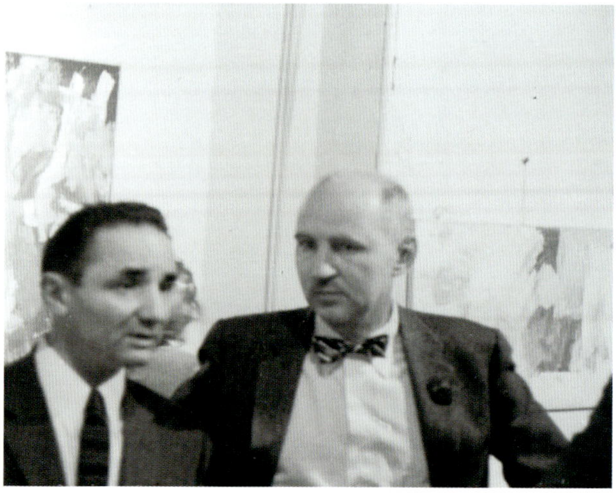

FIGURE 18. Sam Feinstein (left), organizer of the New York painters exhibition, with unidentified attendees.

CENTER CITY LOCATIONS OF SELECTED GALLERIES AND MEETING PLACES

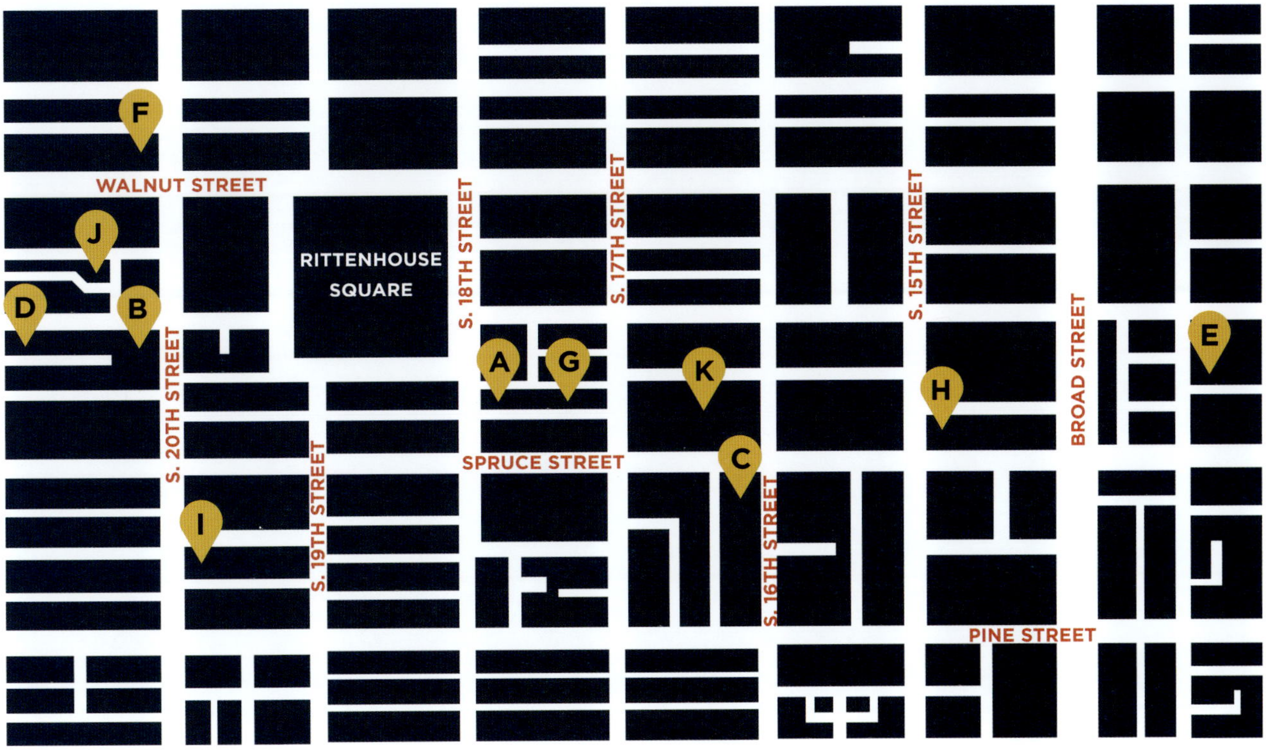

A Philadelphia Art Alliance
251 South 18th Street

B Dublin-Lush Galleries
2016 Locust Street

C Dubin Galleries
312 South 16th Street

D Dubin Galleries
2046 Locust Street

E Dubin/Gallery '55
1319–21 Irving Street, between Locust and Spruce

F Beryl Lush Gallery
2007 Walnut Street

F Carlen Galleries
2007 Walnut Street

G Ellen Donovan Gallery
1716 Rittenhouse Square

H Hendler Galleries
1429 Spruce Street

I Philadelphia Galleries
333 South 20th Street

J Feinstein/Crawford Home
2008 Chancellor Street

K The Print Club
1614 Latimer Street

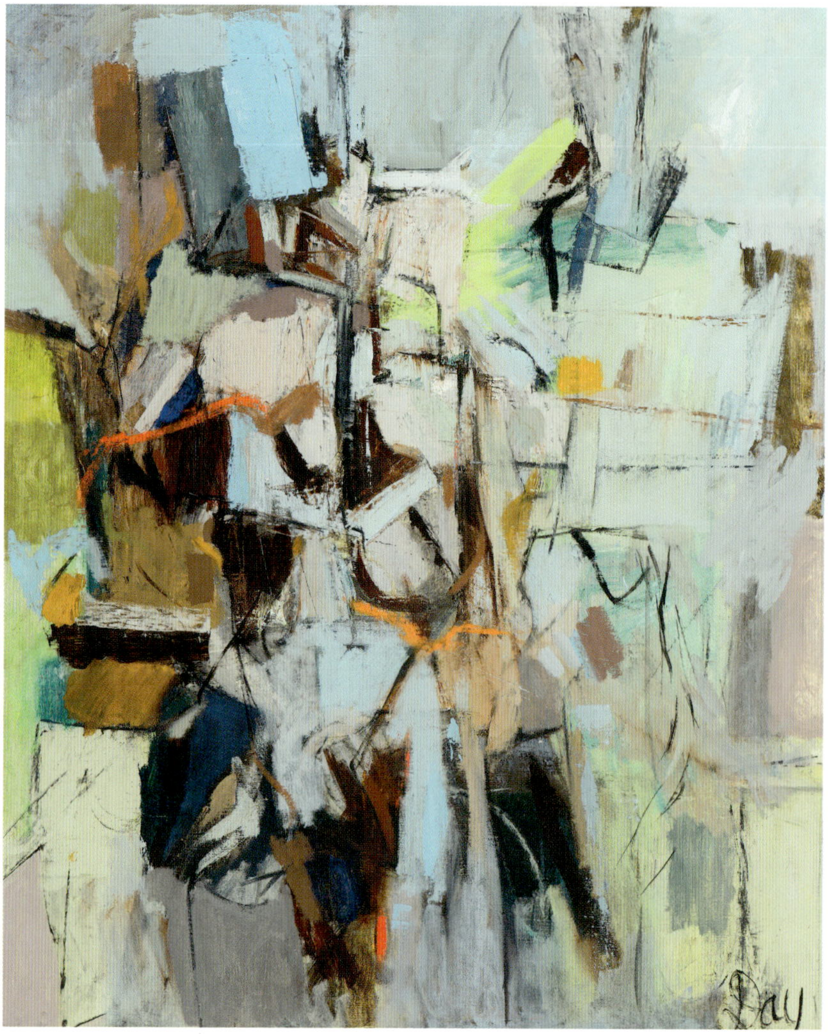

FIGURE 19. Various Asides, c. 1958, by Larry Day (Woodmere Art Museum: Gift of Gregory and Candace Wilkin, 2017) Photograph by Rick Echelmeyer

Dubin's final move, in 1957, was to 1319–21 Irving Street, between Locust and Spruce, in what had been a municipal horse stable (fig. 48); this new location would become the home base for Group '55 (and, in another iteration, would host one exhibition of the Philadelphia Abstract Artists). Without ownership of a building, life for a gallery owner was precarious, and Dubin was fortunate to have kept his gallery going, even if in different locations. Dubin evidently was able to purchase this space. In 1971, after being "quiescent since the 1950s," he opened again as Dubin-Manning Galleries.[29] He lived at that address the rest of his life.[30]

Dubin's business partner Lush, a cotton merchant, had been simultaneously exhibiting work in his own gallery at 2007 Walnut Street since 1952. Like Dubin, he was open to showing new art, beginning with a show of Freid, Whitehill, Abraham P. Hankins, and Patricia Evans (later Mangione), all of whom would join Group '55 or Philadelphia Abstract Artists. Lush also had a summer gallery in Provincetown.[31]

Robert Carlen would later present the first exhibition of the Philadelphia Abstract Artists at the Carlen Galleries, founded at 2007 Walnut Street in 1937. He specialized in American folk and "primitive" art, but he showed Piper, a modernist painter, as early as 1943.

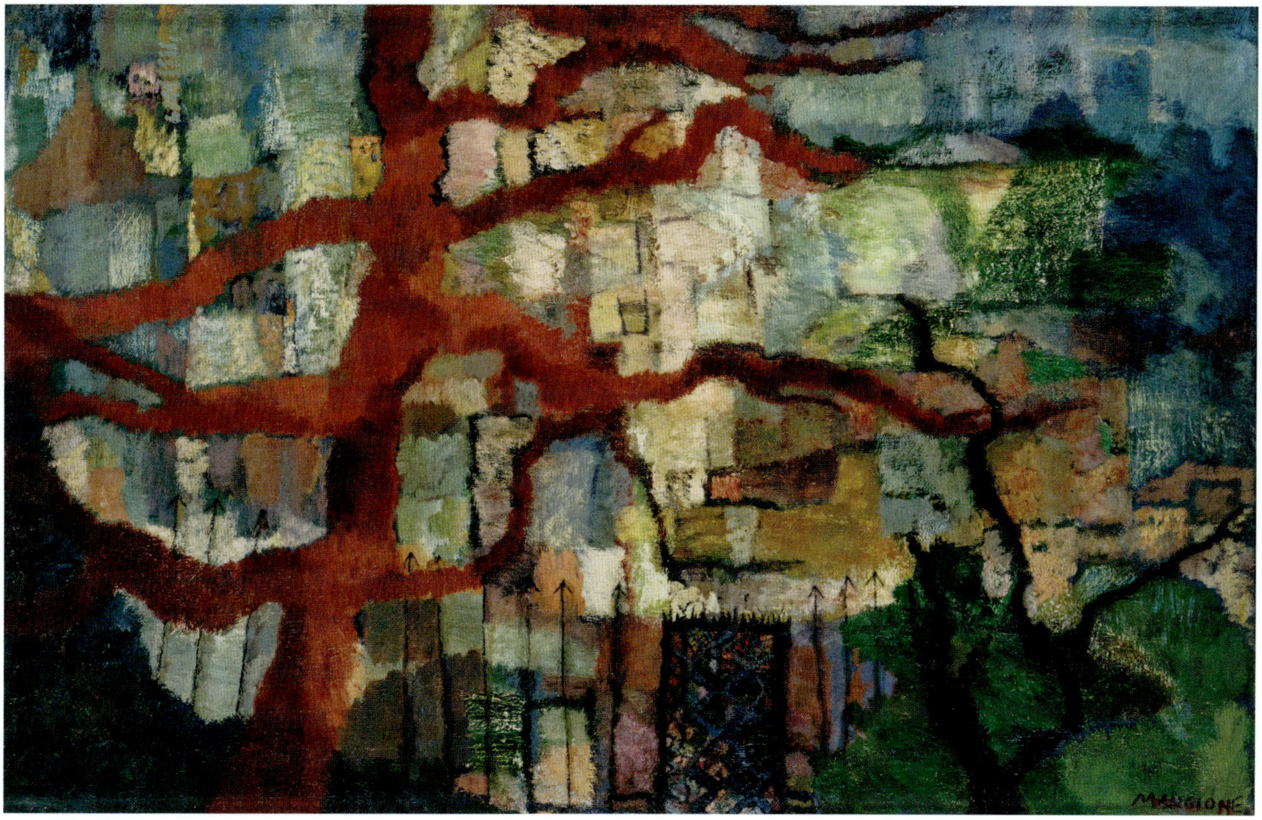

FIGURE 20. **Garden Gate**, c. 1955, by Patricia Evans Mangione (Woodmere Art Museum: Museum purchase, 2019)

Painter and art teacher Ellen Donovan opened a gallery in her name at 1716 Rittenhouse Square in 1950, co-run by English sculptor Barbara Phillips. Her goal was to show and sell the work of living Philadelphia artists, and she was successful with sales.[32] She was receptive to showing abstract art, as she did in solo exhibitions of Feinstein, Whitehill, and Francis Jennings in 1951, as well as various group shows. Later that year she asked Feinstein to join "an informal group to discuss the latest trends in the arts." This led to a program on February 15, 1952, called "Today's Trends in the Arts," possibly another precedent for the Group '55 forums. Feinstein spoke, along with a University of Pennsylvania professor of American civilization, an interior designer, and an architect.[33] Feinstein was then asked to teach painting in the gallery. Early in 1955, Donovan gave up the gallery to show work by appointment only in her studio.[34] The loss of her space may have made Dubin's gallery the logical choice for Group '55.

Hendler, a co-founder of Group '55, opened Hendler Galleries at 1429 Spruce Street in October 1952; it was noted as the "first in Philadelphia to concentrate on avant-garde artists."[35] In the approximately year and a half that it was open, Hendler showed mostly leading New York artists, including de Kooning, Kline, Pollock, and George McNeil, along with Feinstein, Greenberg, and Price, as well as his own work. Feinstein praised Hendler: "It is a brave and pioneering effort in a city where polite indifference to 'radical' art has often succeeded in channeling the artists' viewpoint into safe and socially cozy academicism."[36]

Also in 1952, future group member Wagman opened his own Philadelphia Gallery at 333 South 20th Street, near Delancey Place, close to Rittenhouse Square (figs. 22). He would show the Philadelphia Abstract Artists in 1961 and include them in group shows. Framing services helped support the gallery. In 1963, he moved to 1911 Walnut Street and offered art workshops; the gallery would remain at that location until closing, in 1974.

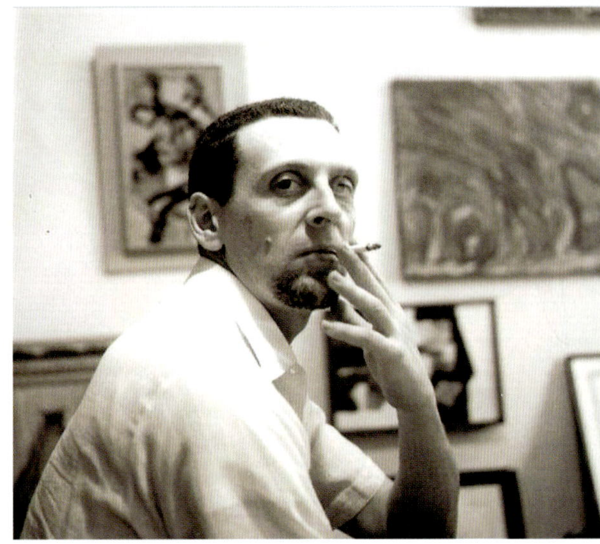

FIGURE 21. Mitchel G. Wagman in his Philadelphia Gallery on Walnut Street (Courtesy of the Estate of Mitchel G. Wagman)

Despite these galleries showing some new art in the city, Feinstein was disappointed with the level of art discourse in Philadelphia and the lack of interest in abstract art. In an article in the February 15, 1955, issue of *Art Digest*, he responded to the art festival at the Philadelphia Museum of Art and was harshly critical of local newspapers and critics. He saw them as avoiding abstract art, with reviews being only "a catalogue of friendships" that left the "laymen" "numbed but unenlightened" and yearning "for some objective basis upon which to orient his artistic judgment. Yearning for applause, the artists, in notable instance, are numbing their talents, forfeiting their search for significant pictorial utterance and subjecting their work to prettifying, recognizably safe techniques." (Feinstein and other Group '55 artists often referred to "laymen," meaning people who were not artists or had no specialized knowledge of art, a profession they felt was sacred. These were the people they wanted to educate.) He then praised the work of Leonard Nelson being shown at the Dubin Galleries. Three of the five letters to the editor the following month responded positively, including one by Feinstein's student Margaret Milliken and another by Bechtle.[37]

It was this resistance to and lack of understanding of nonobjective art, despite awareness of New York Abstract Expressionism, that made Philadelphia artists feel there was a need to educate the public about what they were doing. Although, as described, there was a small number of venues where abstract art could be shown in Philadelphia, such work was rarely exhibited or purchased by museums in the city. The Philadelphia Museum of Art acquired contemporary prints, and some important examples of European early modern art were donated by Louise and Walter Arensberg and A. E. Gallatin, assuring the museum's prominence. It exhibited the work of Carles along with that of Franklin C. Watkins in 1946, but it would not hire a curator of contemporary art until 1972. At PAFA, it was rare to have abstract paintings selected for juried exhibitions. An exception was Piper's

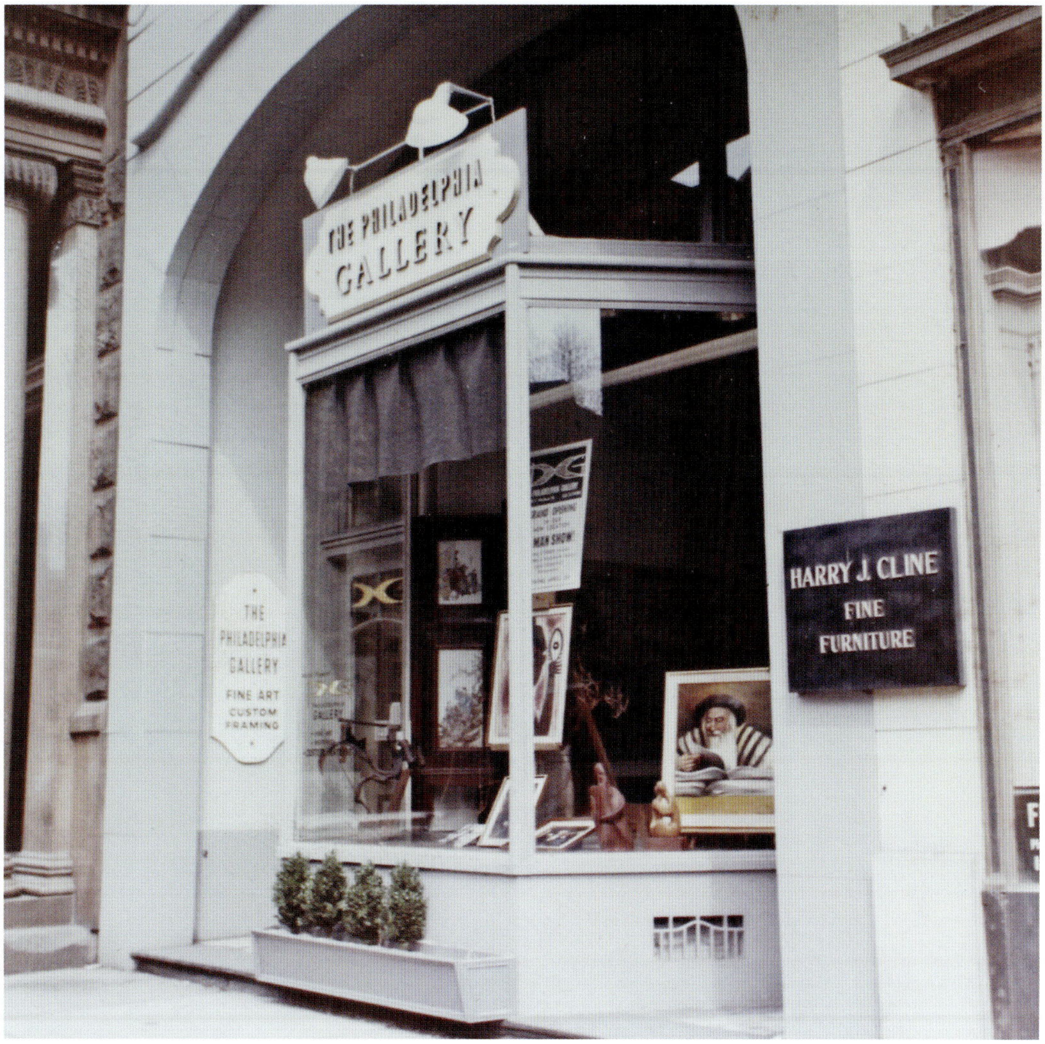

FIGURE 22. Mitchel G. Wagman's first gallery on 20th Street (Courtesy of the Estate of Mitchel G. Wagman)

Study in Red, which the museum purchased in 1954. When Hofmann's *Red Hat* won a prize for "a painting of special importance to the exhibition" at a show juried by abstract artist Vaclav Vytlacil, the *Philadelphia Inquirer* referred to it as "spectacularly empty of deeper meaning." Feinstein described the viewers as "somewhat bewildered by the barbarisms housed at the Academy. . . .I suspect that this superb Hofmann will survive the *Inquirer*'s autopsy; that the analysis will ultimately rank with a contemporary valuation of Renoir's painting which declared it insensitive and inept."[38]

The Formation of Group '55

Group '55 was born with a postcard inviting selected artists to a "meeting at the Dubin Galleries this Friday, May 20, 8 pm." (Postcards would be the medium of choice for communication about meetings in the days of frequent deliveries.) The group decided to meet monthly, on third Fridays. Officers and a governing board were elected, and meeting minutes were taken by the secretary. At the meetings, members worked to improve rules and procedures, even once proposing the idea of a constitution. Attempts were made to be democratic by rotating who led meetings and whose work was discussed after day-to-day business was complete. Future members were to be voted in based on the quality of their work. Artists selected what they wanted to exhibit. Dubin indicated that he hoped to give each member a solo show. Membership dues were ten dollars a year, and each artist contributed two dollars to an exhibition fund to cover expenses, like refreshments at openings.[39] The Philadelphia artists' concern for rules and votes to gain consensus was very different from the spirit of the Club in New York, where "there were no formal rules, no agreed charter, in fact the first organizational meeting was mostly concerned with how to remain unorganized."[40]

Feinstein was elected as president, Freid as vice president, and Brodhead as secretary. A year later, Frances Lachman was chosen as secretary, and Milliken as treasurer. A governing board of additional members met with the officers in between the monthly meetings, often at Feinstein and Crawford's home, on Chancellor Street. The governing board worked with officers on planning and decision-making.

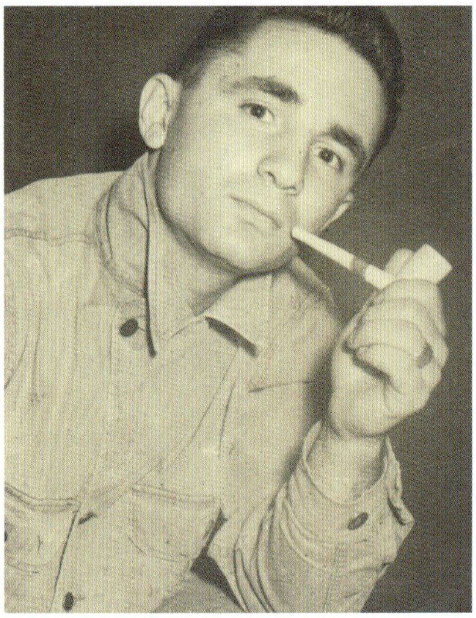

FIGURE 23. Photo of Sam Feinstein used for Group '55 publicity, c. 1957 (Courtesy of Samuel L. Feinstein Trust)

The energetic leader of and spokesman for Group '55, Feinstein (fig. 23) had evolved from a painter of semiabstract harbor scenes to one of thickly textured Abstract Expressionist canvases built entirely on color relationships. He was a charismatic teacher, usually privately, although he had served for a year as director of the art program at the Philadelphia Museum of Art. One reviewer summarized his credentials: "His professional background, beyond his work as a painter and teacher, includes motion picture animation and photography for documentary films for the government, the Federation of Atomic Scientists and the United Nations, writing art criticism as contributing editor of *Art Digest*, and as a professional filmmaker."[41] Thoughtful and articulate, he was connected with the art scenes in New York and Provincetown as well as in Philadelphia. He authored more than three hundred articles and reviews for *Art Digest* from 1953 to 1955 and wrote about a number of the artists he would later invite to join him in Group '55. Without Feinstein writing about Philadelphia exhibitions after 1955, they were generally overlooked by New York critics and art magazines.

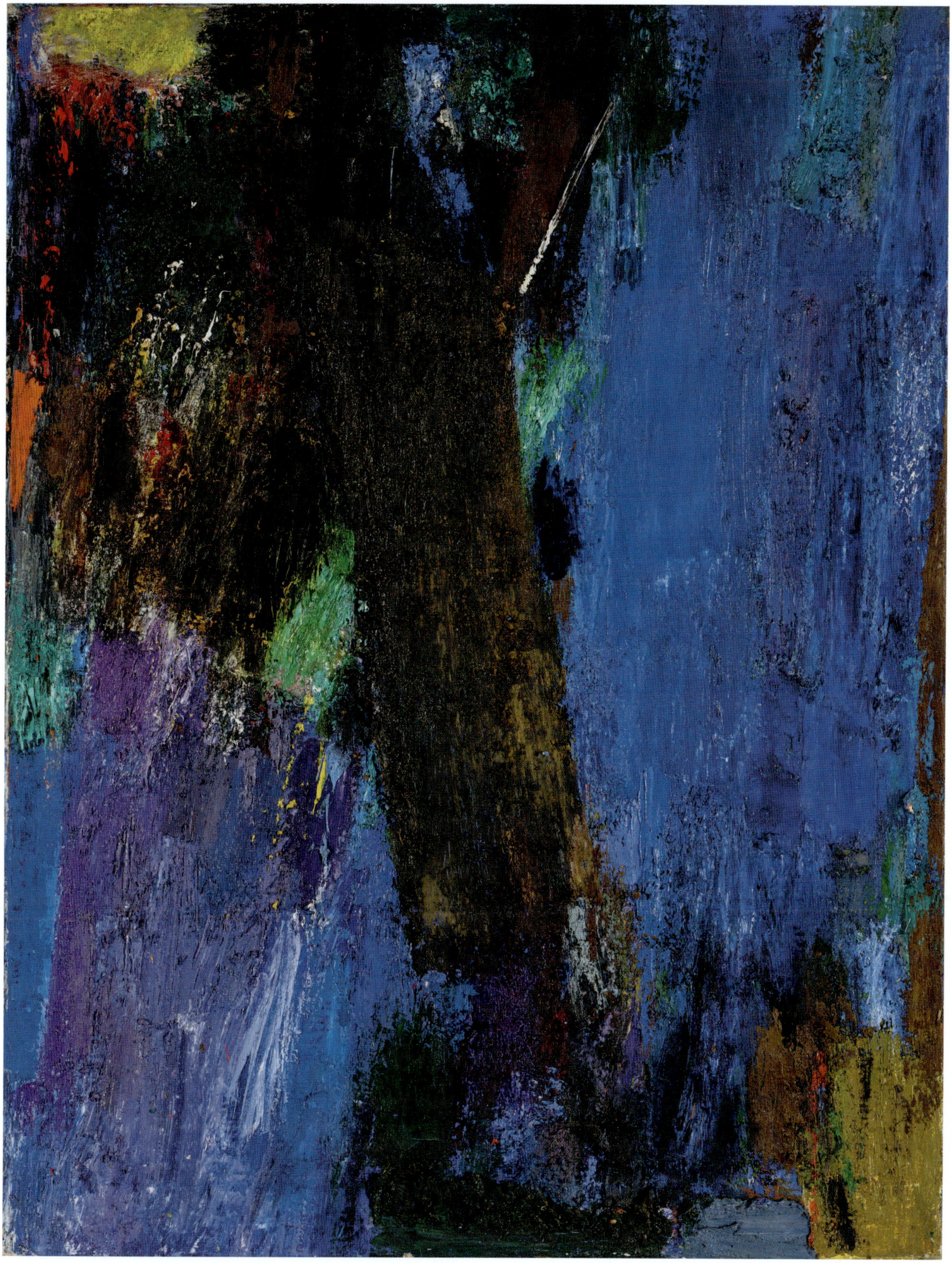

FIGURE 24. **Pieta II**, 1957, by Sam Feinstein (Samuel L. Feinstein Trust)

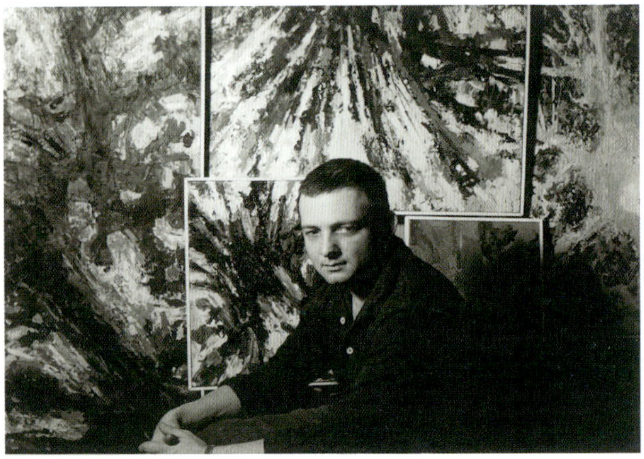

FIGURE 25. Raymond Hendler—with *(No. 9)*, at left—in his studio, 1952 (Courtesy of the Estate of Raymond Hendler)

FIGURE 26. **(No. 9)**, 1952, by Raymond Hendler (Woodmere Art Museum: Gift of the Estate of Raymond Hendler, 2020)

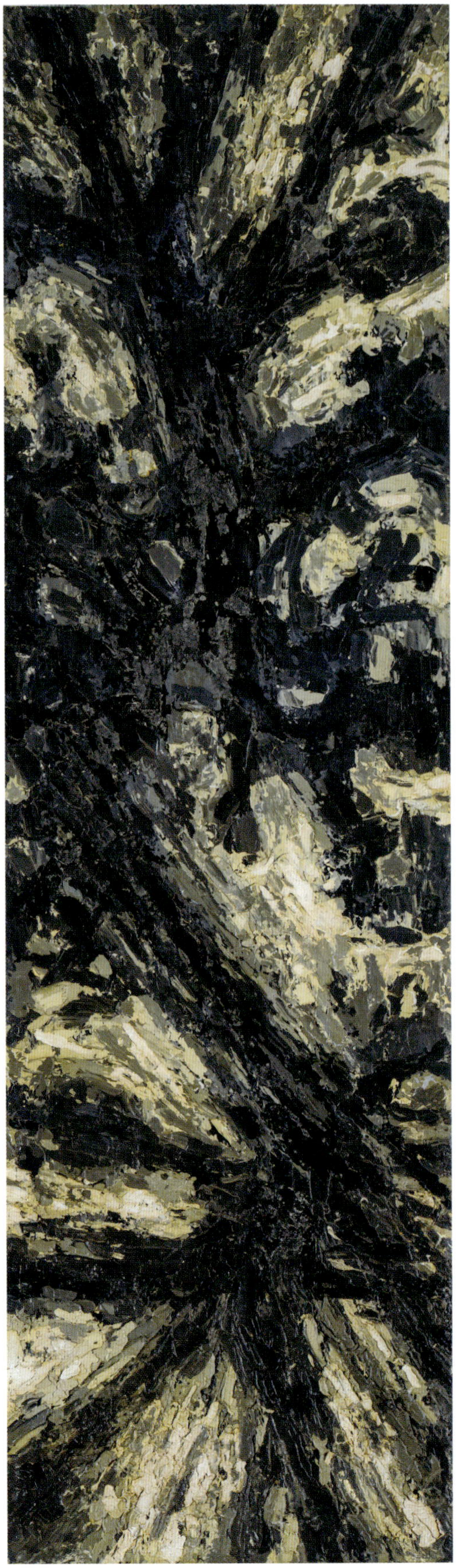

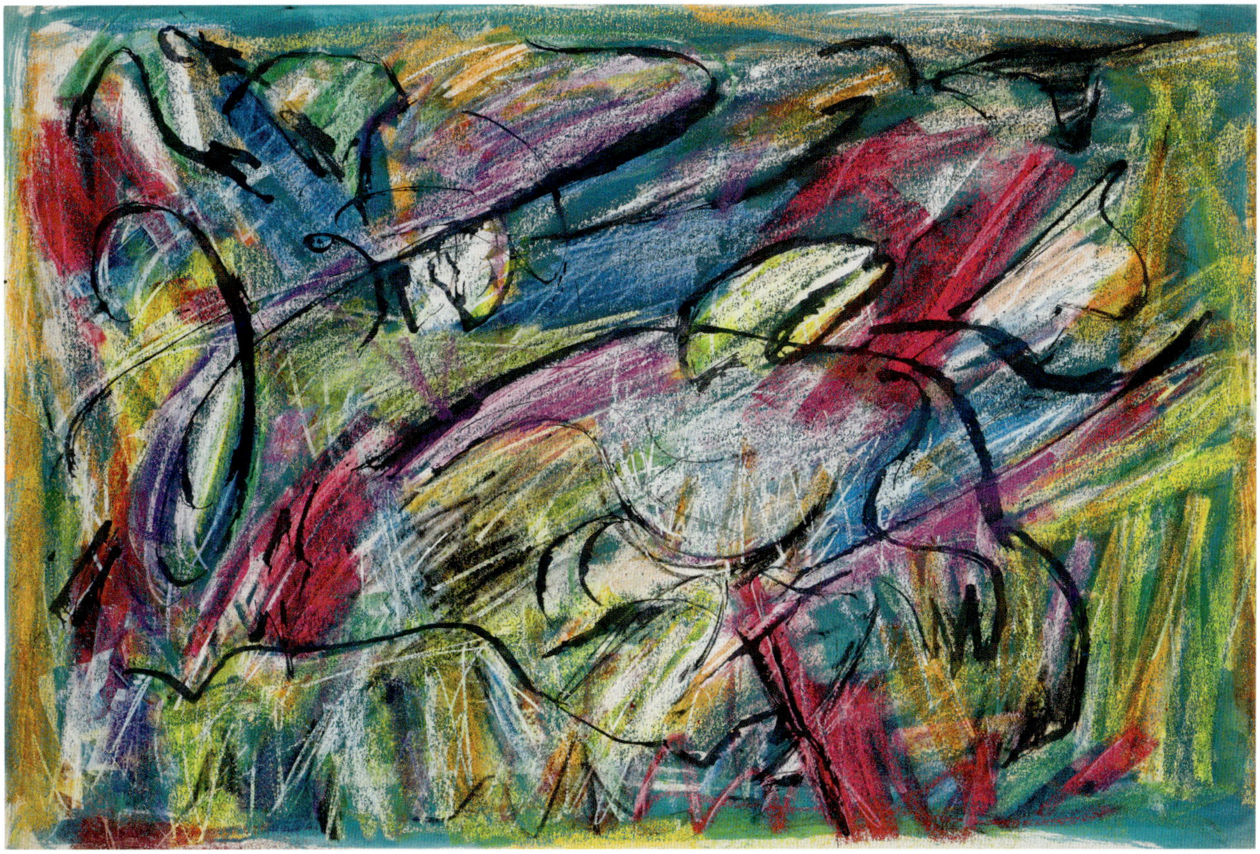

FIGURE 27. **Hawks over Appomattox**, June 24, 1955, by Sam Freid (Woodmere Art Museum: Museum purchase with funds generously provided by Patricia Stark Feinstein, 2019)

If Feinstein was an artist who was also a teacher and a critic, his energy and contributions to the art scene were complemented by those of the group's co-founder Hendler. Hendler brought experience as an artist in Paris and at the Club in New York, as well as lessons learned from running his own gallery. Hendler was producing large black-and-white, freely brushed abstractions in black, gray, and whites, such as *(No. 9)* (fig. 26). He was a good speaker and had served on panels at the Club, one of them introduced by Clement Greenberg. He closed his gallery in 1954 to concentrate on painting and was a participant in the first Group '55 exhibition and forum. In 1957, he moved to Minnesota, thus ending his involvement with the group.

Freid was described by Laurie Wagman as "a lovely bear of a man."[42] He had been exhibiting his paintings since the late 1930s, and he and his wife, Hilda Berger Freid, sometimes collaborated on work and showed his paintings and drawings with her jewelry and wire sculpture.[43] He had moved from scenes of coal miners into exuberant abstractions, such as his energetic, allover, almost wildly stroked pastel *Hawks over Appomattox,* June 24, 1955 (fig. 27). Feinstein praised Freid's 1950s work: "Sam's abstract oils have evolved from his earlier, hard-edged forms to a more intuitively felt poetic imagery, enriched by color nuances."[44] Freid had shown with other artists in the group and taught at the Samuel S. Fleisher Art Memorial, at 715–19 Catharine Street in Philadelphia. A fluent and effective writer, he was interested in poetry and drafted letters and statements to help publicize the group's ideas and efforts. Bechtle noted: "Sam did more for me in art and poetry than anyone else. His understanding was first class."[45]

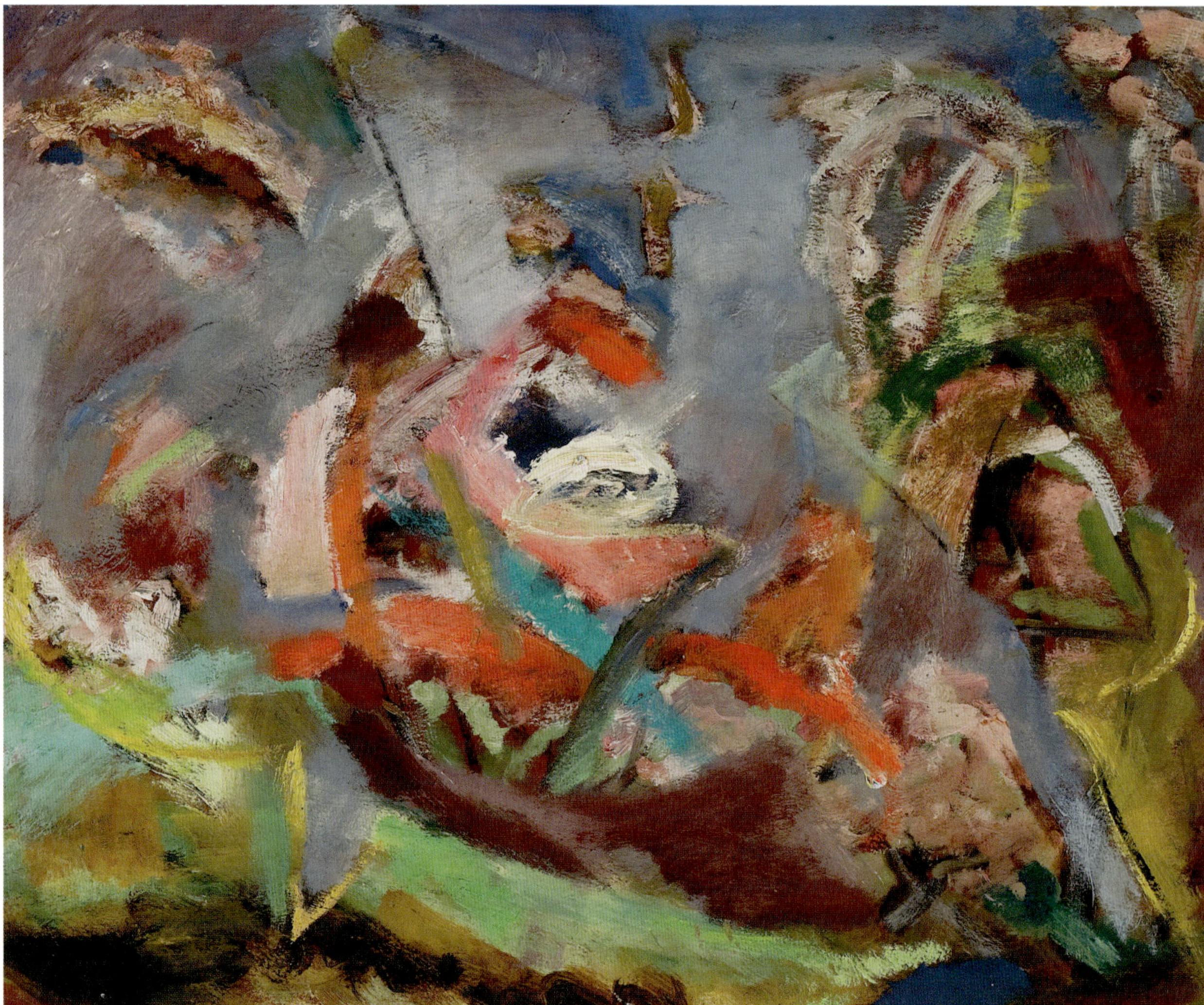

FIGURE 28. **From a Peach Orchard**, 1954, by Quita Brodhead (Woodmere Art Museum: Gift of Bill Scott, 2011)
Photograph by Rick Echelmeyer

Brodhead had studied at PAFA and in Paris. She had enjoyed Carles's class at PAFA and continued to study with him privately until he could no longer paint. She had been exhibiting still lifes and portraits in New York since the late 1930s and was being praised for her abstract work such as *From a Peach Orchard* (fig. 28), filled with rough swathes of color and bursting with implied movement. She continued to develop personal abstract modes over the next half century and enjoyed a retrospective exhibition at Hollis Taggart Galleries, New York, that marked her one hundredth birthday, in 2001.[46] Lachman had studied at Moore College of Art, at PAFA, and with Feinstein. She was praised for some of her

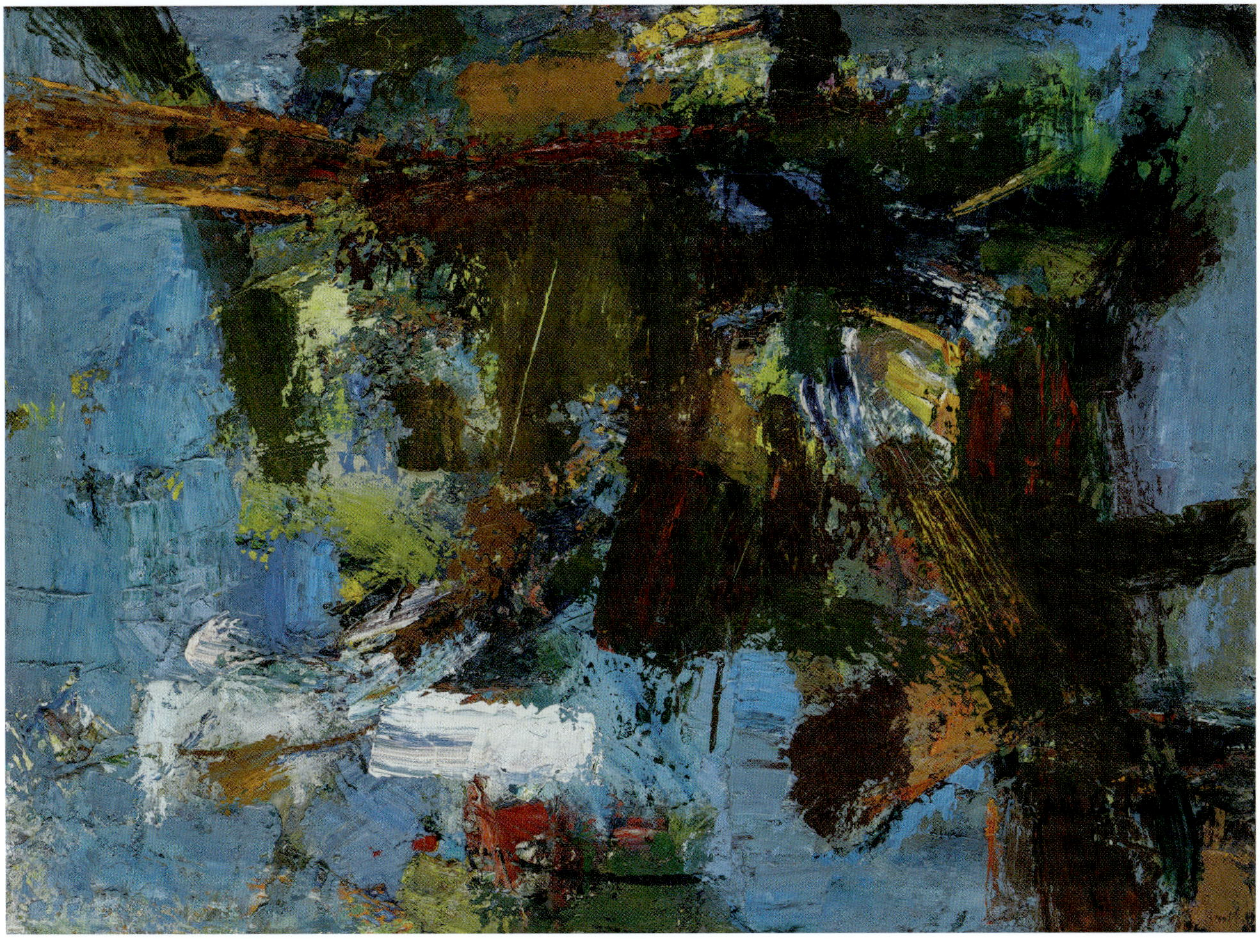

FIGURE 29. **September**, 1957, by Frances Lachman (Woodmere Art Museum: Gift of the Lachman Family, 2020)

semifigurative work and for paintings like *September* (fig. 29), built of strokes and patches of pure color. She ended up being one of the most frequently exhibited in the group shows of both Group '55 and Philadelphia Abstract Artists. Milliken was also a student of Feinstein. A reviewer in 1956 noted that her work had "cut loose from conventional picturization and has found a natural expression in highly individualized abstraction, mostly executed with a palette knife," and commented on her "unusually acute color sense".[47]

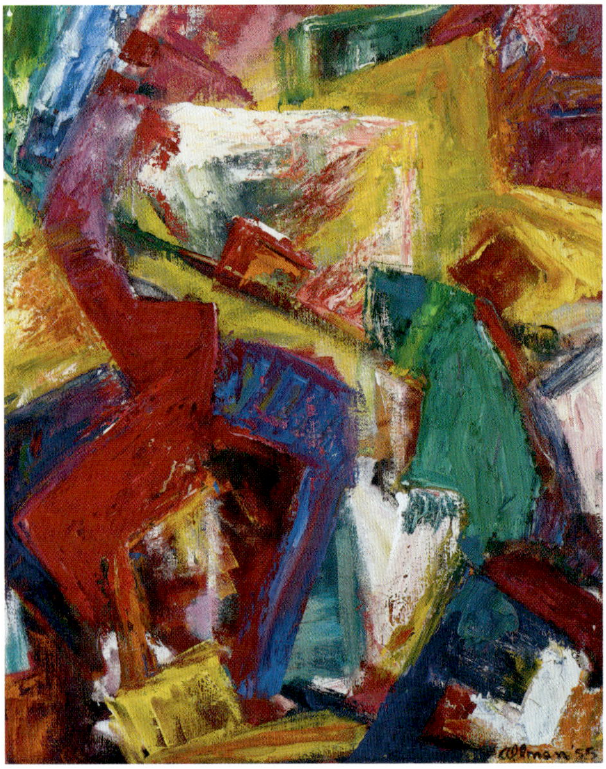

FIGURE 30. **Nicht Wahr Hans Hofmann,** 1955, by Margo Allman (Courtesy of the artist)

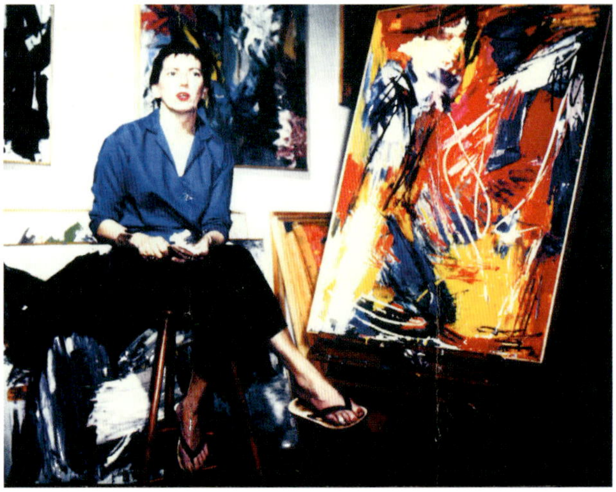

FIGURE 31. Margaret Milliken in her studio (Courtesy of Sydney Milliken)

Group '55 members were carefully selected. It was never a large group—twenty-seven at most, with members resigning and new ones being accepted. Up to sixteen active members attended monthly meetings. In early 1957, there were seventeen members, including Dubin,[48] all of whom were painting in Abstract Expressionist or nonrepresentational styles. They ranged in age. The oldest—Whitehill, Brodhead, and Hankins—were born at the turn of the century and had strong exhibition records. Most of the others were born between 1910 and the mid-1920s, with Margo Allman the youngest.

Women were welcome and active members from the start. Almost half of the artists listed on the first exhibition poster were women, including Piper and Zion (then known as Wollman). Although the group did follow the norm of the time in filling the offices of secretary or treasurer with women, rather than president or vice president, women played significant roles in supporting events, running meetings, and organizing panels, of which Staffel moderated two. A number were given solo exhibitions. This contrasted with the New York scene—male Abstract Expressionists got the attention of the critics and were highlighted in the first histories of the New York School, and Matter was for a time the only woman member of the Club.[49]

As in the New York art world, a significant number of Group '55 members, including Feinstein, were of Jewish heritage, like him exhibiting strong intellectual curiosity and activist leanings. Several were first- or second-generation immigrants from Russia or Ukraine. Anti-Semitism was pervasive nationwide, although less common among artists and intellectuals. In Philadelphia especially, Jews had established institutions centuries before, and they continued to play an important role in the city. Many members of Group '55 taught at Fleisher Art

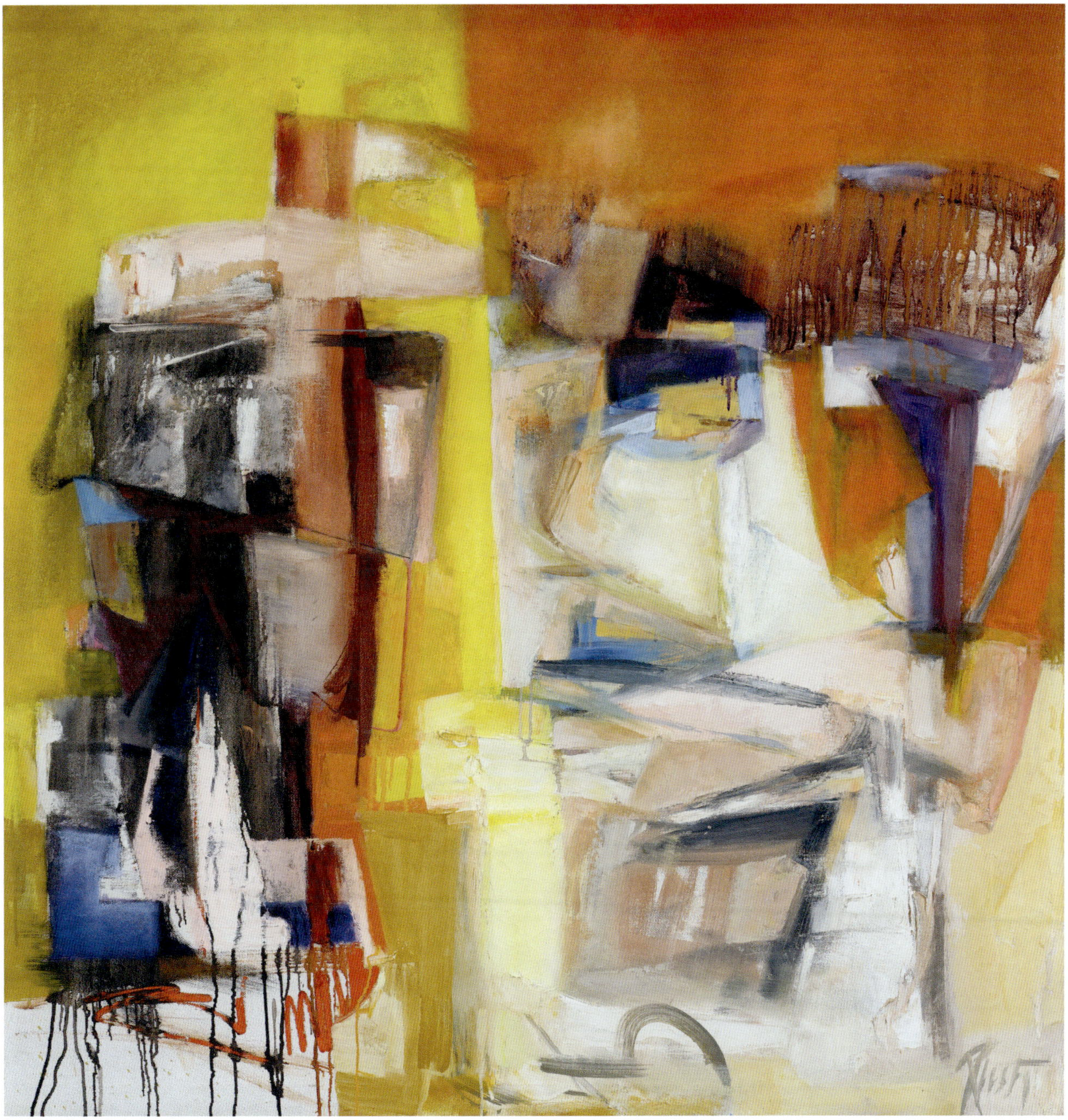

FIGURE 32. **Abstract**, 1959, by Ruth Zion (Private Collection)

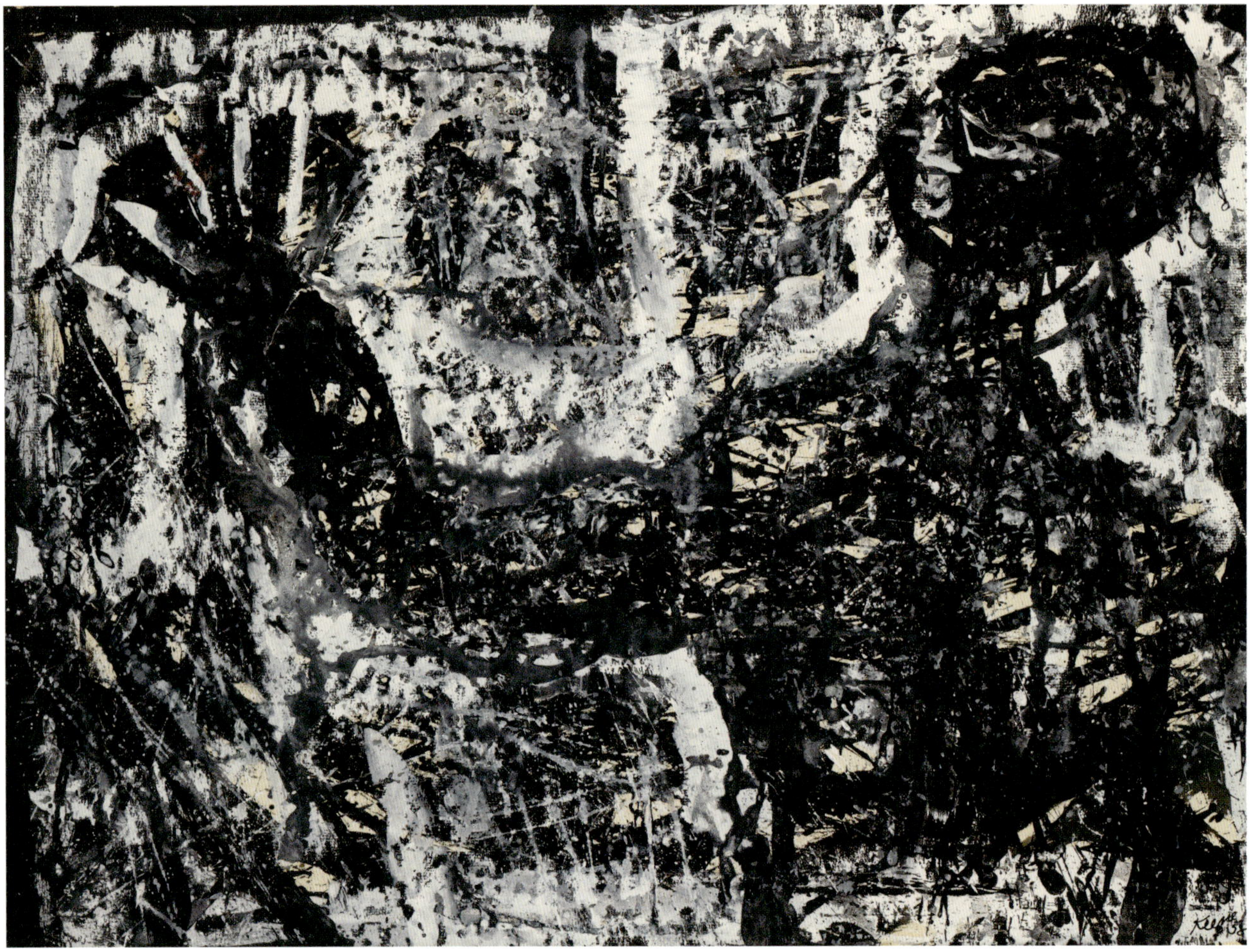

FIGURE 33. **Blues Singer**, 1958, by Paul F. Keene Jr. (Courtesy of Terenchin Gallery)

Memorial, which offered classes to all ages and had been founded by a successful businessman who was the son of German Jewish immigrants. Group '55 also had strong ties to the University of Pennsylvania, where, unlike other Ivy League schools with restrictive quotas, forty percent of students at the time were Jewish.[50]

The group was not racially diverse, but several of the members were close friends with and exhibited alongside African American painters. African American artist Paul F. Keene Jr. and Hendler were founders of Galerie Huit in Paris; at the time, Keene and Sanford Greenberg shared housing. They remained friends later in Philadelphia. Keene also taught at the Philadelphia College of Art, where he was a colleague of Group '55 members Piper and Staffel. Along with them, Keene was invited to join the Philadelphia Abstract Artists in 1957. Some Group '55 artists exhibited at the Pyramid

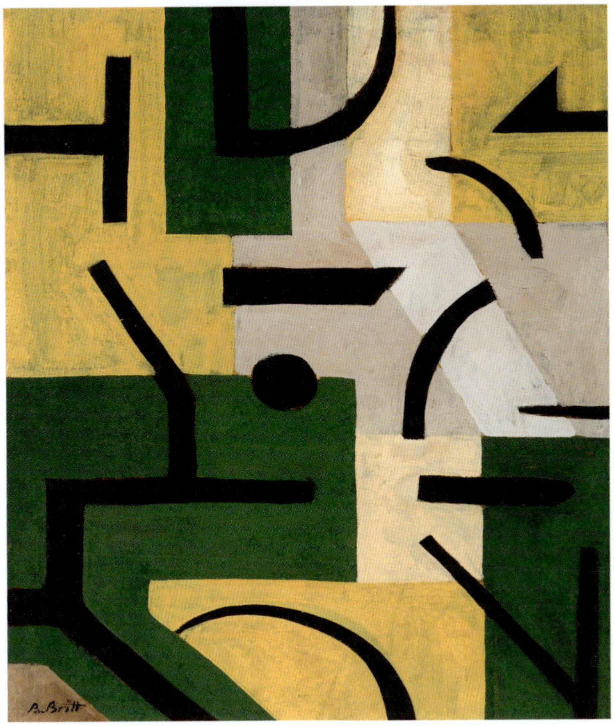

FIGURE 34. **Untitled (Abstract)**, c. 1950s, by Benjamin Britt (Woodmere Art Museum: Museum purchase, 2015) Photograph by Rick Echelmeyer

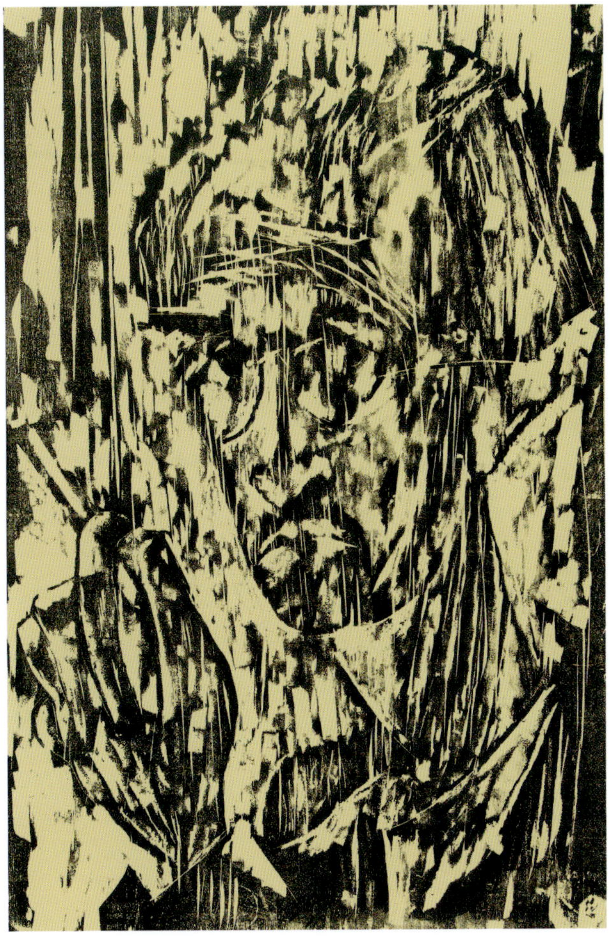

FIGURE 35. **Self-Portrait**, 1953, by Itzhak Sankowsky (Woodmere Art Museum: Gift of Roslyn Silverman Hahn, 2013) Photograph by Rick Echelmeyer

Club, a social club formed by African American professionals that sponsored annual art exhibitions from 1941 to 1957.[51] Many Philadelphia African American artists focused primarily on figurative work and social realism. Keene described himself as an abstract realist, as in *Blues Singer* (fig. 33). Benjamin Britt, who painted in a variety of styles during his career, was one of the few African American artists exploring abstraction at the time in Philadelphia. The 1957 Group '55 programs included performances by African American concert pianist Natalie Hinderas.

Group '55 members were connected and knew one another in a variety of personal and professional ways. In addition to teaching together, they frequently exhibited together in group shows. Allman, Anderson, Lachman, Milliken, and Jack Mayerson were all students of Feinstein. Brodhead, Freid, Hankins, Lachman, Jack Gerber, Paul Greenwood,

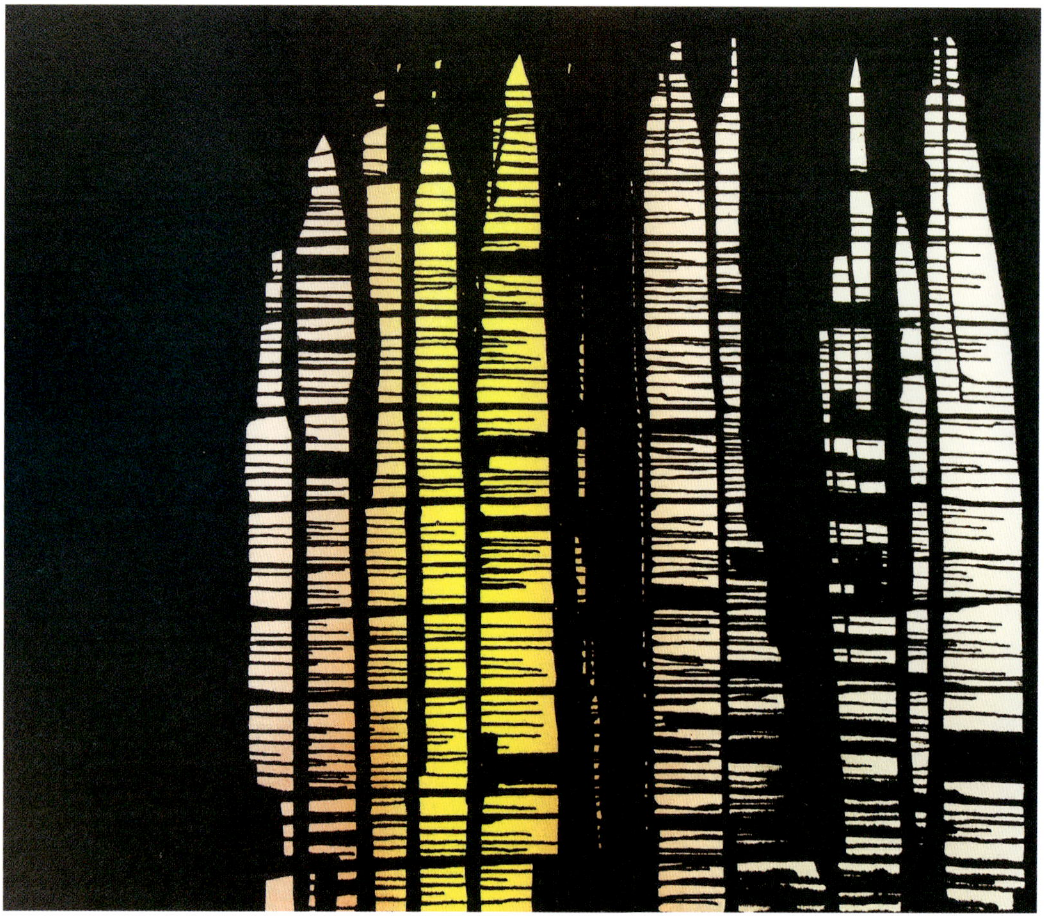

FIGURE 36. **Drip Print**, 1956, by Eugene Feldman (Woodmere Art Museum: Gift of Rosina Feldman, 2008) Photograph by Rick Echelmeyer

and Itzhak Sankowsky all studied at PAFA and showed together in Fellowship exhibitions. Brodhead, Piper, and Sankowsky were students of Carles. Piper, Feinstein, Allman, Staffel, and Laura Goodman studied with Hofmann. Some of the printmakers, including Hankins, Sankowsky, and Feldman, often exhibited together (figs. 35–37). In addition, a number of them lived in Center City, not far from Rittenhouse Square, also the location of most of the galleries.

Group '55 artists had genteel meetings where white wine and cheese and crackers were served; wine and perhaps sherry and port or a vodka-spiked punch were available at openings.[52] Their behavior contrasted with the New York scene; the Philadelphia artists in the group did not meet at bars and did not indulge in heavy drinking and interpersonal and romantic drama. At the Club, the New York artists engaged in informal rap sessions and parties after openings with lots of drinking and dancing and sometimes brawls.

First Group '55 Exhibition and Forum

As noted previously, the Dubin-Lush Galleries provided a space for the new group to carry out its goals. Grafly, who listed all the gallery's exhibitions in *Art in Focus*, alerted her readers: "Plans are to devote a rear gallery to a group of nonfigurative painters of the area." She gave Feinstein, Hendler, Staffel, Greenberg, Price, and Zion as examples of "artists who paint in abstract idea." All but Price joined. The outer gallery would show art of "various complexions."[53]

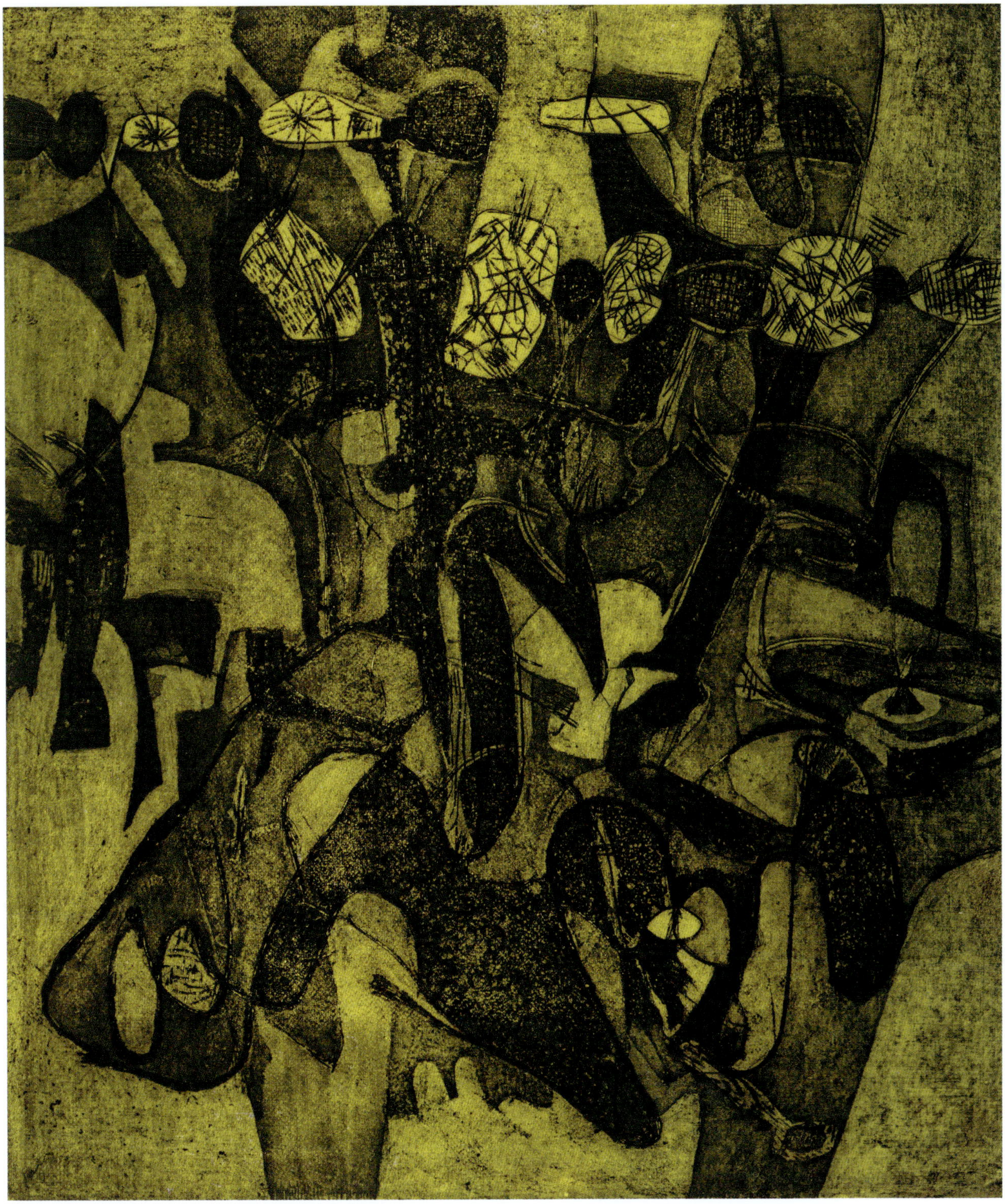

FIGURE 37. **Halibut Point**, 1951, by Abraham P. Hankins (Woodmere Art Museum: Museum purchase, 2018)

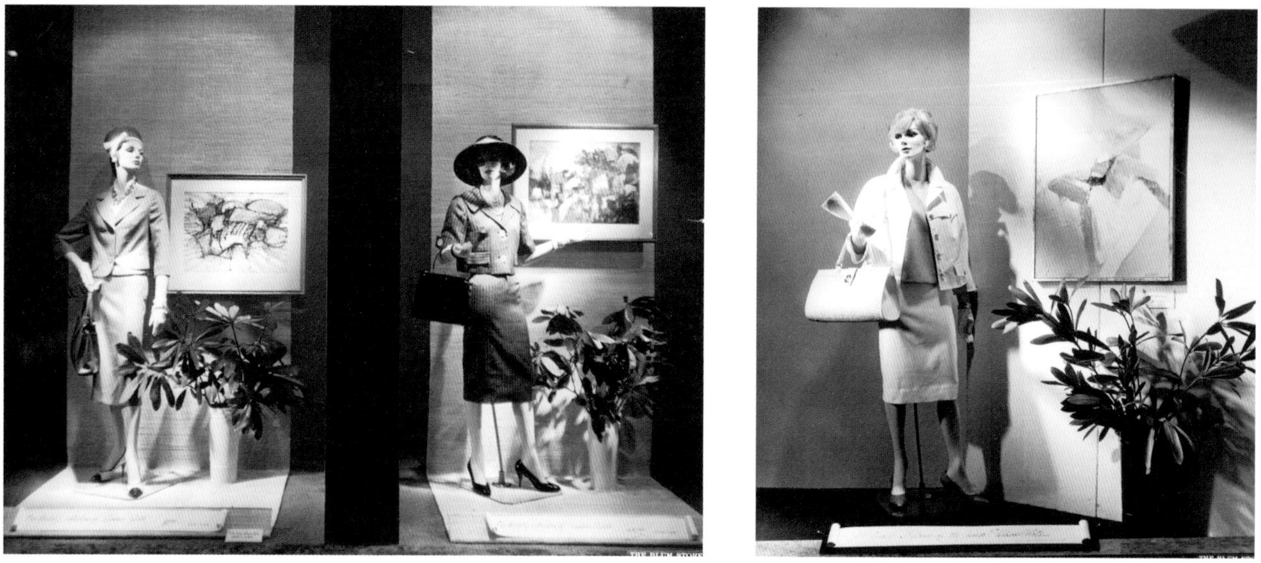

FIGURE 38. Blum Store windows, January 1956, designed by Michael Ciliberti. (Estate of Michael V. Ciliberti)

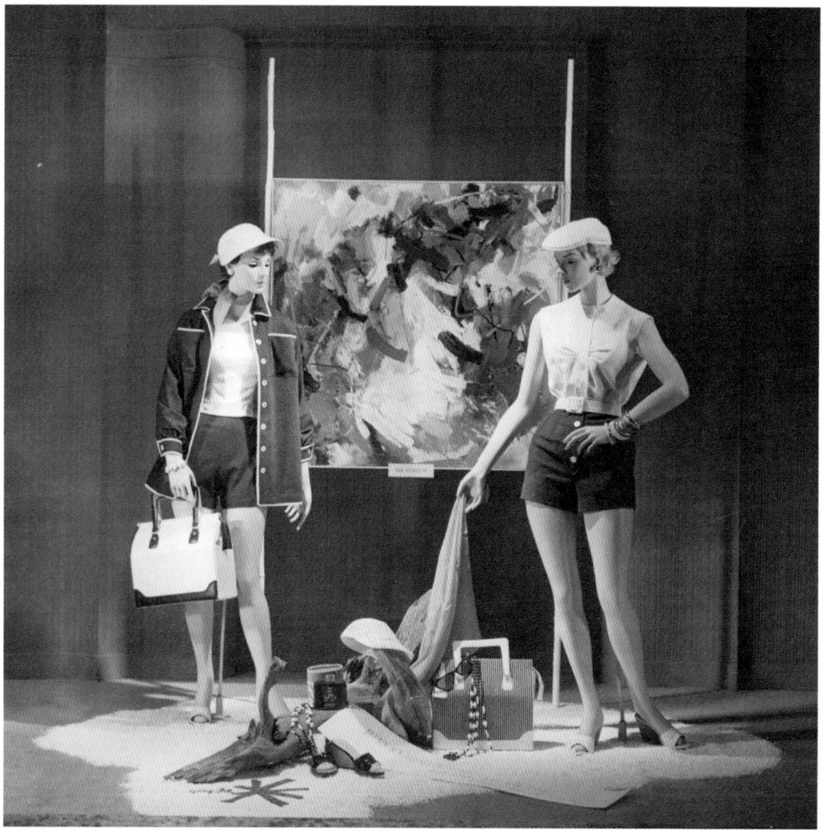

FIGURE 39. Blum Store window featuring a painting by Sam Feinstein and the Group '55 burst logo on the floor, January 1956, designed by Michael Ciliberti (Estate of Michael V. Ciliberti)

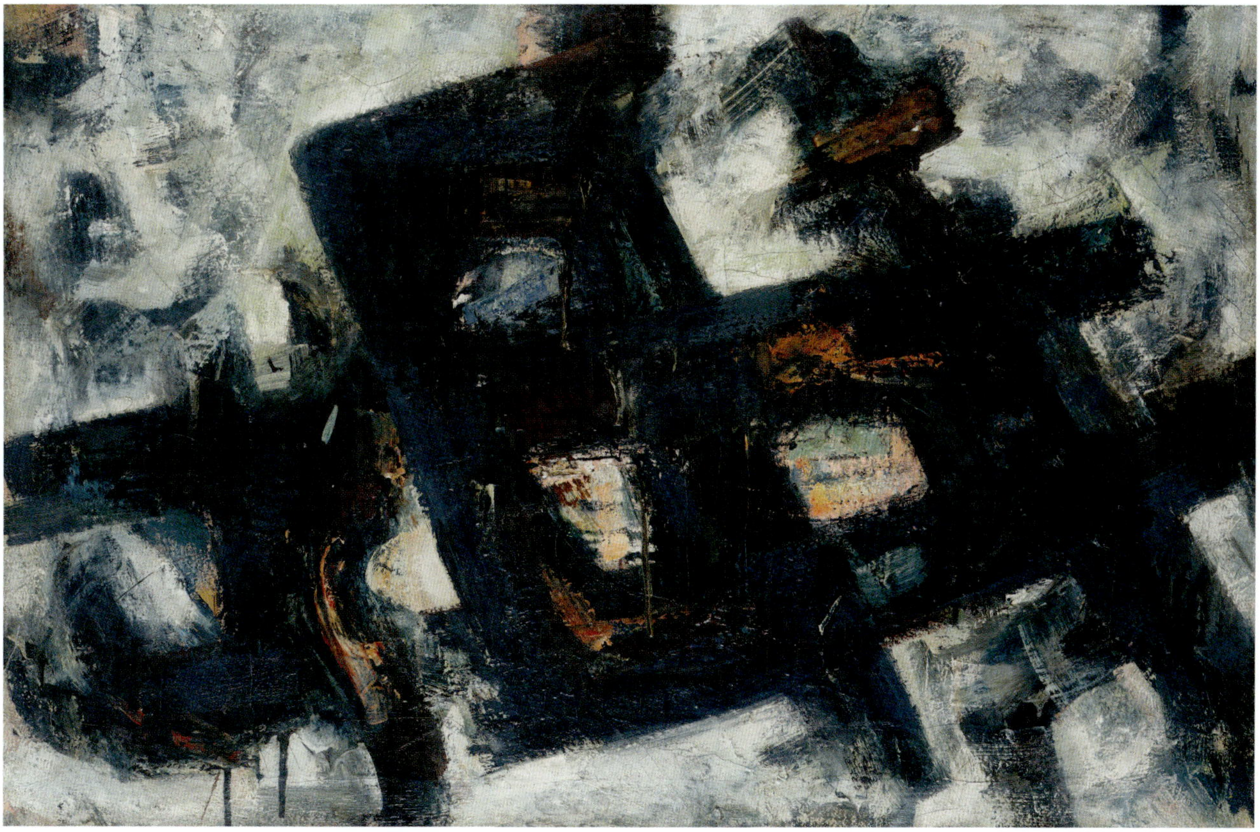

FIGURE 40. **The Tornado**, 1954, by Melville Price (Woodmere Art Museum: Gift of Barbara Gillette Price, 2020)

Grafly included Price in her announcement about the new group as one of the Group '55 artists.[54] This strongly suggests he was invited to join. Price had been a member of the Club and was in the *Ninth Street Show* in New York. There he and Kline became lifelong friends. Price was then teaching at the Philadelphia Museum School of Industrial Art and persuaded Kline to do so as well. Price's powerful abstractions, like *The Tornado* (fig. 40), suggest the inspiration of Kline, but the work has its own drama, with gesture counterbalancing overlapping forms. A painting like this would have more than qualified him for the group. His work was exhibited by Dubin and Hendler, and he attended forums. Price often exhibited in group shows with Group '55 members and was invited by Bechtle to join the Philadelphia Abstract Artists in 1957.[55] He left Philadelphia in 1958 to begin teaching in Alabama.

In advance of the first exhibition in January, each member was invited to bring two canvases, each not more than four feet wide, to the December meeting. The size limit is significant: unlike many in the New York School, the Philadelphia abstractionists were traditional easel painters, working in sizes that would fit into Philadelphia galleries and homes. Feinstein's four-foot-high canvases (figs. 6 and 24) were larger than most in the group were painting. Each artist would have one canvas hung in the gallery and one in a store window. Paintings were brought in by twenty-four members. Freid read his "excellent clarifications of the aims of the group for presentation to the critics" and moved that "each member write a statement about his work." Artist

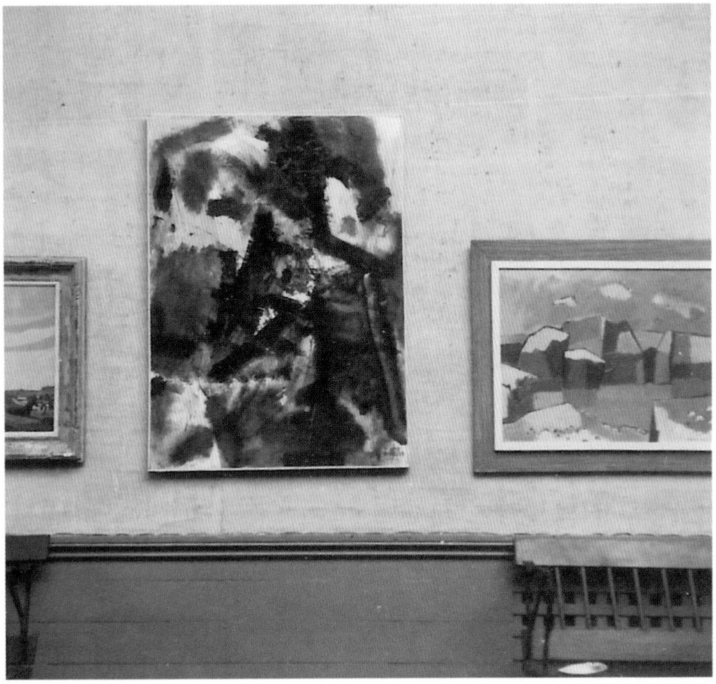

FIGURE 41. First Group '55 exhibition with Sam Feinstein's *Black Dominant* (Samuel L. Feinstein Trust)

statements were to be made available in the gallery, but it is not known whether this practice continued in future exhibitions. Feinstein kept his statement about *Black Dominant* (fig. 41), explaining that it "pertains to August nights in Provincetown."

Ciliberti, a friend of Wagman and soon to officially join the group, was in charge of the street-front windows for the Blum Store, at 13th and Chestnut Streets. The gallery exhibition and forum were publicized by including fifteen paintings by some of the artists and even the Group '55 logo in the store window displays for two weeks (figs. 38–39). Freid commented, "This alone was seen by many thousands who don't normally attend art exhibitions."[56]

The group's collaged "burst" logo, designed by Feinstein, was incorporated into posters and flyers for each event. Officers reached out to area art critics, publications, and radio stations to publicize exhibitions and forums. Freid wrote press releases that contributed to mentions in the *Philadelphia Inquirer*, *Art in Focus*, and suburban newspapers. Anticipating the group's historic importance, Feinstein arranged to have some of the forums recorded, and Crawford typed up transcripts of the audio.

The inaugural Group '55 exhibition opened on January 4, 1956, and received several reviews. Benson of the *Philadelphia Inquirer* reported favorably: "Practically all of the twenty-four exhibitors use the nonfigurative approach of the Abstract Expressionists. A serious effort has been made by many of the artists to explain in words their intention and direction. . . . The most impressive aspect of the show is the wholesome diversity in the use of color as a language to suggest light, tension, space, movement, volume, mood, emotion, ideas and experience with nature."[57]

More skeptically, Grafly commented, "It is well to consider that a work of art depends for lasting value on more than words and paint tubes." However, she accurately stated that the "dual objective is to show their work and through discussions and forums to bring about better understanding, not only between artist and public, but also between artist and artist. The Group hopes, in fact, that other professionals, perhaps a different slant, will band together so that there may be intergroup discussions." She generalized the stylistic scope as "predominantly abstract-nonobjective, with a thin sprinkling of those not yet weaned from an objective base."[58] (She did not announce or report on any of the other forums and may not have attended them.)

Much of what is known about the participants in any of the group exhibitions is thanks to reviews. Fortunately for this show, Walter E. Baum, who was also a landscape painter, described many of the paintings. For example: "Sam Fried's [sic] own painting, a large canvas in vigorous color forms, is in itself the artist's interpretation of a French poem that has to do with the overtones of a jungle. . . . Sam Feinstein's *Black Dominant* suggests in an epic way, the sea and scenes around Provincetown." Baum also let his readers know about "the first public discussion forum," explaining, "In view of the fact that any departure from conventional art forms brings with it surges of criticism that range from violent abuse to shoulder-shrugging neglect, the new organization feels the need for a clearing house of ideas—not so much to soften criticism as to combat apathy."[59]

The group planned to have paintings on view during forums. Shortly after the opening of the show, the first forum, "Changing Forms in Art," took place in the gallery on January 12. Kahn and serial music composer George Rochberg, both good friends of Feinstein and Crawford, were featured speakers, along with four painters. So great was the interest in the speakers that two hundred people had to be turned away, a measure of how hungry Philadelphians were for what Group '55 was offering. Moderator Feinstein apologized for the lack of a larger space, then explained why the group was formed:

> Our purpose is to help each other as artists by discussing our work with each other and to help to lessen that very wide gap which we feel exists between the layman and the artist in terms of a kind of communication which perhaps is not immediately felt in our work. Obviously, on a verbal level you cannot talk art, but you can talk around it and perhaps in that way to develop some insights, [even for work that is seen as] relatively barbaric.

Each speaker talked at length, with the whole forum lasting over an hour and a half. Rochberg, chairman of the music department at the University of Pennsylvania, spoke first: "Most people, including many musicians, painters, writers themselves, are resisting change in art. There are always with us those who believe in the status quo." He presented an overview of experimental twentieth-century composers from Stravinsky and Schoenberg up to John Cage and those creating then-current electronic music using tape recorders. To connect with abstract painting, he said some composers were creating "an abstract score."

Kahn talked in an abstract way about creating space through architecture and made memorable statements such as, "That which a thing wants to be is a powerful beginning of a problem. . . . We must decide what a thing wants to be. It's the spirit of it, the WHY aspect of the whole problem. And the WHAT aspect is the order and design is the means." An audience member questioned him about the new Penn Center, for which he did not win the design competition and was very critical of what was built.

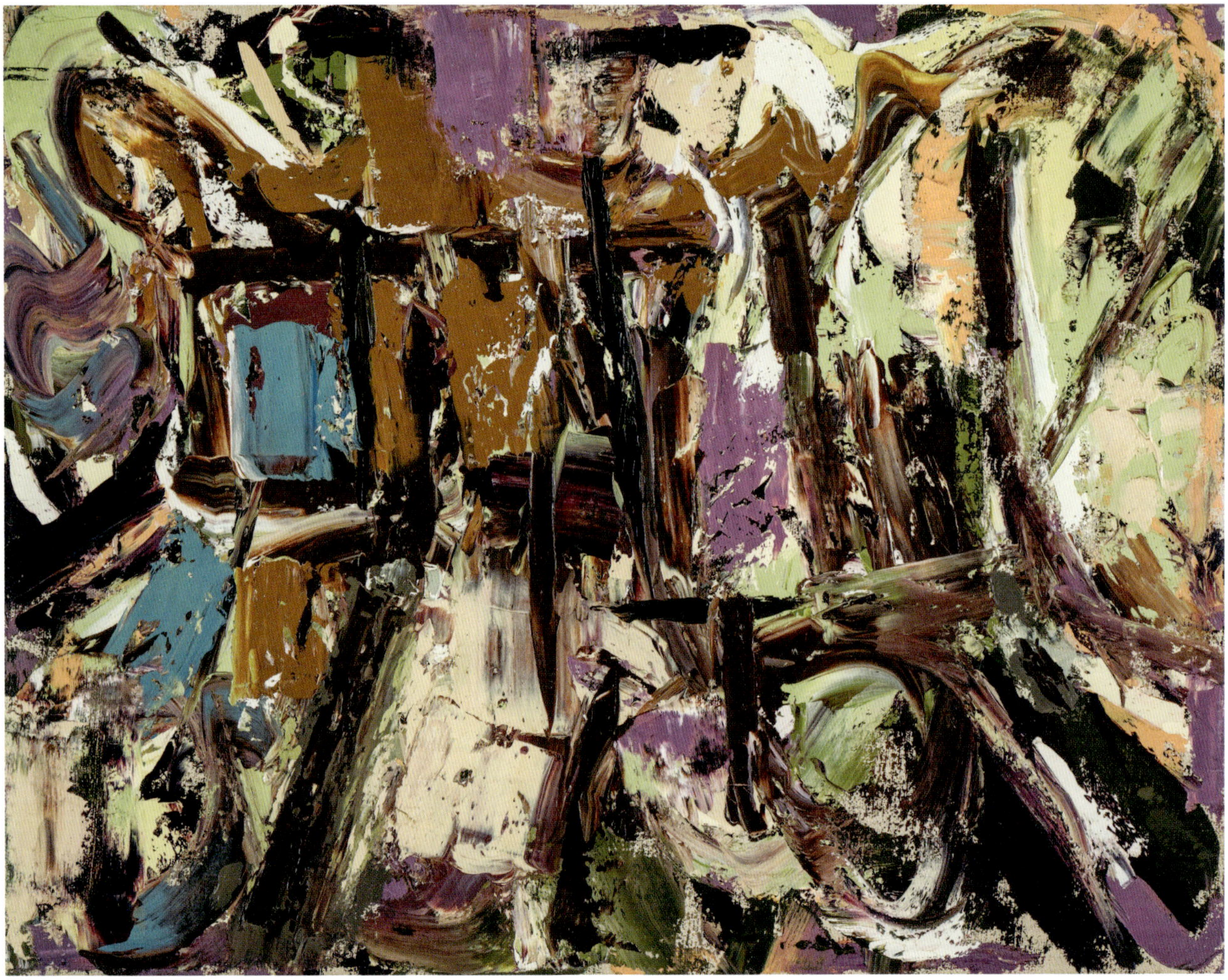

FIGURE 42. **Grand Marais (No. 3)**, 1955, by Raymond Hendler (Woodmere Art Museum: Gift of the Estate of Raymond Hendler, 2020)

Freid spoke about the outrage provoked by performances of the Ballets Russes in 1913, and how Stravinsky had challenged the expectations for a ballet, implying but not spelling out a parallel with the advent of Abstract Expressionist painting. He said that Cocteau concluded that "insult to habit is the thing that keeps art from stagnating and becoming a mere game." He provided insights about the aesthetic impact of poetry, such as how the sounds of words create a sense of movement: "by the rivering waters of—hithering, thithering waters of—Night." Poetry suggested "perfumes, sounds and colors. These are the dimensions in which painters and poets deal today. They are seemingly intangible things but that is what the poet-painter has in mind a great deal of the time."

Staffel described how some painters are interested in structure: "There is no such thing as the structure and the flesh of a painting. The structure is the flesh of a painting." She explained how the combination of feelings and awareness, expressed through patterns, movement, tension, space, and feeling and defying gravity, plus the direct use of materials, show the artist's "willingness to be intimate with himself and with his audience. He is breaking apart so many of the absolute and enclosed concepts that were so comfortable before. The structure and the flesh become one." She concluded, "I think every painter who paints today, to a more or less degree, goes through all these stages in a painting. [One starts with] free-floating attention [to feelings and experiences] and then out of the paint and ourselves grows a new form. . . . I think that there is an intimacy that is now being felt in American painting that is very important."

After talking about various forms of communication, Hendler explained that art can communicate without telling a story. He pointed out the "great variety among the work here represented," contrasting his own approach to painting, as in *Grand Marais (No. 3)* (fig. 42), to that of Freid and Feinstein. He focused on art terms used to describe paintings, or sometimes misused: "There's a difference, artistically speaking. . . between an abstract painting, an Abstract Expressionist, a nonobjective painting, nonrepresentational, and many other terms." After asking the audience to look around to see if they "could identify the terms relative to the pictures," he pointed out how Piper's was abstract because she started with specific objects, unlike his painting, which he called nonrepresentational. Piper agreed.

Finally, Feinstein talked about space: "One of the prime considerations of a contemporary painter. If he has given up the outside forms of things, he is concerned very much with space as an active, vital factor in terms of making his pictorial transformations as a parallel as to what his experience has been in nature . . . space is not simply dead areas. . . . All the spaces are servants of each other." He described actual objects as being three-dimensional while the canvas is two-dimensional and is an object in itself. "The canvas is a nature in itself," not just an echo of nature. He continued, "For that, just take a photograph."

The recording suggests that the question-and-answer session that followed was the most interesting for the audience. (Grafly reported: "Authentic enthusiasm detained the artist speakers long after the close of the program. And what of

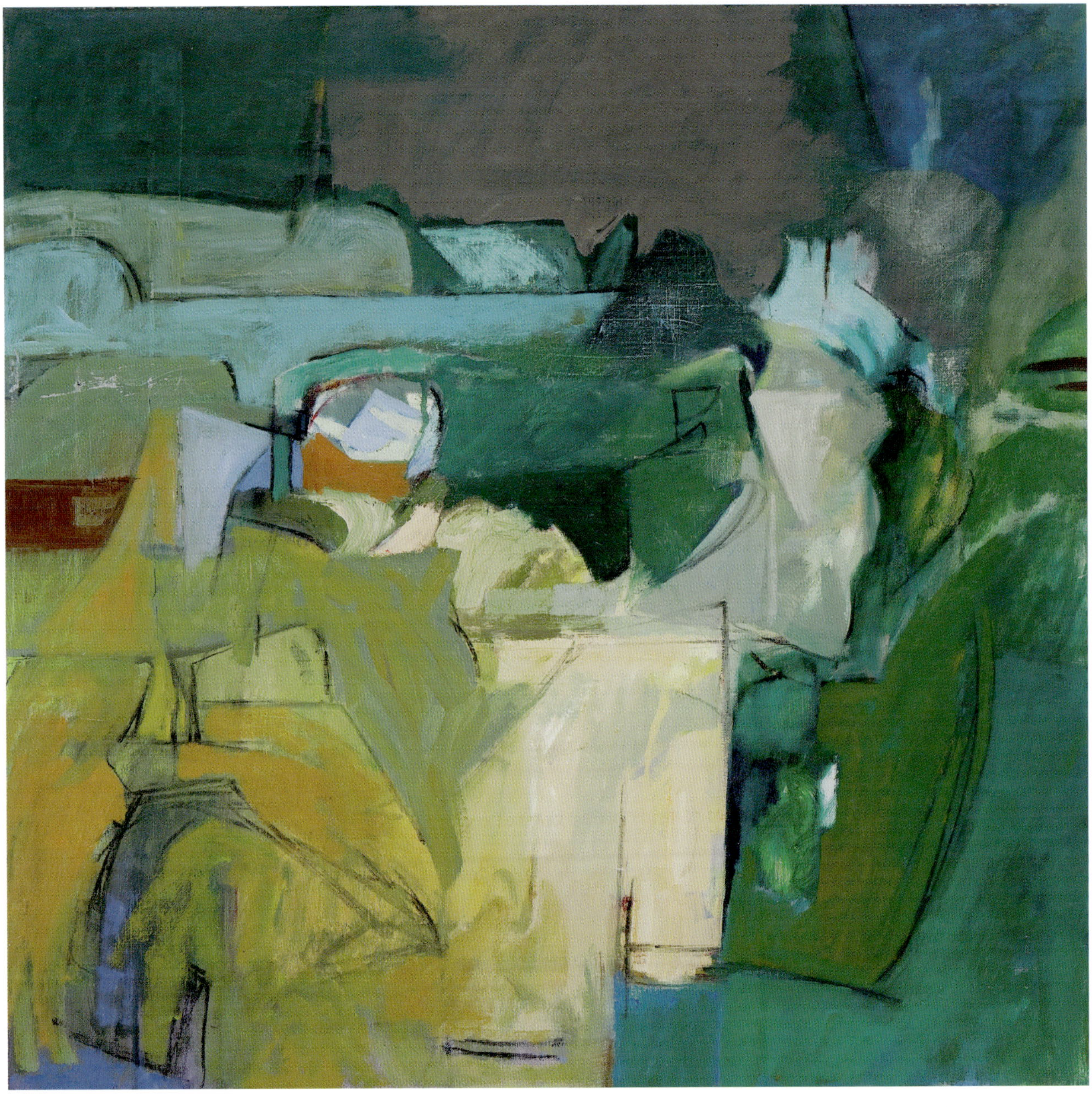

FIGURE 43. **Untitled**, c. 1950, by Doris Staffel (Woodmere Art Museum: Gift of the artist, 2011) Photograph by Rick Echelmeyer

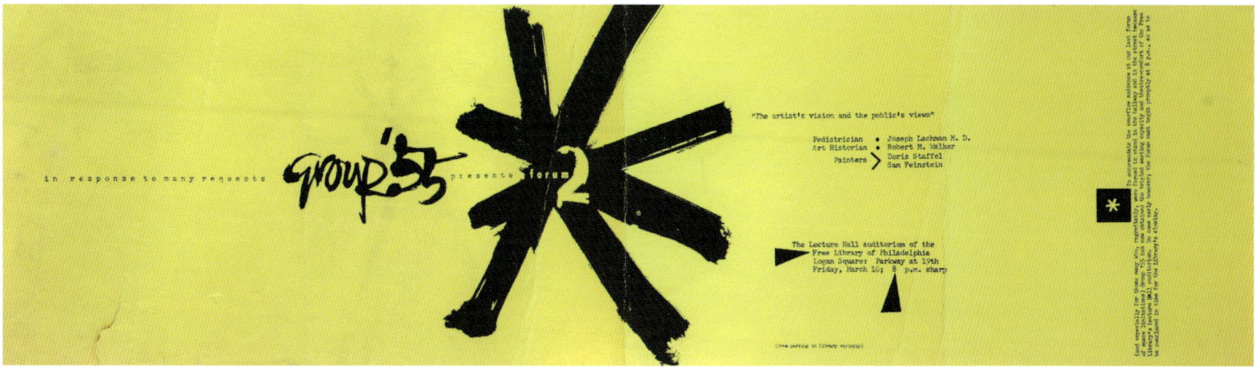

FIGURE 44. Invitation for the second Group '55 forum (Samuel L. Feinstein Trust)

sales? One watercolor, one print, no oils."[60]) Toward the end of the evening Feinstein asked for a show of hands of who was getting something out of the discussion. Because the artists had to pay for it to make it free, he asked people to contribute and to put their names on the mailing list for the next forum. The spirit of the forums was altruistic: there is no evidence that speakers expected to be paid, though there were some expenses for advertising, renting chairs, and other minor purchases.

A Series of Successful Forums

Group '55 members experimented with different formats for their forums over the first year. In response to the many attendees who could not be admitted to the first forum, the second forum, on March 16, was moved to the much larger lecture hall at the Free Library of Philadelphia, which could seat almost four hundred people. Unfortunately, many seats were left empty, with only one hundred attendees, as a heavy snowstorm hit the area that night. Paintings were arranged on easels as subjects for the discussion.

The topic of the second forum was "The Artist's Vision and the Public's Views." Staffel served as moderator, and the panel consisted of Feinstein, Dr. Joseph Lachman (a pediatrician and husband of Frances Lachman), and Swarthmore College art historian Robert M. Walker, who had participated from the audience at the first forum. Dr. Lachman's presence prompted a discussion of the common notion that even a child could make a good abstract painting; this was countered by the observation that a child cannot sustain the same level of quality over time. In answer to a question of how one can tell a good nonfigurative painting from a bad one, Feinstein explained:

> So, ask yourself this, when you're in front of the picture, so well now, does this really have to go together in this way? I see a bunch of colors and a bunch of forms here, and presumably the artist has wanted to set up some sort of rhythmic organization here. Does it have to go together this way? Try it. Block off a form. Block off a color. And if it doesn't change its meaning for you, if the rhythm isn't upset, then for you that painting isn't working.

> If that painting is really working, it should be profoundly affected by even the slightest change, by even the change of an inch.

Staffel added her perspective:

> I think that you might say amongst longtime painters or master painters or painters who are very committed, they develop an awareness on levels which are not intellectual or a mental level. Once you've had an experience you can recognize many things which are not on a verbal level. And I think this is awfully true in the area of painting.

Piper's paintings were the focus of discussion at both of the first two forums. The discussion of quality was illustrated by looking at three paintings by Piper, one of which Feinstein considered not as good as the others. She had been a student of Carles, who suggested she study with Hofmann, which she did in 1941. Like Carles, Paul Cézanne and Matisse guided various phases of her art. Her paintings were often inspired by something she experienced in nature, most often a still life but also, in the 1950s, by landscape. White, starting in the early 1950s, became actually her primary color, creating a sense of both air and light. Pointing to a successful work, possibly similar to the later *Landscape towards Abstraction (Torremolinos)* (fig. 45), where she captured a sense of radiant color and light from a vacation in southern Spain, Feinstein articulated what he saw happening:

> You'd be amazed how much of this has been painted out, painted over, redone. You'd have to get close to it to see what is underneath this work, before finally, a specific order is created, a specific tension, one which both begins to expand and at the same time, is held back by the four edges of the rectangle. Just as you expand when you breathe and at the same time, you are held in by your own structure. And so, this painting works. This painting exists because it really is radiant at you.

At the follow-up discussion, group members "generally agreed that the presence of laymen on the panel to ask pertinent questions was a definite step in the right direction, and [because the] primary function of Group '55 [was] the mutual discussion of painting at this meeting, the business was disposed of as quickly as possible to allow time for this purpose."

But Grafly questioned the value of talking about art and the new art itself: "Today abstractionists are eager to throw a book at the audience in hope that those who take time to read may learn a new vocabulary of color-form symbols. . . . Too many avant-garde compositions bog down in pyrotechnics or in a desire to challenge or to shock."[61]

Announcing the third forum, to be held on April 13, a *Philadelphia Evening Bulletin* critic commented on the previous event: "Group '55, a local artists' group, began its public forums to explain modern art (no easy task, that) to the laymen. . . . Apparently, the laymen want to solve some of the mysteries of modern art."[62] The third forum was a follow-up of the second on the same topic, "The Artist's Vision and the Public's Views," and was again held in the lecture hall of the Free Library of Philadelphia, with the same moderator and speakers.

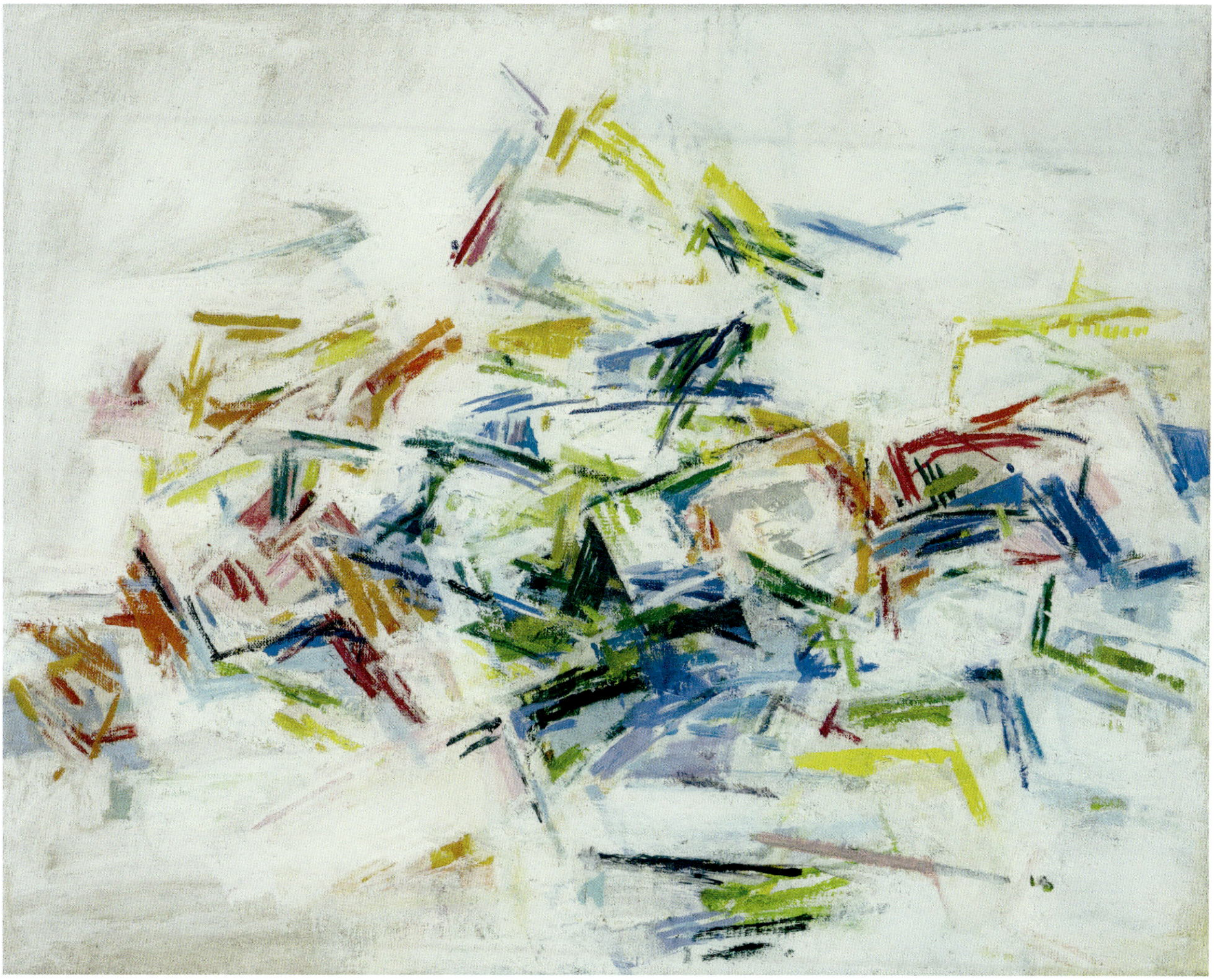

FIGURE 45. **Landscape towards Abstraction (Torremolinos)**, 1958–59, by Jane Piper (Woodmere Art Museum: Gift of Karen Segal, 2017)

At their April 21 meeting, group members "felt that there was a sympathetic relationship between panel and audience for the first time in the last forum, though some people objected to laymen participating as part of the panel." Because the panelists who were not artists were knowledgeable about art, "the meeting was rigged." Some thought the event was "too orderly, without enough play between panel and audience." So, the group moved to have another forum with only artists on "a panel of four with one painting apiece. . . . the paintings to be displayed upon the stage as before. Questions directed to the panel to be written on slips of paper and answered by any of the panel."

The group asked Feinstein to be on the panel, along with Brodhead, Crawford, and Wagman, and that he repeat a short slide talk on the history of art that he had recently given at Swarthmore College. Meetings were now to take place twice a month. Pictures by potential new members were to be voted in with the required three-quarters majority. Two weeks later, on May 2, Freid chaired a meeting of sixteen members. In line with the desire for clear rules, some suggested "a constitution embodying the basic purpose and regulation of Group '55 be drawn up in a cohesive, compact form."

Looking over the accomplishments of the group's first year, Freid expressed pride in a letter to critic Baum: "Judging by the response thus far we have filled a void which existed in the Philadelphia art world. People in ever-increasing numbers seem eager and thirsting for just such informative meetings with the artists. . . . Aside from painting itself, what more vital function could we perform in the interest of art? The general public is still so illiterate concerning the art of painting. . . . I honestly do believe that Group '55 was the most important thing that developed in Philadelphia in the art season 1955–56." He asked Baum to let people know about the upcoming forum. "We members of Group '55 work long and hard to prepare these forums—we do so as a civic responsibility. Our reward is none other than the satisfaction derived from knowing that we are doing our utmost to enlighten the public."[63]

As planned, the topic of the fourth forum, held on May 18, was "Four Abstract Painters Analyze Their Pictures," focusing on paintings by "four outstanding abstract artists of the Philadelphia area with audience participation encouraged," according to the *Delaware County Daily Times*.[64] Brodhead's face would light up almost half a century later when talking about her pride in having her painting focused on by the large audience that attended the event.

Nevertheless, group members suggested afterward that "for next year fewer painters speak longer and more specifically about their work. The reading of papers was considered unadvisable." It is clear that the members were idealistic and actively engaged, working to create formats and rules that worked well, constantly striving to foster meaningful and open dialogue between artists and the public—not easy to achieve in a large lecture hall. But dissatisfaction was mounting among the members.

Discontent

After a summer out of the city, on September 28, 1956, only nine months after the launch of Group '55, tensions among members surfaced at the first fall meeting. Feinstein faced pushback: some disliked having his students and other "unknown painters" included with "professionals." In a letter to

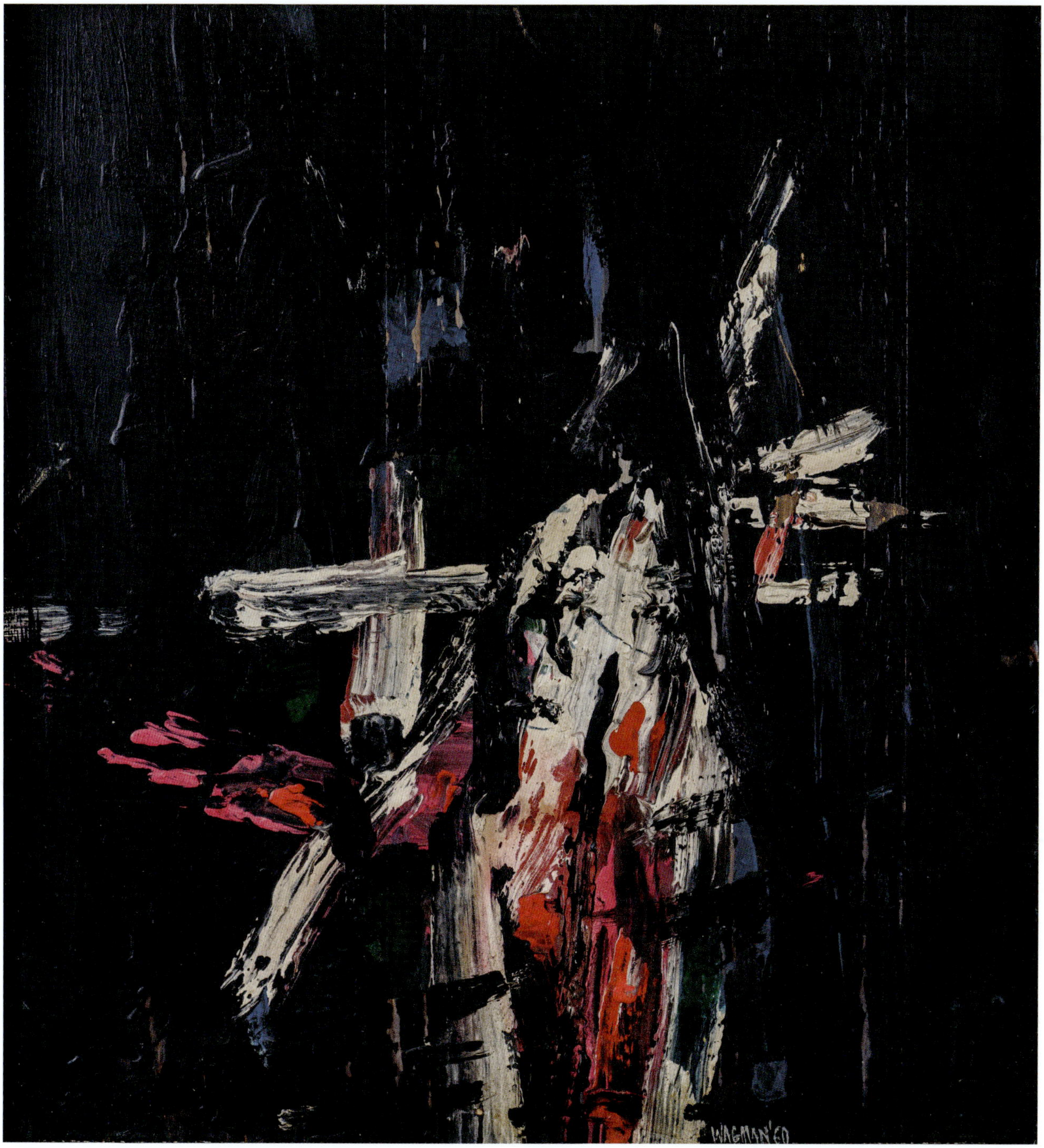

FIGURE 46. **Untitled**, 1960, From *Zen Series 2*, by Mitchel G. Wagman (Courtesy of the Estate of Mitchel G. Wagman)

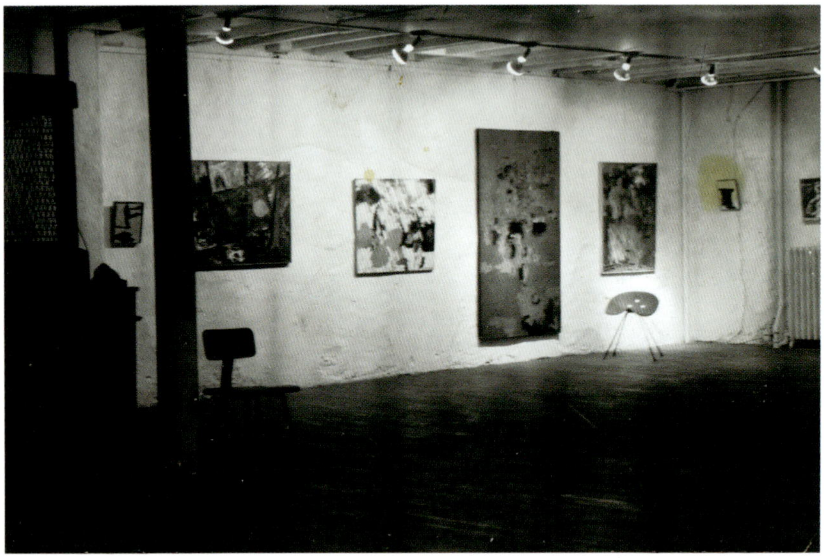

FIGURE 47. Group '55 exhibition of New York abstract expressionist artists organized by Feinstein at Dubin/Gallery '55 that opened on February 15, 1957 (Samuel L. Feinstein Trust)

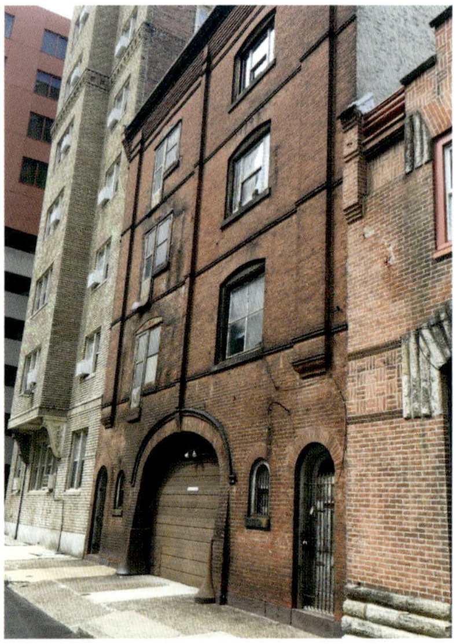

FIGURE 48. This building designed as a stable at 1319–21 Irving Street was the location of Dubin/Gallery '55.

Feinstein the previous spring, Bechtle had conveyed concern about presenting to the public work by mature painters alongside that of students, no matter whether they "possess[ed] seriousness of purpose and potential growth."[65] At the meeting, Jennings moved that "no applicant would be eligible who was still studying with a member of Group '55." After much discussion, the motion was not carried. A proposal that forums be abandoned set off more heated debate. In notes he made of the meeting, Feinstein admitted that there were "personality clashes creating a highly acrimonious atmosphere" and that his own "aggressive manner and undiplomatic expressions brought forth personal hostilities which culminated in threats of resignation." Forums were supported by thirteen of the seventeen members present. A new Forum Committee was formed, consisting of Bechtle, Ciliberti, Anderson, Greenberg, and Crawford. After the three-hour business meeting ended at 11:30 p.m., some stalwarts stayed to discuss Wagman's paintings on view in the gallery.

The postcard sent out for the next meeting, on October 19, raised some hackles: "Absence at this meeting without written notification will automatically indicate your termination of membership. Fran Lachman Per SF." Several active members, including Staffel, neither attended the meeting nor wrote to explain. Bechtle believed that they were "thrown out." He later wrote on the postcard: "(This was the 'End' of Group '55. Sam Feinstein made a mess of it.)"[66] It is possible that Feinstein was trying to ascertain who was still committed to the group and who was resigning. This seems to have been confirmed at the meeting, which included a discussion of how to readmit anyone who had resigned.

A Group '55 roundtable, in effect the fifth forum of the calendar year, took place on November 30 at the Free Library, on the topic "What Do Abstract Forms Communicate?" With the new Forum Committee in charge, the format changed: "A distinctive feature of this roundtable will be the informal exchange of ideas between the lay audience and the panel members, from the very start of the get-together, instead of a short question-and-answer period which was the pattern of our last season's forums."

Freid, Feinstein, and Wagman spoke that evening, and Bechtle presented slides of old master paintings "to foster an awareness of the continuing bases in art—representational or abstract."[67] He was delighted with the outcome of his talk:

> I introduced the "relationship" of Vermeer (1631–75) and Mondrian (1872–1944) in their formal similarities. At the close of this meeting Violette de Mazia, director of the Barnes Foundation, introduced herself to me and because of the unusual and "wonderful position I had created between the two artists" she gave me permission to visit the Barnes Foundation whenever I wished.[68]

In addition to this roundtable, Feinstein had spoken on the panels of all four forums and had given talks about abstract art at the opening of the exhibition in January, at Swarthmore College in April, and at a radio forum titled " Modern Art—Is It Art?" in May.[69] He was clearly the leader and spokesperson for Group '55, and others may have been jealous or resentful of his prominence. Negative feelings were again stirred up at the December 14 meeting. Feinstein proposed that Dubin's new gallery, located on Irving Street, be made the official home of Group '55 and suggested that the members all pitch in to "make the gallery presentable." He further explained that Dubin proposed a partnership with him, giving him half the commissions on sales. While the group did agree to associate with Dubin, some may have been angered that Feinstein could personally profit, and a "heated attack of personal nature on Sam Feinstein precipitated by Sam Freid" ensued.[70] (There is no evidence in his tax records that Feinstein ever received earnings from Gallery '55.)

The new Dubin/Gallery '55, no longer in partnership with Beryl Lush, opened in January 1957. Grafly offered a vivid description:

> [The new location is] one of those quaint, narrow links between streets in Our Town's so-called "Village." . . . The new gallery, once a stable, may be reached from Juniper St. which is intersected by Irving south of Locust; or from 13th St. where Irving intersects it on the west side between Locust and Spruce . . . Plans are to establish a "Village" art center, with the Dubin Gallery and Gallery '55 above stairs, and an intimate theater on the ground floor . . . Walls have been white-washed; lighting is modern; but rafters, open space, and [a] hint of one-time horse stalls, lend atmosphere. Gallery space is so arranged that the two galleries may become one, thus assuring exhibition flexibility, and offering a chance for large shows.

She also described Dubin's new partner:

> "Samuel Feinstein, Phila. Painter, hopes to bring work into the gallery from NYC as well as from this area. Lectures and forums also are being planned; while the walls of a ramp leading from street floor to galleries eventually will be hung with a history of art, tracing via color reproductions (plus explanatory captions) the development of form and color from the days of the old masters to the present.[71]

But despite the change in venue, personal conflicts persisted within the group. Members may have worried that the New York artists Feinstein planned to show in Dubin's galleries would draw attention away from their work. Dubin was upset because members had not helped get the new space ready. And some may have felt that the group was demanding too much of their time and energy. In his journal, Bechtle captured some of the issues that bothered him: "the apparent selfish domination" of the group by Feinstein and the negative feelings of all but Feinstein's students, along with "the lack of a substantial number of talented & interesting personalities since the removal from the Group by Feinstein of such personalities as Hankins, Whitehill, Doris Staffel, Sankowsky, & Wagman." (Feinstein believed they had resigned.) Bechtle expressed confidence that they would be open to joining another group.[72]

Controversy and Rebellion

The arrival of the new year brought two simultaneous Group '55 exhibitions and a breaking apart of the group. A solo presentation in the Dubin Gallery of Brodhead's abstract paintings garnered a review from the *Philadelphia Inquirer*, which noted that her "oils reveal a new exploration of moving three-dimensional space, suggested through accented triangles and arcs of light-filled color and tonally varied planes."[73] Her dynamic *Abstract #1* (fig. 49) would fit this description. The second exhibition, on view in Gallery '55 was a group show. It included paintings by Anderson, Lachman, Mayerson, Milliken, and Goodman—Feinstein students—along with Crawford and Feinstein.

Just two days later the *Group '55 Exhibition*, with the work of fourteen artists, opened at the Community Arts Center in Wallingford, Pennsylvania, where Lachman taught. She and Milliken, also a member of the center, were included. The show marked the first time that abstract paintings had been presented at the venue, and it attracted a "record turnout of members and friends" and was considered "provocative" by the *Delaware County Daily Times*. Feinstein gave a version of his illustrated talk "Abstract Painting." A reviewer noted that the artist used his early "representational pictures" and sketches to illustrate his process of moving to abstraction, and that he spoke about color as "an entity in itself [and how] it is possible to create emotions and concepts without familiar forms or structures."[74]

Abstract art was controversial in that suburb just nine miles southwest of Philadelphia. A *Chester County Daily Times* reviewer wrote with anticipation, "A burning issue at the Community Arts Center for almost a year may come to a climax on Jan. 26, when a panel discussion, 'What Does Modern Art Mean to Me?' opens at 3:30." Feinstein was the only artist on the panel, which was moderated by an editor at the newspaper. The panel included representatives of various professions from the Wallingford area, including a physicist, an architect, an assistant manager at the *Philadelphia Inquirer*, and scientist T. Harry Milliken, husband of Margaret Milliken.[75]

A week before the panel took place, there was a profound shift in the fate of Group '55. At a meeting at Feinstein and Crawford's home, Feinstein resigned as president in light of his new responsibilities at the gallery. Bechtle was elected president by the fourteen members present. He understood that the group would not be able to

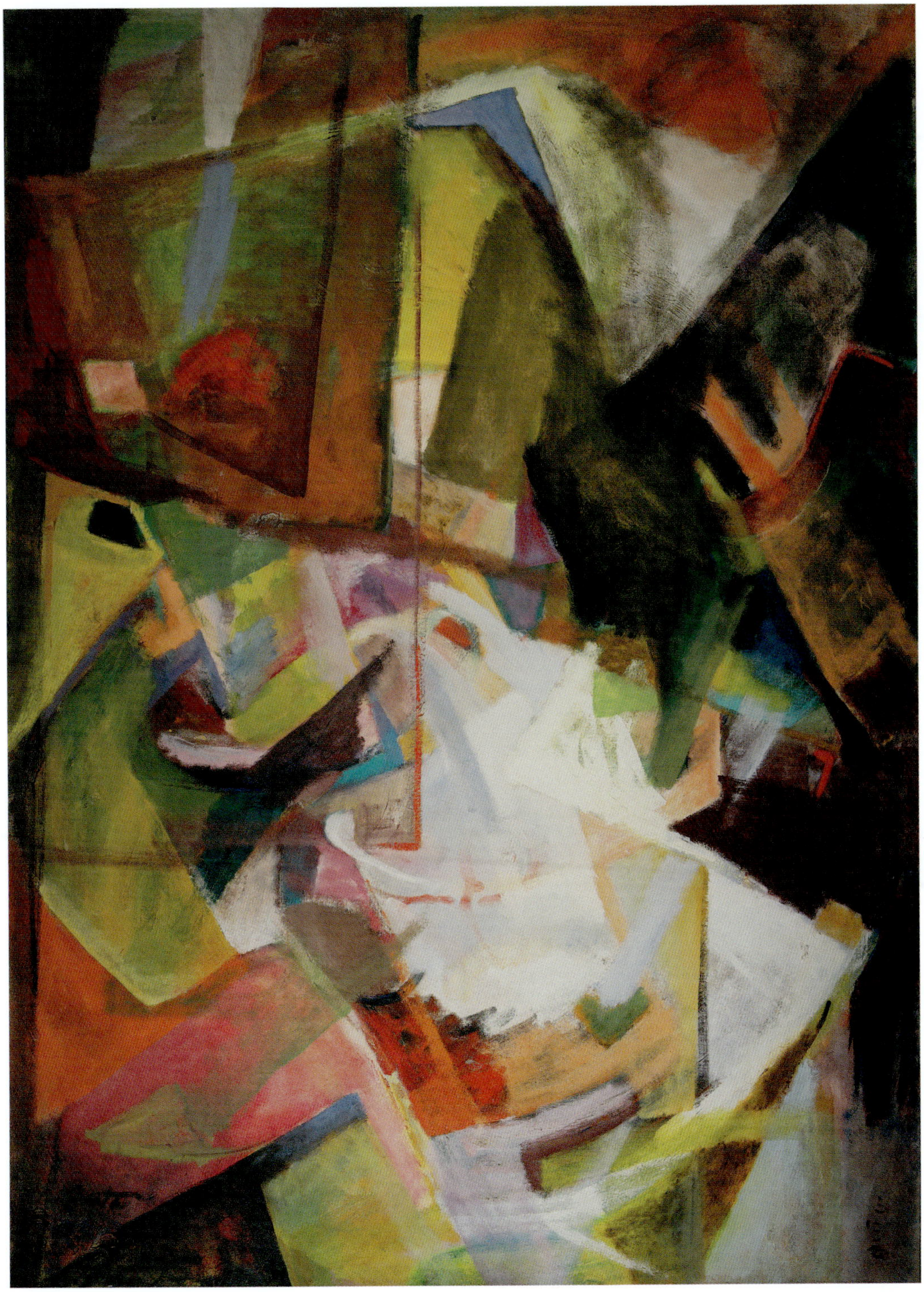

FIGURE 49.
Abstract #1, c. 1955, by Quita Brodhead (Woodmere Art Museum: Gift of the Brodhead Family, 2013) Photograph by Rick Echelmeyer

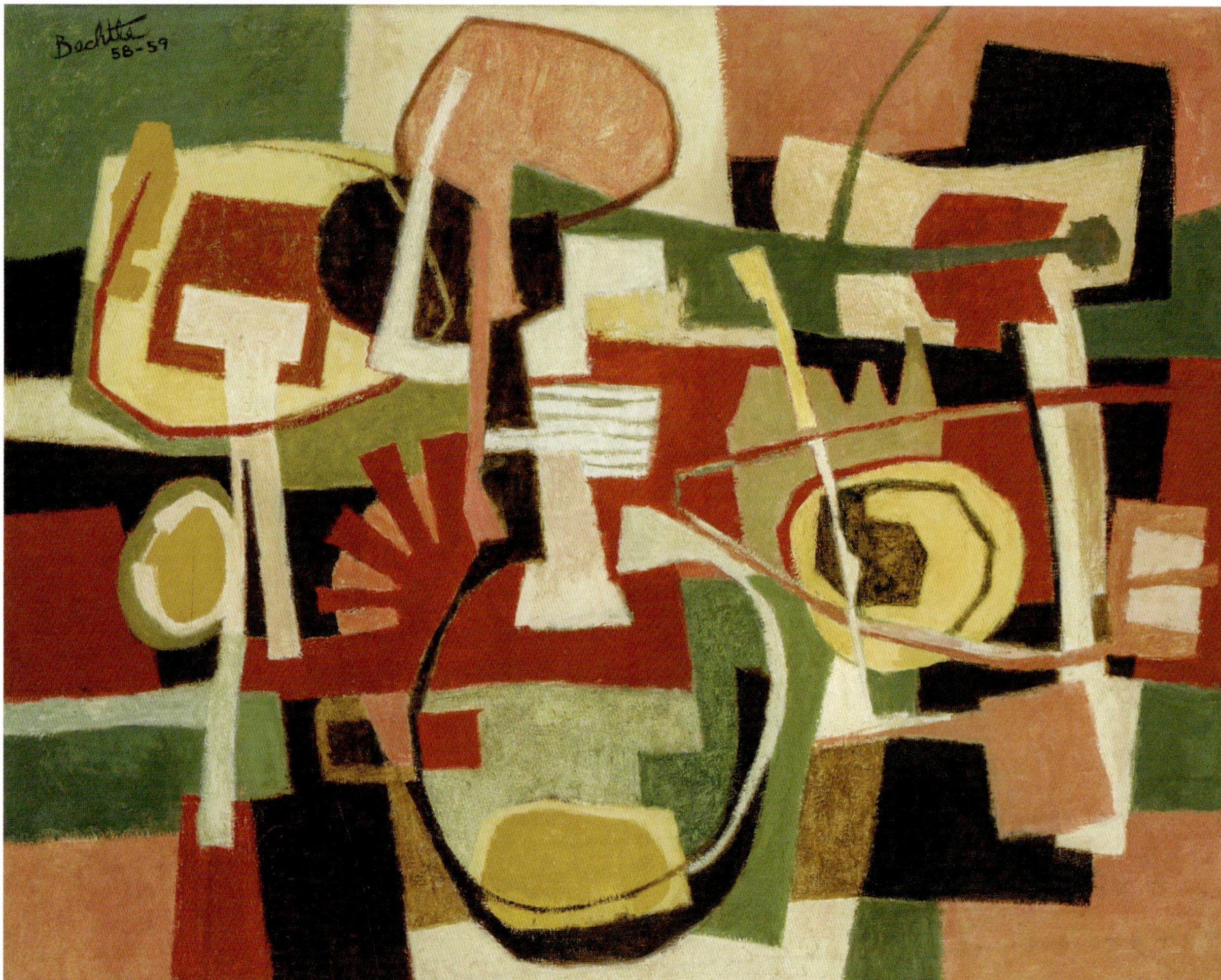

FIGURE 50. **Untitled**, 1958–59, by C. Ronald Bechtle (Woodmere Art Museum: Gift of Reid and Dorothy Bechtle, 2020)

meet in the new space because "the organization did not do physical work on the preparation of said gallery."[76]

One of the group's younger members, Bechtle was an engineering design consultant and not a full-time artist. He first had a painting, *7th Street Cellar* (fig. 168), accepted for a juried exhibition at Woodmere Art Museum in 1952. Although he had been exhibiting in group shows for five years, his first solo show was at Red Door Gallery in 1956. Grafly described his work as "precisely organized. Each canvas has developed from innumerable preliminary sketches. . . . Forms are abstract, although one may find a point of take off in objects on a draughtsman's table."[77] His only known exhibition with Group '55 was the one that month in Wallingford. An article on Bechtle described him as "a quick-smiling man" and went on to say:

> Bechtle does not fit too well into the stereotype of the painter of modern art. He goes to work every morning at the Philco Corporation where he is manager of the cost estimating department of the appliance division. "I'm a mathematician," he grinned. He said he liked to paint abstractly to make people think and compared abstract art with music.[78]

Bechtle's abstract paintings of the mid-1950s were carefully composed. Starting with a drawing, he made changes as he was painting, using a limited palette and clearly defined shapes. *Untitled* (fig. 50) seems inspired by a still life, not of fruit and flowers but rather of gears and machine parts. His attention to the picture plane, creating flat forms in shallow space, shows his basis in cubism, and perhaps awareness of Marcel Duchamp, whose work had just recently been donated to the Philadelphia Museum

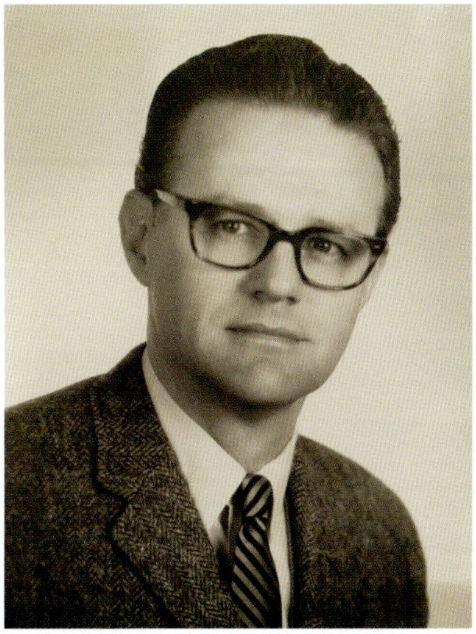

FIGURE 51.
C. Ronald Bechtle, c. 1950s (Courtesy of Reid and Dorothy Bechtle)

of Art. Bechtle's rational approach to the canvas was diametrically opposed to Feinstein's intuitive process based on accretions of strokes of color growing without a preconceived result.

As the group's newly elected president, Bechtle took immediate steps by requesting members' addresses and records of the financial account, which showed a balance of only seventy dollars, mostly from donations at the November forum.[79] But instead of acting as president of Group '55, he, along with Ciliberti, Freid, Greenberg, and Wagman, sent a formal resignation letter, dated February 1, to all Group '55 members. The next day they followed with letters inviting each recipient to join them at a meeting at the Print Club, at 1614 Latimer Street in Philadelphia, "for the express purpose of forming a new group within the framework of which we may more readily realize the manifestation of those principles upon which Group '55 was originally established."[80] Nine additional members accepted the invitation, leaving Feinstein, his students, and a handful of others in Group '55.

Those interested in the new group met at the Print Club on February 15, the same day as the opening of Feinstein's show of New York artists at Dubin/Gallery '55. In attendance were Bechtle, Brodhead, Ciliberti, Hankins, Greenberg, Freid, Jennings, Staffel, Wagman, and Whitehill, with Bechtle noting that he considered Lachman, Nelson, Piper, and Sankowsky members as well. All but Whitehill and Nelson joined the core group of twelve members who would show together until at least 1969 as Philadelphia Abstract Artists, with some additions over the years.

Nelson, an active abstract painter exhibiting and teaching in Philadelphia, was given a solo exhibition in the Dubin Galleries in December 1956 and later exhibited once with Philadelphia Abstract Artists. Bechtle also planned to invite Zion, Warren Rohrer, and Keene. Day attended a March meeting, but never joined, although his work at the time would have fit in well.

At that first meeting, Bechtle asked everyone to write a statement of what they wanted from the group, saving the scraps of paper. Common themes were the desire to discuss their art in one another's homes, socialize, and mount exhibitions. Staffel wrote: "Exhibiting group—not sure what kind of discussion group. Chance to see each other's work—partly social including husbands and wives at studio meetings." Jennings stated his goal: "To know and understand ourselves and the others. To formulate our ideas. No projects. When the time comes and we feel we wish to we will have an exhibit or exhibits. No officers, no chairman. Assume we are all ladies and gentlemen." Hankins was looking for "mutual communication on an informal basis." The artists did meet at the homes of different members, including Hankins's in March and Brodhead's in May. Staffel's turn on December 31 was a New Year's party.

As director of the new group, Bechtle distributed typed mimeographed letters and notices as well as guidelines for hanging exhibitions, all of which provide invaluable information about the organization. Meetings were mostly informal discussions about art in members' studios. An Exhibition Committee distributed clear procedures, stipulating how many works each artist could submit, what information to supply, and who was responsible for which tasks. The committee did not consider itself a jury and aspired to hang work "with the lens of continuity, variety, and personal dignity of a member in mind."

The philosophy of the group was articulated by Freid in the press release for exhibitions (which started and ended with poetry):

> Each of these poet-painters feels the compelling need to use art as a means of attaining spiritual growth. They probe nature . . . wrest secrets from nature . . . transform nature. The poet-painter is a sensitive and perceptive experiencer of the human situation who is able to create within his own work the pattern of a new order, from which other men may learn.[81]

A 1959 letter drafted by Bechtle stated that the painters had joined "in order to consolidate their efforts in the exhibition of their work and to further develop themselves individually through discussion etc. of the names and philosophy of modern art that such a group embraces." He emphasized their professionalism, which had been his concern for Group '55: "The group is composed of eleven

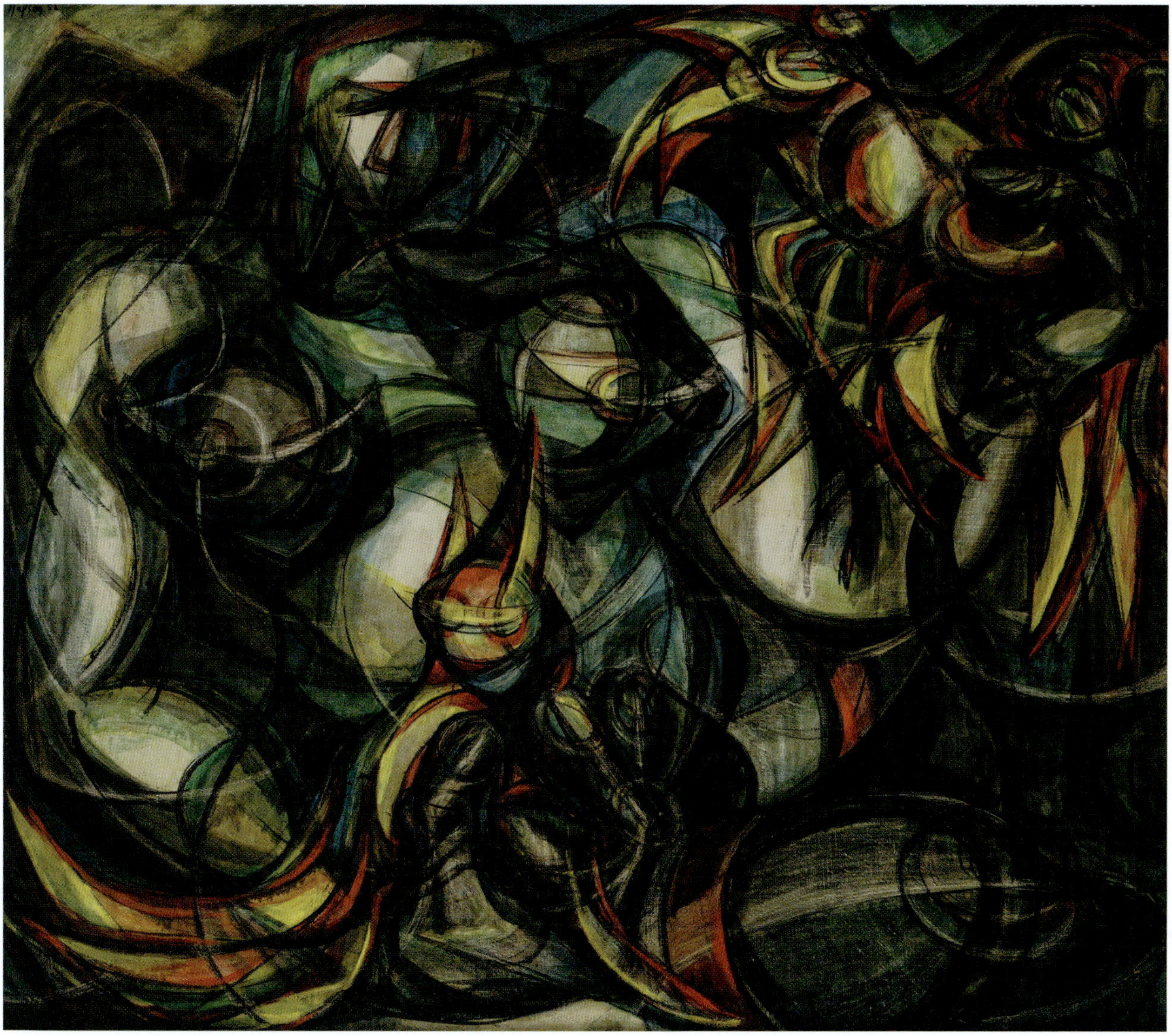

FIGURE 52. **Woman and Birds,** 1952, by Leonard Nelson (Woodmere Art Museum: Museum purchase, 2019)

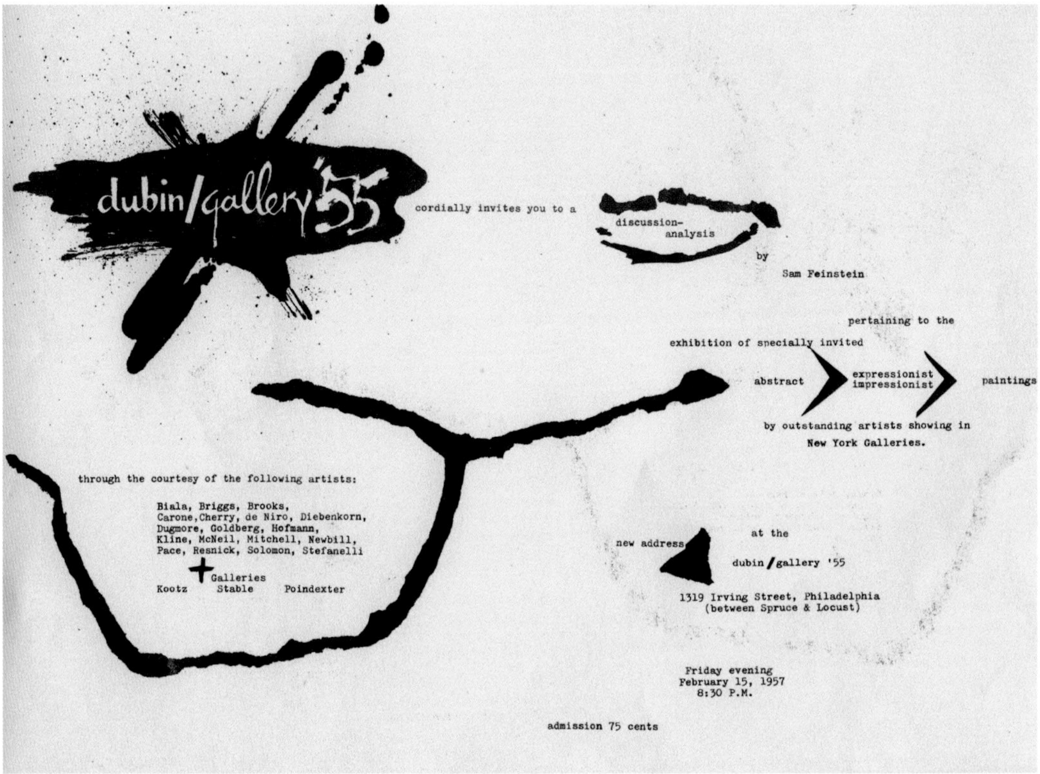

FIGURE 53. Invitation to a discussion by Sam Feinstein on February 15, 1957 at Dubin/Gallery '55 (Samuel L. Feinstein Trust)

professional painters (the term 'professional' pertains to the degree of commitment) who have been painting for a considerable period of time in abstract or the nonrepresentational idiom. The majority of these people have exhibited broadly at the local level (Phila. & New York) and a few of them are represented in such collections as the Pennsylvania Academy of the Fine Arts, the Barnes Collection, and the Museum of Modern Art, etc."[82]

Evidently following up on the success of the Group '55 forums, the Print Club offered Philadelphia artists the opportunity to gather on second Fridays beginning in October 1957 for discussions in a variety of fields. Speakers included Sankowsky, Kahn, Persichetti, and sociologist E. Digby Baltzell (Piper's husband), in a series called "The Creative Process in the Arts and Sciences." Staffel believed that these talks "sprang from Group '55" and remembered them going on for four or five years, with Whitehill organizing the "Print Club Group."[83]

Meanwhile, Feinstein and the remaining Group '55 members forged ahead with the group's educational mission by organizing exhibitions, performances, and discussions at Dubin/Gallery '55. Some members, including Lachman, also joined Philadelphia Abstract Artists, and members of Philadelphia Abstract Artists, such as Ciliberti, continued to attend and support Feinstein's events.

In February, Feinstein installed a significant show of New York artists at Dubin/Gallery '55, likely bringing the work of many to Philadelphia for the first time. The show was probably hung in the main gallery, with paintings by Lachman and Milliken in the back room. Feinstein drew on his connections to mount the "exhibition of eighteen specially invited Abstract/Expressionist-Impressionist paintings by outstanding artists showing in New York galleries," among them Hofmann, Kline, Robert De Niro Sr., Richard Diebenkorn, Michael Goldberg, and Joan Mitchell. The opening event included discussion and analysis by Feinstein.

That spring, Feinstein organized the first in a series of contemporary music recitals followed by discussions with him and composer Joseph Castaldo at Dubin/Gallery '55. On March 24, a harp and horn performance by Philadelphia Orchestra members Marcella DeCray and Leonard Hale was followed by a discussion between music director Castaldo and Feinstein on the topic "The New Artist-Audience Relationship in America," comparing "related problems in contemporary music and painting." Castaldo commented:

> The concrete aspect of any art form, especially music, is that one can say that a piece of music presents itself and only itself as a sunset would present itself. We don't ask the sunset to represent anything. You don't ask the sunset to be an abstraction of anything. It just is. Just as a piece of music just is. And we must not come to it with any preconceived idea of what it should be. We should listen to it, or we should see a painting just as itself. Just as an order exists. So, a piece of music exists. A painting exists.

Feinstein agreed, saying, "People expect music to be music. People still somehow expect painting to be a reference to nature, a notation of nature, if you will. It is very logical really." He suggested reflecting on the history of painting, where what has made painters great is not the subject, "but the structure in their work which has emanated a meaning."

In April, Dubin/Gallery '55 showed *New Work by Members of Group '55*. That same month, perhaps because Brodhead was on the jury, PAFA's Fellowship show included more abstract work than usual, and awards were given to Hankins and Nelson.[84]

On May 22, pianist Hinderas performed contemporary music by Castaldo, Alban Berg, Edward Clark, and Paul Hindemith. The avant-garde composers were using twelve-tone systems, incorporating dissonance, and moving away from recognizable melodies, suggesting comparisons with Abstract Expressionist paintings that may have been on the walls. The concert was followed by a continuation of the discussion from the March event.

From today's perspective, one might wonder why jazz was not part of the Group '55 recitals, since it was the music that many Abstract Expressionist painters were listening to at the time and Philadelphia itself had a strong jazz culture. Although popular, jazz did not have the academic credibility it has now or connections to the topics selected for the Group '55 programs, where many of the participants had ties to the University of Pennsylvania and the Philadelphia Orchestra.

A Season of Lively Competition

The fall of 1957 was the start of an active art scene for Philadelphians interested in abstract art, with exhibitions being organized by Group '55 and its offspring. The first of three planned Philadelphia Abstract Artists exhibitions opened at the Carlen Galleries in October. All the members except Sankowsky participated, with more than one painting each and members contributing to the expenses. Hedley H. Rhys in the *Philadelphia Inquirer* wrote, "The first impression here is one of strict stylistic unity, not to say conformity," and found the paintings "not communicable verbally." He thought Wagman's work "much influenced by the late Jackson Pollock," perhaps referring to a painting like *Time #4* (fig. 55). He noted that Bechtle's presented "numbered compositions," similar in style to *Untitled* (fig. 54). Bechtel's untitled composition seems to allude to figures and to suggest his affinity to Duchamp's *The Bride Stripped Bare by Her Bachelors, Even (The Large Glass)*, first on view at the Philadelphia Museum of Art in 1954. He could find no "trace of representation" in Freid's work, and he found Piper's *Study of Flowers* a "surprise for being representational."[85]

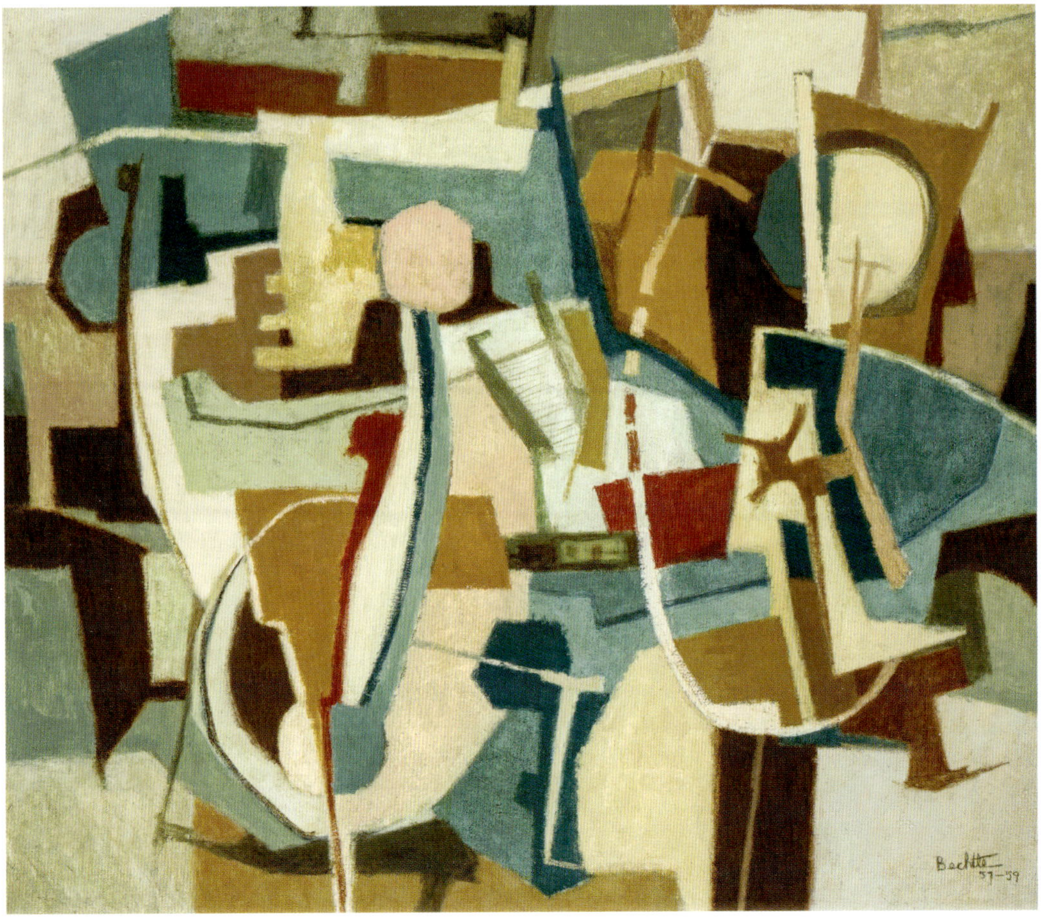

FIGURE 54.
Untitled,
1957–59, by C. Ronald Bechtle (Woodmere Art Museum: Gift of Reid and Dorothy Bechtle, 2020)

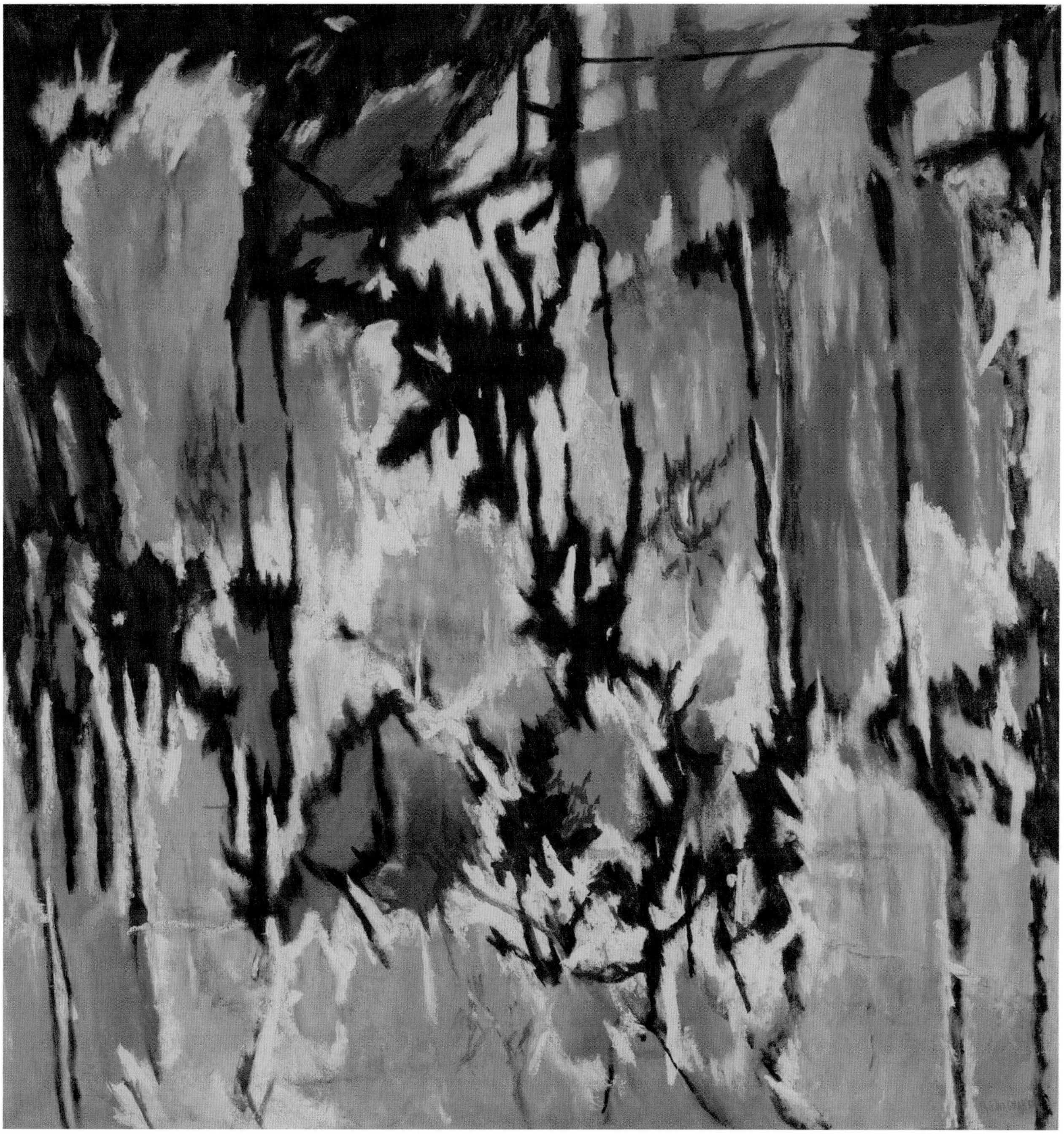

FIGURE 55. *Time #4*, 1955, by Mitchel G. Wagman (Collection of Laurie Wagman)

FIGURE 56.
Poster for the first Philadelphia Abstract Artists exhibition (Estate of Mitchel G. Wagman)

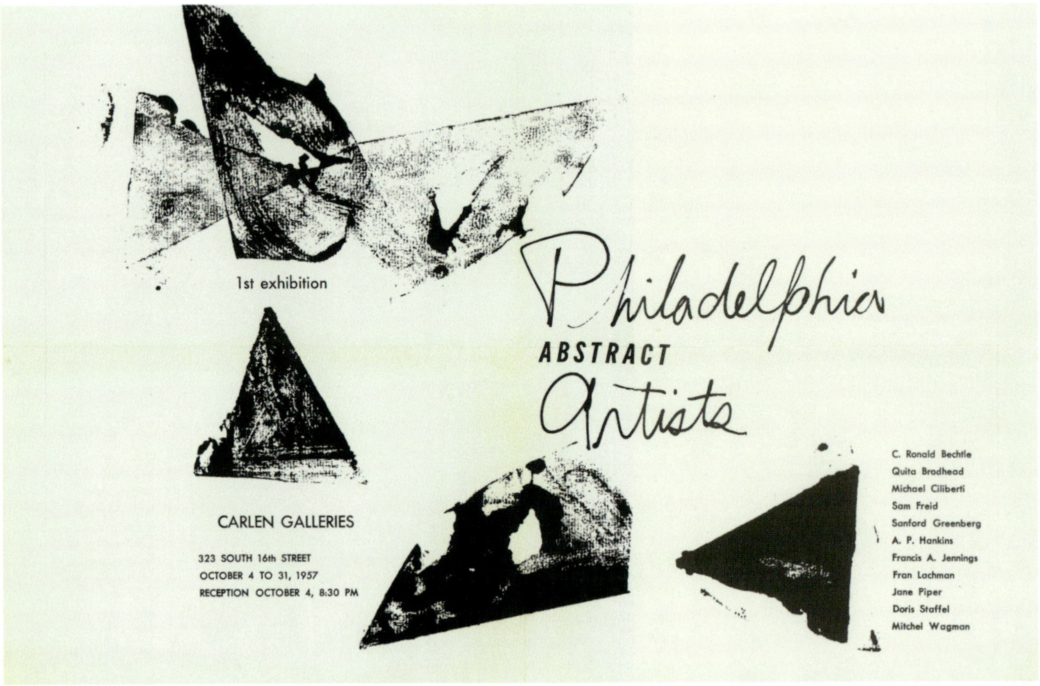

Grafly, drawing from Freid's press release, explained the artists' view:

> The paintings are not paintings of things as such. They are not stories. Nor are they political or social tracts. These paintings are a distillation of some of our life experiences. . . . Each painting grows according to the laws of its own nature: like a flowering plant, bearing leaves, bearing flowers, bearing fruit—a fusion of spirit and nature.[86]

One would think Feinstein would have readily agreed with these ideas, suggesting that the motivation for the people breaking away from Group '55 was more personal than philosophical.

The group followed up in December with *Philadelphia Abstract Artists Second Exhibition* at the Fleisher Art Memorial, with work by twelve members. Art historian Walker, who had been part of the second Group '55 forum, wrote a sympathetic review for the *Philadelphia Inquirer*. He explained the philosophy of the group and stated that the work exemplified "the desire to break up the surface and develop strong spatial sensations," as seen in Greenberg's *No. 24* (fig. 57). He noted that the work could be considered realist because "reality lies behind the surface of natural appearances," a philosophy tinged with existentialism.[87]

That same fall, Feinstein hung three exhibitions in Dubin/Gallery '55, two in the same months as those of the new group: *Group '55* in October, a solo show of nonobjective paintings by Milliken in November, and *Abstractionists: Group '55* in December.[88] Which artists exhibited in the group shows is not known.

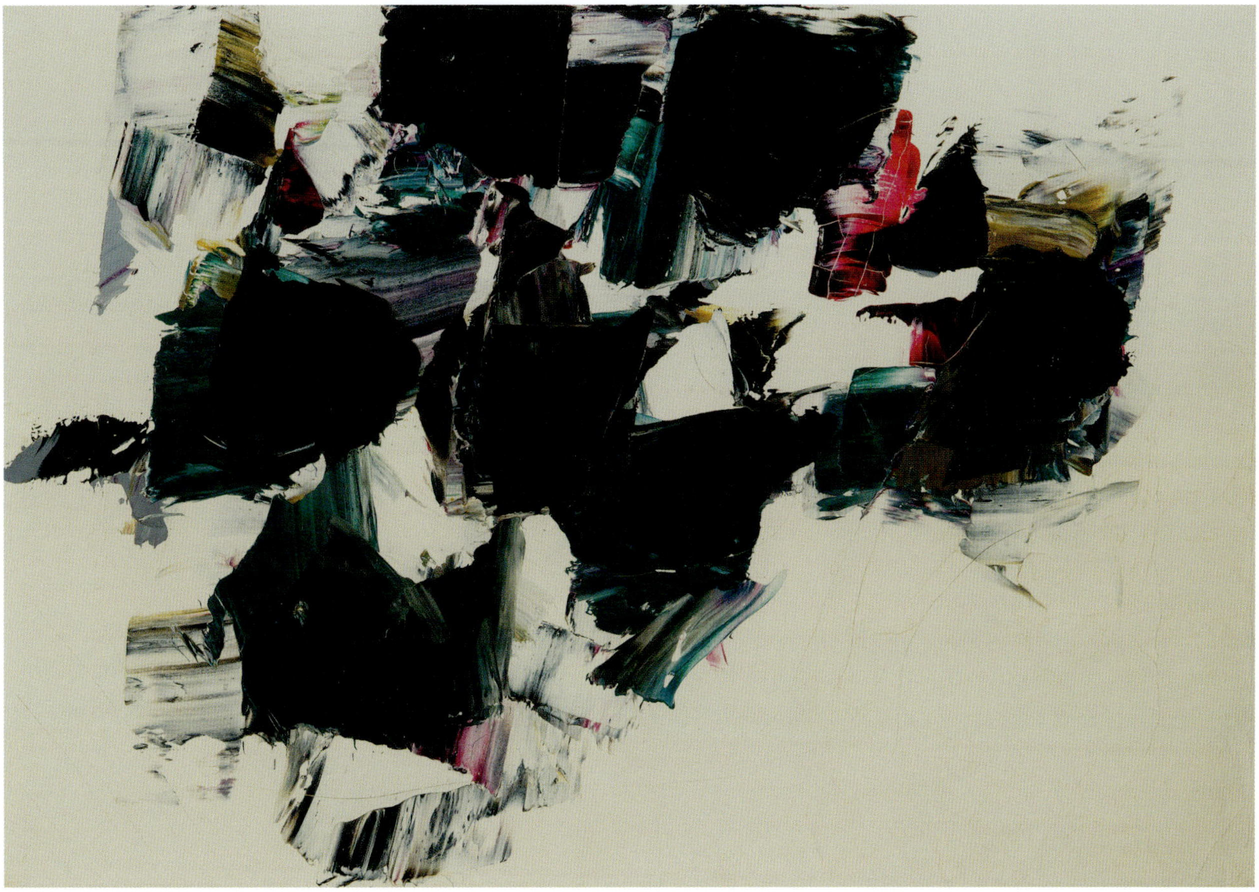

FIGURE 57. No. 24, 1955, by Sanford Greenberg (Woodmere Art Museum: Museum purchase, 2014) Photograph by Rick Echelmeyer

A New Series of Group '55 Forums

Because the third Philadelphia Abstract Artists show did not take place until October, the excitement in Philadelphia's abstract art scene for much of 1958 was provided by Feinstein's exhibitions and four stimulating forums, presented by Group '55 and held at Dubin/Gallery '55. Tickets were sold to recoup costs, and the artists were encouraged to sell them to friends: $4.00 for all four forums, or $1.50 for single tickets. On February 14, Group '55 opened a savings account to hold funds from the sale of the forum tickets and to pay for equipment rentals, with Feinstein listed as president, Anderson as secretary, and Milliken as treasurer.

A solo exhibition of oils and mixed-media work by Feinstein was on view Dubin/Gallery '55 for three weeks in February, his last solo exhibition in Philadelphia. The *Philadelphia Inquirer* review conveyed the artist's thoughts on his work: "The paintings in this exhibition are my impressions relative to landscape around Provincetown, Mass., where I have spent the past ten summers. . . . My primary aim has been to help structure their color-form relationships so as to activate each painting

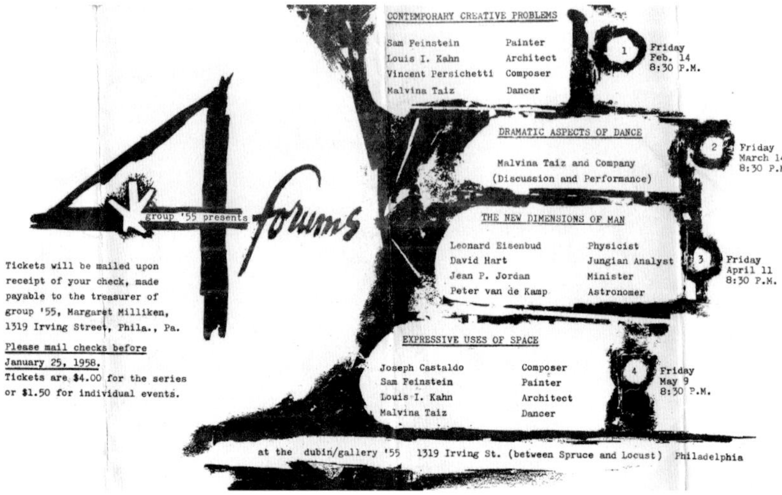

FIGURE 58. Announcement for Group '55 1958 forum series (Samuel L. Feinstein Trust)

toward its own pictorial presentation."[89] These paintings were the setting for the first forum of 1958, "Contemporary Creative Problems," held on February 14. Feinstein interacted with Kahn, Persichetti, and dancer Malvena (then spelled Malvina) Taiz,[90] following up on the performances of the previous spring. Anderson's paintings were on view in March and provided the backdrop for the second forum, "Dramatic Aspects of Dance," with a performance by Taiz and her company on March 14.

In April, Dubin/Gallery '55 mounted an exhibition of colorful work by Carles. Rhys reviewed the show for the *Philadelphia Inquirer*:

> Carles' modest fame is an inadequate index of the extent of his influence and of the quality of his paintings. An impressive percentage of today's leading Philadelphia artists studied under him at the Pennsylvania Academy. He brought to them, direct and unsullied from impeccable sources in Paris, the gospel of modern art. The city's flourishing harvest of nonobjective painting is in part the fruit of his labor.[91]

The Carles show was the setting for the third forum, "The New Dimensions of Man," on April 11. This time the discussion expanded into science, with physicist Leonard Eisenbud, Jungian analyst David Hart, astronomer Peter van de Kamp, and the Rev. Jean P. Jordan. Eisenbud talked about the social significance of changes such as population growth and whether atomic energy would fulfill the growing need, with hope that "the individual would be able to survive the powerful socialization predominant in the future." Hart spoke about the new psychology and how understanding oneself must come before understanding others. Van de Kamp talked about his reasons for being in the field and the astronomer's place in society, noting that human beings "are a slight imperfection in the universe." Finally, Rev. Jordan discussed how existentialism "comes closest to present-day philosophy," pointing out that more people were going to church in light of anxieties.

The next exhibition at Dubin/Gallery '55 showed work by two nonmembers Constance Contry and Robert Kristler Allen. Following that was a summer group show,[92] presumably of Group '55 members,

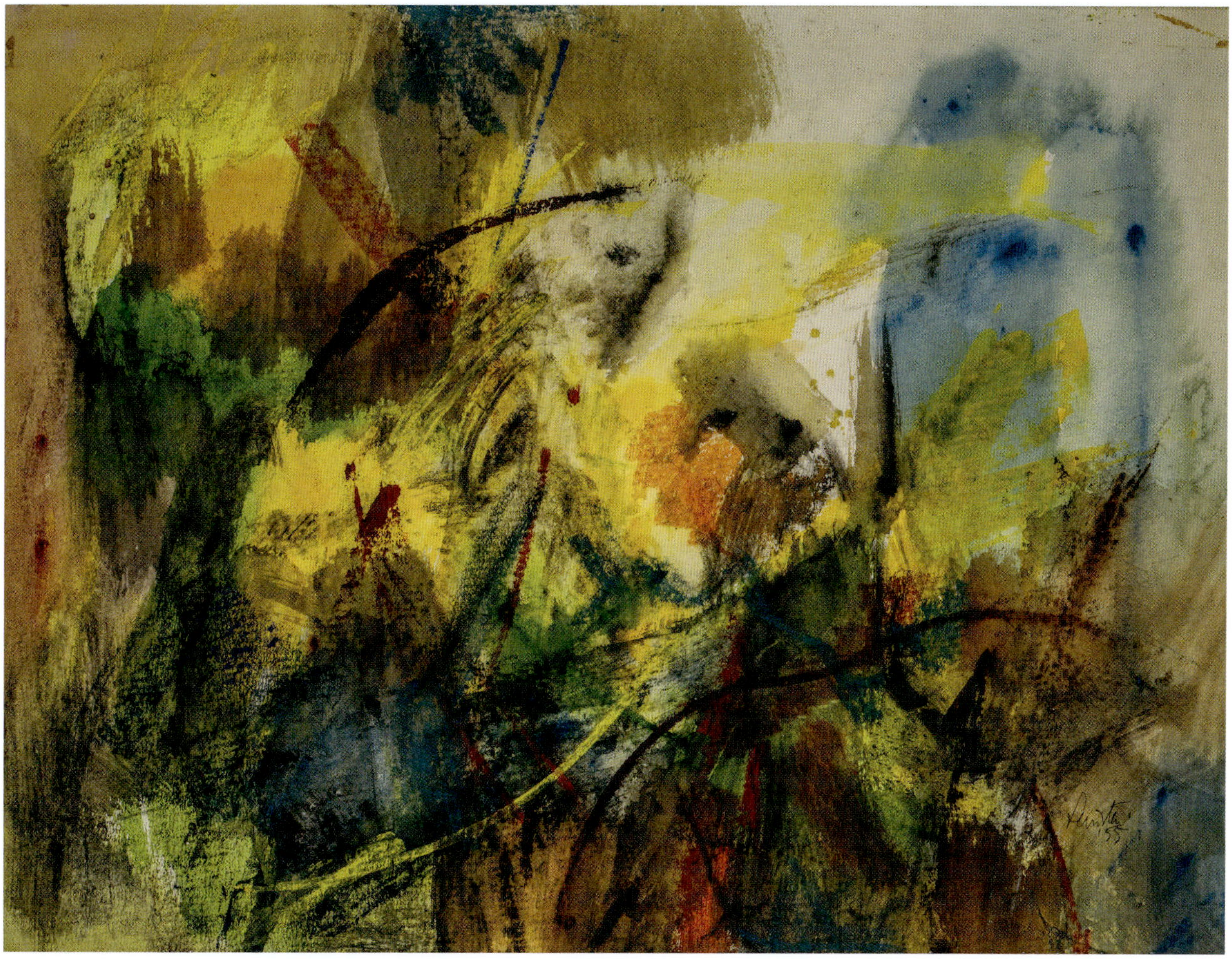

FIGURE 59. **Untitled**, 1955, by Sam Feinstein (Samuel L. Feinstein Trust)

which was on the walls on May 9 for the fourth forum, "Expressive Uses of Space." Feinstein was on the panel along with Castaldo, Kahn, and Taiz. The summer group show, not reviewed, was apparently the last for Dubin/Gallery '55.[93] The last evidence of Group '55 as an organization was a payment made to Castaldo in November, apparently for costs associated with the last forum, authorized by officers Feinstein, Anderson, and Milliken on November 3, 1958.

Feinstein and Crawford separated that summer, and Feinstein moved permanently to New York, although he still taught one day a week in Philadelphia. After the last forum and exhibition, Feinstein showed work in Provincetown that summer, but he then suddenly stopped exhibiting or selling his paintings. He was discouraged by the commercialism of galleries, particularly those in New York, but possibly highlighted during his time helping manage one with Dubin. Although he organized *Tradition in Evolution: Abstract Expressionism* with paintings by Hofmann and four others in 1965 in Princeton, where he taught

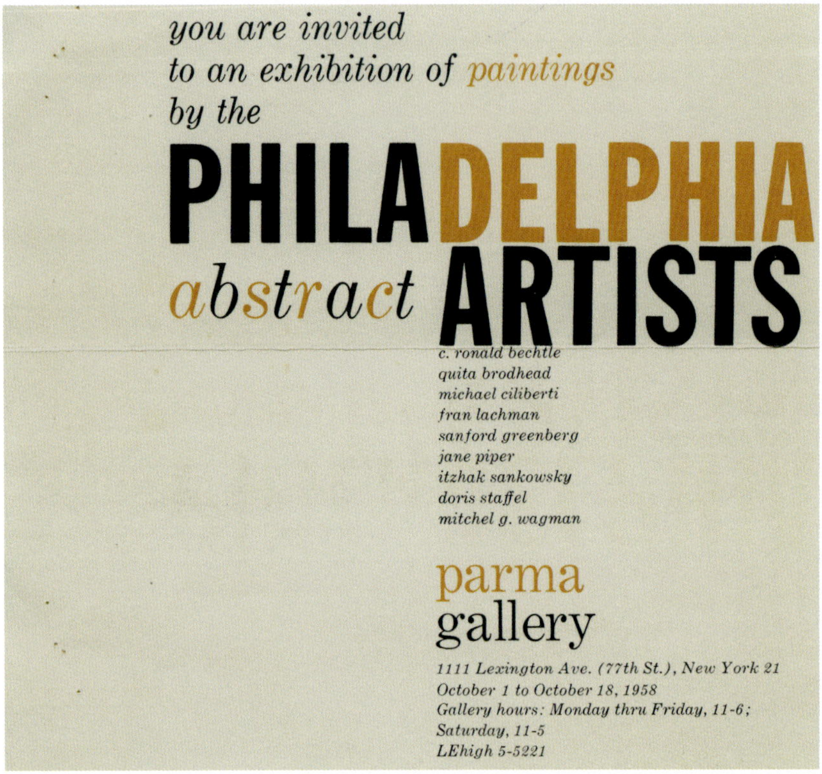

FIGURE 60. Invitation to Philadelphia Abstract Artists exhibition (Estate of Mitchel G. Wagman)

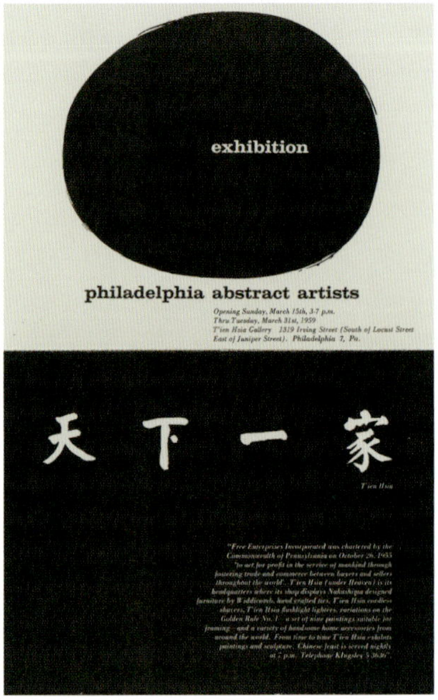

FIGURE 61. Announcement for Philadelphia Abstract Artists exhibition at T'ien Hsia Gallery (Charles Ronald Bechtle Jr. Papers, 1951–1998, Archives of American Art, Smithsonian Institution)

privately, he had given up his leadership role in Philadelphia.[94] Yet he remained dedicated to the principles and philosophy he had espoused while running Group '55. He painted hundreds of large canvases up to his death, in 2003, unseen by the public or critics until relatively recently through the efforts of his widow, Patricia Stark Feinstein.

Philadelphia Abstract Artists Carry On

In late 1958, the Philadelphia Abstract Artists were organizing their third show; they continued to organize about one exhibition a year, as was their goal. *Paintings by the Philadelphia Abstract Artists* was on view in October at the Parma Gallery in New York. Showing there was undoubtedly a plus for the résumés of the nine former Group '55 members. Grafly reported that the show garnered "sales and, largest preview crowd," the largest in the history of the gallery.[95]

Then, in March 1959, Philadelphia Abstract Artists announced an exhibition at a new venue called T'ien Hsia Gallery, meaning "under heaven" in Chinese. Its address was 1319–21 Irving Street, the same as the former Dubin/Gallery '55. While he continued to show art, Dubin had converted his gallery into a shop, selling furniture and a variety of other items.[96] Each artist paid ten dollars for expenses.

Almost a year after the fourth exhibition, in late February 1960, *Exhibition by the Philadelphia Abstract Artists* was on view at the Fleisher Art Memorial. To promote the show, Bechtle wrote:

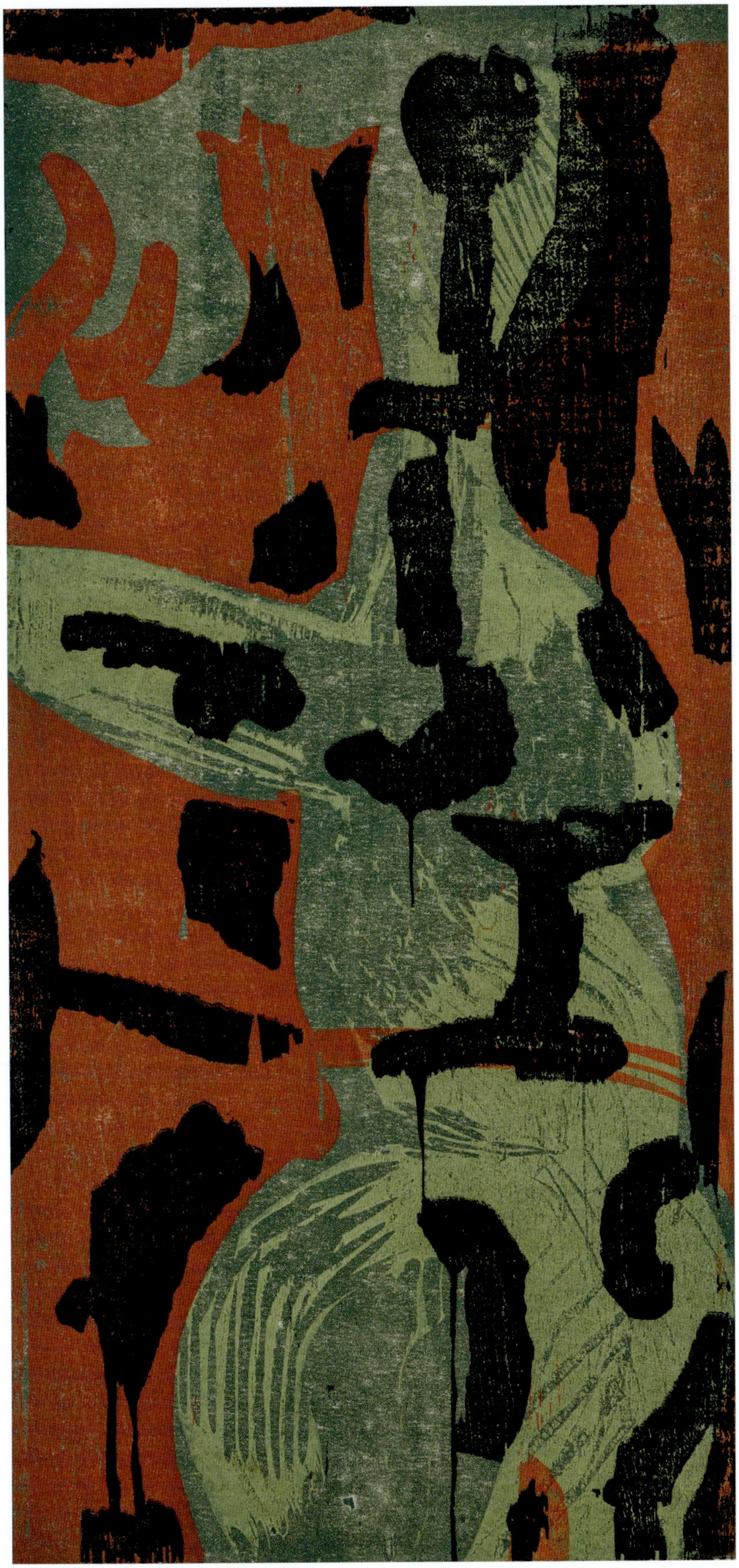

FIGURE 62. **Figure of a Woman**, 1956–57, by Samuel Maitin (Woodmere Art Museum: Gift of Ronald Rumford, 2002)

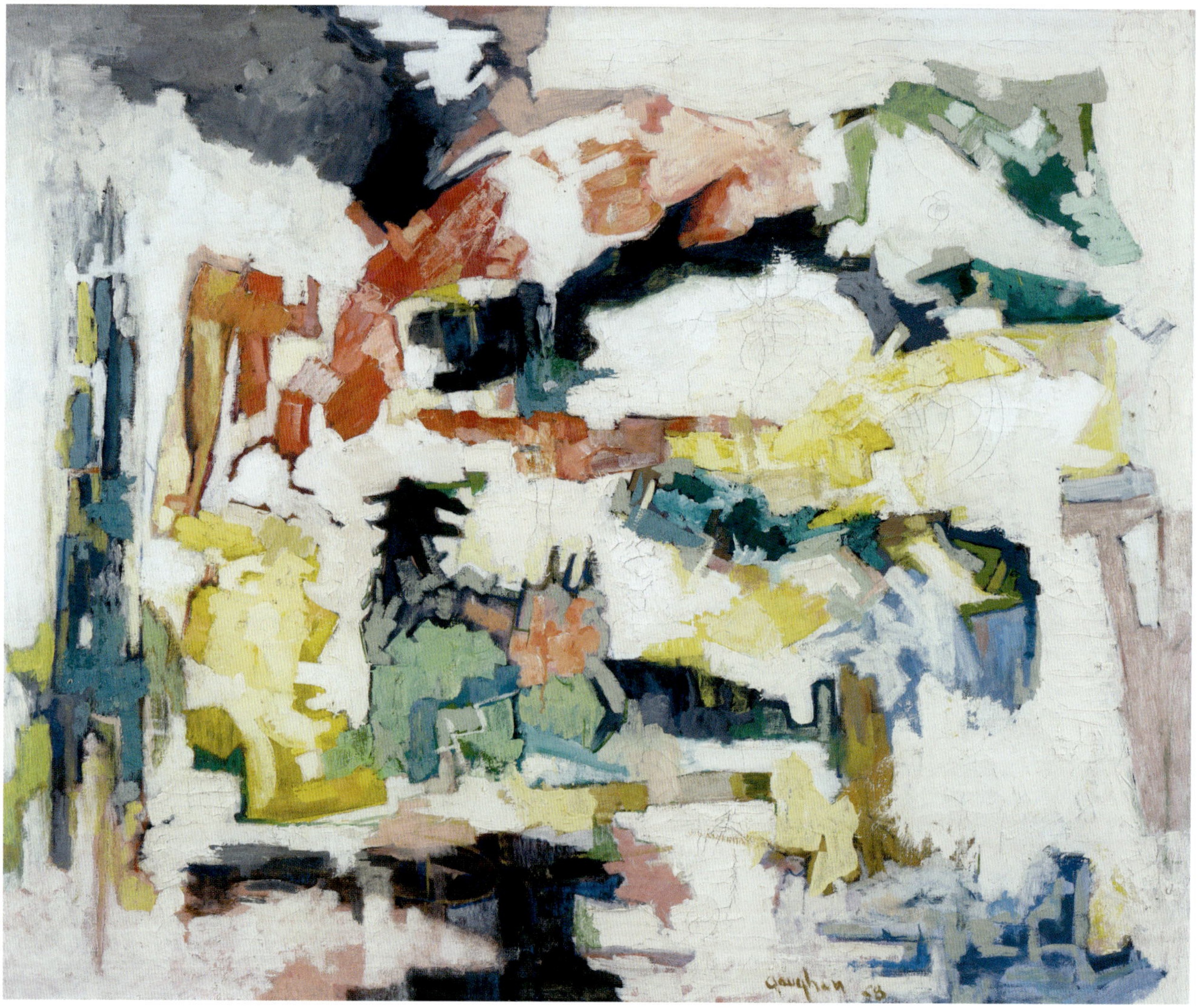

FIGURE 63. **Winter Landscape**, 1958, by Thomas Gaughan (Courtesy of Esther and Stephen Hrabrick)

> "Those of you who attended the openings of our last four annual group exhibitions know why we received such exciting critical reviews. Not to boast, bombast, or ballyhoo, there just isn't any other place to see the most interesting, serious group of living artists work in Phila."[97]

The exhibition of thirty works by fifteen artists was expanded to include a number of artists who had never joined Group '55, among them Adolph Dioda, Thomas Gaughan, Jack Gregory, Samuel Maitin, Nelson, and Walter Redding, thus significantly expanding the group. Reviewer Dennis Leon of the *Philadelphia Inquirer* described three different approaches to abstract art among the paintings. Some paintings he called "abstract," such as Lachman's *The Mirror* with discernible figures. He categorized Gaughan's painting as "non-figurative," as is his *Winter Landscape* (fig. 63) that has a "pictorial" organization suggesting landscape.

Gaughan's *Cascade* (fig. 149) fits best into Leon's third category. Leon categorized Greenberg's work as "action painting, with "flat, tight space and non-figurative forms to permit only a limited association external to the canvas itself."[98]

Greenberg's *No. 24* (fig. 57), fits that description with its striking patches of black and touches of color on a white field, in sympathy with Kline's work. His *No. 4* (fig. 156), with its large scale and roughly brushed reds and yellows, has calligraphic dripped black lines only slightly suggestive of figures.

A year later, in February 1961, Wagman opened his Philadelphia Galleries at 333 South 20th Street for the sixth Philadelphia Abstract Artists exhibition. Of the eleven artists, who showed three oil or watercolor paintings each, seven were former members of Group '55, along with Gaughan, Goodman, Carmine De Vivi, and Harold Mesibov (showing as Mesa). Leon of the *Inquirer* was less complimentary this time, again considering Greenberg and Lachman the best, but complaining that "neither reveals a profound personal vision." He called the rest "a third- or fourth-hand rehash" of abstract ideas and declared that "the spirits of spontaneity and individualism are completely lacking in the exhibition."[99]

Grafly, reviewing the show for the *Sunday Bulletin*, dealt with the question of how to tell whether abstract art is good. Her continuing skepticism was evident, even after attending all the Group '55 exhibitions and at least one forum: "What too often happens is that the artist paints first and thinks afterward. Then, because he wants to establish contact with the public, he fishes around for a name." She was critical of most of the paintings in the exhibition:

> Acid test for an abstraction is the ability of the artist to organize colors and forms in a given space. Not all the abstractions in the current show can pass the test. Sanford Greenberg's softly poetic color brushings, for instance, seem to be groping toward a yet un-achieved organization. Quita Brodhead's paintings (not her best) are similarly unconvincing, while a strange mechanistic figure analysis by Mesa [Mesibov] leaves one cold.[100]

Interestingly, at just this time, in the exhibition *Young Artists of Philadelphia* at Woodmere, Gaughan was one of the three out of five painting abstractly, perhaps an indication of growing acceptance of nonrepresentational art.

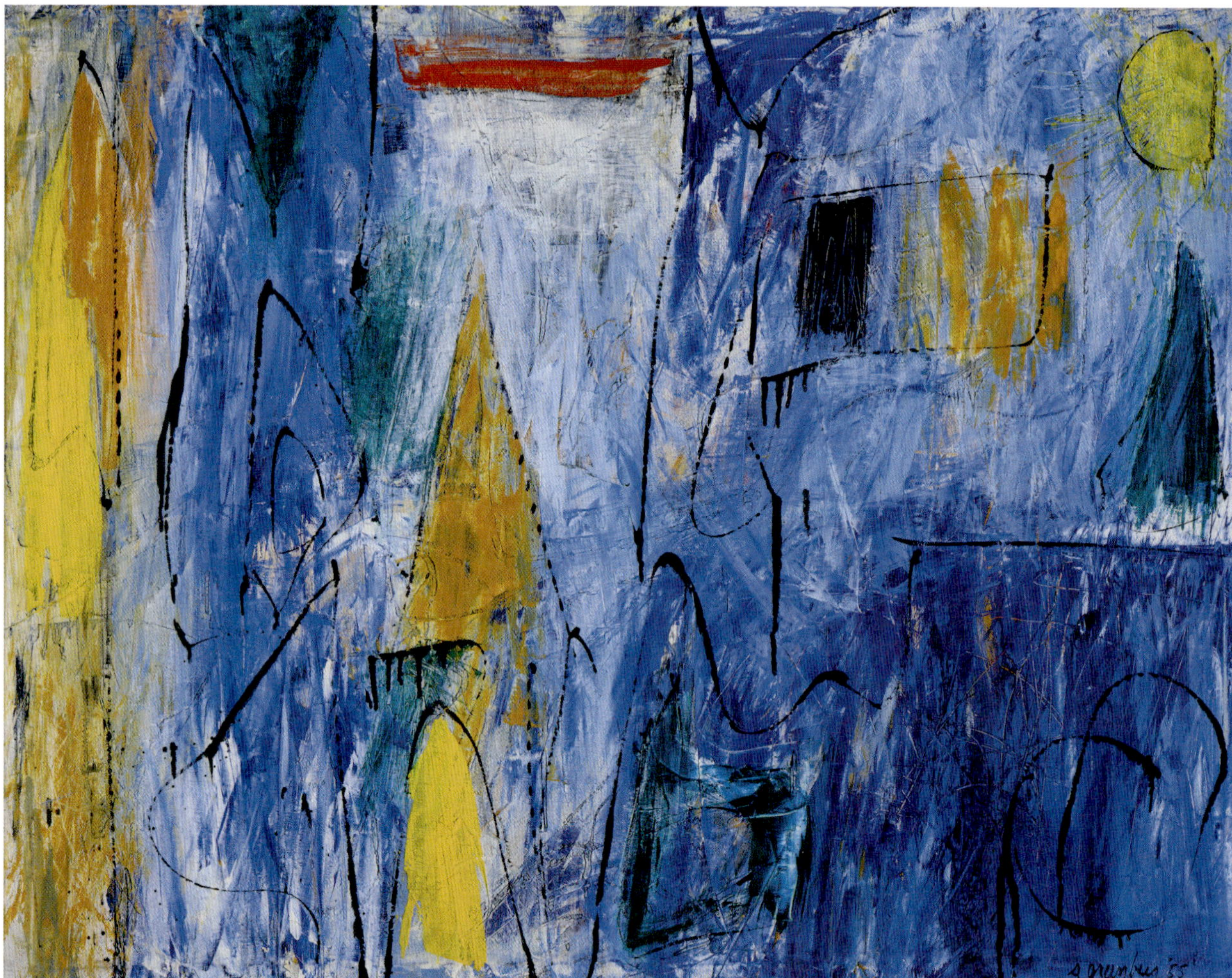

FIGURE 64. **Untitled,** 1955, by Sanford Greenberg (Private Collection)

After seeing these less-than-favorable reviews, Bechtle began to question whether Philadelphia Abstract Artists was on the right track. He wrote on the list of the original twelve members, noting those that had moved, were not painting, or had returned to "figure," and described only himself as still "abstract." In March, he invited Ciliberti, Freid, Gaughan, Greenberg, Hankins, and Lachman to meet at Gaughan's home "to discuss formation of a new group." He was looking for members who "are dedicated to the principle that painting is a way of life, and not primarily a route to financial reward," with the goal of at least one "first-class exhibition each year."[101] Such a group was not formed, but Bechtle's inquiry is evidence that he was still striving for a group that fully met his standards.

The last exhibition that Bechtle counted as one of the seven organized by his group, *Abstract Artists of Philadelphia*, opened in January 1962 at the Penn Center Galleries. It showed work by just seven artists: Bechtle, Ciliberti, Freid, Gaughan, Greenberg, Hankins, and Lachman. One review that month titled "Omni-present Philadelphia Abstract Artists" also made reference to a concurrent Philadelphia Galleries exhibition of fifteen artists, including Bechtle, Gaughan, Greenberg, Lachman, Milliken, Wagman, Nelson, and other Philadelphia and New York artists. Grafly titled her short review "Abstraction Takes Over," commenting that "the art of swinging color through space is as personal as handwriting, but more emotionally motivated."[102] The latter exhibition, organized by Wagman, certainly made an impression on the city and demonstrated the still-vital commitment and connections among the artists. At that time Bechtle was dealing with family issues that may have made it impossible for him to continue as director, with no one else taking the reins. But he would remain "dedicated to the principle that painting is a way of life" and continued to paint for hours each day for most of the rest of his life, focusing on watercolor and seeing his work enter a number of museum collections.

In the spring of 1962, Freid and two others organized a series of six forums and discussions in the spirit of Group '55 along with exhibitions at the Bryn Mawr Art Center, where Freid was a director. The topic was "Creative Achievements in the Arts and Its Relation to Contemporary Man."[103]

Many of the artists associated with Group '55 and Philadelphia Abstract Artists continued to exhibit regularly in juried shows and in new galleries that opened. A number of the former members of both groups took part in annual faculty exhibitions at the Fleisher Art Memorial, where they were all teaching, with shows in 1967, 1968, and 1969.[104] One review was illustrated with a painting by Lachman and concluded, "What the eight seem to say as a group is that, whatever means of expression the present-day creative artist may choose, he is a creator rather than a translator."[105]

Conclusion

Feinstein and Bechtle, leaders of Group '55 and Philadelphia Abstract Artists, respectively, were intelligent and strongly principled men who clashed over leadership styles and criteria for membership. They also had different approaches to painting. Grounded in his association with Hofmann, Feinstein's was spiritual and intuitive. Bechtle's was more cerebral and analytic. Yet the two had a lot in common. They were both well organized, well read, and thoughtful. They were both interested in placing contemporary art in the context of art history, as evidenced by Feinstein's many talks and statements, and Bechtle's later development of his own course on modern art. Both were so dedicated to their vision of painting that they devoted their lives to it even after they stopped exhibiting and selling their work.

In the late 1950s, Feinstein expanded the scale of his paintings into monumental works, as seen in Woodmere's concurrent exhibition, *Sam Feinstein: Immersive Abstraction*. He continued the challenge of painting abstractly with pure color to the very end of his life. Bechtle also saw painting as a way of life, and he continued to paint for hours each day. In the early 1960s he turned his attention to watercolor. Experimenting with squirting or dripping inks or pigments on paper, he used chance as a starting point for his striking experiments, as in his watercolor and collage *Puerta Del Sol II* (fig. 65). The work contains an upside-down, torn fragment of a review of a show of Kenneth Noland's paintings, with the circular forms suggesting Noland's target series. Bechtle may have met Noland, then painting in an Abstract Expressionist style, who signed his name in the first Group '55 exhibition guest book and came to at least one forum. Bechtle arranged to get a number of his own works on paper accepted into museum collections, as were some of Feinstein's.

Both Feinstein and Bechtle knew the groups they led were important, and they both preserved documentation that made researching and understanding the history of the groups possible. Strikingly, on the outside of the expanding file of folders Bechtle organized to be donated to the Archives of American Art, he wrote adamantly: "Group '55 & Philadelphia Abstract Artists exhibitions were the *first* meaningful nonrepresentational shows in Philadelphia."

Greater acceptance of abstract art in Philadelphia exhibitions was likely strengthened by the activities of Group '55. In early 1964, Grafly noted the ascendance of nonrepresentational art in a national exhibition where "abstract and nonobjective compositions are still much in the majority."[106]

But the art world had already changed. Clement Greenberg had promoted post-painterly abstraction as the latest thing and even encouraged Feinstein to move on from Abstract Expressionism.[107] Robert Rauschenberg and Jasper Johns were transitioning into what would become Pop art. In 1962, the Y Arts Council at Philadelphia's Young Men's and Young Women's Hebrew Association, instead of presenting a show of Abstract Expressionist painting, pioneered in presenting innovative Pop, Fluxus, and Nouveau Réaliste, work and an Allan Kaprow happening. The same year, the Institute of Contemporary Art opened at the University of Pennsylvania.[108] Both Feinstein and Bechtle were dismayed by the new movements gaining critical attention, as the abstract art they believed in so strongly was on the road to being deemed passé.

Another factor was that the art world was increasingly emphasizing sales and sale prices, and galleries felt more and more commercial. This distressed dedicated abstract artists like Feinstein, who were focused on the spiritual impact of their paintings. Both Feinstein and Bechtle thus kept creating art but withdrew from showing or selling it. Many of the artists in their groups earned their living through teaching or other means and could never count on sales.

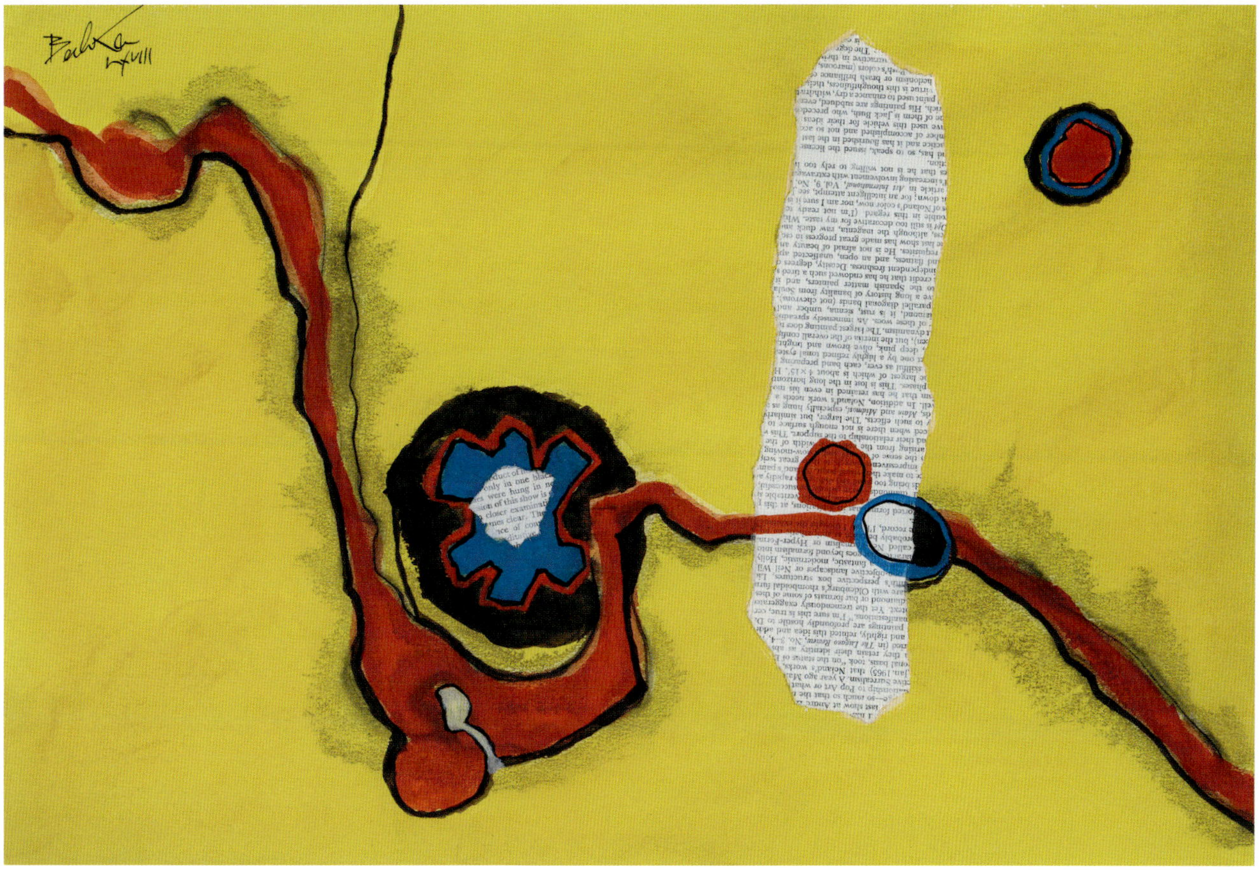

FIGURE 65. **Puerta del Sol II**, 1968, by C. Ronald Bechtle (Woodmere Art Museum: Gift of Reid and Dorothy Bechtle, 2020)

In addition to the arrival of the new kinds of avant-garde art then being taught at the Philadelphia College of Art and art departments, representational painting regained prominence in Philadelphia in the 1960s and 1970s. Piper was always primarily concerned with form and color in her paintings even after becoming known for her signature still life compositions (fig 66). Often repainting areas, she felt that changing one area could change the whole painting, as was expressed in the Group '55 forums. In the 1960s her friend Day found recognition for his refined figures and architectural settings. Ciliberti soon focused on realist landscapes and continued painting them until the end of his life. Mitzi Melnicoff began teaching at the Philadelphia College of Art and gained recognition for her figurative work. Peter Paone, also a teacher, became known for his compelling images that grow out of figure studies. Next generation artists such as Eileen Goodman and Martha Mayer Erlebacher began attracting attention for their detailed still lifes and classical figures, as Edith Neff did with her complex figured scenes.

However, the principles of the visual language of painting continued to be taught and passed on to future generations. Many of the group members were teachers, and they continued to convey their

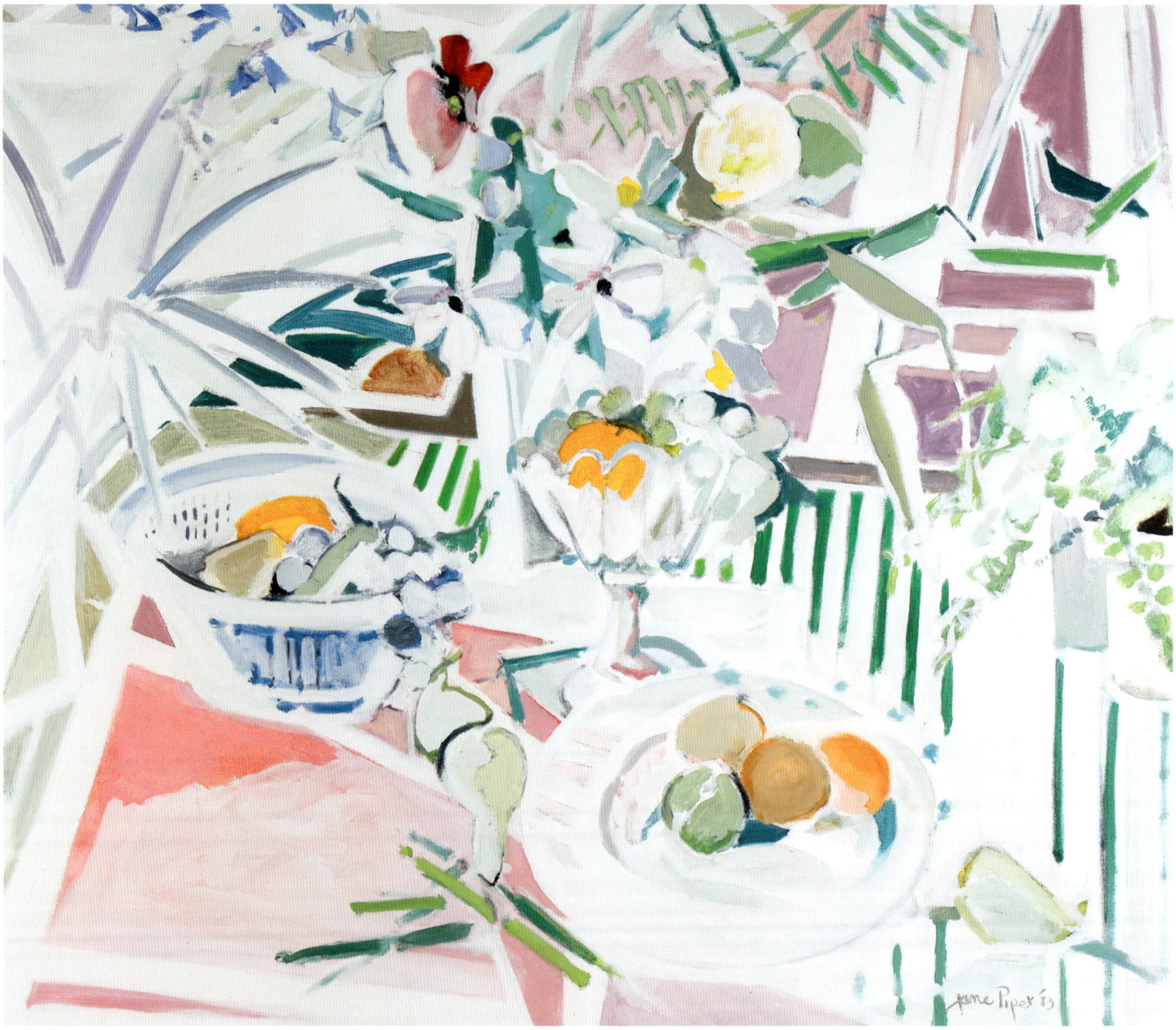

FIGURE 66. **Three Bowls of Fruit**, 1983, by Jane Piper (Woodmere Art Museum: Gift of Bill Scott, 2011) Photograph by Rick Echelmeyer

understanding of the principles of painting to their students for decades. A number of them were on the faculty of the Fleisher Art Memorial. Feinstein taught classes in Philadelphia for half a century, with many of his students becoming teachers themselves. Hankins and Hendler taught for years at major art schools and universities. Piper and Staffel were on the faculty of the Philadelphia College of Art for decades. Piper's daughter Jan Carles Baltzell taught for many years at PAFA. Lachman taught at the Wallingford Arts Center and at Fleisher Art Memorial. Her daughters, who also studied with Feinstein, became teachers of art themselves. Maitin taught at the University of Pennsylvania and was known as Philadelphia's "mayor of the arts."

An artist writing for *Art in America* once described "the Philadelphia Triangle," suggesting that Philadelphia artists, so close to New York, seem to just disappear, like ships in the Bermuda Triangle, from the national art scene.[109] Although many of the artists are represented in the collections of Philadelphia museums, when looking at major New York museums, there are only works on paper by Piper, Feldman, and Maitin (in the Museum of Modern Art) and by Feinstein (in the Metropolitan Museum of Art). Thus Woodmere Art Museum, with its mission to bring attention to Philadelphia artists, serves an important role in preserving evidence of their accomplishments and legacies.

The artists who joined Group '55 and Philadelphia Abstract Artists were hungry to talk about their work with other painters, thinkers, and individuals in other art fields and to deepen their own understanding. They remained proud of their participation in the groups' exhibitions and forums, and in untold ways their belief in the importance of making their art was reinforced. Like Feinstein, Brodhead and Piper kept painting and exhibiting until the last year of their lives, still working with an understanding of color gained from Carles and the artists he most admired. Brodhead's art kept evolving into daring abstractions such as *Implosion* (fig. 67), perhaps grounded in Group '55 discussions as well as her continuing interest in new discoveries in space. The range of her explorations documented in the retrospective celebrating her hundredth birthday, in 2001, as well as in posthumous exhibitions including *Quita Brodhead: Bold Strokes,* at Woodmere Art Museum in 2014.[110]

Numerous Philadelphia artists are still exploring abstraction today. Piper's daughter, Baltzell, and Scott continue to explore abstract color in their paintings, as does Louise Fishman, who studied with Piper. Dina Wind, who began as a student of Feinstein and later became an abstract sculptor, would always be inspired by his discussions of the dynamics of paintings and dedication to art as a sacred pursuit.

The artists in this exhibition could be considered second-generation Abstract Expressionists. Like most of their contemporaries, none are credited with breakthroughs that changed the history of art. None of them made it into the multitude of books on Abstract Expressionism, much less surveys of the history of American art. Yet each was serious and thoughtful about painting and evolved a distinctive philosophy and voice. Many continued to exhibit. Their beautiful and distinctive work continues to be enjoyed by collectors and acquired by museums. The youngest member, Allman, was honored with her own exhibition at the Delaware Art Museum this year.

Woodmere's ongoing program of exhibitions and installations featuring its collection includes many of the artists who were part of Group '55, as well as younger artists inspired or mentored by them. In his essay for the catalogue for *Flirting with Abstraction*, which included many of these artists, Scott explained that the questions about what abstract painting means and the lack of understanding by much of the public are still with us today: "I'm always a little bit surprised at how sad I feel when, from time to time, someone approaches me at one of my exhibitions and proclaims that they have never really understood abstraction. They'll point to a painting of mine and in a cavalier tone ask, 'What's it supposed to be?'"[111]

The exhibitions, forums, and teaching of Group '55 and Philadelphia Abstract Artists had an impact on countless people. People today could still benefit from a Group '55 forum discussion, with the understanding of abstract art still predicated on an open mind, careful looking, and personal response.

The Group '55 artists created a center of gravity for abstraction and opened minds to the art of their time. They enlivened and changed the art scene in Philadelphia, bringing attention to the validity of abstract painting and its connection to other avant-garde art forms. They raised the level of discussion, showing that abstract art was a force to be reckoned with in contemporary life and thought.

ACKNOWLEDGMENTS

This essay would not have been possible without the years-long efforts of Patricia Stark Feinstein and her curatorial assistant Victoria Schuh in organizing and scanning the vast archive left by Sam Feinstein. They also interviewed and researched his students and many of the artists in the exhibition. It has been rewarding for me to work with them and with Woodmere's director, William R. Valerio, and curator Rachel Hruszkewycz, who believe in the importance of Group '55, in envisioning this exhibition. I am grateful for the assistance of family members of many of the artists, including Reid Bechtle, Laurie Wagman and her daughters, and the Greenberg daughters, and for Sid Sachs's generous sharing of sources. This essay is dedicated to Michael Ciliberti, who had long suggested there should be an exhibition about Group '55 and so hoped he would live long enough to see it.

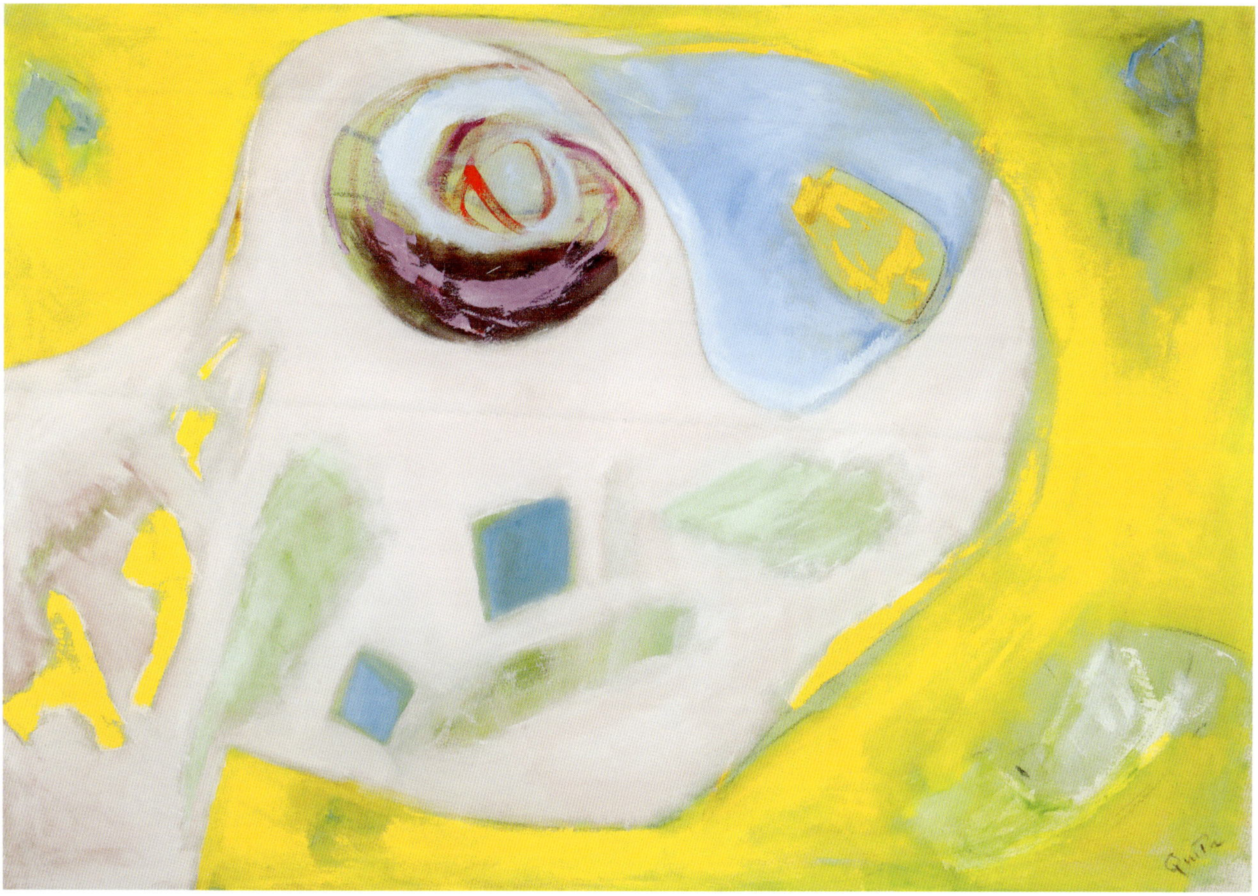

FIGURE 67. Implosion, c. 1980, by Quita Brodhead (Woodmere Art Museum: Gift of Bill Scott, 2011) Photograph by Rick Echelmeyer

NOTES

1 Email communication to the author, April 12, 2020, just three days before he died, at age ninety-four. See the brief biographies starting on page 178 for life dates and information about individual artists.

2 Telephone interview with the author and Patricia Stark Feinstein, September 26, 2019, and emailed statement May 2020.

3 Selected notes by Joyce Jackson from telephone conversations with Ben Herr, 2012–16.

4 Transcript from recording of Group '55 forum, January 26, 1956, Samuel L. Feinstein Trust Archive (hereafter SLFTA).

5 Postcard postmarked May 16, 1955, SFLTA.

6 Carbon copy of letter to Frank Brookhouser, *Philadelphia Bulletin*, April 7, 1956, SLFTA.

7 The SLFTA is maintained by Patricia Stark Feinstein in Brewster, Massachusetts, with plans to donate it to the Archives of American Art, Smithsonian Institution, where the Charles Ronald Bechtle Jr. Papers, 1951–1998 (hereafter CRB AAA) are preserved.

8 Carroll A. Osborne, "A Difference of Opinion," *Art Digest*, May 1, 1954.

9 Interview by Patricia Stark Feinstein, August 17, 2006, SLFTA.

10 *Life*, August 9, 1949, www.life.com/people/jackson-pollock-early-photos-of-the-action-painter-at-work/.

11 Recent vivid descriptions of this time drawn on here include Norman L. Kleeblatt, ed., *Action/Abstraction*, Jewish Museum (New Haven: Yale University Press, 2008) and Mary Gabriel, *Ninth Street Women* (New York: Little Brown and Company, 2018).

12 Oral history interview with Jane Piper, January 16–17, 1988, Archives of American Art, Smithsonian Institution.

13 Emily Grenauer, "Critic Deplores New Art of Nothingness," *Herald Tribune*, March 11, 1958, Book Review section.

14 John Canaday, "Happy New Year: Thoughts on Critics and Certain Painters as the Season Opens," *New York Times*, September 6, 1959.

15 *Art in Focus* 6, no. 6 (March 1955). *All Art in Focus* articles were written by Dorothy Grafly (1896–1980).

16 "'True Art Emotional,' Carles Says," *Philadelphia Press*, July 21, 1913.

17 Barbara A. Wolanin, *Arthur B. Carles: Painting with Color* (Philadelphia: Pennsylvania Academy of the Fine Arts, 1983), 134.

18 Sam Feinstein, "Philadelphia," *Art Digest* 27, no. 13 (April 1, 1953): 12.

19 Philadelphia Museum of Art, "First Art Festival," 1955, no. 27; Pennsylvania Academy of the Fine Arts, "Twentieth-Century American Paintings and Sculpture from Philadelphia Private Collections," 1958, no. 84.

20 Telephone conversation with the author, April 30, 2020.

21 In Feinstein's review, "Pennsylvania Academy National," he mentioned six future Group '55 members. *Arts Magazine*, February 15, 1954.

22 *Art in Focus* 1, no. 2 (November 1949), and 1, no. 5 (February 1950): 2.

23 C. H. Bonte, "News of City's Art Galleries," *Philadelphia Inquirer*, November 17, 1935, 14.

24 October 7–14, 1953, sponsored by the United World Federalists.

25 Sam Feinstein, "Behind the Serene Façade," *Art Digest*, October 1, 1953, 7.

26 *Art in Focus* 1, no. 1 (October 1949) and no. 3 (December 1949); *Art in Focus* 3, no. 1 (October 1951); *Art in Focus* 4, no. 1 (October 1952); and *Art in Focus* 5, no. 2 (November 1953).

27 Gertrude Benson, *Philadelphia Inquirer*, December 3, 1952, 48.

28 Exhibition on view January 5–22, 1955; *Art in Focus* 6, no. 4 (January 1955).

29 *Philadelphia Inquirer*, April 30, 1971, 14.

30 I met Hank Dubin (1905–1987) in person in 1976 when I was doing research for my dissertation on Carles. I remember him as a man small in stature, full of stories about Carles, many exaggerated. He told me that he sold mostly to New York dealers and galleries. I unfortunately did not think to ask him why and when he started his gallery. On the second floor, up a ramp was a large space filled with antiques and objects piled everywhere. He and his younger wife had a bedroom in a back room. Of course, I had no idea then that this was where the Group '55 exhibitions had been shown two decades before, or how important he had been in showing abstract art in Philadelphia.

31 In 1952 his gallery was directed by widow Mrs. Leonard Gechtoff, and in 1955 by Janet Goodfried. *Art in Focus* 3, no. 3 (December 1951); "New Gallery," *Art in Focus* 3, no. 4 (January 1952).

32 Her gallery was established by her husband, L. V. Heilbrunn, a professor of biology at the University of Pennsylvania. "Donovan Gallery," *Philadelphia Inquirer*, September 28, 1952, 86.

33 Letter from Ellen Donovan to Sam Feinstein, December 28, 1951, program, SLFTA.

34 1822 Cherry Street, *Art in Focus* 6, no. 6 (March 1955).

35 *Art in Focus* 4, no. 2 (November 1952).

36 Sam Feinstein, "Philadelphia," *Art Digest* 27, no. 13 (March 15, 1953).

37 Sam Feinstein, *Art Digest*, February 15, 1955, 17; letters to the editor, *Art Digest*, March 15, 1955.

38 Sam Feinstein, "The Pennsylvania Academy National," *Art Digest*, February 15, 1954, 14.

39 All information quoted henceforth from Group '55 meeting minutes and forum transcripts is preserved in SLFTA and will not be individually noted.

40 Gabriel, *Ninth Street Women*, 280.

41 Unidentified clipping, January 1957, shared by Michael Ciliberti.

42 Telephone interview by Patricia Stark Feinstein and the author, September 26, 2019.

43 *Art in Focus* 1, no. 3 (December 1949).

44 Sam Feinstein, "Philadelphia," *Art Digest*, March 1954, 28.

45 Noted on his undated handwritten list of Philadelphia Abstract Artists members, CRB AAA.

46 *Quita Brodhead: Celebrating a Century* (New York: Hollis Taggart Galleries, 2001).

47 "Art Work of Two County Women in Phila. Exhibit," *Philadelphia Inquirer*, January 13, 1956.

48 Membership list sent to Bechtle, CRB AAA.

49 Gabriel, *Ninth Street Women*, 280.

50 Corey Stern, "The Chosen Ivy," in *34th Street*, October 27, 2016.

51 "Pyramid Club (Philadelphia)," Wikipedia; "A Conversation with Phil Sumpter," *We Speak: Black Artists in Philadelphia, 1920s–1970s* (Philadelphia: Woodmere Art Museum, 2016), 166ff.

52 Telephone interview with Laurie Wagman, September 26, 2019, and exhibition expense accounts kept by Bechtle, CRB AAA.

53 *Art in Focus* 7, no. 2 (November 1955).

54 *Art in Focus* 7, no. 2 (November 1955).

55 Letter from C. Ronald Bechtle to Sam Freid, Mitchel G. Wagman, Michael Ciliberti, and Sanford Greenberg listing names of artists to be invited, January 29, 1957, CRB AAA.

56 Letter from Sam Freid to Walter E. Baum, April 5, 1956, SLFTA, and Michael Ciliberti, interview by Patricia Stark Feinstein, March 21, 2018.

57 Walter E. Baum, "Memorial Display Honors John Sloan: Group 55," *Philadelphia Inquirer*, January 8, 1956, 119.

58 "Group '55," *Art in Focus* 7, no. 4 (January 1956).

59 Baum, "Memorial Display," *Philadelphia Inquirer*, January 8, 1956, 119.

60 "Full House," *Art in Focus* 7, no. 5 (February 1956).

61 Dorothy Grafly, "Camera vs. Brush," *Art in Focus* 7, no. 7 (April 1956).

62 Frank Brookhouser, "Man About Town," *Philadelphia Evening Bulletin*, April 13, 1956.

63 Sam Freid to Walter E. Baum at the *Philadelphia Evening and Sunday Bulletin*, May 5, 1956, sent to Sam Feinstein for review, SLFTA.

64 "Discussion on Painting Set Friday," *Delaware County Daily Times*, May 16, 1956.

65 Copy of letter from C. Ronald Bechtle to Sam Feinstein, April 7, 1956, CRB AAA.

66 Handwritten note on postcard, CRB AAA.

67 Carbon copy of letter from Margaret Milliken's address to Mrs. Gertrude Benson at *Philadelphia Inquirer* announcing the event, November 18, 1956, CRB AAA. Letter from C. Ronald Bechtle to Sam Feinstein requesting he borrow specific twelve slides, November 7, 1956, SLFTA.

68 Handwritten notes on roundtable poster, CRB AAA.

69 Feinstein delivered the annual Benjamin West Lecture at Swarthmore College on April 17, 1956, and was part of the radio forum on station WFIL on May 6, 1956.

70 Feinstein's own notes about the meeting, SLFTA.

71 "Dubin Gallery Moves," *Art in Focus*, January 1957.

72 "The Personal Reflections of C. Ronald Bechtle," 1957, CRB AAA.

73 "At Dubin Gallery," *Philadelphia Inquirer*, January 13, 1957, 101.

74 "Records Wallingford Turnout on Hand for Abstract Show," *Delaware County Daily Times*, January 7, 1957, 14.

75 *Chester County Daily Times*, January 16, 1957, 58; "Jan. 26 Panel Art Controversy May Have Climax," unidentified newspaper clipping, SLFTA.

76 "The Personal Reflections of C. Ronald Bechtle," 1957, CRB AAA.

77 "Bechtle Debut at the Red Door Gallery," *Art in Focus* 7, no. 7 (April 1956).

78 Ruth R. Russell, "Modern Art a Challenge Exhibitor Bechtle Says," 1956 clipping, CRB AAA.

79 Group '55 financial report as of January 23, 1957 (Milliken), CRB AAA.

80 Mimeographed letter, February 2, 1957. This and any Philadelphia Abstract Artists business communications referred to henceforth were archived by Bechtle, CRB AAA.

81 Typed press release saved by Michael Ciliberti and CRB AAA.

82 Abraham P. Hankins was represented in the collection of the Barnes Foundation by works from the 1940s, but it is not clear who in the group might have been represented in the Museum of Modern Art at that time.

83 Interview by Patricia Stark Feinstein, August 17, 2006. Staffel remembered Melville Price and his wife were among the attendees. Typed schedule of planned talks, SLFTA.

84 "New Works by Members of Group '55" and "Fellowship Awards," *Art in Focus* 8, no. 7 (April 1957).

85 Hedley H. Rhys, "Virile Entries Appear: Abstractions Shown," *Philadelphia Inquirer*, October 20, 1957, 7.

86 "New Abstract Group," *Art in Focus* 9, no. 1 (October 1957).

87 Robert M. Walker, "Phila. 'Abstractionists' in View," *Philadelphia Inquirer*, December 8, 1957, D15.

88 "Through Artist's Eye," *Art in Focus* 9, no. 2 (November 1957); "Abstractionists Group '55" *Art in Focus* 9, no. 3 (December 1957).

89 "Feinstein Exhibit," *Philadelphia Inquirer*, February 9, 1958, 71.

90 While her first name was usually spelled Malvina in Group '55 posters and newspaper articles at the time, the artist's preferred spelling was Malvena, as shown here, per her children.

91 Hedley H. Rhys, "Carles Works Showing Here," *Philadelphia Inquirer*, April 6, 1958, D5.

92 "Calendar," *Art in Focus* 9, no. 8 (May 1958).

93 "Dubin/Gallery '55 Group Show," *Art in Focus* 9, no. 9 (Summer 1958).

94 Clipping about exhibition at the Princeton Art Association at McCarter Theatre Center, December 9, 1965, SLFTA.

95 *Art in Focus* 10, no. 2 (November 1958).

96 Exhibition invitation, CRB AAA, and *Art in Focus* 10, no. 7 (April 1959).

97 Handwritten draft of promotion for Fifth Annual Exhibition, undated, CRB AAA.

98 Dennis Leon, "Abstract Artists on Display at Fleisher," *Philadelphia Inquirer*, February 28, 1960, 76.

99 Dennis Leon, "Abstract Artists," *Philadelphia Inquirer*, February 12, 1961, 78.

100 Dorothy Grafly, "Interpretations of Nature Offered in Two Exhibits," *Sunday Bulletin*, February 12, 1961, B5.

101 Typed statement dated February 17, 1961, CRB AAA.

102 "Omni-present Philadelphia Abstract Artists," *Philadelphia Inquirer*, January 28, 1962, 40, and February 4, 1962, 60; *Art in Focus* 13, no. 5.

103 *Art in Focus* 13, no. 7 (April 1962) and *Art in Focus* 13, no. 9 (June 1962).

104 *Philadelphia Inquirer*, March 3, 1968, 109, and *Delaware Valley Art*, February 1969 (clipping CRB AAA).

105 "Watermelons and Mops? Believe It or Not, They're Art," clipping saved by Michael Ciliberti.

106 "The National Show—Problem in Selection," *Art in Focus* 15, no. 5 (February 1964).

107 As told to Patricia Stark Feinstein.

108 Jennie Hirsh, "Lox, Salami, and a Danish: The Avenue of the Arts," in Sid Sachs, *Invisible City: Philadelphia and the Vernacular Avant-Garde*. The 2020 multivenue exhibition and catalogue organized by Sachs cover the years 1956–76 and provide important content.

109 Bill Richards, "The Philadelphia Triangle," *Art in America* 64 (July 1976).

110 *Celebrating a Century* and *Quita Brodhead: Bold Strokes*, Woodmere Art Museum, 2014.

111 Bill Scott, "An Artist's Thoughts on Abstraction," *Flirting with Abstraction* (Philadelphia: Woodmere Art Museum, 2012), 4.

LOUIS KAHN AND GROUP '55

IZZY KORNBLATT

Of all those associated with Philadelphia's Group '55, only architect Louis Kahn went on to achieve global renown. A short Philadelphian with a scarred face and a penchant for speaking in opaque terms, Kahn made for an unlikely celebrity. But by the time of his sudden death, in 1974, he had designed a national capitol, a university, Jonas Salk's medical research center, and several museums and performing arts centers—all from a small office in Center City. Scholars in search of explanations for Kahn's success have often minimized his connection to Philadelphia (along with his Judaism), instead finding the key to his work in his visits to the ruins of Rome and in the neoclassical tradition in which he was trained. Kahn thus becomes a European in American clothes, a closet classicist.

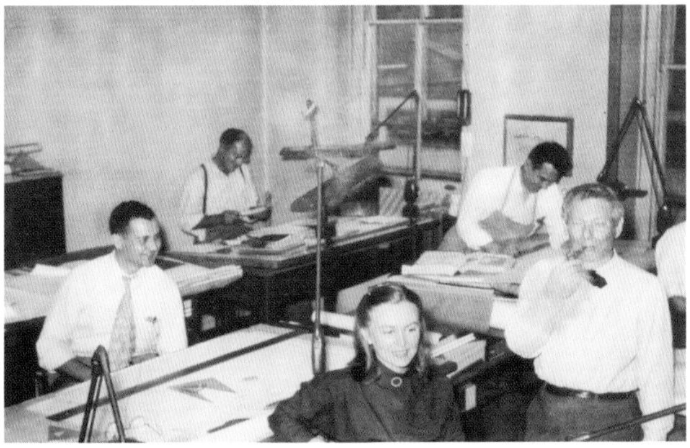

FIGURE 68. Anne Tyng, Louis Kahn, and others, 1728 Spruce Street office, 1947 (Courtesy of the Anne Griswold Tyng Collection, The Architectural Archives, University of Pennsylvania) Photographer unknown

Given the prevalence of this interpretation, it comes as no surprise that Kahn's involvement in Group '55 has received scant attention in Kahn scholarship. It is important nonetheless, not least because it illuminates the scope of the impact Philadelphia architects and artists had on his thought and his work. It also offers a window into Kahn's understanding of modernism—in architecture and in art—at the moment his career was beginning to take off. Kahn was by no means a leader of Group '55, and his architectural work was not exhibited alongside his colleagues' abstract paintings. He was, however, involved with the group throughout its existence, and he spoke at three of its events. He maintained friendships with a few of its members afterward and retained records of the group. Although archival materials do not paint a complete picture of Kahn's Group '55 activity, they do suggest an outline that can be filled in through examination of the architect's contemporaneous thinking and work.[1]

Kahn's interest in visual art began early on. As a child he adored drawing and attended art classes at what is now the Samuel S. Fleisher Art Memorial in South Philadelphia. During his years at Central High School, his drawings were exhibited at the Pennsylvania Academy of the Fine Arts (PAFA), and in his senior year there the academy even offered him a scholarship. Instead Kahn chose to pay full tuition for an architecture degree at the University of Pennsylvania (Penn).[2] The training he received there was rigid and traditional, but the Beaux Arts curriculum introduced to him a crucial notion: that architecture, in its ornamentation and decoration as well as the graphics used to represent it, relied heavily on painting, drawing, and sculpture. Kahn

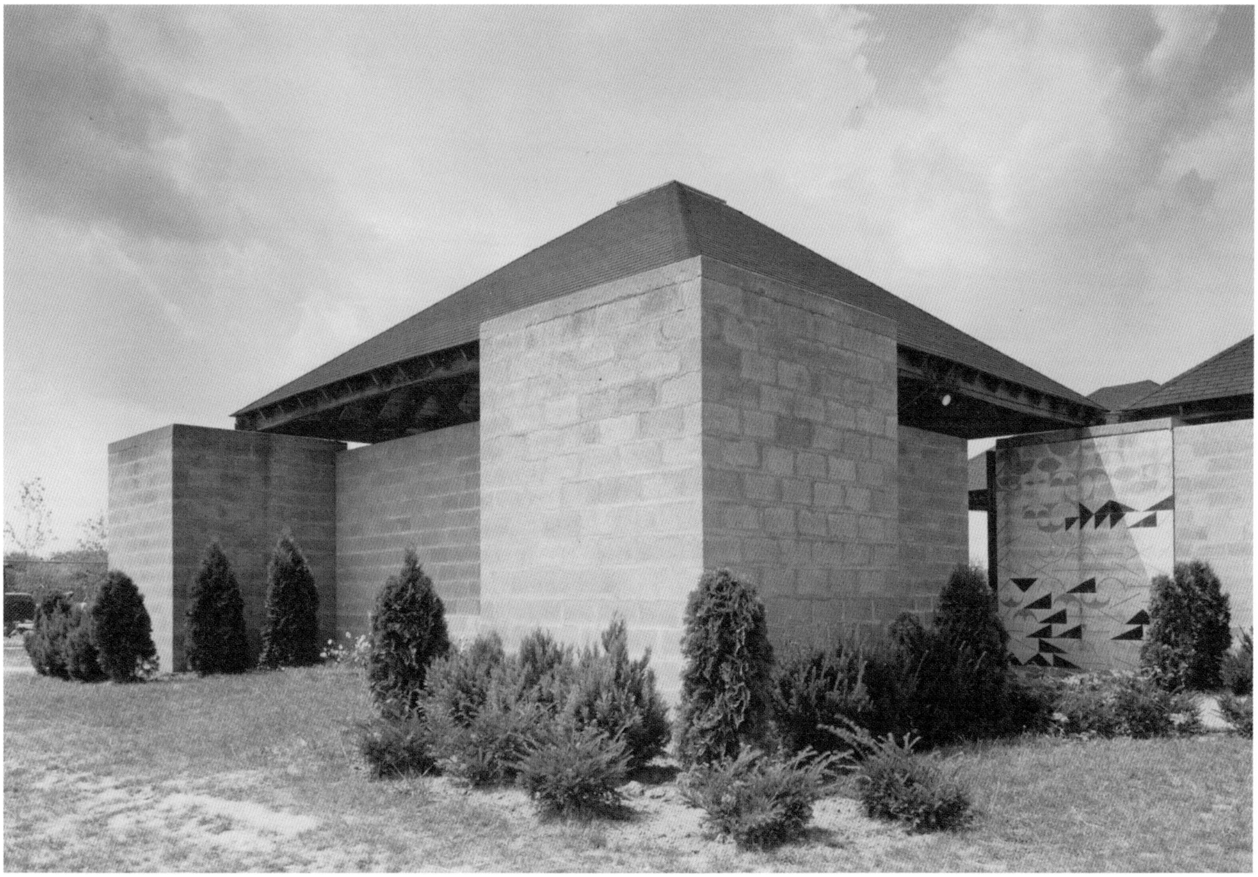

FIGURE 69. Trenton Bathhouse. Photograph by John Ebstel

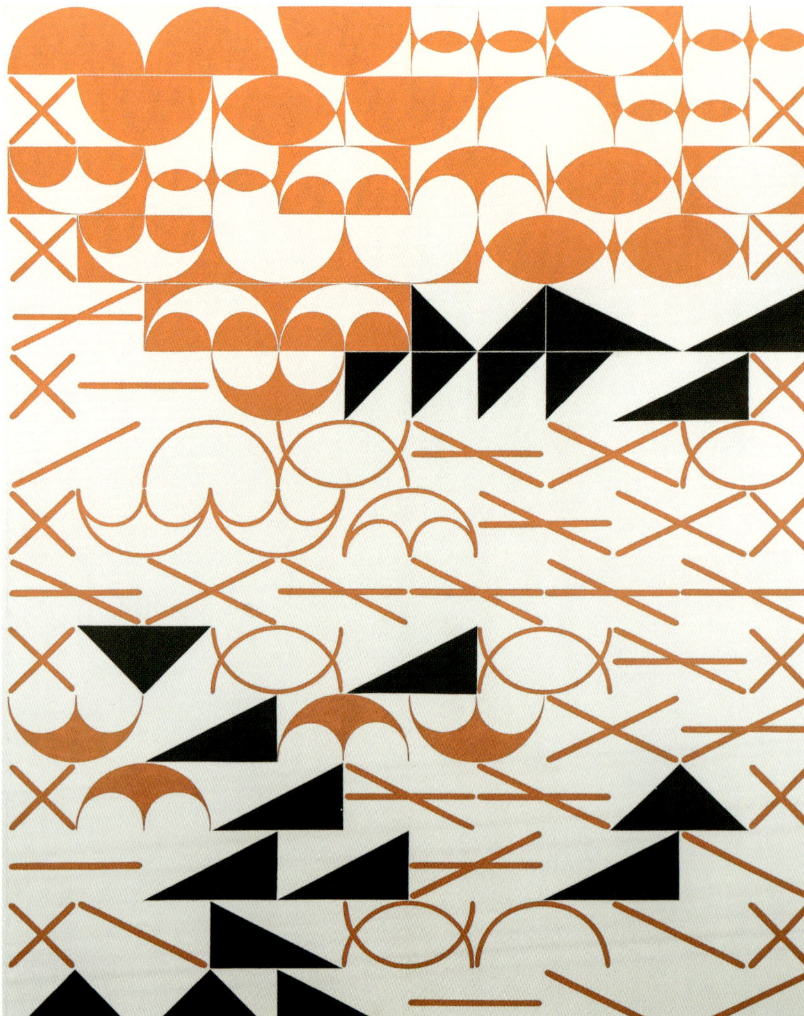

FIGURE 70.
Replica of the Trenton Mural, 2012, by Canning Studios (Architectural Archives, University of Pennsylvania, by the gift of the Vitra Design Museum)

continued to draw and paint on his own, soon moving beyond the traditional styles prescribed in the curriculum. As architectural historian Vincent Scully has noted, the drawings and watercolors Kahn created on a trip through Europe a few years after his graduation are stylish and slick, evidently influenced by the likes of Georgia O'Keeffe and Charles Demuth.[3]

Not long after his European tour, Kahn abandoned the dictates of his training and became a convert to architectural modernism, then a loosely affiliated set of convictions and aesthetic ideals drawn largely from architects practicing in France, Germany, and the Netherlands. The Great Depression had set in, and the decadence of neoclassicism must have seemed badly out of touch with the needs of ordinary people. George Howe and William Lescaze's landmark headquarters for the Philadelphia Savings Fund Society (now the Loews Philadelphia Hotel) eschewed historical styles for

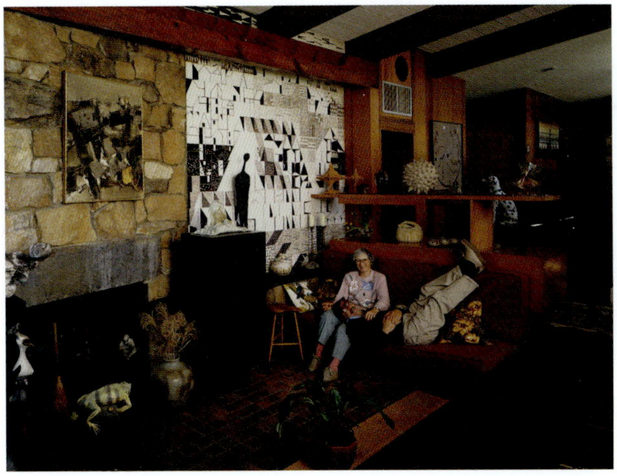

FIGURE 71. Kahn and Tyng's mural in the Morton Weiss House. Photograph by Lewis Tanner

that very reason; upon its completion, in 1932, it became the nation's first modernist skyscraper.[4] Howe became Kahn's close friend and lifelong mentor, and the two worked together to promote modernism in Philadelphia through a joint firm and a magazine called the *T-Square Club Journal*.[5] Howe later chaired the architecture department at Yale University, where he oversaw a modernist curriculum and retained Kahn as an instructor. At Yale, the duo came into contact with leading modernist figures such as Anni and Josef Albers, and Kahn received his first prominent commission: a sharp, modern addition to the university's neo-Gothic art gallery (1951–53).[6]

Kahn, then, was a natural fit for Group '55. Like the artists who initiated the group, he struggled with the bias against novel styles endemic in aesthetically conservative Philadelphia. Also like them, he sought to make a case for new artistic modes that would be relevant and valuable in the postwar era. Important too was the notion of art's significance within architecture that Kahn had learned at Penn. Following the Bauhaus ideal, modern architects took this notion even further with their dream of integrating all the visual arts, from graphic design and painting to sculpture and architecture. Kahn was no different, and around the same time he became involved with Group '55, he was working to incorporate murals into his architectural projects. Next to the fireplace at the Morton Weiss House (1948–50), Kahn and his associate Anne Tyng painted a large, abstract mural that incorporates symbolic references to the Weiss family's dog and the Pennsylvania landscape.[7] And in 1955 at the bathhouse for the Trenton Jewish Community Center (1954–59), which Kahn and Tyng designed together, he and another associate, Marie Kuo, painted another abstract mural on the wall adjacent to the entrance. This second project lacks any obvious representation—it consists of red and black geometric shapes arranged dynamically on a white background—though some scholars have interpreted it as echoing the tile floors of the Roman Baths of Caracalla.[8]

All this shows the depth of Kahn's modernist convictions and places him in the company of Philadelphia's most progressive artists and architects of the era. It does not, however, explain the more important question of what ultimately set Kahn so far apart from his architectural contemporaries. Just as Kahn was beginning his involvement with Group '55, he was developing the novel philosophy of architecture that would come to guide his writings as well as buildings such as the Trenton bathhouse. The talk he gave at the first Group '55 exhibition, in early 1956, illustrates this thinking in vivid terms and hints at its origins in Philadelphia.[9] In typical Kahn fashion, its themes are lofty—nothing less than the very nature of art and architecture—but its language is crisp and clear.

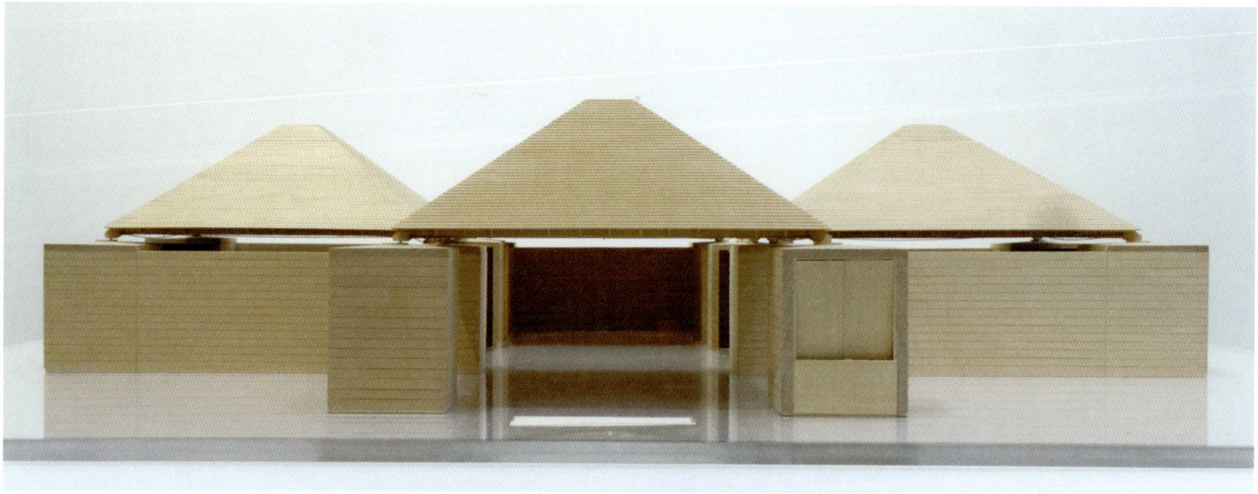

FIGURE 72. Model for the Trenton Bath House, 1991, by Bill Christensen, Linda Brenner, and Laurie Kass (Architectural Archives, University of Pennsylvania, by the gift of the Museum of Contemporary Art, Los Angeles)

Kahn began his talk with the argument that architecture derives from a comprehension of the "order" of a building.[10] The order of *house*, he suggests, is different from and far more important than any particular house. Only when order is grasped can one begin the process of *design*, the reconciling of order with the circumstances of the given project. As he put it, "Architecture essentially is a matter of designing spaces—and so the organization which it is designed from—which is derived out of order of space and which is a concept or a grasp of what space is like."[11] Aesthetics, then, is a vehicle for revealing truth rather than an end in itself. To illustrate this point, Kahn imagined a skyscraper of the future that would not have "arbitrary shape" but would instead follow "the forces which tend to shape it, economic, order of construction, order of spaces, and order, also, of economy."[12] In sum, the architect's goal is to express the facts of a building's creation rather than to re-create a conventionally beautiful object. It is to express "what a thing wants to be."[13]

This view placed Kahn squarely at odds with his contemporaries, most of whom were then in the thrall of the glossy International Style that had grown out of early modernism. A savvy audience member at the Group '55 event, recognizing this, asked Kahn his view of the Penn Center office development planned for Center City. Kahn, who repeatedly clashed with Ed Bacon of the City Planning Commission over the project and had earlier in his talk even alluded to his own alternative designs for Center City, did not hold back. "It's a gigantic real estate thing," he responded. "And if I were to describe it as nothing, I think I would describe it very accurately."[14] Nor did he have anything positive to say of the recently completed United Nations headquarters in New York, describing it as a "toy enlarged" and lacking in the expression of the "fabric . . . of construction."[15]

Kahn's rejection of the International Style linked him to the American architects whose ideas had helped launch the modernist movement: Frank Lloyd Wright, Louis Sullivan, and fellow Philadelphian Frank Furness. It was Sullivan, a former employee of Furness, who famously commented that "form ever follows function,"[16] and it's no accident that his phrase better describes Kahn's working method than it does that of the practitioners of the International Style who adopted it as a slogan. Kahn's break from his contemporaries was not so much a return to antiquity as to an earlier

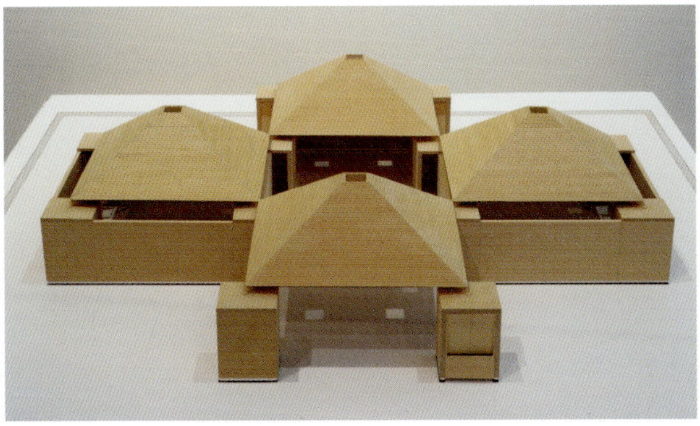

FIGURE 73. Model for the Trenton Bath House, 1991, by Bill Christensen, Linda Brenner, and Laurie Kass (Architectural Archives, University of Pennsylvania, by the gift of the Museum of Contemporary Art, Los Angeles)

American idea of what it means to be modern. He all but admitted as much at the Group '55 event; in response to an audience member asking where in Philadelphia one might find buildings that fulfilled his ideal, he replied:

> There are buildings, old buildings, buildings which were built before the so-called International Movement, buildings which have every evidence of the process of building about them. They are not necessarily what we may call beautiful buildings, but there are more architects today who after having gone through a certain amount of practice recognize them suddenly as being very good. They are good, because they are so easily readable, from the standpoint of how they were built. . . . And in back of that, you see, there is more beginning of beauty than there is in any kind of design-making which is purely temporal, which is purely stylish.[17]

Kahn famously refused to admit his influences, and his phrasing here carefully avoids particular architects or buildings. (In response to a follow-up request for an example, Kahn demurred: "Offhand, I'm very poor on the names of buildings."[18]) But his meaning is clear: he is referring to the industrial architecture of the nineteenth century—buildings created prior to the International Style that were not widely considered to be beautiful in 1956 but that had recently started to gain the attention of some progressive architects, Kahn among them.

Most notable among Philadelphia's industrial-era buildings were the neglected works of Furness, which most modernists saw as offensively decadent. What Kahn found in this architecture, by contrast, was a living precedent for buildings that reveal how they were made and what purpose they serve, buildings that set aside conventional aesthetics to be what they want to be. There is good reason to think that Furness in particular was on Kahn's mind when he made his remarks: a 1953 exhibition at the Philadelphia Art Alliance on the city's nineteenth-century architecture had featured work by Furness, and Kahn's close friend Howe had given a speech at the exhibition in which he cited Furness as the most notable local architect of the era.[19]

Kahn's interest in Furness seems to have begun in earnest around the time of that exhibition, perhaps prompted by the planned demolition of several Furness-designed banks for the creation of Independence National Historical Park. (One of Kahn's engineers recalled him remarking that he "would rather see them tear down Independence Hall" than a Furness bank.[20]) In subsequent years, Kahn's interest grew only stronger, culminating in his successful efforts to save Furness buildings from demolition at the Philadelphia College of Art and to prevent Furness's PAFA from the potentially worse fate of being sold to an aggressive local developer.[21]

Kahn may not have mentioned Furness by name at the Group '55 event, but his remarks offer confirmation of the formative influence of nineteenth-century Philadelphia architecture on

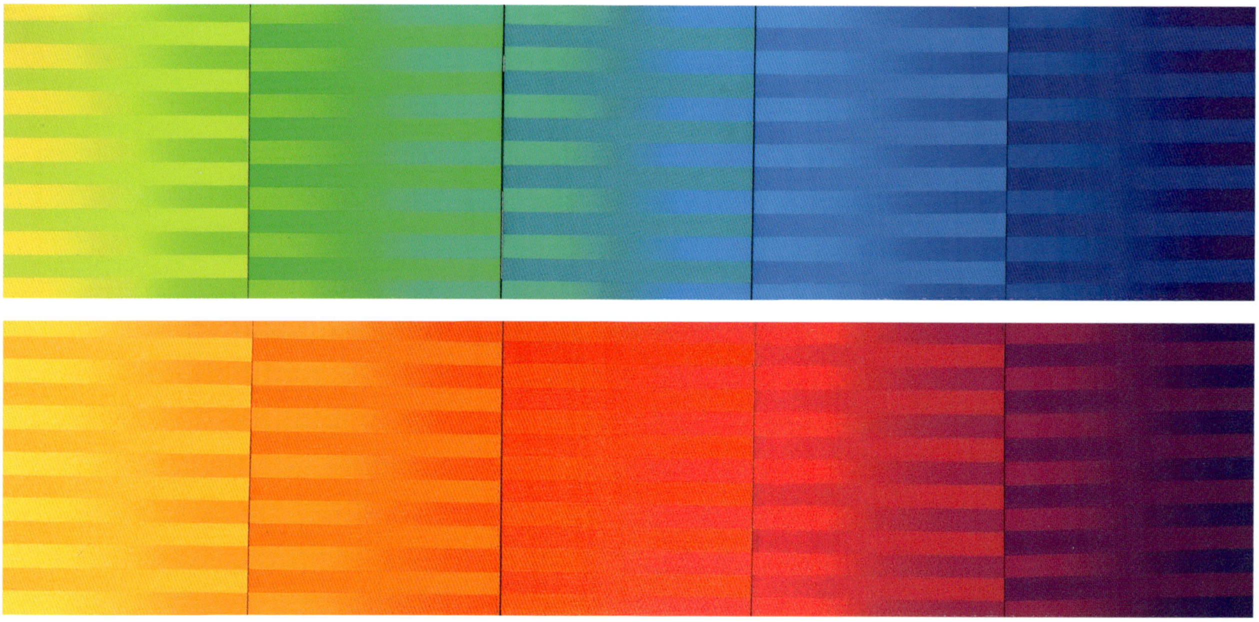

FIGURE 74. **Spectrum Study, Warm to Cool**, c. 1974, by Elaine Kurtz (Private Collection) The five panels called *Warm Spectrum* were installed in the Korman house designed by Kahn. Photograph by Rick Echelmeyer

his mature architectural thought. And they capture Kahn engaging with his fellow artists: at one point, Kahn had a spirited exchange with Raymond Hendler when he suggested that painters should not make corrections to their work but instead start with fresh canvases.[22] They also set the stage for the deeper exploration of the relationship between art and architecture that characterized much of Kahn's subsequent work, including the tapestries for the sanctuary of the First Unitarian Church of Rochester, New York (1958–68), designed in their original iteration by Anni Albers, as well as great oriental carpets daringly hung on the walls of the common areas of Erdman Hall at Bryn Mawr College (1960–64). And at the Korman House in Fort Washington (1971–74), Kahn and his clients selected a set of paintings by abstract artist Elaine Kurtz (fig. 74) to grace prominent walls in the foyer and the living room.[23]

Of equal importance are Kahn's later museums, the Kimbell Art Museum in Fort Worth (1966–72) and the Yale Center for British Art (1969–74), both of which were shaped by their collections. Both take cues from Furness's skylit galleries at PAFA, and both seek to integrate art and architecture for the disciplines' mutual benefit. At the Center for British Art, a dramatic, 140-foot-long gallery and entrance court recall those found in English country houses; at the Kimbell, vault-like bays suggest at once Roman ruins and the American industrial vernacular, a fitting combination for a Fort Worth museum centered around antiquities. These two buildings achieve a feat rare in the world of museum architecture: they assert themselves as artworks in their own right without upstaging the art housed within. And it is this remarkable balance, perhaps more than anything else, that speaks to the importance of the dialogue between art and architecture sparked by Group '55.

NOTES

1 Research for this essay in the Louis I. Kahn Collection held in the Architectural Archives, University of Pennsylvania, Philadelphia, was limited due to the COVID-19 pandemic of 2020.

2 For Kahn's early biographical information, see Wendy Lesser, *You Say to Brick: The Life of Louis Kahn* (New York: Farrar, Straus and Giroux, 2017), 47–61.

3 Vincent Scully, "Introduction," in *The Travel Sketches of Louis I. Kahn* (Philadelphia: Pennsylvania Academy of the Fine Arts, 1978), 13.

4 George Howe, "Architectural Design of the Proposed PSFS Building at 12th and Market Streets" (n.d.), Columbia University, New York, Avery Architectural and Fine Arts Library, George Howe papers, 1926–1974 bulk 1926–1955, box 2, folder IV B.

5 See David Brody, "The Functionalist's Agenda: George Howe, the *T-Square Club Journal*, and the Dissemination of Architectural Modernism," *American Periodicals: A Journal of History and Criticism* 20, no. 2 (2010): 241–68.

6 David B. Brownlee and David G. De Long, *Louis I. Kahn: In the Realm of Architecture* (Los Angeles and New York: Museum of Contemporary Art, 1991), 127.

7 The mural may have been painted after the house's completion; the first extant photograph of it appeared in 1953. See Jane Murphy, "Drawing on Walls: Louis Kahn's Murals," https://knowlton.osu.edu/sites/default/files/2018_Murphy_Drawing-on-Walls_PDF%282%29.pdf, accessed June 27, 2020.

8 Susan G. Solomon, *Louis I. Kahn's Trenton Jewish Community Center* (New York: Princeton Architectural Press, 2000), 95–97.

9 This is unfortunately Kahn's only recorded Group '55 talk.

10 Kahn's use of this term varied over time. See Izzy Kornblatt, "Architecture for a New World: Louis Kahn and Philadelphia" (master's thesis, Harvard University Graduate School of Design, 2019), 5 and n7.

11 Group '55 Forum: "Changing Forms in Art," January 12, 1956, reel 1 transcript, 18.

12 "Changing Forms in Art," reel 2 transcript, 2.

13 "Changing Forms in Art," reel 2 transcript, 5.

14 "Changing Forms in Art," reel 4 transcript, 2–3.

15 "Changing Forms in Art," reel 4 transcript, 5–6.

16 Louis Sullivan, "The Tall Office Building Artistically Considered" (1896), in *Louis Sullivan: The Public Papers*, edited by Robert Twombly (Chicago: University of Chicago Press, 1988), 111.

17 "Changing Forms in Art," reel 4 transcript, 6.

18 "Changing Forms in Art," reel 4 transcript, 7.

19 George Howe, "Why Then?—Why Now?" (1953), reprinted in Helen Howe West, *George Howe, Architect, 1886–1955: Recollections of My Beloved Father* (Philadelphia: W. Nunn, 1973), 66–79.

20 Sam Rodell, "The Influence of Robert Venturi on Louis Kahn" (master's thesis, Washington State University, 2008), 78.

21 The Kahn-Furness connection is examined in depth in Kornblatt, "Architecture for a New World," 114–46.

22 "Changing Forms in Art," reel 4 transcript, 11–12.

23 On the Unitarian Church, see Susan G. Solomon, *Louis I. Kahn's Jewish Architecture: Mikveh Israel and the Midcentury American Synagogue* (Waltham, MA: Brandeis University Press, 2009), 80. The carpets at Erdman Hall and the paintings at the Korman House remain in place.

THE COMPOSERS OF GROUP '55

THOMAS PATTESON

In music, as in other arts, the period after World War II was one of dizzying possibility. Musicians of all stripes shared the feeling, in the words of Italian philosopher Antonio Gramsci, that "the old is dying, and the new cannot be born."[1] In these extreme conditions, the search for orientation was paramount, for the audiences encountering bewildering new art forms as well as the artists creating them.

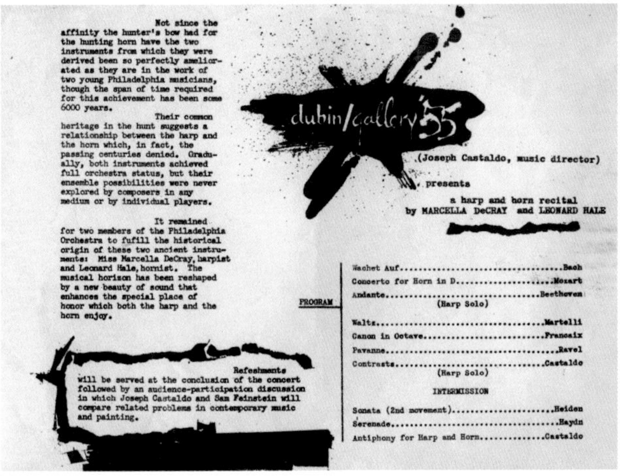

Not since the affinity the hunter's bow had for the hunting horn have the two instruments from which they were derived been so perfectly amelior-ated as they are in the work of two young Philadelphia musicians, though the span of time required for this achievement has been some 6000 years.

Their common heritage in the hunt suggests a relationship between the harp and the horn which, in fact, the passing centuries denied. Gradu-ally, both instruments achieved full orchestra status, but their ensemble possibilities were never explored by composers in any medium or by individual players.

It remained for two members of the Philadelphia Orchestra to fufill the historical origin of these two ancient instru-ments: Miss Marcella DeCray, harpist and Leonard Hale, hornist. The musical horizon has been reshaped by a new beauty of sound that enhances the special place of honor which both the harp and the horn enjoy.

Refeshments will be served at the conclusion of the concert followed by an audience-participation discussion in which Joseph Castaldo and Sam Feinstein will compare related problems in contemporary music and painting.

dubin/gallery '55

(Joseph Castaldo, music director)

presents

a harp and horn recital
by MARCELLA DeCRAY and LEONARD HALE

PROGRAM

Wachet Auf..Bach
Concerto for Horn in D.........................Mozart
Andante..Beethoven
(Harp Solo)

Waltz..Martelli
Canon in Octave................................Francaix
Pavanne..Ravel
Contrasts......................................Castaldo
(Harp Solo)

INTERMISSION

Sonata (2nd movement)..........................Heiden
Serenade..Haydn
Antiphony for Harp and Horn....................Castaldo

Figure 75. Program for Group '55 Harp and Horn Recital (Samuel L. Feinstein Trust)

Although Group '55 was led by painters, three composers numbered among its members: Joseph Castaldo, George Rochberg, and Vincent Persichetti. For these men, the group offered a public platform to foster the understanding of contemporary music, seek common ground with artists working in other mediums, and grapple with the challenge of bringing music "up to date" with the modern age. And while they were young and relatively unknown in the 1950s, all went on to have significant careers not only as creative artists, but also as teachers, administrators, and public figures.

Born in New York to Italian immigrants, Castaldo moved to Philadelphia in the early 1950s to take a teaching position at the Philadelphia Musical Academy. Castaldo was deeply involved in Group '55's operations and served briefly as music director of Gallery '55, where he curated performances of his own and others' music. His work from this period can be heard in the 1956 composition *Contrasts*, a series of six short études for the harp based on Persichetti's hymn "Purer Than Purest Pure," which set to music a poem by e. e. Cummings. The piece gradually shifts from the shimmering Debussyesque harmonies of the earlier movements to the dissonant spareness of the end. Beyond describing a general feature of the music, its title is typical of modern composers' avoidance of generic labels such as symphony or sonata and the overly descriptive titles of Romantic program music, which led to the midcentury proliferation of titles consisting of isolated nouns and adjectives.

Castaldo and Group '55 founder Sam Feinstein shared an interest in aesthetics and engaged in an ongoing conversation about the implications of abstraction for painting and music. Feinstein, like many other visual artists of the time, believed that abstract art captured a higher, purely formal truth that transcended painting's traditional function of representing the world as it appears to our everyday perception. Accordingly, the preeminence of abstraction—setting aside the many fractious debates about what the term could mean—was taken almost as an article of faith by modern artists. Among musicians, however, there was much less consensus about the way forward; no single approach possessed the talismanic power of abstraction, in part because music's dominant paradigm—its counterpart to representation in the visual arts—was less clear. Since European Romanticism emerged in the early nineteenth century, artists and aestheticians had celebrated instrumental music as the abstract medium par excellence, one whose tenuous link to the empirical world gave free rein to the auditor's imagination. (Indeed, in the early twentieth century, instrumental music was widely held up by painters such as Mondrian, Klee, and Kandinsky as a model for nonrepresentational art.) But many also ascribed to music a function that could be called "psychomimetic," arguing that its proper aim was the imitation or "expression" not of outward appearances (as was the case for painting) but of inward states of being. Many twentieth-century composers rebelled against this idea; while few rejected the ideal of expression outright, they sought to escape the familiar orbit of emotional representation as it had been formalized in the aesthetic theory of the so-called common practice period (roughly 1650–1900).

Attempting to outline a unified notion of abstraction that could encompass modern painting and modern music, Castaldo argued that both must be seen as fundamentally presentational rather than representational. He pointed out that modern art should be called not "abstract" but "concrete," because it sought to treat color, shape, tone, and timbre as objects of attention rather than signs or symbols of something else. Thus, from different directions, Feinstein and Castaldo each arrived at an aesthetic position that could be very loosely labeled "formalist." Painters took as their model so-called absolute music (exemplified in particular by genres such as the symphony and string quartet), while composers pursued musical equivalents to the unfettered play of line and color found in modern visual art.[2] Ultimately, however, formalist art fled into the arms of that which it had hoped to escape. In eschewing representation and seeking a state of aesthetic self-sufficiency—in Castaldo's words, "an independent reality, analogous to, rather than an imitation of, nature"—modern art ironically aspired to the condition of nature itself.[3]

While the relationship between music and painting loomed large for the composers of Group '55, even more pressing was the need to reconnect with international currents in the wake of the Great Depression and World War II. This feeling was perhaps especially intense for composers in Philadelphia, who chafed at the city's somewhat provincial artistic culture. Enthusiasts of modern music could point to Leopold Stokowski, conductor of the Philadelphia Orchestra from 1912 to 1940 who led the American premieres of works by modernist composers such as Schoenberg, Shostakovich, and Varèse, but by the 1950s they might reasonably have felt that the action was elsewhere.

The question of the state of the musical arts was addressed by Rochberg in the first Group '55 forum, in January 1956. Born in Paterson, New Jersey, he attended the Mannes School of Music, in New York. After serving in the military during World War II, he moved to Philadelphia, where he studied at the Curtis Institute of Music and the University of Pennsylvania (Penn), and later taught at Curtis. Among the composers associated with Group '55, Rochberg was uniquely well informed about recent developments in Europe, having traveled to Italy on

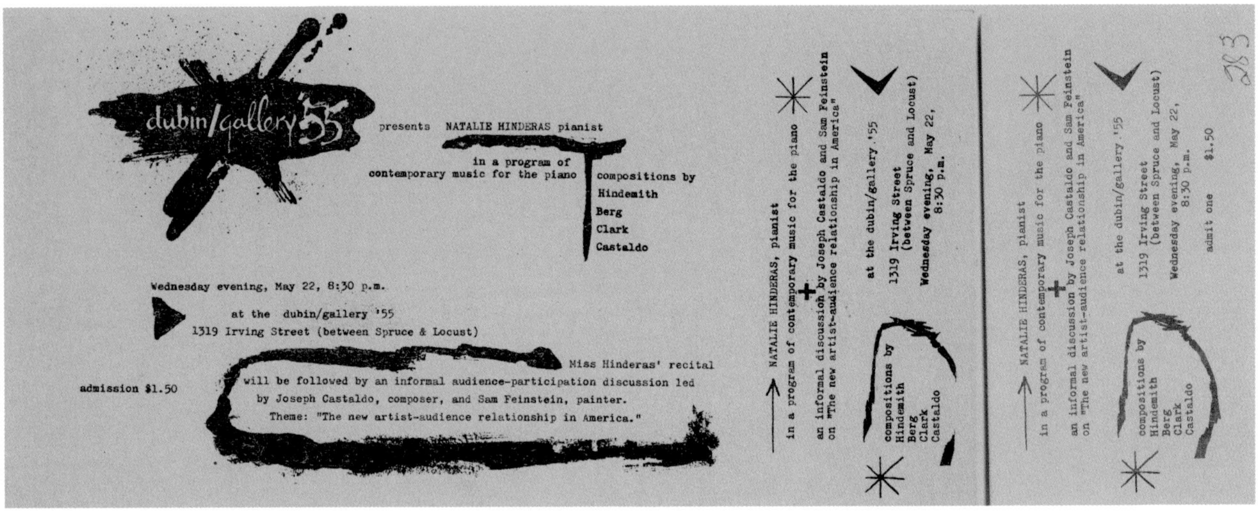

FIGURE 76. Flyer and ticket for Natalie Hinderas concert (Samuel L. Feinstein Trust)

a Fulbright scholarship in 1950, where he studied under composer Luigi Dallapiccola. His presentation at the 1956 forum was something of a crash course in musical developments since 1945 in which he sought to convey both the weight of the musical past—"the nineteenth century is still very much with us," he noted—and a typically modernist sense of unlimited possibility.

The dominant international style in music in the 1930s and 1940s had been neoclassicism, as composers such as Stravinsky, Hindemith, and Prokofiev, sought to temper the unruly energies unleashed at the turn of the century with the reintroduction of pre-Romantic forms such as the fugue, the sonata, and the concerto. (While neoclassicism in painting looks back to Greco-Roman antiquity, neoclassicism in music seeks its models in the late eighteenth and early nineteenth centuries.) Although neoclassical composers' invocations of the musical past were tinged with varying degrees of ironic distance, the movement was attacked by critics as a refutation of modernity. In line with this view, Rochberg's historical survey framed the first half of the twentieth century as a confrontation between neoclassical nostalgia and the progressive atonal movement led by Schoenberg. (This polemical opposition of "Schoenberg and progress" versus "Stravinsky and restoration" had been advanced by Theodor Adorno in his 1949 book *Philosophy of New Music*, whose argumentation Rochberg likely encountered in Europe.) Noting that Stravinsky himself had recently adopted the twelve-tone technique, Rochberg issued the verdict that "Schoenberg has won out," and, with the demise of neoclassicism presented as a fait accompli, he sketched three distinct yet closely related paths out of the postwar impasse.

For many composers in the 1950s, the way forward was serialism, a technique developed by Luigi Nono, Karlheinz Stockhausen, and Pierre Boulez in Europe and by Milton Babbitt in the United States. Serialism was an extension of the twelve-tone technique

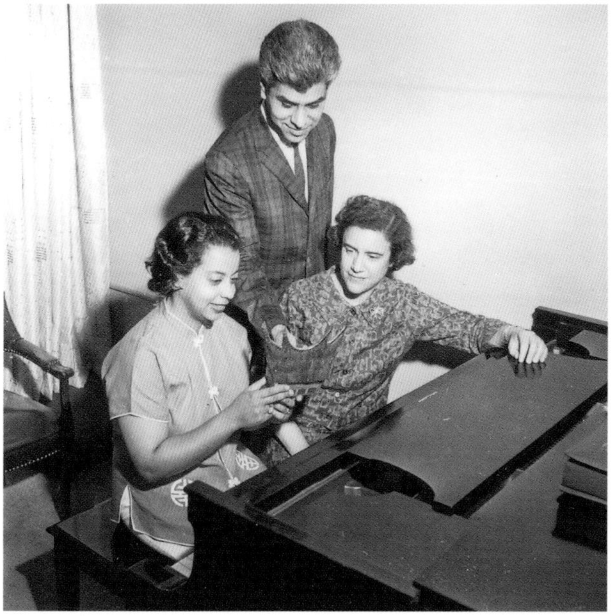

FIGURE 77. Natalie Hinderas (left) and Joseph Castaldo (standing) with unidentified woman at piano, date unknown (Natalie Hinderas Collection, Charles L. Blockson Afro-American Collection, Temple University Libraries, Philadelphia) Photographer unknown

developed by Schoenberg in the 1920s, in which a composition was based on a twelve-tone row, or series—a pre-compositional ordering of the twelve pitches of the octave—that was manipulated to generate the melodic and harmonic structure of the piece. (Because the twelve-tone row requires all pitches to appear with equal frequency, twelve-tone music tends strongly toward atonality; however, the two terms are not synonymous.) The powerful allure of serialism after 1945 was twofold: it freed composers from what many felt to be the inescapable clichés of the major and minor scales of tonal music, and it seemed to guarantee structural coherence through the derivation of all the musical material from a single source, almost like a magic formula. Rochberg's music of the 1950s weds the chromatic richness of atonal music with a sweeping lyricism that the work of Schoenberg and his school rarely possessed. His Symphony No. 2 (1955–56), the first twelve-tone symphony by an American composer, is a bracing introduction to serial music in a broadly traditionalist idiom.

Another alternative was offered by John Cage and the younger composers in his circle in New York. Drawing on the teachings of Zen Buddhism, Cage used chance methods to remove his ego from the creative process and enjoined composers to "let sounds be themselves rather than vehicles for man-made theories or expressions of human sentiments."[4] With its luminous silences and radical discontinuities, the music of the so-called New York School has often been viewed as a parallel to the Abstract Expressionism that then dominated the visual arts. Although Cage's approach is often seen as the antithesis of serialism, the music that resulted from these two approaches was often startlingly similar. Both the serial composers and the Cage circle were entranced by the music of Schoenberg's pupil Anton Webern—the former by the tightness of its compositional logic, the latter by its spaciousness and unpredictability.

Finally, the new medium of electronic music, whose technological foundations were developed in the early twentieth century and became widely available after 1945, offered a way for composers to bypass conventional scores and instruments altogether and work directly with sound in a hands-on fashion. Rochberg's talk touched on the emergence of this new form in numerous centers around the world: the *elektronische Musik* of Stockhausen and Herbert Eimert in Cologne, the *musique concrète* of Pierre Schaeffer in Paris, and the manipulation of taped instrumental sounds by Otto Luening and Vladimir Ussachevsky at Columbia University in New York. While reactions to this music tended toward the extremes of either adulation or disdain, Rochberg remained agnostic, stating flatly, "We don't know yet whether to call this music or not." Regarding changes in music technology, however, he presciently noted "indications that live music is suffering considerably from the impact of recording [and] the increased number of people who own private record collections, who prefer to stay home and listen to their own recordings rather than go to a concert and hear a recital or hear an orchestra."

Of the three composers associated with Group '55, Persichetti was the only native Philadelphian. He studied at Curtis, at the Juilliard School in New York, and at the Philadelphia Conservatory of Music, where he later taught. He appeared on a couple of discussion panels in the late 1950s but otherwise seems to have been less engaged with the group than Castaldo and Rochberg. Persichetti left the Philadelphia Conservatory upon its merger with the Philadelphia Musical Academy in 1962. The same year, he was appointed chair of the composition department at Juilliard, a post he held—commuting all the while from his native city—until his death, in 1987.[5] By virtue of his force of personality and his talent as a teacher, Persichetti was arguably the most influential of the three composers of Group '55. And while Rochberg and Castaldo explored the avant-garde extremes of midcentury music, Persichetti remained more firmly anchored in the American mainstream, as seen in compositions such as "Pageant for Wind Band" (1953), one of his many contributions to an ensemble that retains strong ties to vernacular musical styles.

After their involvement with Group '55, Rochberg and Castaldo took on significant leadership and administrative duties in addition to their creative work. Castaldo became the president of the Philadelphia Musical Academy in 1966 and used his position to invite a number of major composers to give guest lectures at the school, including Babbitt, Boulez, Cage, and Morton Feldman. While he built up Philadelphia's standing as a destination for avant-garde music, Castaldo cautioned against the tendency toward hyper-specialization and argued for a broadly humanistic approach to music education that integrated performance and composition.[6] As an administrator, he oversaw the expansion of the academy and its eventual metamorphosis into the Philadelphia College of the Performing Arts. A few years after Castaldo's retirement in 1983, a further merger created the University of the Arts, fulfilling his long-held dream of a unified arts college in the city.

Rochberg, like Persichetti and Castaldo, assumed an academic leadership role, serving for several years as chair of Penn's music department and developing its national profile by recruiting composer George Crumb and musicologist Leonard Meyer to join the faculty. He remained at Penn until 1983. As a composer, Rochberg became a figurehead in the postmodern turn of the 1970s, abandoning what he saw as the austerities of the avant-garde to embrace a broad spectrum of historical and expressive resonances, a project he dubbed *ars combinatoria*.[7] Rochberg's abandonment of modernism was all the more surprising given his earlier position as one of the most prominent twelve-tone composers in the United States.

In considering the stature and influence that these three composers would later attain in American musical life, it is remarkable that their paths should have converged during the fleeting existence of Group '55. They cannot in any sense be viewed as a unified school; they shared no collective mission on par with the championing of abstraction undertaken by Feinstein and the painters of the group. Their efforts to introduce new ideas and techniques into the conservative world of classical music would take decades to bear fruit. Still, their engagement on behalf of modern music in Philadelphia in the late 1950s is a testament to the shared vision that animated the members of Group '55, and Castaldo, Rochberg, and Persichetti carried the spirit of the group on throughout their diverse and distinguished careers.

NOTES

1 Antonio Gramsci, *Selections from the Prison Notebooks*, ed. and trans. Quintin Hoare and Geoffrey Nowell Smith (New York: International Publishers, 1971), 276.

2 In fact, the stance of visual arts theorists such as Clement Greenberg had been anticipated a century earlier by the Austrian music critic Eduard Hanslick, who famously argued that music fundamentally consists of nothing but "tonally moving forms." See Lee Rothfarb and Christoph Landerer, *Eduard Hanslick's "On the Musically Beautiful: A New Translation"* (Oxford: Oxford University Press, 2018).

3 Castaldo's argument here is remarkably similar to the roughly contemporaneous statements of Pierre Schaeffer, with which he was likely not familiar. See Pierre Schaeffer, *In Search of a Concrete Music*, trans. Christine North and John Dack (Berkeley: University of California Press, 2012).

4 John Cage, "Experimental Music" (1957), in *Silence* (Middletown, CT: Wesleyan University Press, 1961), 10. Rochberg dryly noted in his 1956 talk, "This is the first time in the history of music that anyone has seriously considered leaving the progression of sounds up to chance."

5 For more on Persichetti's influential career, see Andrea Olmstead, *Vincent Persichetti: Grazioso, Grit, and Gold* (Lanham, MD: Rowman and Littlefield, 2018).

6 Joseph Castaldo, "Creativity Can End Our Musical Isolationism," *Music Educators Journal* 56, no. 3 (November 1969): 36–38.

7 A collection of Rochberg's writings can be found in *The Aesthetics of Survival: A Composer's View of Twentieth-Century Music*, rev. ed. (Ann Arbor: University of Michigan Press, 2004).

MODERN DANCE AND GROUP '55

VICTORIA SCHUH

"Dancing is at once the abandon of physical joy and movement with spiritual thought and purpose."
—Malvena Fried Taiz

In 1958, Group '55 looked to modern dance in its efforts to further the public's understanding of contemporary creative challenges, to examine the relationship between artist and audience, and to explore new uses of space and visual language. Modern dance echoed the changes then happening in many fields of creative endeavor, which were rejecting classical rigidity in favor of innovative forms better suited to individual expression and aligned with the social idealism and dynamism of the times.

Malvena Fried Taiz (1907-1979) was invited to participate in two Group '55 forums and to perform with her dance group at a third event.[1] Described as an "outstanding exponent of modern dance in Philadelphia," Taiz was an educator who brought an obsession with creative practice to her teaching, and a well-networked professional in the performing arts community.[2] She was a second-generation modern dancer who learned from pioneer Martha Graham, much as Sam Feinstein was a second-generation abstractionist inspired by Hans Hofmann. Taiz's thirty-year career paralleled the arc of modern dance, which would develop new techniques, movement, space, and stagecraft.

Dance in Philadelphia in the early twentieth century had been largely limited to professional performances, such as those audiences might see at concerts, musical theater, or the opera, and the social dances that people of all classes engaged in for fun. But in this period of rapid change, that distinction began to blur. The tightly bound social conventions and class stratifications that had long defined how and where people danced, with whom, what they wore, and how they behaved were giving way.[3] San Francisco–born Isadora Duncan, often considered the first "modern dancer," for example, cast off pointe shoes and stiff-corseted costumes in favor of bare feet and gauzy, flowing gowns. Inspired by folk dances, nature, and classical art,[4] she introduced humor, emotion, and a new athleticism to her performances. Duncan was the first American dancer to develop a philosophy of dance, one that relied on use of the breath and that was defined by spiritual rather than formal considerations.[5] Professional dancers in Europe and the United States alike were inspired to adopt and adapt her innovations.

Simultaneously, Philadelphians were going wild for "ragtime dances," among them the Grizzly Bear, the Castle Walk, and especially the tango. Young women met for "tango teas" after work to practice dance steps. "Wanamaker's, Strawbridge's and Lit Brothers sold 'tango shirts' and 'tango shoes' for men and 'tango sashes,' 'tango hats' and even flexible 'tango corsets' for women. Bolts of brilliant orange fabric that had sat unsold in dry goods

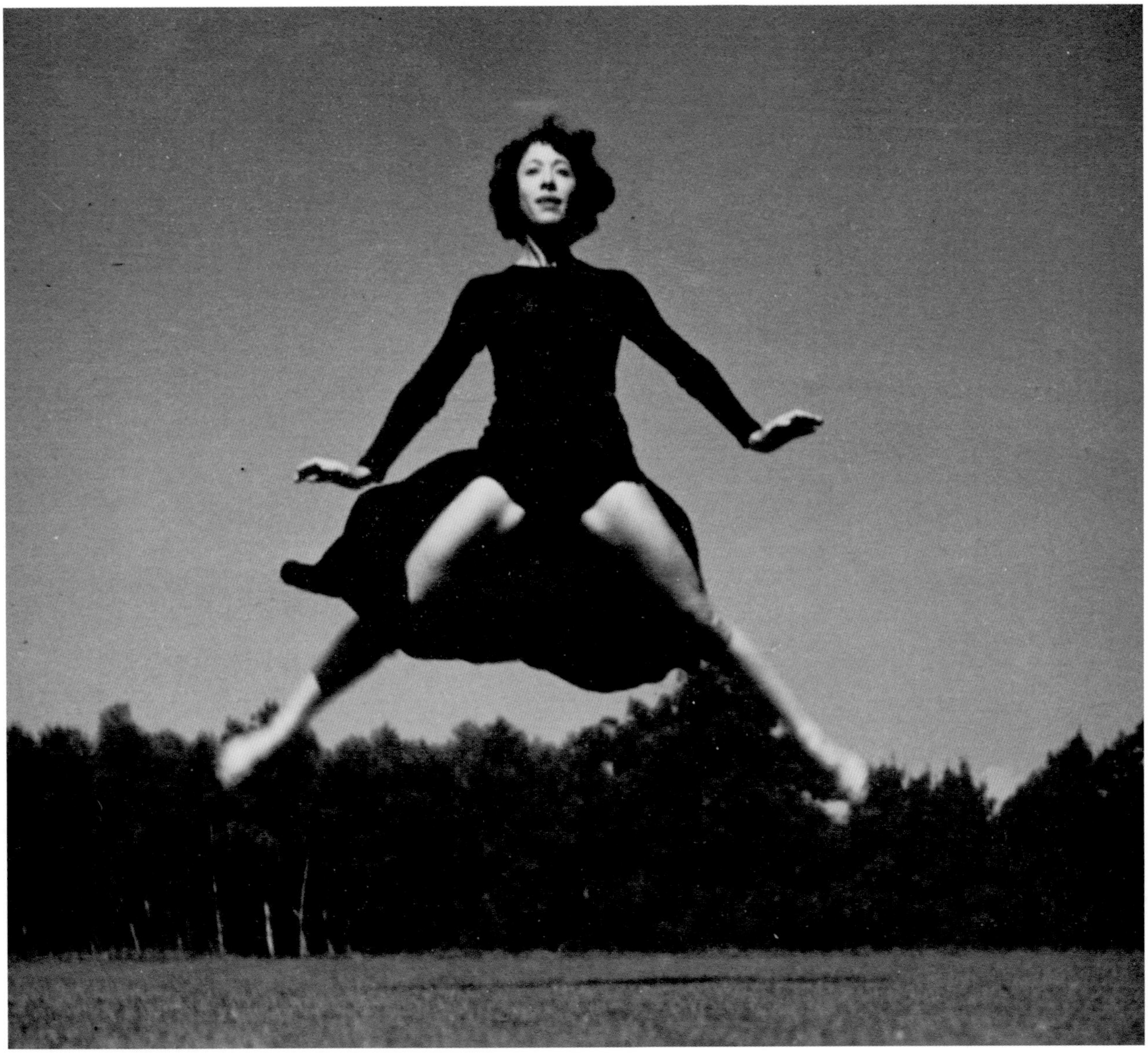

FIGURE 78. Malvena Fried Taiz in Fairmount Park, Philadelphia, 1937 (Courtesy of Lincoln and Lillian Taiz)

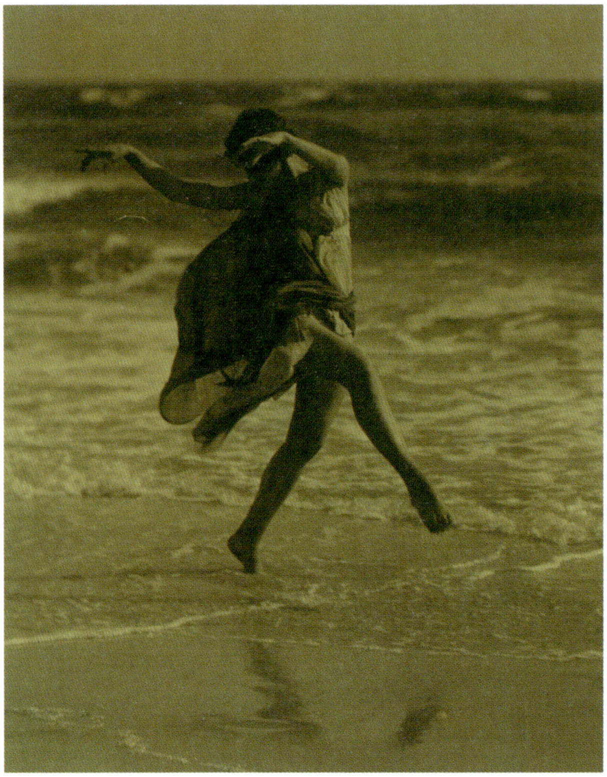

FIGURE 79. Isadora Duncan dancing on Long Beach, CA, c. 1915 (Courtesy of the New York Public Library: Jerome Robbins Dance Division) Photograph by Arnold Genthe

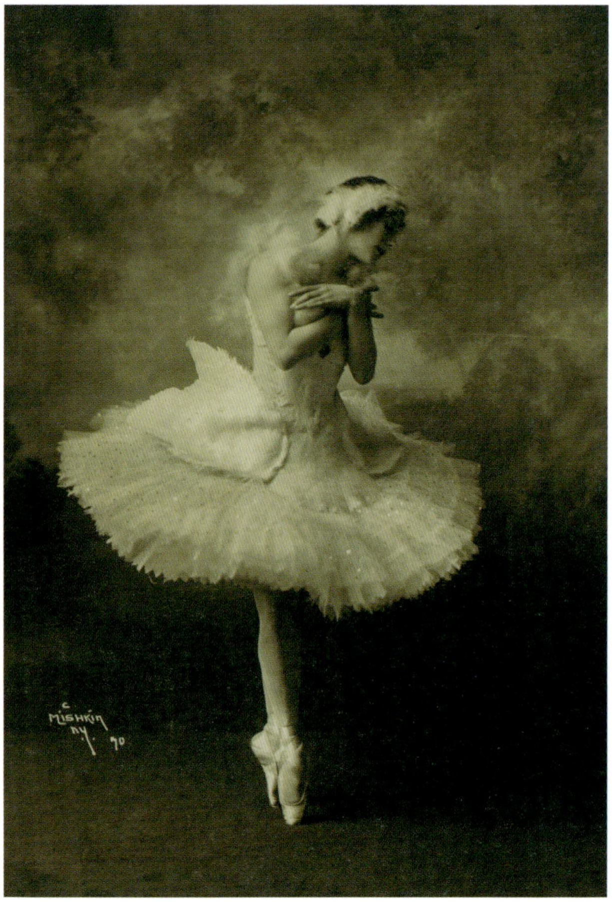

FIGURE 80. Anna Pavlova, costumed as the dying swan, c. 1905 (Courtesy of the New York Public Library: Jerome Robbins Dance Division) Photograph by Herman Mishkin

stores flew off the shelves when the color was dubbed 'tango.'"[6] Step-by-step instructions in daily newspapers and mail-order classes made social dance even more popular. People could practice in their own parlors to recorded music from their hand-cranked Victrolas.[7] Even ballerina Anna Pavlova, known to Philadelphians from her many tours with the Russian Imperial Ballet, published her dance instructions in the *Evening Public Ledger*, validating social dance and increasing her own celebrity in the process.[8]

Dance became a lesser priority with the advent of World War I and the arrival of a new strain of flu, which by the fall of 1918 had mutated and become even more contagious and deadly. Unaware of the threat, on September 28, 1918, more than 200,000 Philadelphians of all ages jammed the streets for a rally promoting government bonds to help pay for the war. Thousands were stricken and died. By its conclusion, the pandemic had killed an estimated 50 million people worldwide and 675,000 Americans, far more than the war itself—and in 1918, Philadelphia was the hardest hit of all American cities.[9]

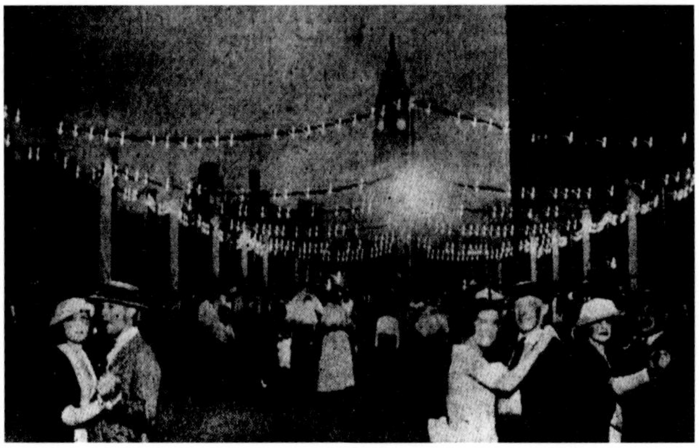

FIGURE 81. "An Evening of Tango at the Swann Memorial Fountain," *Evening Public Ledger*, July 8, 1921 (Association for Public Art)

But by 1921, with the war and the pandemic having passed, Philadelphians were once again looking to have a good time. Weekly open-air "Parkway dances" blossomed throughout the summer on what is now Benjamin Franklin Parkway.[10] As many as twenty-five thousand waltzed, fox-trotted, and tangoed to live music by the Philadelphia Firemen's or Police Band. An official censor enforced strict codes of behavior, but ultimately fewer than a handful of warnings were issued. This wider participation in social dance spurred public interest in other performance styles, including modern dance.

California-based Ruth St. Denis toured the United States extensively throughout the 1910s and 1920s, including many small towns. With its Hindu, Middle Eastern, and Japanese influences, her work featured a "free use of the torso and expressive use of the arms."[11] She was the primary creative force behind the Denishawn School of Dancing and Related Arts,[12] formed with her husband, Ted Shawn. Later in life, St. Denis focused on the relationship between spirituality and dance. Her students, including Martha Graham, Doris Humphrey, and Charles Weidman—all of whom would have a direct impact on Taiz's work—seized this radical form and made it their own, giving it individual flavor while developing a distinctly authentic American style.

Humphrey, who was a Denishawn soloist and rehearsal mistress for eight years, left the company in 1928 due to artistic differences and established her own school with Weidman. The Humphrey/Weidman technique was characterized by "fall and recovery"—a dramatic use of gravity displaying the conflict between the human desire for security (balance) and the urge for progress and adventure (imbalance). Humphrey "was a master of abstraction and stylized gesture" and was committed to creating dance that was highly individualized and expressive of the contemporary American character.[13]

Graham had moved to New York in 1923 and performed in vaudeville, one of the few options for non-ballet dancers. She also pursued her real interest: choreography. Working out of a small studio in midtown Manhattan, she focused on the center of the body (as opposed to ballet's focus on the limbs), contract and release, and movements that were "sharp, angular, jagged, and direct."[14] She was an ingenious choreographer who created 181 works broadly influenced by Greek mythology, Native American rituals, and the American West, and she portrayed many great women in history. Exploring the concept of her ballet *Frontier*, Graham wrote, "I had the idea of *Frontier* in my mind as a frontier of exploration, a frontier of discovery and not one of limitation. . . . It makes me triumphant to think that nothing lasts but the spirit of man and the union of man. People cross the border from East to West to shake the hands of those they have not seen before. In a way, they have become each other's frontier."[15] Graham was declared a "national

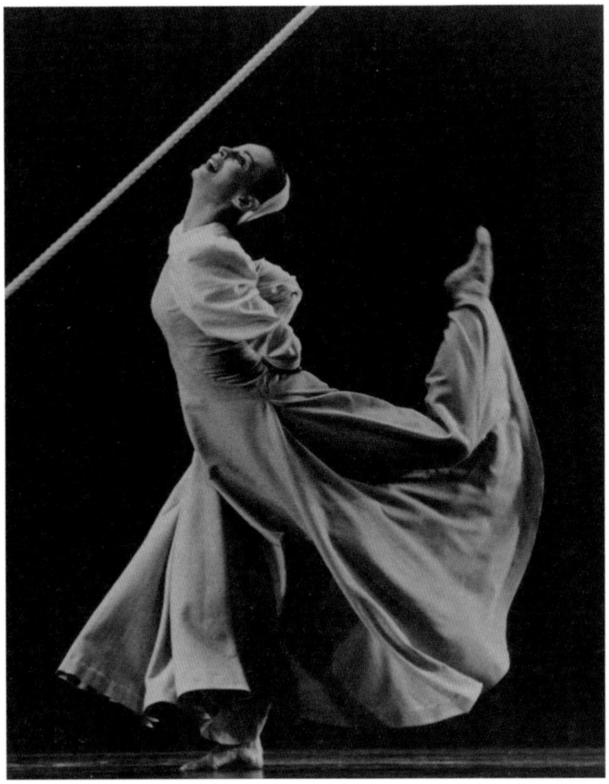

FIGURE 82. Ethel Winter in *Frontier*, c. 1960s, Choreography by Martha Graham (Courtesy of Martha Graham Resources, a division of the Martha Graham Center of Contemporary Dance, Inc.) Photographer unknown

treasure" in 1976, becoming the first dancer and choreographer to receive the Presidential Medal of Freedom, the highest civilian award given in the US.[16]

Around the time Humphrey and Graham were emerging as creative forces in their own right, in the late 1920s, Taiz was a young dance major at New York University. She had grown up in Alabama, playing the piano and violin and studying ballet as "proper" young women did to prepare for a graceful introduction into society. Exposed to New York's wider world and new forms of dance, Taiz rejected her ballet training to study with Graham, absorbing the choreographer's prejudices against ballet's formulaic sequences and the way it "squashed people's creativity."[17]

After graduating, she continued with Graham's company during the performance season, and in the summers she danced at Tamiment, a resort for socialists and their families in the Pocono Mountains of Pennsylvania. For five summers, she choreographed and danced in the resort's productions, directed by Max Liebman, who eventually created *Your Show of Shows*, a television variety program featuring Sid Caesar and Imogene Coca. Clement Greenberg, the critic most associated with Abstract Expressionism, spent summers at Tamiment and remembered Taiz vividly. He wrote: "At night I tag after a revolutionary dancer, Malvena Fried. . . . She likes me but likes the brightness of her own shining more. But she has something on the ball, makes her own dances, etc. She's something out of a modern novel."[18]

Taiz toured the country with vaudeville companies until the late 1930s, when she married, moved to Philadelphia, and, with other former Graham students, established the city's first resident modern dance company, the Dance Center of Philadelphia.[19] In June 1939, she choreographed several shows, including *Prelude to Swing* at the Walnut Street Theatre as part of the Federal Theatre Project in Philadelphia.[20]

Taiz intersected with another great catalyst for modern dance at this time, the Bennington School of the Dance, in rural Vermont. Bennington, a liberal arts college, offered a six-week program during the summers of 1934–42 that became "a rallying point for a new American art."[21] It was a "highly influential training program, creative laboratory and performance venue" for early modern dancers

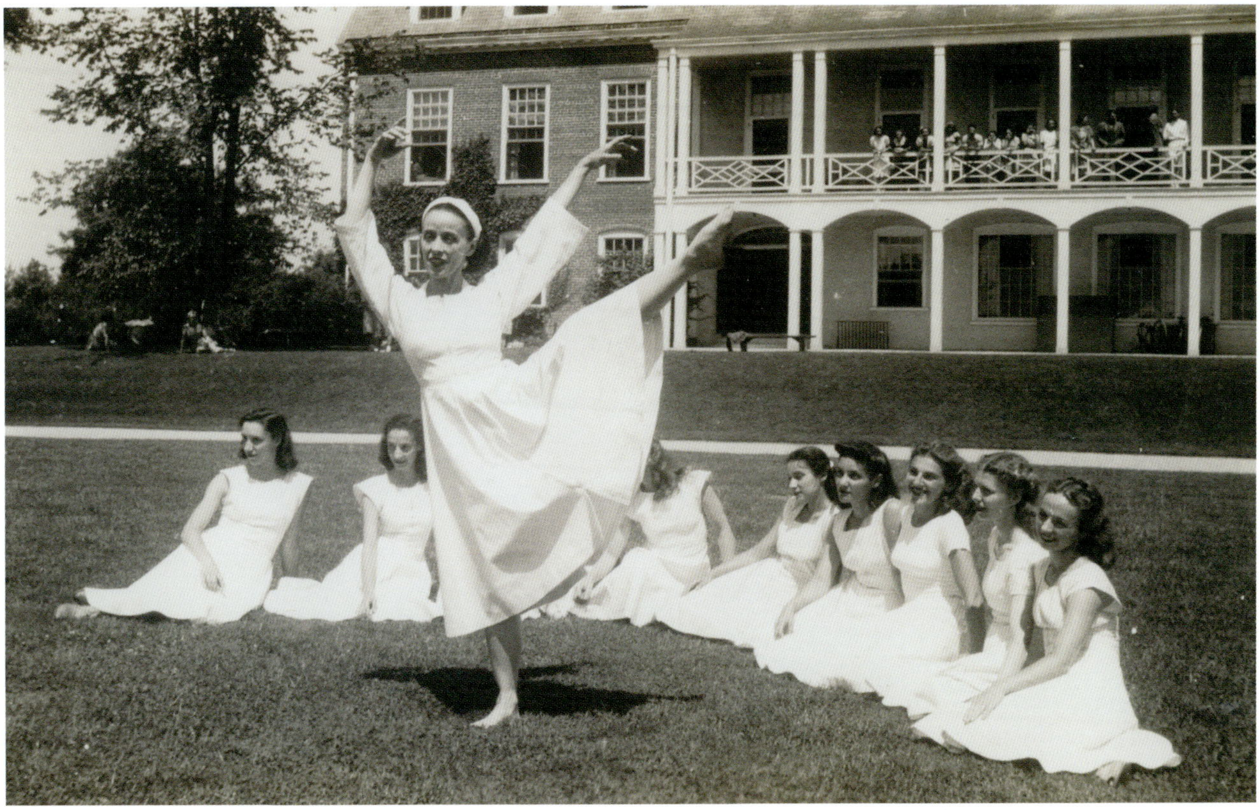

FIGURE 83. Martha Graham at the Bennington School of Dance, 1940 (Courtesy of the American Dance Festival Archives) Photograph by Patricia Edison Powers Jones.

and dance educators, as well as an "incubator for the production and presentation of new works by modern dance's most distinguished exponents."[22] It is not clear whether Taiz attended as part of the Graham company or independently, but she was among students from forty-eight states who flocked to Bennington to study with four modern pioneers—Graham, Hanya Holm, Humphrey, and Weidman—along with a dance critic, a composer, and a stage/lighting designer. Humphrey would later teach at Bryn Mawr College in Pennsylvania—as would Taiz, in 1945.

Bennington dance school founder and Graham company member Martha Hill Davies recalled, "We concentrated on modern dance, which has always prided itself on being, not a system like ballet at that time, but rather a point of view."[23] Davies acknowledged the difficulty of getting highly competitive professional dancers to work together but felt that to be effective, dance educators had to expose students to the most progressive and creative artists. She continued: "One unique thing about Bennington was that our performing arts productions didn't depend on one discipline or one

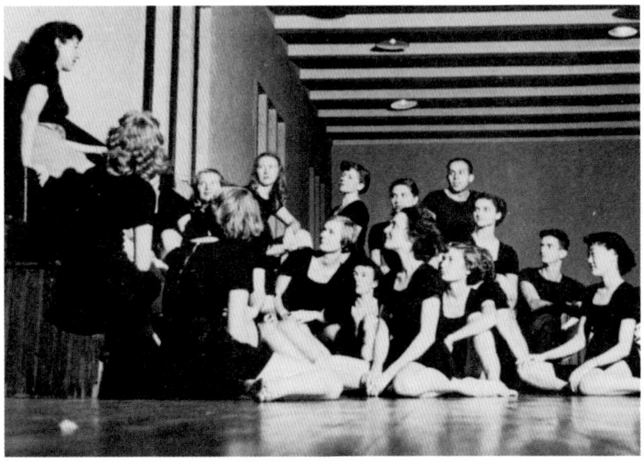

FIGURE 84. Malvena Taiz and her modern dance class, 1952. Published in the *Dolphin*, the women's annual yearbook (Courtesy of the University Archives, University of Pennsylvania)

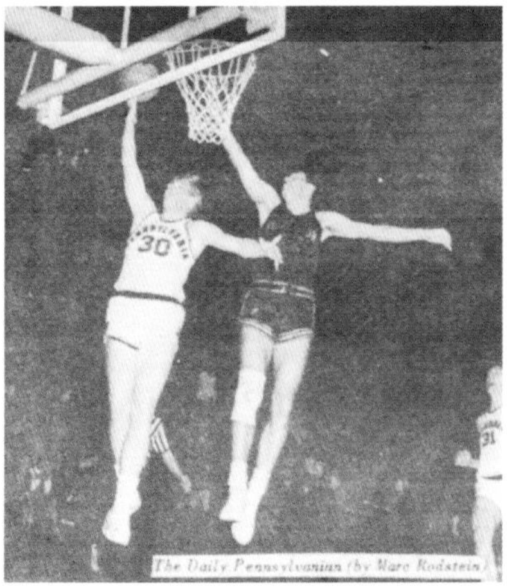

FIGURE 85. "Get ready, get set, go!" from an unpublished manuscript by Malvena Fried Taiz on sports as dance (Courtesy of Lincoln and Lillian Taiz)

person. *Everything* was collaboration. We wouldn't simply do a play—we did plays that combined dance, drama, music, literature."[24] She highlighted one especially challenging project based on a Hart Crane poem, "The Bridge," which included speaking and singing choruses, a solo speaker, a solo dancer, and an orchestra and original score. This kind of collaboration had a significant influence on Taiz's later creative work in Philadelphia.

While not accepted everywhere, modern dance was also emerging in other university curricula in the early 1930s, first for gym credit and later as a performing art. Taiz brought theatrical experience, professional training, and a strong choreographic vision to her position as assistant professor of physical education at the University of Pennsylvania (Penn) in Philadelphia. She headed the new dance program and taught theory, composition, and stagecraft there until 1973. The pay was modest, but the studio was enormous, and she had a great deal of creative freedom. She opened her classes to nonmatriculated students. She is remembered for inviting African American students into her classes. She also taught on various occasions at Connecticut College for Women, New London; Swarthmore College, Pennsylvania; Temple University, Philadelphia; and Bryn Mawr College, all while running a dance academy and choreographing and performing her own work.[25]

Taiz loved the human body and understood dance as a combination of movement and intellect. She had high expectations of her students: her choreography demanded athleticism, expert technique, preparation, attitude, and poetic interpretation. A 1944 review described her dance *Shadrack* as a "skillful study in the shadings of a Negro spiritual," noted that her solo in *Go Down Moses* was executed "with restraint and plasticity," and added that Taiz "danced an extremely fine bit of social satire to the reading of e. e. cummings' '[My sweet old] etcetera.'"[26]

Penn's football coach often sent his least nimble players to Taiz to help develop their footwork. She

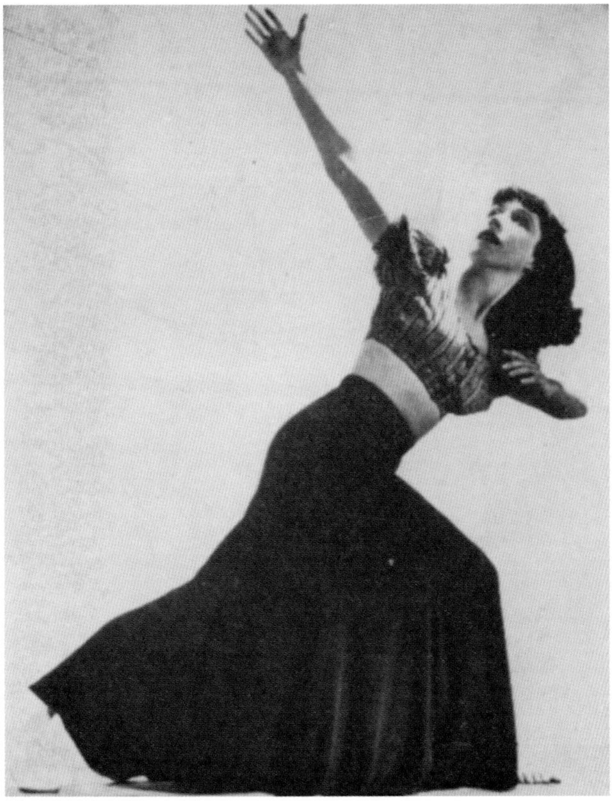

FIGURE 86. Malvena Fried Taiz, date unknown (Courtesy of Lincoln and Lillian Taiz)

saw sports as a form of dance and was thrilled to work with these strong, motivated students. In an unpublished manuscript written years later, she compared athletes to dancers, illustrating her points with photographs of sports figures leaping, falling, reaching, and sliding (fig. 85).[27]

"Like all theater arts," she wrote, "sports will extol in one way or another, the strength and frailty of men in individual or collective action. In spite of the preparation and pitiless drilling; in spite of the strategy and wishful logistics of the coach, there may occur the heartbreaking accident, the casual heroism, the startling error to produce the shock of unexpected victory or defeat." Taiz saw each performance as a singular experience in time and space, open to discovery and serendipity, re-creating the dance each time.

Throughout these artistic and academic pursuits, Taiz was also a wife and a mother. But her husband was not supportive of her career and, after the bitter breakup of their marriage, he visited her Penn department chair and accused Taiz of being a communist. She feared losing her job and the custody of their two children. Like many intellectuals, in the aftermath of the Great Depression she had supported a variety of liberal causes. She had spent those summers at Tamiment, where communist ideology was openly discussed. She had supported unions and politically outspoken theater friends with whom she raised funds for the Abraham Lincoln Brigade, a force of largely communist US volunteers—organized by Communist International—fighting against Francisco Franco in the Spanish Civil War. In 1944, Taiz taught at the Philadelphia School of Social Science and Art and was considered one of a group of "radical dancers."[28] She partnered with an African American dancer, John Hines, well before doing so was widely accepted. The anti-communist, anti-immigration managing editor of the *National Republic*, Walter S. Steele, added Taiz's name to the record of the hearings of the House Un-American Activities Committee in 1947.[29] Taiz's son, Lincoln, recalls a tense night when he was ten years old, during which he and his mother secretly took wheelbarrows full of supposedly "suspicious" books to the backyard and burned them. Penn supported Taiz throughout the controversy, eventually promoting her to tenured associate professor. Temple, however, fired her immediately upon hearing the accusation.

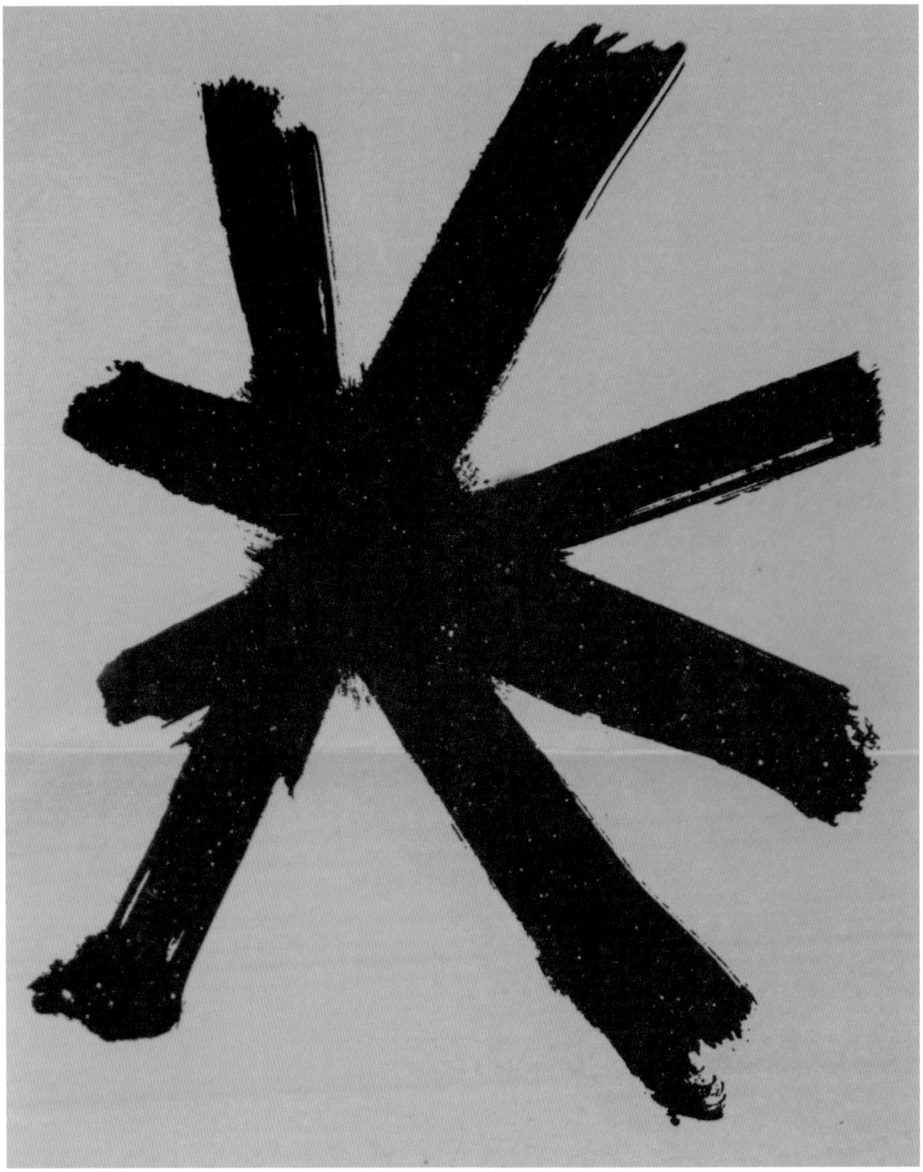

FIGURE 87. The Group '55 logo, created by Sam Feinstein, gestures like a dancer, symbolizing the group's artistic energy. (Samuel L. Feinstein Trust)

A musician, amateur poet, and aesthete as well as a dancer, Taiz was a talented collaborator. Her tireless pursuit of opportunities to showcase Penn's Modern Dance Group gave students access to important figures in classical music. They danced in an annual children's concert with the Philadelphia Philharmonic Orchestra. Pianist/narrator Dorothea Persichetti and her husband, composer Vincent Persichetti (later a Group '55 forum panelist), joined the company for the performance of *Two Fables—The Hare and the Tortoise and The Swan and the Raven* at Philadelphia's Academy of Music and for several productions of *Peter and the Wolf*.[30] Students experienced Taiz's choreographic vision firsthand in their performances of *Shadrack, Parade, The Babe Ruth Ballet*, and *Improvisations to Pete Seeger*. Taiz demonstrated the relationship of dance and the spoken word in her work through the integration of poetry by W. H. Auden and e. e. cummings. In 1953, her program "The Dance and the Spoken Word" was featured on the WFIL-TV series *Exploring the Fine Arts*.[31] Taiz created an entire dance inspired by haiku in 1961, with original music provided by Group '55 panelist Joseph Castaldo and sets by Group '55 artist Mitchel G. Wagman.[32]

In addition to performances, Taiz was a sought-after speaker. In 1949, as part of the first symposium of the Philadelphia College Dance Council, she moderated a panel that included a choral conductor, a painter, a dancer, and a choreographer. She opened with the thoughtful question: "Is it possible to reunite the various arts as they once were in primitive society?" The panel ended with an attempt to define "abstraction"—a lively point of discussion in the Group '55 forums years later.[33] In 1962, as part of the third Philadelphia Festival of Art, Taiz participated in a series titled "Creative Achievement in the Arts and Its Relationship to Contemporary Man" with former Group '55 member Sam Freid, as well as architects, artists, composers, and a poet.[34] In her unpublished manuscript "Creative Dance as an Introduction to the World of Art," she continued her lifelong investigation of the role of dance in the arts.

Taiz was a logical choice to represent dance to Group '55 audiences. As a choreographer, she could relate to the Abstract Expressionists' use of exaggeration for emotional effect. And where the painters pushed the limits of form and color within a two-dimensional space, Taiz similarly pushed the limits of the human form—movement, weight, gesture, interaction—within a defined three-dimensional space. She was experienced in the use of other mediums to enhance her dance expression: music, spoken word, and sound to establish content, mood, or rhythm; costume to suggest personality, extend a line, or establish relationships; and lighting and set elements to build environment. (Interestingly, the Group '55 logo (fig. 87)—created by the group's founder, Feinstein—gestures like a dancer, symbolizing the group's artistic energy. Gesture, so readily associated with dance, is in fact common to all the arts. The explosive burst is confident, unapologetic, sincere. It appears excited for connection, open to influence and inspiration. It suggests an eruption of diverse ideas from a common center.)

Taiz first participated in a Group '55 forum in February 1958. She was well known in the performing arts community and may have been introduced to the group by member Barbara Crawford (then Feinstein's wife), who created costumes for Taiz's 1941 Dance Center of Philadelphia concert, or perhaps by Persichetti, with whom she had also collaborated. But she would also have been familiar with many Group '55 artists from her work on committees at the Philadelphia Art Alliance. The forum was a panel with Feinstein, architect Louis Kahn, and Persichetti, addressing "Contemporary Creative Problems." A month later, in the forum "Dramatic Aspects of Dance," Taiz and her group performed at Dubin/Gallery '55, likely focusing on gesture and movement as communication. Taiz later explained: "My field is human drama. We should communicate. My art may cut deeply into unexpressed emotions."[35]

Taiz knew that creative use of space could contribute to the eloquence of dance. In the forum "Expressive Uses of Space," she may have addressed new ways in which dancers were relating to their performance venues and audiences, as they shifted from frontal presentations to facing away from viewers, moving on multiple levels, from the floor to the air. Dancers also created visual spaces as they interacted with gravity, suggesting directions, areas of focus, and rhythms. And there were spaces within the music and in the absence of music when the dancers' movements provided the score.

Taiz was energetic, passionate about dance, prolific in her choreography, nurturing to her students, and committed to progressive social change through the arts. Her openness to experimentation and collaboration contributed significantly to the progression of modern dance in Philadelphia. *New York Times* critic Anna Kisselgoff spoke to this most active period, when dance and painting shared a common truth: "America's golden dance age . . . was golden precisely because it acknowledged that a choreographer, like a painter, needed an unfettered vision—one beholden to no specific social or moral truth . . . no whims of patrons."[36] This sincerity and unrestrained exploration was epitomized by Taiz and many Group '55 artists in their commitment to enlightening the public.

ACKNOWLEDGMENTS

Many thanks to Lincoln Taiz and Lillian Taiz for kindly sharing their remembrances and rare photographs of their mother. Thanks too to Joan Myers Brown, director emerita of Philadanco, and Terry Fox, director of Philadelphia Dance Projects.

NOTES

1 Malvena is misspelled as "Malvina" in many documents, a source of great frustration to her, according to her son, Lincoln Taiz.

2 Lise Metzger and Lucretia Duncan (Bryn Mawr College students), letter to the editor, "Gym Dept.'s Treatment of Modern Dance Defended," *College News* 31, no. 19 (March 14, 1945).

3 Elizabeth Robins Pennell, *Our Philadelphia* (Philadelphia: J. P. Lippincott, 1914).

4 Peter Kurth, *Isadora: A Sensational Life* (Boston: Little, Brown, 2001), 28–29.

5 Susan Gillis, "Chapter 2: The Solo Dancers—Isadora Duncan (1877–1927)," The Early Moderns, tutorial, www.pitt.edu/~gillis/dance/disp.html, accessed June 11, 2020.

6 Bob Skiba, "In Philadelphia, Everyone Was Doin' It . . . or Not," *Philadelphia Dance History Journal*, April 17, 2012, https://philadancehistoryjournal.wordpress.com/category/•-20th-century/.

7 Skiba, "In Philadelphia."

8 Bob Skiba, "When Philadelphia Went to the Ballet," *Philadelphia Dance History Journal*, March 1, 2012, https://philadancehistoryjournal.wordpress.com/category/•-20th-century/.

9 Thomas Wirth, "Influenza ('Spanish Flu' Pandemic, 1918–1919)," *Encyclopedia of Greater Philadelphia*, 2011, https://philadelphiaencyclopedia.org/archive/influenza-spanish-flu-pandemic-1918-19/.

10 "An Evening of Tango at the Swann Memorial Fountain," *Evening Public Ledger*, July 8, 1921.

11 "Ruth St. Denis," New Jersey Women's History, http://njwomenshistory.org/discover/biographies/ruth-st-denis/, accessed June 11, 2020.

12 Jane Sherman, *Denishawn: The Enduring Influence* (Boston: Twayne, 1983).

13 "Doris Humphrey," Encyclopaedia Britannica, updated October 13, 2020, www.britannica.com/biography/Doris-Humphrey.

14 "History," Martha Graham Dance Company, https://marthagraham.org/history/, accessed June 11, 2020.

15 Martha Graham, *Frontier*, 1935, https://www.beyondthenotes.org/blog/martha-graham-frontier-1935/, accessed June 25, 2020.

16 Anna Kisselgoff, "Martha Graham Hailed by Nation; Given Freedom Medal by Ford," *New York Times*, October 15, 1976, 12.

17 Lincoln Taiz, conversation with the author.

18 Clement Greenberg, *The Harold Letters, 1928–1943: The Making of an American Intellectual* (Washington, DC: Counterpoint, 2000), 176.

19 "Dance Center Program," *Philadelphia Inquirer*, April 7, 1941, 114.

20 "Malvena Fried Taiz papers relating to Federal Theater Project, 1938–1940," Archives of American Art, Smithsonian Institution, www.aaa.si.edu/collections.

21 Anna Kisselgoff, "Dance View; Bennington Nurtured the Moderns," *New York Times*, September 19, 1982, section 2, 18.

22 M. Candace Feck, "Bennington School of the Dance (1934–1942)," *Routledge Encyclopedia of Modernism*, January 10, 2016, www.rem.routledge.com/articles/bennington-school-of-the-dance-1934-42.

23 Rebecca Godwin, "Martha Hill on Early Dance at Bennington," *Quadrille* 25, no. 1 (winter 1992–93): 17.

24 Godwin, 19.

25 Students of Bryn Mawr College, "Taiz to Teach Modern Dance," *College News* 32, no. 4 (October 24, 1945), 4 .

26 "Modern Dance Club Joins Taiz's Troupe with Recital in Gym," *College News* 30, no. 25 (May 10, 1944), https://repository.brynmawr.edu/cgi/viewcontent.cgi?article=2021&context=bmc_collegenews.

27 Malvena Fried Taiz, "Sports/Dance," unpublished manuscript, courtesy of Lincoln Taiz.

28 Terry Fox, conversation with the author, March 2020. Fox is the director of Philadelphia Dance Projects.

29 *Hearings on H.R. 1884 and H.R. 2122, Session 1, Before the Committee on Un-American Activities*, 80th Cong. (1947) (testimony of Walter S. Steele).

30 "Two Fables—The Hare and the Tortoise, The Swan and the Raven," *Philadelphia Inquirer*, November 11, 1950, 17.

31 Dorothy Grafly, "The Dance and the Spoken Word," *Art in Focus* 7, no. 5 (February 1955): 2. Taiz and her Modern Dance Group performed on WFIL-TV as part of the Board of Public Education's TV series "Exploring the Fine Arts."

32 "Haiku Experimental," *Philadelphia Inquirer*, March 26, 1961, 60.

33 Sherrill Cowgill (Bryn Mawr College student), "Barefoot Dancers Gyrate, Slide at Penn; Discuss Dance as Art," *College News* 36, no. 9 (December 7, 1949), 3.

34 Samuel L. Singer, "Drama and Music Highlighted during Arts Festival Week," *Philadelphia Inquirer*, June 10, 1962, 71.

35 S.L.S., "'Dance Showcase' at Fleisher," *Philadelphia Inquirer*, May 5, 1961, 88.

36 Anna Kisselgoff, "Golden Ages: Dance; 1930s to 1960s, When Dance Grew Strong," *New York Times*, May 15, 1994, section 2, 38.

Sam Feinstein

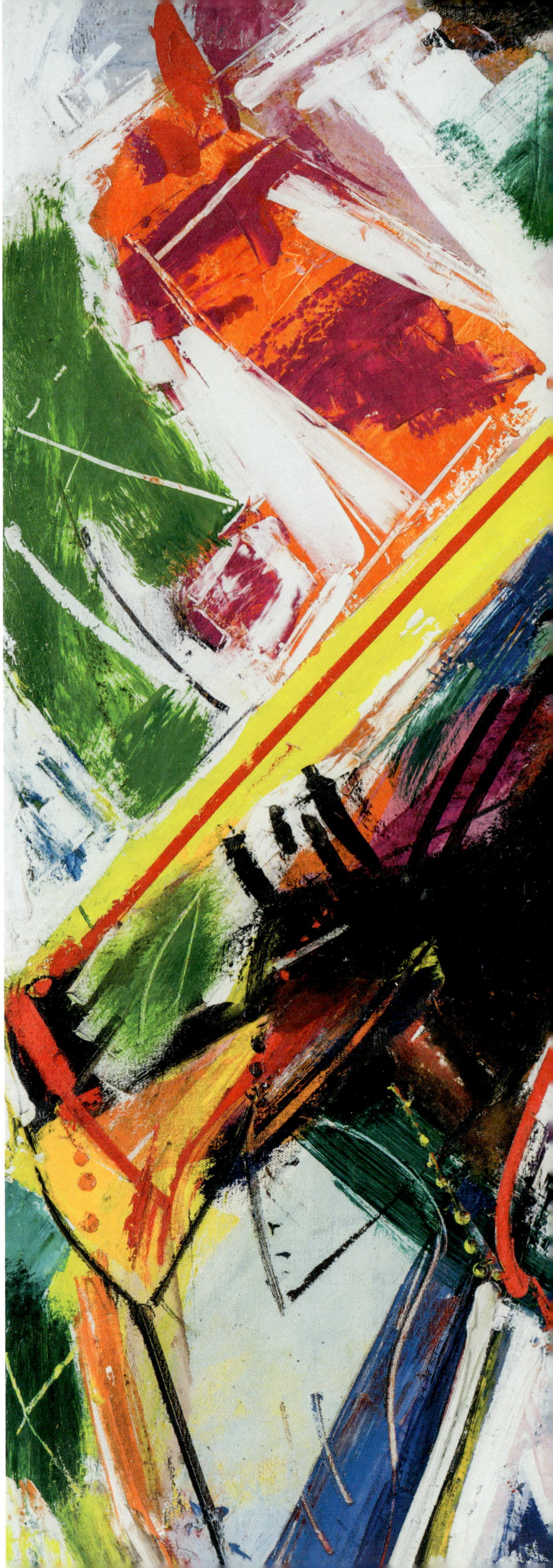

FIGURE 88. Untitled (detail of Fig. 104) , c. 1952, by Sam Feinstein (Samuel L. Feinstein Trust)

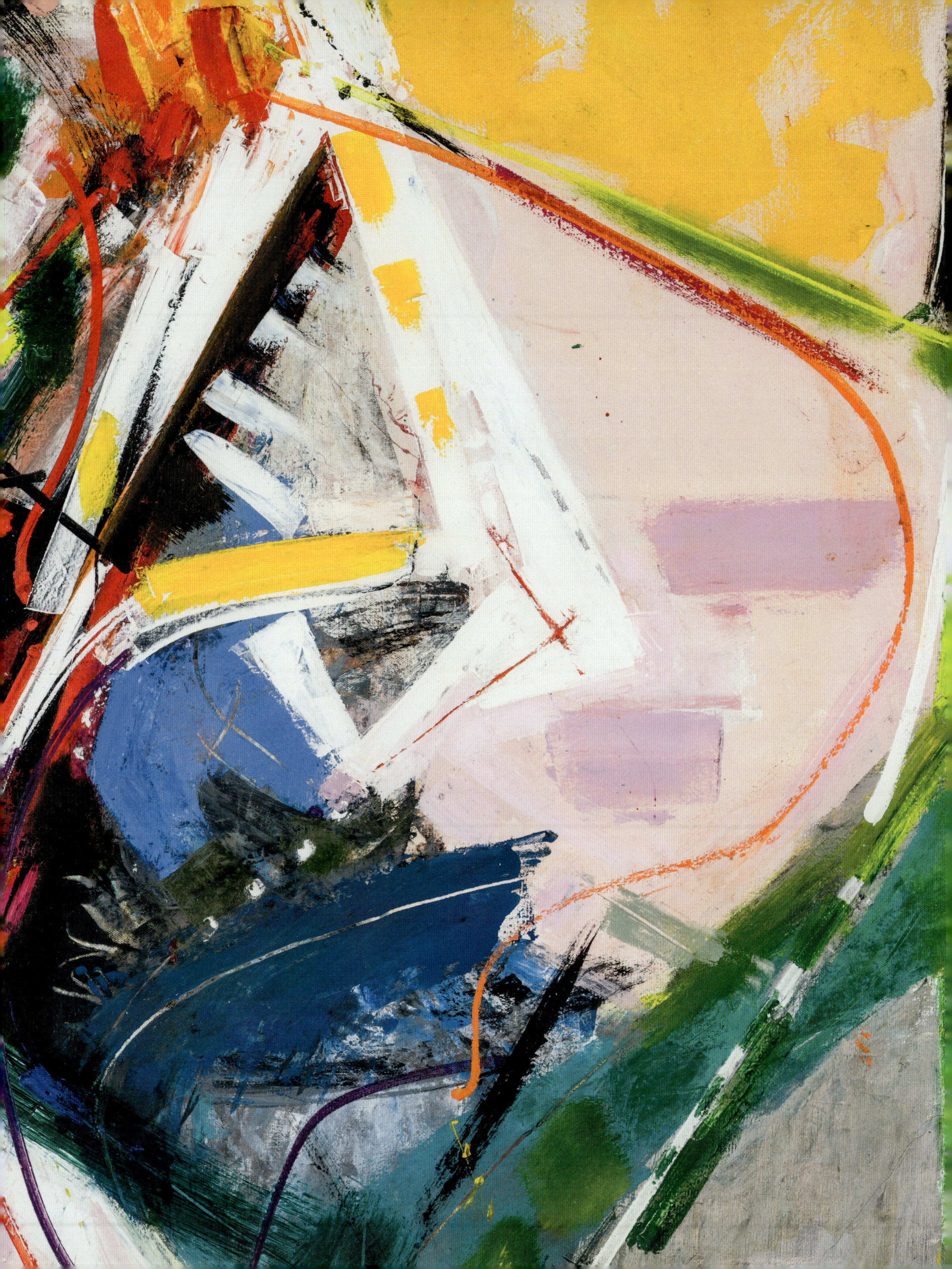

UNDERSTANDING SAM FEINSTEIN

PATRICIA STARK FEINSTEIN

It is with great joy that I witness Sam Feinstein being rediscovered in Philadelphia. I am still stunned when I look around my home at his paintings and realize how few people have seen his work. It has been my mission for the past fifteen years to bring Sam's legacy to a wider audience and to share his life-affirming views about art.

The three exhibitions documented in this catalogue—focused explorations of Sam's early social realist and expressionist work, his leadership of Group '55, and his later immersive abstractions—represent distinct phases of his work with different, but intentional, modes of social engagement. At the same time, they are bound together by the philosophy that guided him throughout his life. As a young man, Sam wrote of being "endowed with potential" and "obliged toward its fulfillment."[1] In his high school yearbook, he was described as an "athlete, artist, scholar, linguist, orator, prophet, actor, journalist." His life could have gone in many other directions, but he saw art as his calling. Painting became "a stubborn necessity," and teaching another forum for his many strengths.

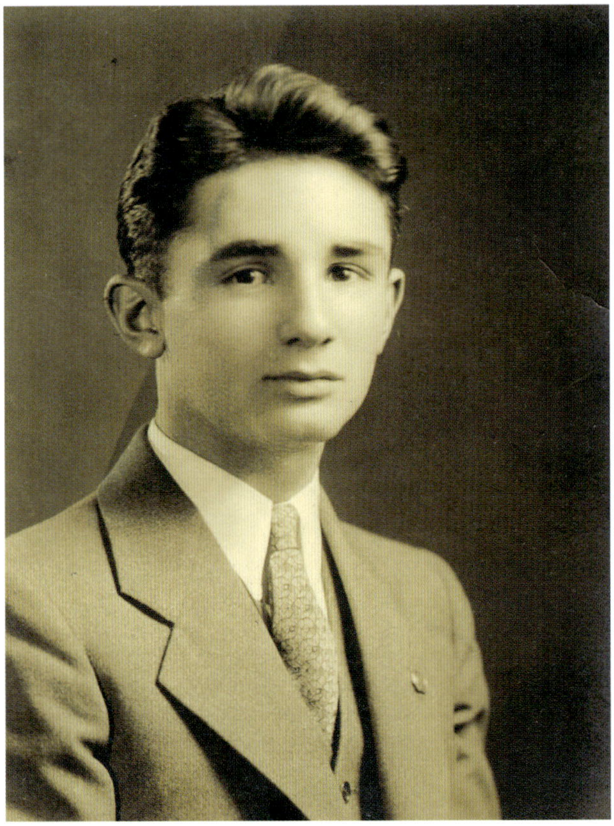

FIGURE 89. Sam Feinstein's senior portrait, Central High School, Philadelphia, 1932 (Samuel L. Feinstein Trust)

Sam aimed to convey in his work "some significant utterance," while avoiding "superficially appealing effects." This is evident both in the art of his early, exploratory years and in his later abstract paintings, which he called "evocations." As he wrote, "Creativity is spirituality looking for a form. It is a quest of the human spirit to find somehow a way of flowing with the universal pulse that runs through all things."

Sam believed that making art was not a special skill possessed by a select few. He saw the process of creation as essential to the mental and spiritual health of every human being; "You might as well be talking about breathing," he would say. The hands-on making of things was a means of individual education, a drawing out of oneself, a deepening of awareness and intelligence. It was,

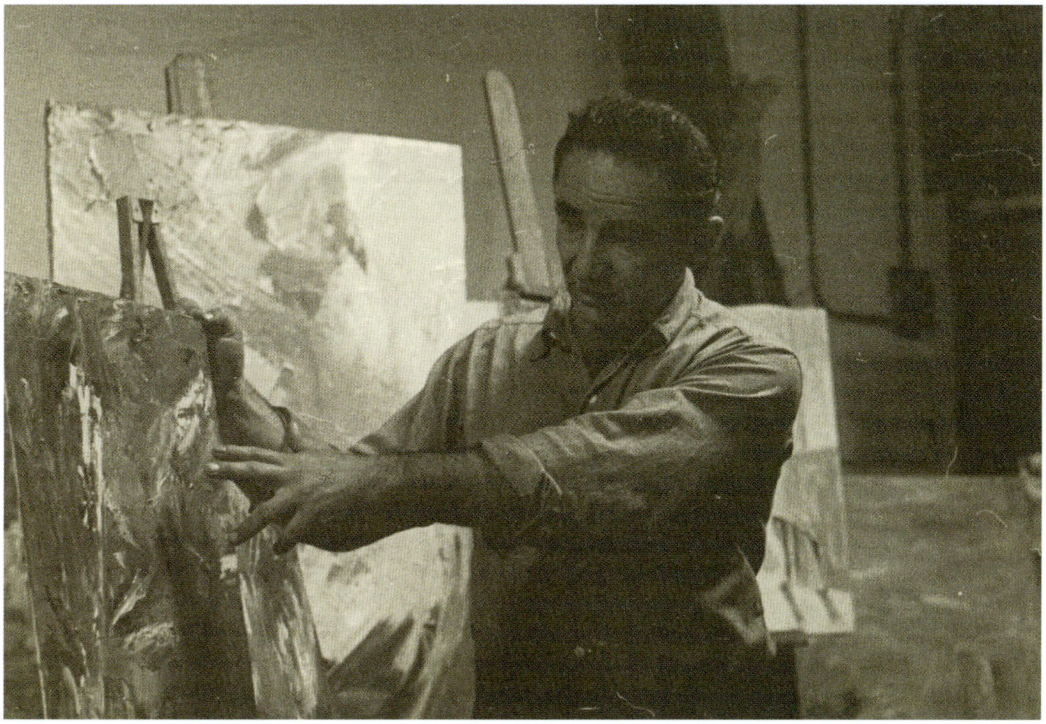

FIGURE 90. Sam Feinstein pointing out expressive gestures to a class, late 1950s (Samuel L. Feinstein Trust)

for everyone, a logical extension of nature's own creative drive—not an endeavor confined to an elite minority called "artists." As a teacher, Sam said he was "constantly trying to find ways of talking more and more clearly about art, because it's bigger than all of us and should be seen that way."

I met Sam in 1964, when a friend took me to his loft/studio in New York. At the time I was studying art and art history at Mount Holyoke College, in Massachusetts. I graduated that spring, and in the summer I joined Sam's class on Cape Cod. I had already been painting large, colorful abstractions. What I absorbed over time—and it did take time to understand—is that Sam was teaching much more than the principles of art or picture making. He was offering a way of living based on a reconnection with nature—its rhythms, its logic, its sense of order. His classes were workshops, gymnasiums in which to stretch the spirit, intelligence, awareness, and soul. Paint was just the vehicle. Sam was my mentor and teacher long before I was his wife. In class we—like Sam in his studio—were all on the same challenging path, trying to bring our paintings to life, cracking open the shells of our understanding to let in more light.

I became an art teacher, like Sam, and our life together revolved around our teaching schedules. We shared ideas and the successes and challenges of our classes and individual students. We read and discussed recent findings. Sam buoyed me with his experience and advice, and I introduced him to new ideas. The readings from a course I taught on the history of Western culture, including philosophy, literature, science, music, and art, led to many wonderful conversations. I introduced him to Gary Zukav's *Dancing Wu Li Masters*, and

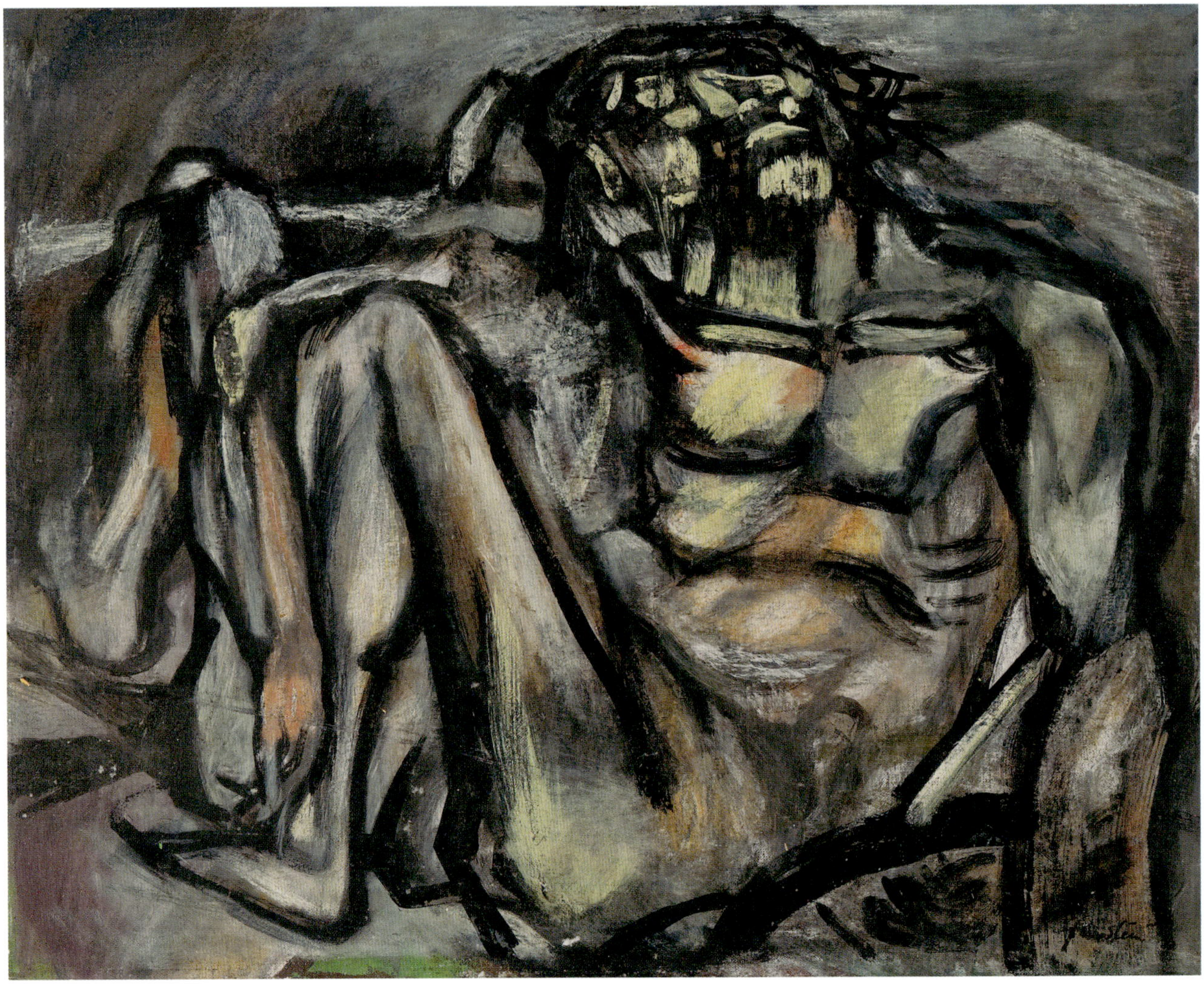

FIGURE 91. **Crucified**, 1935–39, by Sam Feinstein (Woodmere Art Museum: Gift of the Samuel L. Feinstein Trust, 2011)
Photograph by Rick Echelmeyer

he introduced me to Stanley Burnshaw's *Seamless Web* and George Leonard's *Silent Pulse*. I remember Sam reading passages aloud in class and expanding on ideas that linked modern science with human biology, psychology, and art. When we were not teaching, we painted in our respective studios and did not intrude on each other. If I asked for Sam's eye and counsel, he was frank and astute, and I often returned to his classes.

Art filled our lives at home and inspired our trips abroad. In 1992, we traveled for a month to see art throughout Europe, starting in Amsterdam and ending in Madrid. The painting Sam most wanted to see was the Isenheim Altarpiece, by Matthias Grünewald, so we left Paris and took the five-hour train ride east to the town of Colmar. The small museum there held many exquisite works, most anonymous and from centuries ago—and then there was the room that held the altarpiece, its haunting crucifixion on one side, its glorious resurrection on the other. Standing there, tears welled in Sam's eyes, one of the few times I saw him cry. He was deeply spiritual, though he adhered to neither the Jewish faith in which he was raised nor any other specific doctrine or sect. But the image of Christ, such as *Crucified* (fig. 91), likely inspired by the work of George Rouault, figured large in his early work. Later the twin themes of the suffering of humankind and the transcendence or resurrection animated many of his paintings.

Sam was always creating—everywhere, and with everything. The streets of New York provided many materials: scrap metal became a lamp, a candelabra, and jewelry; discarded lumber became mosaic floors and a spiral staircase. On Cape Cod, tree limbs, honed and shaped, became a sculpture dancing across the lawn. He saw potential everywhere, and if an object's use was uncertain, he added it to the studio's still life. His largest recycling project was an enormous wall: he embedded the cut domes and flanks of an old oil tank into concrete chunks of a former sidewalk to create a breathtaking backdrop for his garden. His creative use of found objects led to a friendship with his trash collector. For favors received, Sam offered to make a portrait for the man if he provided Sam with a photograph from which to work. Months later, to the delight of his co-scavenger, Sam presented him with a portrait of Martin Luther King, Jr. (fig. 92).

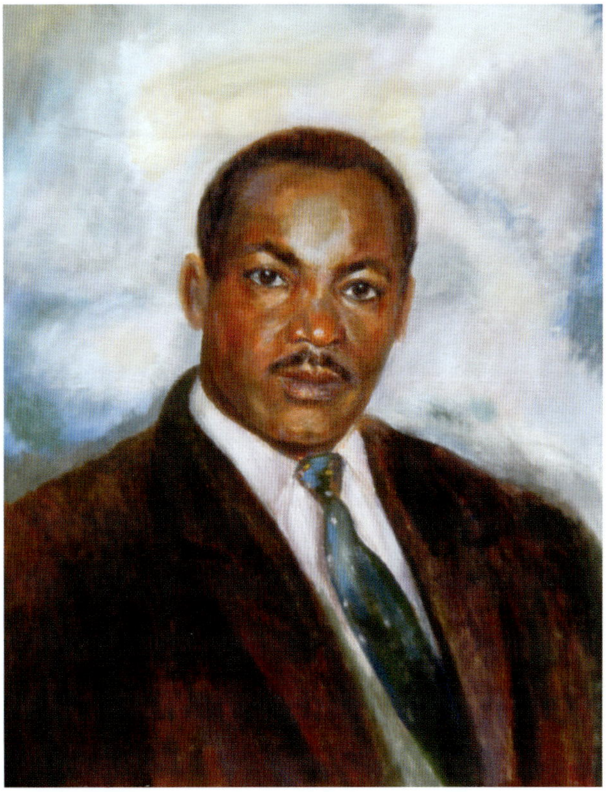

FIGURE 92. **Martin Luther King**, 1987 by Sam Feinstein (Private Collection)

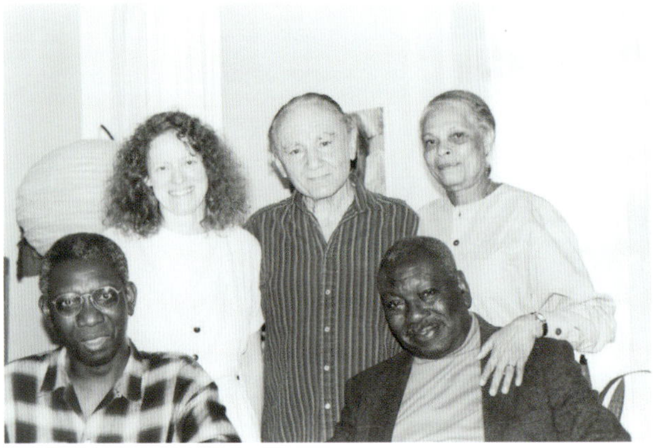

FIGURE 93. Gathering in New York, 1994. Top row from left to right: Patricia Feinstein, Sam Feinstein, and artist Gwendolyn Knight; Bottom row from left to right: poet Yusef Komunyakaa and artist Jacob Lawrence. (Samuel L. Feinstein Trust)

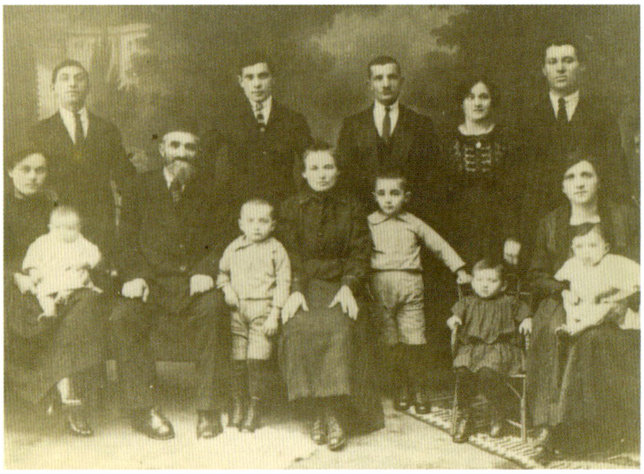

FIGURE 94. The Feinstein family, 1920, Sam is standing in the front row, his arm outstretched, in front of his father. (Samuel L. Feinstein Trust)

Sam's friendships centered around those committed to the arts and to creative endeavors. On one special occasion in 1994, we held a brunch at our New York brownstone with poet Yusef Komunyakaa; his wife, Australian writer Mandy Sayer; artist Jacob Lawrence; and his wife, artist Gwendolyn Knight. Mandy, requested we pose for a picture (fig. 93).

Sam was a perpetual student and a spiritual pilgrim. Society and commerce interested him very little; it was the life of the mind that engaged him. He knew every bookstore in New York and Philadelphia. For holidays, we gave each other art books and shared them page by page at the kitchen table. Sam was a delightful punster, and on one occasion when the table seemed to me too cluttered with writings, crossword puzzles, and books, I requested a clearing. With a glance up he countered, "But this is my table of contents."

Sam and I were married for eighteen years. After his death in 2003, I was swept up in the care of his legacy, but I couldn't have anticipated the scope of the project. I discovered entire rooms filled with artworks I had never seen before. I had studied painting with Sam, transcribed recordings of his teachings, and taught workshops with him in Michigan and Toronto. But I had never seen the trove of paintings carefully stored in rooms near his studio on the fourth floor of our brownstone.

A sabbatical from my position teaching art and art history at Riverdale Country School, in the Bronx, gave me time to explore, time to look. Besides paintings, drawings, and prints, I found a vast archive of writings, clippings, and memorabilia, which led to my discovery of Group '55 and informed the monograph I wrote prior to Sam's 2008 retrospective at the Cape Cod Museum of Art.[2] The short biography that follows is based on these resources and my own experiences with him.

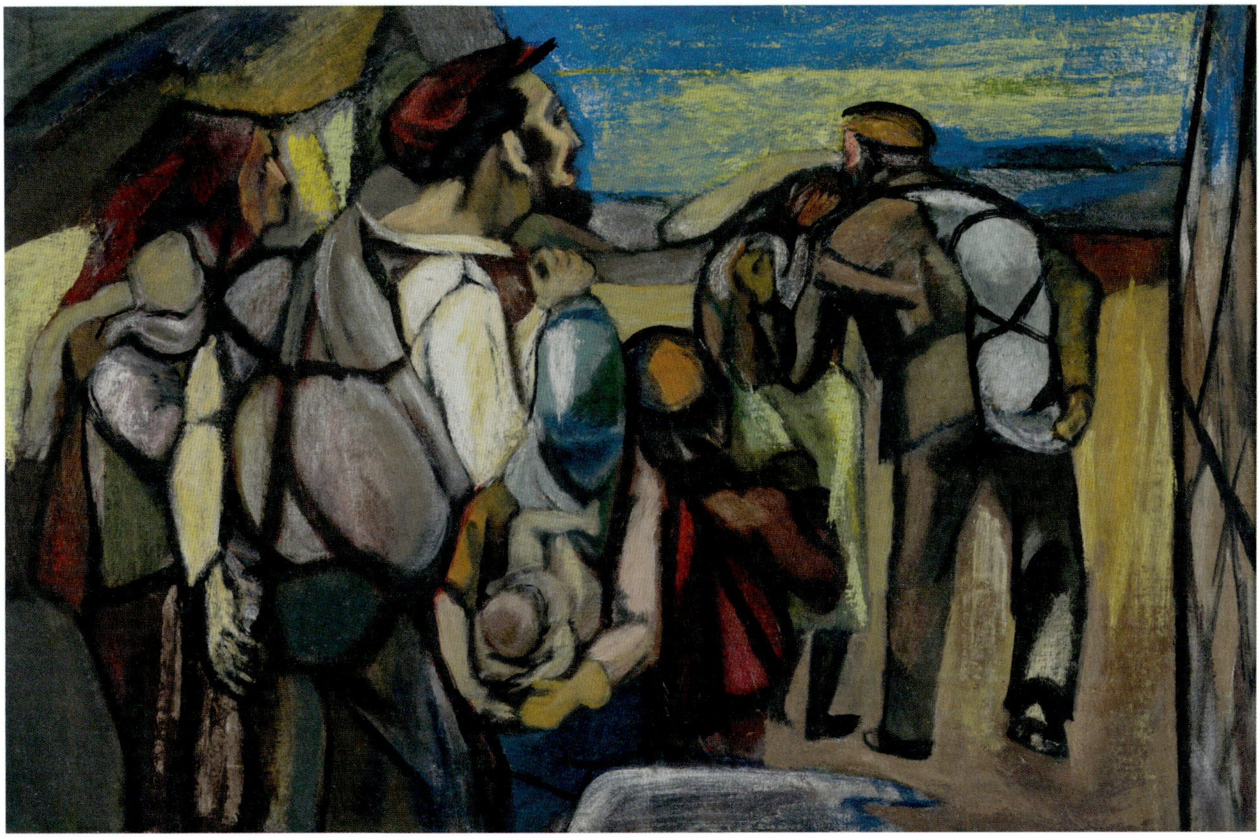

FIGURE 95. **Immigrants**, 1930s, by Sam Feinstein (Samuel L. Feinstein Trust)

Early Years

Born in Russia in 1915, Sam was the eldest son in a scholarly Jewish family. Fleeing oppression and hostility, they ultimately found a new, if impoverished, home in Philadelphia. Sam was called "a little old man," as he was frail as a young child and spent much of his time alone drawing, though his later weightlifting hobby lent him considerable strength. A painting Sam created many years later, which I call *Immigrants* (fig. 95), portrays a family looking to the horizon as they trudge across a field.

To his parents' dismay, Sam rejected a scholarship to the University of Pennsylvania in favor of a scholarship to the Pennsylvania Museum School of Industrial Art (now the University of the Arts). He was a superb draftsman, as can be seen in his 1932 *Self-Portrait* (fig. 96), one of many he created over time. His exquisite use of color—later the focus of his abstract paintings—is also already apparent in his early fairy tale illustrations.

Barbara Crawford, a fellow art student who became his wife, teased him about his sixty-four versions

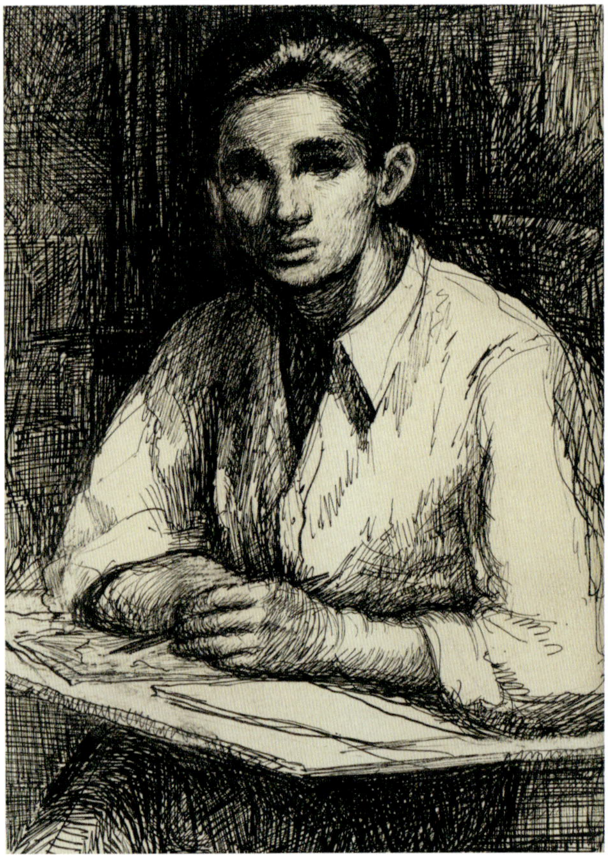

FIGURE 96. **Self-Portrait**, 1932, by Sam Feinstein (Samuel L. Feinstein Trust)

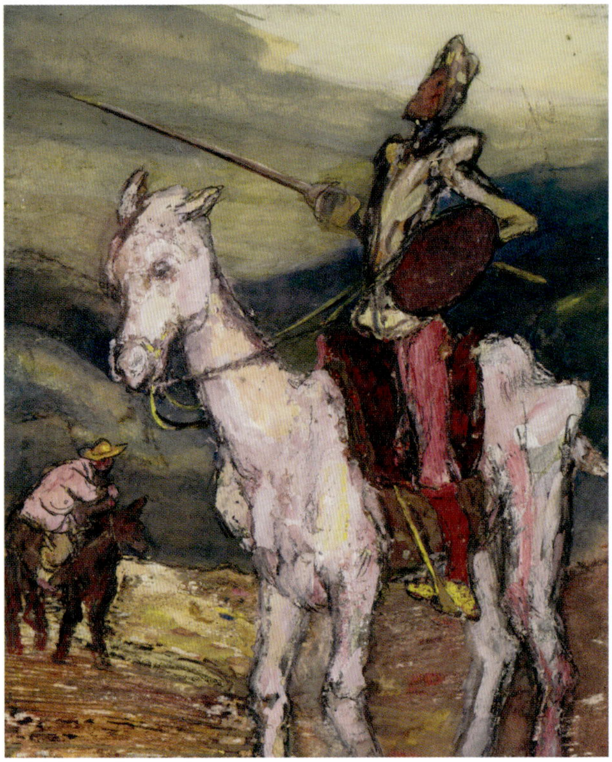

FIGURE 97. **Don Quixote**, 1935, by Sam Feinstein (Samuel L. Feinstein Trust)

of Don Quixote, including the color image in the exhibition *Sam Feinstein: The Early Years* (fig. 97) and a similar black-and-white version that was published in the school catalogue. Sam sometimes thought of himself as the fabled knight, tilting at windmills. He was an idealist, like Quixote, aiming to make the world a better, nobler place. He insisted, "If you are going to create, you use the purest aspect of yourself, the noblest aspect of yourself as human spirit. . . . It is the most religious thing you can do."

Sam graduated with a degree in commercial art but made a name for himself with his paintings and prints. He recalled with pride his solo show at the age of twenty-one at the Philadelphia Art Alliance and his place in the 1936 *American Masters* exhibition at the Philadelphia Museum of Art. To earn a living, Sam created illustrations for ads, a tedious occupation from his point of view. He preferred the freedom of the watercolors he painted all around the city: his scenes of the morning market are soft and sleepy, while his views of the factories contrast textures and details, and bright and shaded space (fig. 98).

Sam was blessed with mentors who smoothed his path. The first was his teacher Franklin C. Watkins, who had him teach a painting class at art school and in 1938 sent him to Chestnut Hill Academy

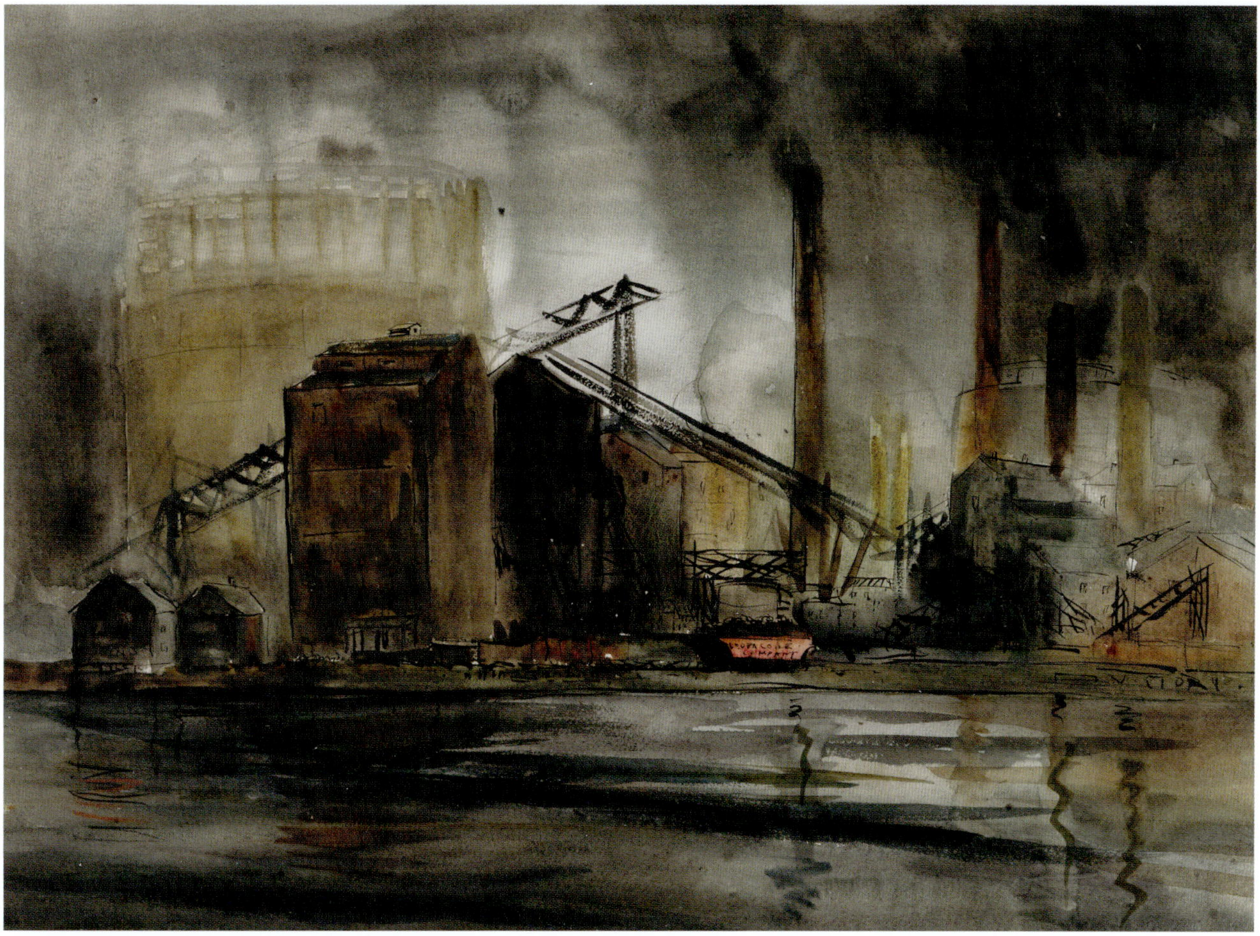

FIGURE 98. **Factories**, 1930s, by Sam Feinstein (Samuel L. Feinstein Trust)

(CHA) to take up his first major teaching position. Working with boys of all ages over the next four years, Sam became fascinated by the process of creativity and its varied aspects at different stages of life, and his interest in art education deepened. He established the school's community gallery, now named the Crawford Gallery, after Barbara, where he installed compelling and inspiring exhibitions.

About this time, a second mentor came into Sam's life. Sam Rosenbaum—lawyer, composer, jazz musician, vice president of the Philadelphia Orchestra Board, head of WFIL studios, and parent of a Springside student—invited Sam to teach a private class in his home. Rosenbaum's wife was a renowned harpist, whose portrait had been painted by Arthur B. Carles. The entire family became friends of Sam's and opened new avenues into Philadelphia's cultural world. It is likely that Sam met the composers (and future Group '55 panelists) Joseph Castaldo, Vincent Persichetti, and George Rochberg through the Rosenbaums. The Group '55 harp and horn recital in 1957 included a piece composed by Castaldo and probably commissioned by Rosenbaum, who honored his wife with a new piece of harp music every year for two decades.

When summoned by the draft board in 1942, Sam claimed conscientious objector status based on the "study and practice of art, with its fundamental philosophy of beauty, construction and order, as against any form of destruction, especially that of man by man."[3] The request was denied, and Sam spent the next three years serving in the Army, while Barbara took over his teaching position and began her own long career at CHA.

Sam's paintings and prints from this time became more distorted and expressionistic—visions of pain, sorrow, and terror. *The Threat of War* (fig. 99), a charcoal drawing, combines imagery from World War I in a powerful composition similar to those of Mexican muralists. In the Army, Sam began working as a designer of camouflage but soon became an illustrator of instructional booklets and posters for the medical corps. The exaggerated scale and dynamic interactions of form and space foretell the drama of his later abstract canvases. For a time he was stationed in Queens, where he learned film production. He must have reveled in his proximity to the city's museums and galleries, where the early works of New York Abstract Expressionists could be seen and Picasso's *Guernica* was on view at the Museum of Modern Art.

After his honorable discharge Sam taught art history at Springside School, borrowing slides from the Philadelphia Museum of Art, but he struggled to find a full-time teaching position. He turned to his painting with greater vigor and immersed himself in reading about creativity, art, and art's relationship to nature and to human life. He wrote to Ralph M. Pearson, author of *The New Art Education*:

> If it is agreed that design is inherent in human nature, and if man is physiologically impelled towards self-expression . . . is it not logical to assume that his design sense is rather nature's design, or universal law, making him its medium? . . . (Since we are living in a materialistic age where scientific proof is the key to public acceptance) isn't it time for the artist to do some research as well? What are nature's laws? How specifically do they operate? How are they to be interpreted for a two-dimensional rectangle so as to evoke a genuine esthetic response?[4]

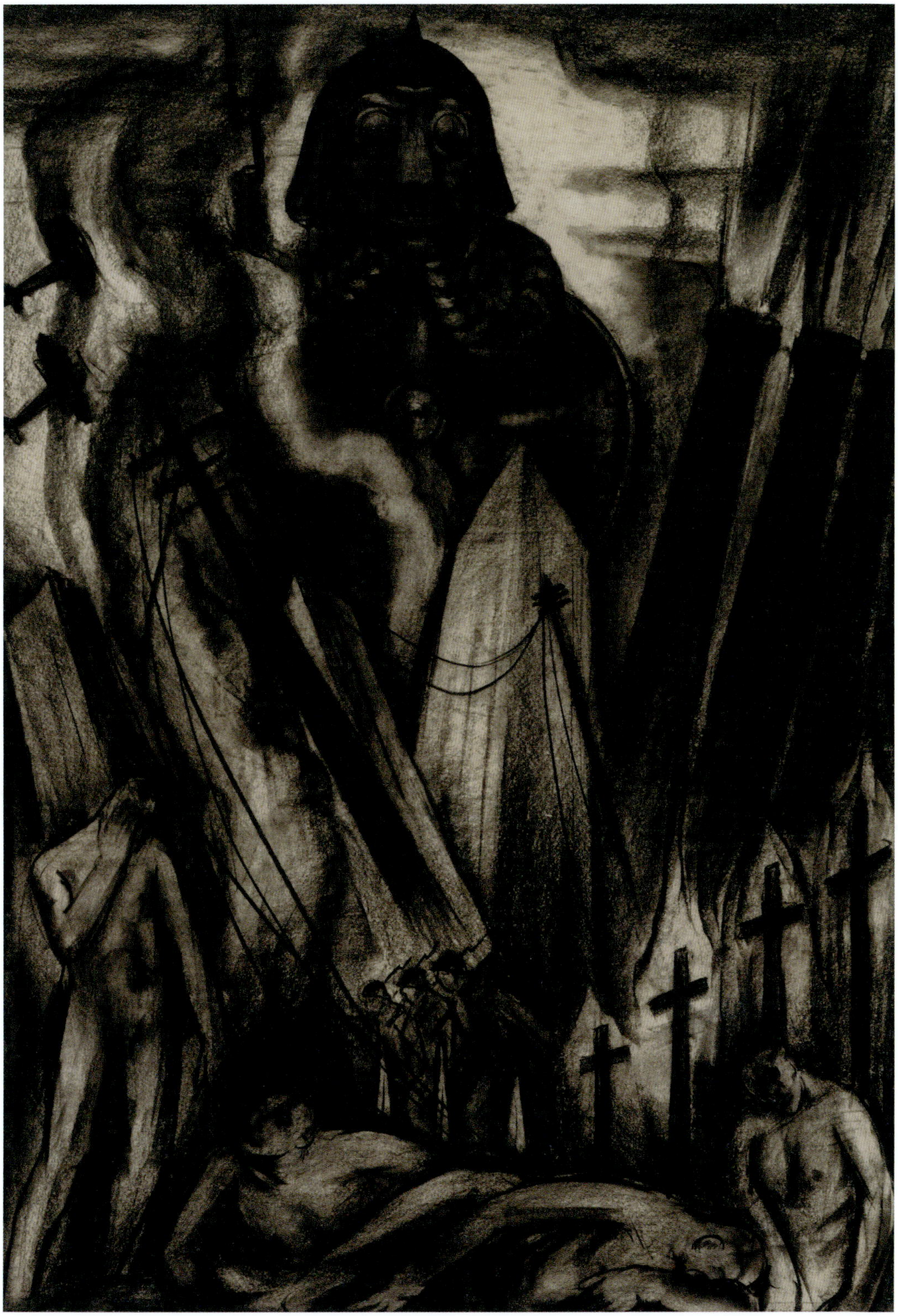

FIGURE 99. The Threat of War, c. 1941, by Sam Feinstein (Samuel L. Feinstein Trust)

Serendipitously, a filmmaking job that required knowledge of modern physics reinforced his emerging beliefs. For the film *One World or None*, commissioned by the United Nations, Sam created the first animation of atomic fission.[5] To do this accurately he studied physics with a professor from the University of Pennsylvania. The film won awards and can still be seen today. Sam was fascinated with the unseen world of the atom and the pulsing energies beneath the visual realm:

> All phenomenon is made of atomic energy—smaller and smaller units—vibration—vibrance or bubbling that is the life process—that is plasticity. . . . Human beings are temporary traffic jams of atoms. . . . Everything is made out of vibrance; vibrance is a continuity through all the life forces at work; plasticity is the forming power that runs through nature, a flow of energies that are all pulsing.

For Sam, painting was an attempt to reconnect with nature's rhythmic drive, to align with nature's "plasticity," a term Sam often spoke about in painting classes and spent chapters of his book trying to explain.[6] He thought of the brain as a bottleneck, a compendium of habits, taste, and data that narrowed our natural intelligence. He saw the creative process as breaking through that narrowing, a straw that draws forth a more profound intelligence that flows from nature.

Sam made his living at this time working on films, but his commitment to his own painting had solidified. He wrote to a friend:

> For me, painting has become a stubborn necessity, a reason for existing. I can no longer question (as I once did) its validity—

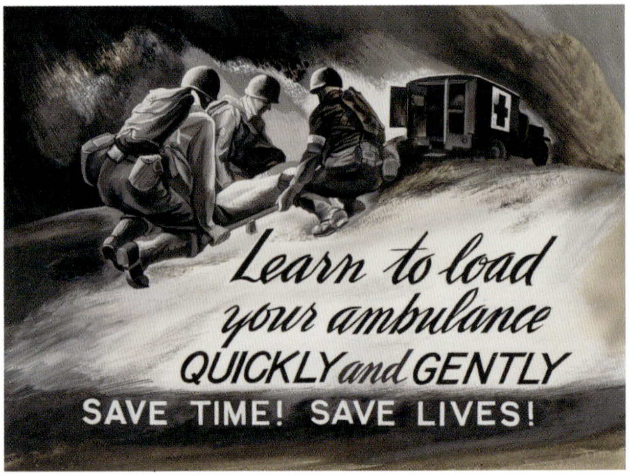

FIGURE 100. **Loading Ambulance**, 1943, by Sam Feinstein (Samuel L. Feinstein Trust)

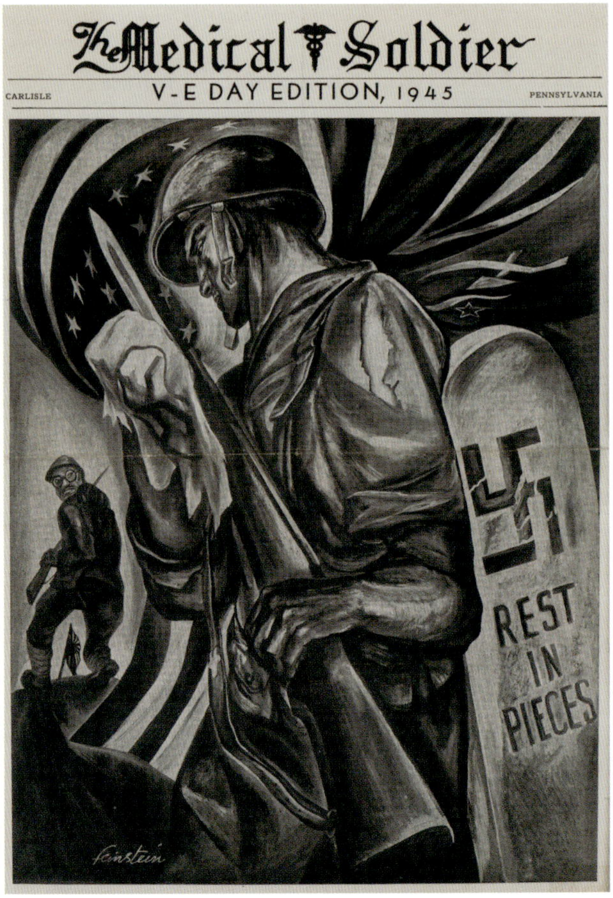

FIGURE 101. **Rest in Pieces**, 1945, reproduction of the cover of the V-E Day edition of *The Medical Soldier*, by Sam Feinstein (Samuel L. Feinstein Trust)

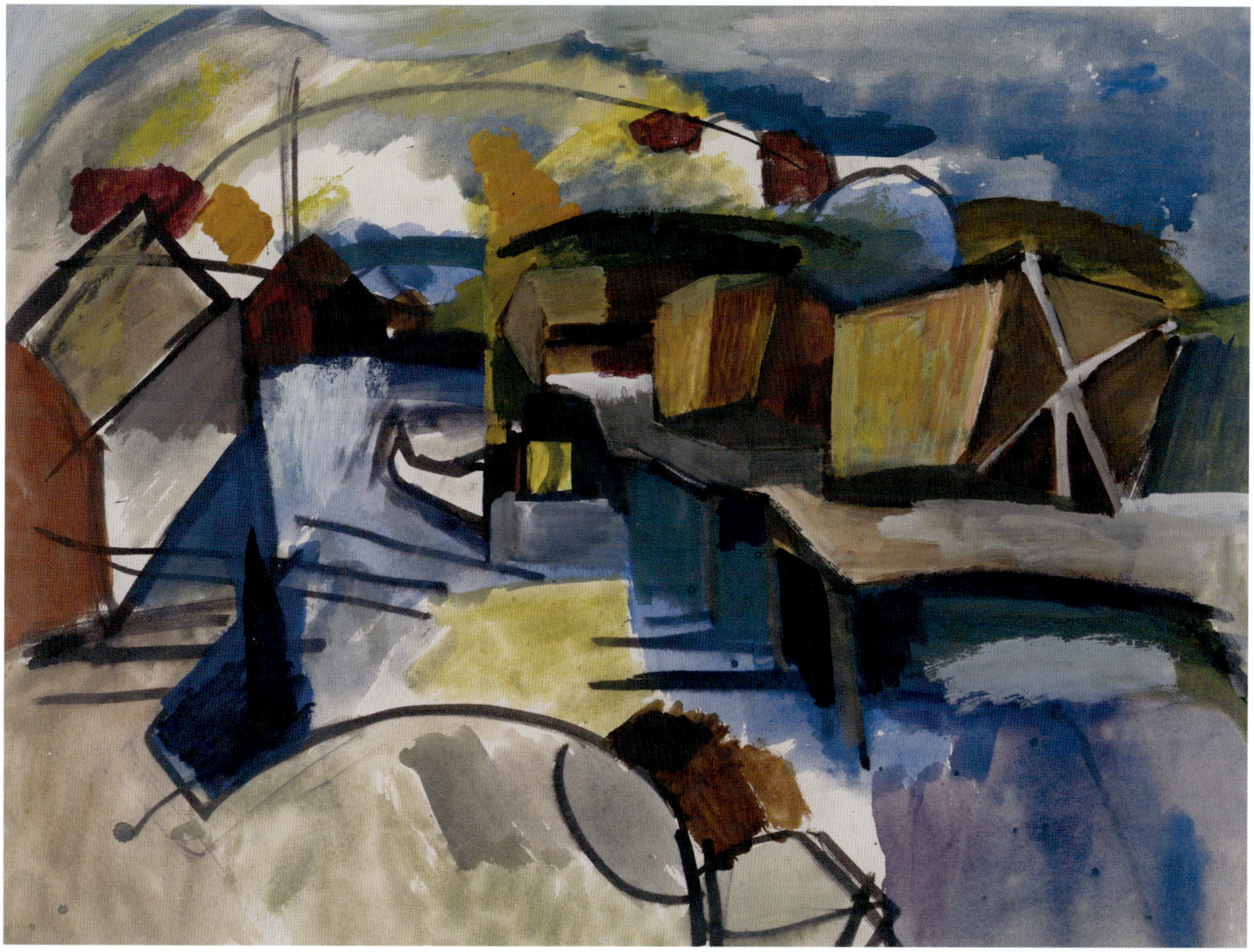

FIGURE 102. **Harbor**, 1947, by Sam Feinstein (Samuel L. Feinstein Trust)

its need by society in a wholly new and more important sense than ever before: as a means by which human beings, mass molded by the atomic age, reduced to targets on a war map, can yet express an individuality, can as participants in painting extend through themselves some spark of the marvelous cosmic force which powers all natural phenomena, and in that extension raise man's evolution to a plane beyond that of the animal.[7]

From 1946 through 1948, Sam spent two to three weeks each summer in Gloucester, Massachusetts, where he explored dynamic new compositions of form and space. Stimulated by the imagery of the old working harbor, he created dozens of paintings in watercolor, casein, and pastel, several of which courted abstraction. Later he explained: "I found that in my own work I seemed to be heading toward more abstract forms without really knowing why. . . . I needed to find reasons why this was happening or to give up abstraction."[8]

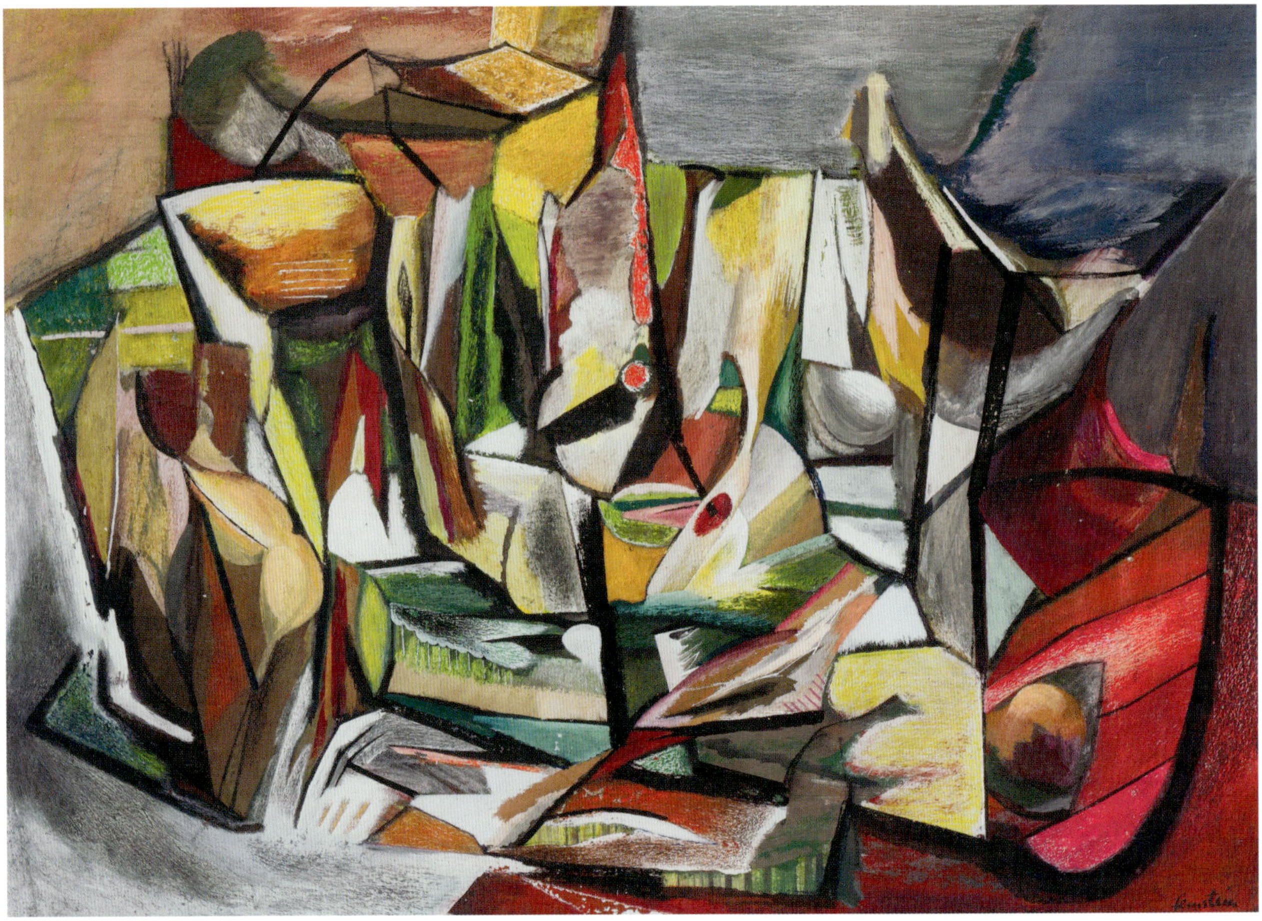

FIGURE 103. **Untitled**, c. 1949, by Sam Feinstein (Samuel L. Feinstein Trust)

Hans Hofmann

In 1949, Sam's urge to clarify his understanding of abstraction led him to Provincetown, Massachusetts, to study and make a film with artist Hans Hofmann, who would become his most important influence and inspiration. He often spoke of Hofmann in his own classes, telling stories of their time together, contrasting his mentor's work with that of other artists, and explaining his philosophy.

The older artist reinforced Sam's belief in the importance of art and its relationship to nature. Both connected with theories of science and believed that creating art was a form of research, a process of exploration of visual language in relation to nature's own logic and to human aesthetic response. "There are two kinds of reality: physical reality, apprehended by the senses, and spiritual reality," wrote Hofmann in his book *Search for the Real and Other Essays*, published the year before Sam arrived in Provincetown. "The artist's technical problem is how to transform the material with which he works back into the sphere of the spirit."[9] In *Pieta I*, exhibited at Dubin/Gallery '55 in 1958, this is precisely what Sam aimed to do (fig. 6).

The challenge that Hofmann, Sam, and all of us saw was to bring the entire picture plane to a full, breathing life while maintaining its integrity as a flat, two-dimensional surface. We avoided traditional means of rendering the illusion of depth, such as shading or foreshortening. Instead we used overlapping planes and variations in hue and tone to create a back-and-forth pulsing. We were painting

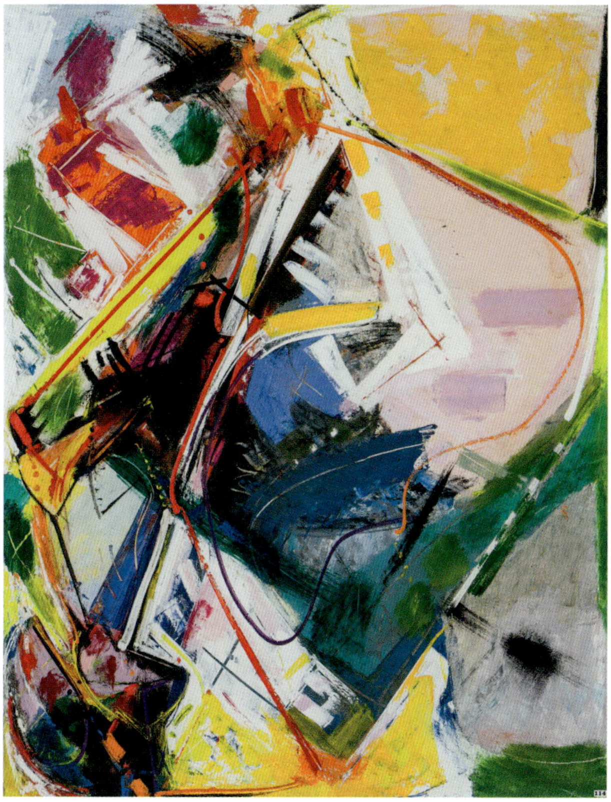

FIGURE 104. **Untitled**, c. 1952, by Sam Feinstein (Samuel L. Feinstein Trust)

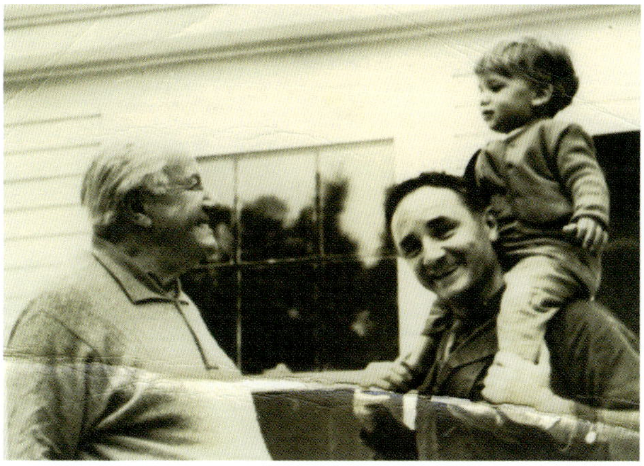

FIGURE 105. Hans Hofmann, Sam Feinstein, and Feinstein's son, Sascha, in Dennis, Massachusetts, 1964 (Samuel L. Feinstein Trust)

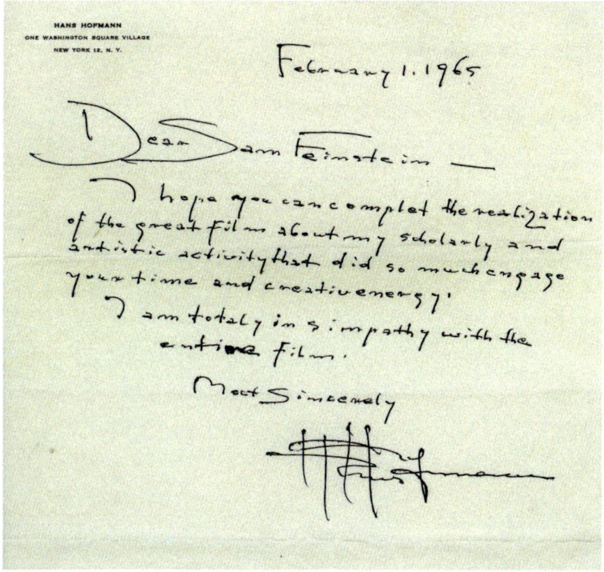

HANS HOFMANN
ONE WASHINGTON SQUARE VILLAGE
NEW YORK 12, N. Y.

February 1. 1965

Dear Sam Feinstein —

I hope you can complet the realization of the great film about my scholarly and artistic activity that did so much engage your time and creative energy.

I am totaly in simpathy with the entire film.

Most Sincerely

FIGURE 106. Letter from Hans Hofmann to Sam Feinstein, February 1, 1965 (Samuel L. Feinstein Trust)

space that was as fully alive as any form and trying to express the dynamic interaction between the two. In a brochure for a Hofmann exhibition in 1953, Sam wrote: "To Hofmann, the canvas is not a passive carrier of appearances from nature. It is a nature in itself: a vibrant being, alive in its own right . . . a gesturing anatomy . . . a palpitating, breathing organism."[10]

Inspired by a film about Watkins that he had helped produce at the Philadelphia Museum of Art a few years earlier, Sam suggested the creation of a film about Hofmann.[11] In a 1950 letter, Sam enthusiastically explained its educational value to his intended subject: "Such a film could be of immense interest to people everywhere who are involved in either creation or appreciation of painting and of special significance to laymen who would like to understand more fully the interpretation of the artist's vision . . . as a creative rather than imitative art."[12]

Little did Sam realize that he would spend decades completing what Hofmann called "the great film about my scholarly and artistic activity."[13] He worked on it consistently throughout the 1950s, 1960s, and early 1970s. Due to a major mistake by a developing company, thousands of splices were needed, and each was done by hand on a small device I still have. Musicians came and went, as did narrators. An attempt to gain funding failed.

But in 1998, at age eighty-three, he Sam brought the film out of storage and began lugging reels of 16mm film to an editor uptown and then to a film company downtown, always traveling by bus or subway. He drew the credits at the end by hand. On one occasion I accompanied him with the reels to a fourth-floor walk-up loft in the East Village, where a former Hofmann student and film editor worked for hours to make minor corrections. After decades of painstaking work, the film, titled simply *Hans Hofmann*, premiered at the Metropolitan Museum of Art, in New York, in 1999.

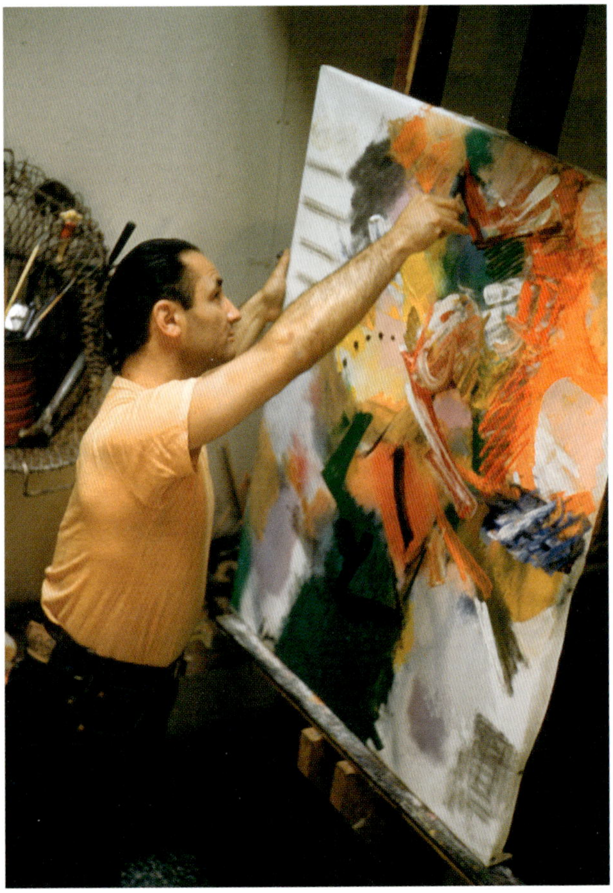

FIGURE 107. Sam Feinstein, early 1950s (Samuel L. Feinstein Trust)

Group '55

"It was a magic time!" Sam reminisced about the early 1950s. The creative energy of artists exploring new nonrepresentational and abstract styles was invigorating. Sam and Barbara took a train from Philadelphia to Provincetown each summer and returned in the fall with new friendships and crates full of new canvases. During their first summer Forum '49 took place at Gallery 200, with weekly panels and speakers—Hofmann among the first—addressing topics such as poetry, film, architecture, jazz, psychoanalysis, and art. Creation and conversation filled the summer. The seed of the idea for Group '55, which took its name from its founding year, and its multidisciplinary discussions may have been planted right then.

Back in Philadelphia, the carriage house Sam and Barbara acquired in 1953 on Chancellor Street near Rittenhouse Square became a gathering place for artists, composers, and architects whose shared momentum led to the formation of Group '55. Certain friendships were key to the spark, including that between Sam and architect Louis Kahn. Both had transformed their work in the early 1950s, lived in realms they had created beyond the everyday, and spoke about the material world in terms of the spiritual. In his classes Sam used Kahn's saying "order is" as a springboard to discuss plasticity. Kahn's colleague Anne Tyng was also a close friend. She called this period in Philadelphia's history "a Renaissance."[14]

Another inspiration for Group '55 came from Sam's ongoing research into the psychology of and language around art. *Feeling and Form: A Theory of Art* by philosopher Susanne K. Langer added depth

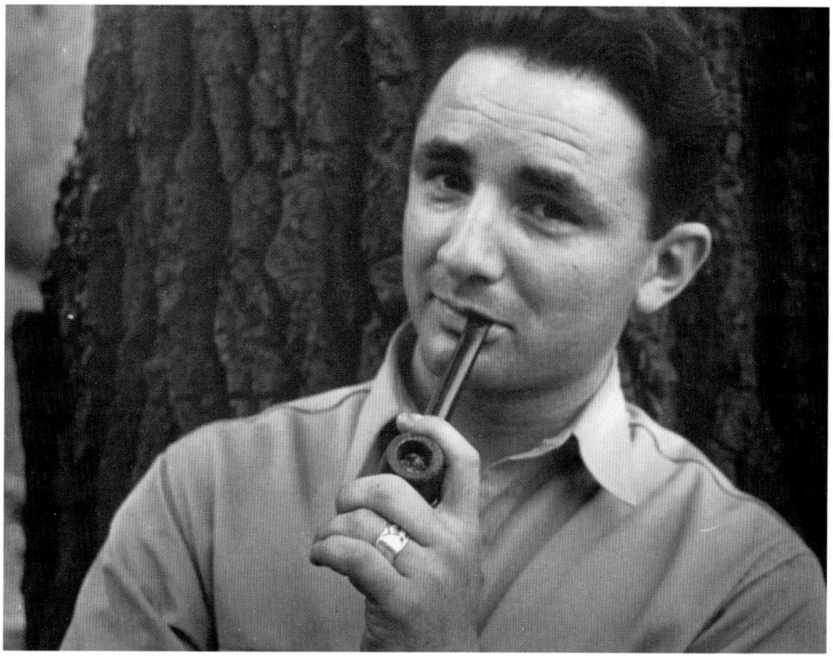

FIGURE 108. Sam Feinstein, 1950s (Samuel L. Feinstein Trust)

to his thinking.[15] Sam echoed her theories about art, aesthetics, and consciousness, as well as her terminology, in his talks. Langer considered symbol-making capacity to be the key element separating humankind from animals, and she described art—whether music, painting, sculpture, architecture, dance, literature, drama, or film—as a symbolic form that by "its dynamic structure can express the forms of vital experience that language is peculiarly unfit to convey."[16] She also noted the difference between "discursive" and "presentational" communication. One of the first books Sam gave me was Langer's *Problems of Art*, which contains one of the clearest explanations of visual art available in print, from my experience. I passed excerpts out to my own students every year.

In the first Group '55 forum, "Changing Forms in Art," Sam emphasized in a variety of ways the difference between "documentary" communication, which shows the look of things or tells a story, and "aesthetic" communication, which conveys the feeling, essence, or spirit underlying the outer appearance. The equation of a recognizable image, a picture, with a work of art was one of the most basic of misunderstandings. As artist and Group '55 member Doris Staffel recalled, "Most of the people that we knew were painting with concern for the essences of things rather than the appearance of things."

In the second forum Sam described the painful situation often faced by abstract painters:

> This poor painter. He's concerned with painting problems. He's an artist. He has his dignity in terms of the profession, in terms of the path to that profession. He knows that

> art is the real landmark in terms of man's development. He goes ahead and does the best he can. And he puts his work out where anybody can come and see it for free. And a person comes and says, "What's that? My kid can do as well."[17]

As previously mentioned, Sam, like many of the Group '55 artists and Hofmann, found support for abstraction in modern science. Here he pointed out that physicists had written that "substance is one of the greatest illusions,"[18] and he quoted Alfred North Whitehead: "If you break down substance to its smallest components, the interaction of the small components, the event, is the unit of reality."[19] Staffel later added, "Immediacy evolving and disappearing, that sense of the impermanence of everything, that interested basically all of us."[20] The artists were concerned with flux and change rather than the fixed image; as a student of Sam's I heard him say, "We don't paint flowers; we paint flowering."

During the second forum, a member of the audience asked if contemporary painting was an extension of the Dada movement, poking fun at art and proposing a negation of reason. This basic misconception resurfaced over the decades, and Sam was adamant in his response:

> No. This is the most affirmative; it is the least kidding kind of painting I know, the most "wearing your heart on your sleeve" painting that I know of, because the artist projects himself fully into the work. . . . It is as if he were the father and the canvas were the mother, and the completed canvas were [the] child—just one thing in which the artist searches for the meaning of his time, pertinent to his time, in the most serious, affirmative way that he knows.[21]

In a 1958 forum, a physicist and an astronomer joined a minister and a Jungian analyst to talk about "The New Dimensions of Man." The selection of these speakers seems to reflect Sam's interest in the micro and macro aspects of the universe as related to the human psyche and soul, as well as their influence on art.

Group '55 exhibitions initially took place at the Dubin Gallery in Philadelphia, and for the first show each member wrote a brief statement about the painting they chose to exhibit. For his *Black Dominant* (fig. 41), Sam wrote:

> My intention as an artist is to synthesize each work into a self-sustaining sensorial experience in terms intrinsic to painting (rather than to illustration or photography); a parallel to those cumulative sensorial experiences in nature which initiate the pictorial transformation. Thus the imagery of the painting and that of nature may, because they differ as media, not necessarily look alike, yet evoke similar meanings. *Black Dominant* pertains to August nights in Provincetown.[22]

In a 2006 interview, Staffel offered this assessment of Sam's role in Group '55: "Sam was very clear and very outspoken, very directive and very critical. He didn't hold back, and I admired that. He was very clear about what he thought, and his responses to painting historically and of his contemporaries . . . [were] not always received well."[23]

The effort involved in putting on forums was not welcomed by all. Sam was more committed to the group's educational mission than those who resigned to focus on exhibiting. But Group '55 survived and programs were added that featured

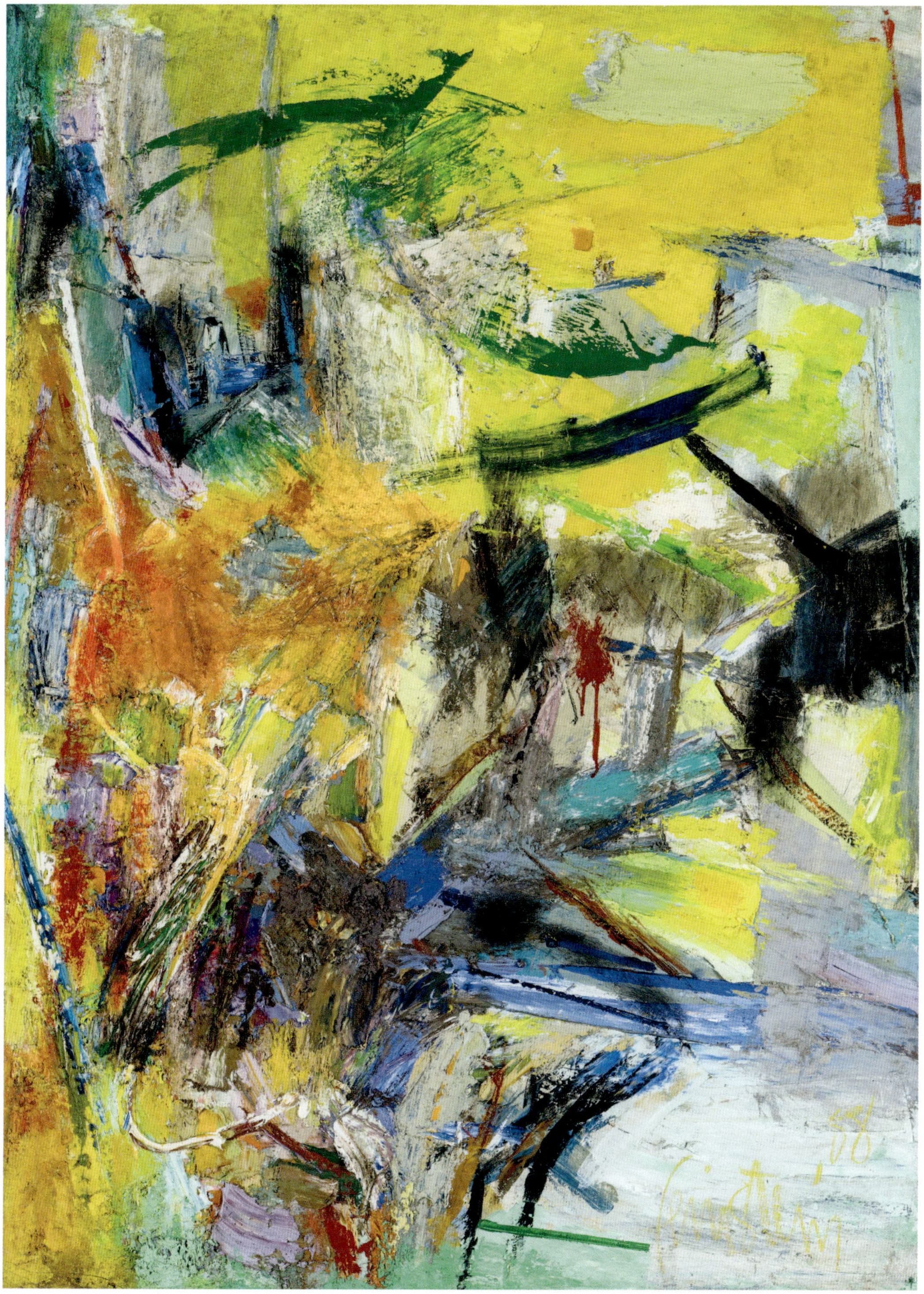

FIGURE 109. *Untitled*, 1958, by Sam Feinstein (Samuel L. Feinstein Trust)

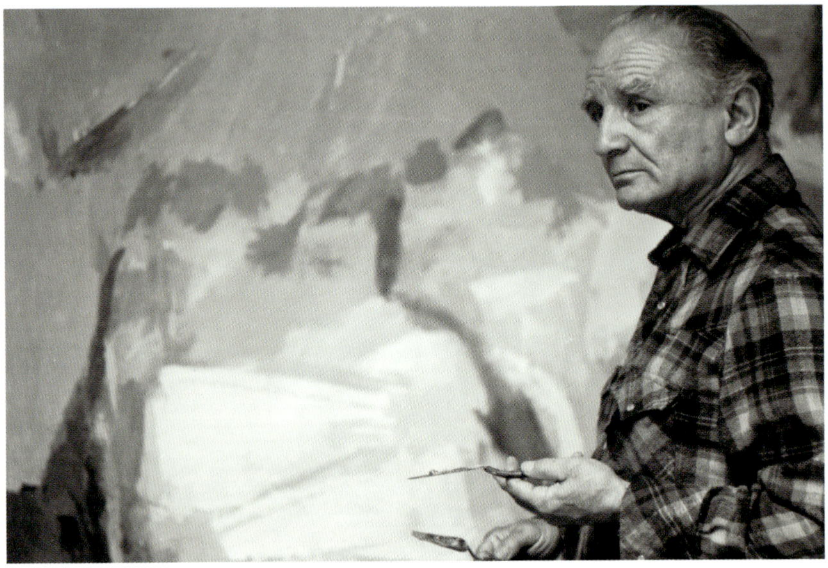

FIGURE 110. Sam Feinstein painting with two palette knives, the second used to hold extra paint, 1990s (Samuel L. Feinstein Trust)

modern music and dance, offering entertainment and real-life experience to connect with the conversations about them. Castaldo discussed the relationship between music and art with Sam for years; Sam often said that "art is simply visual music. It's music that you look at instead of music that you hear." All three art forms present new, independent expressions rather than imitations, each in its own language. Sam suggested that one must be "willing simply to make friends with art which does not immediately tell you something that you already know."

Painting and *Immersive Abstraction*

Sam painted dozens of canvases throughout the 1950s, each unique, nonobjective, and powerfully expressive. While Kahn asked, "What does a brick want to be?," Sam seemed to ask, "What is it that paint wants to be? What can it do?" He believed that the medium provides the means to communicate a huge range of emotional experiences and awareness of life, with its many subtleties and nuances, and that depths of feeling far beyond words can be coalesced into visual imagery. The vigor and complexity of one of his untitled works from 1959 conveys the ambiguous nature of any triumph (fig. 1); the painting stands on its own as a single intelligent eye or, as defined by Sam, a "human utterance attaining separate presence."

Sam's paintings from this period are often characterized by a primary gesture that commands the surface, riveting the edges in an unchangeable final drama. Adjustments of relative size and scale create a sense of monumentality, a feeling of vast space buttressed by powerful forms. These forms are built out of color, some thinly washed, some layered or textured. Sam aimed for the radiance from within seen in works by his hero, Rembrandt.

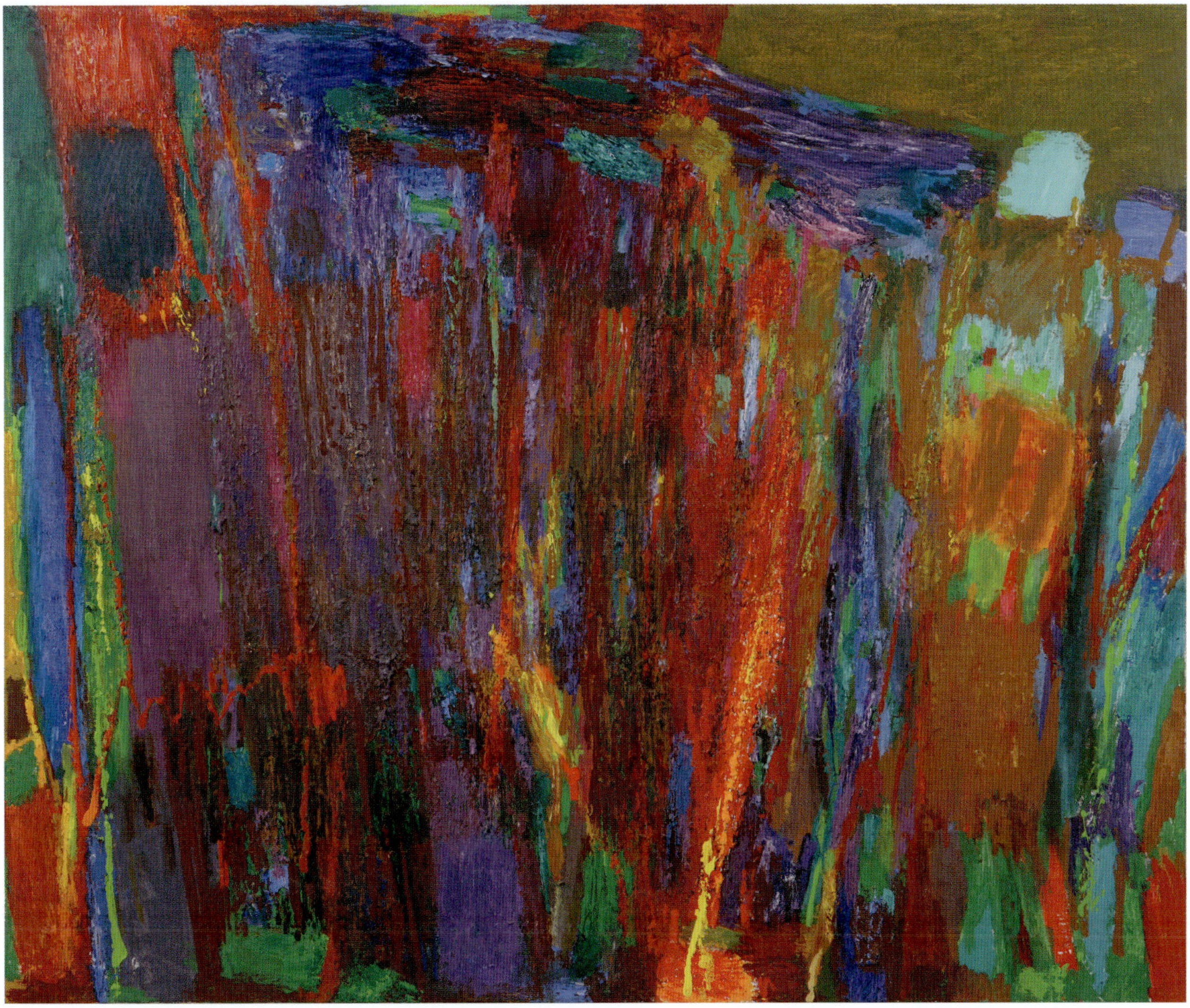

FIGURE 111. **Untitled**, 1988–2002, by Sam Feinstein (Samuel L. Feinstein Trust) Photograph by Laszlo Bodo

The warmth of the sun and summer's glow seem to come alive, for example, in an untitled painting of 1958 (fig. 109).

Sam's process did not vary from painting to painting, and he often worked on compositions over weeks, months, or sometimes even years. He followed what he saw as nature's laws and logic of creation: forms grew from the inside out, gradually over time. The canvas was not a box into which something was placed; the entire surface needed to be activated through the gesture of forms to make it breathe. The outside edges were the activating spines. Contrasting colors advanced or receded to create depth and pulsating life on the flat surface.

For Sam, as for Hofmann, "color-forms" were the building blocks of each composition. But from the early 1960s on, Sam brought a more classical control to each note of color and to the placement of each form, as seen in an untitled painting completed in 2002 (fig. 111). Every large or small stroke of color was set like a mosaic tile to create a "vibrating radiance." Exact hue took on primary importance, while variations of light and dark were secondary. Sam said that "each color is like an atom in the fabric of pictorial form." He saw the energy of light, the quality of vibrance, as a two-dimensional equivalent for the energy and life of the three-dimensional world.

For years Sam painted and repainted his canvases, often with white underpainting, mixing and juxtaposing each subtle, pure hue. He explained that the painter is "like a piano tuner, adjusting each note until it's right. . . . It's not a matter of tinkering with it. It's a matter of living in the realm until you sense what it wants to be." This process of more conscious yet intuitive control can be seen in *Nightscape* (fig. 112). Sam worked in oils until the late 1960s, when he turned to acrylic, whose quick-drying character allowed him to underpaint and repaint repeatedly, adding to the luminosity of his work. "In painting I try to get energy and spirit across through a sense of radiance. All life is radiant, even the darkest hole," Sam said. "Painting is simply working with units of color to make forms emerge that will express the essential spirituality of all life."

Sam's paintings in the *Immersive Abstraction* exhibition convey the range of his decades-long involvement with the composition of color, form, and light. The large golden canvas *Untitled* (1960), (fig. 169) one of his earliest monumental paintings, is part of a series that includes *Untitled* (1959) (fig. 1), in the Group '55 exhibition. Its vigorous brushwork and spontaneous energy are characteristic of many of his 1950s abstractions.

Painted over two decades later, *The Cry* (fig. 115) has an intensified, angular structure, with blocks of color charging in and out of the space. In a film made in 1986, during an exhibition of his paintings, Sam talks about *The Cry*: "It tries to say in its way what in his way, Edvard Munch, the Norwegian painter, tried to say. It's as if, however, you were sort of inside almost the mouth or the throat of the person, whereas he shows the whole figure with the mouth open and screaming. You try to make the painting do the screaming instead of showing somebody doing it on canvas. But that's the purpose of a painting, just as a dancer uses limbs to convey certain emotions."[24] Sam articulates many of his beliefs in this film, and years later, following one of its screenings, a viewer exclaimed to me, "Now I understand abstraction!"

The largest painting in the *Immersive Abstraction* exhibition, the great blue creation displayed on the end wall, was discovered rolled and stored in Sam's

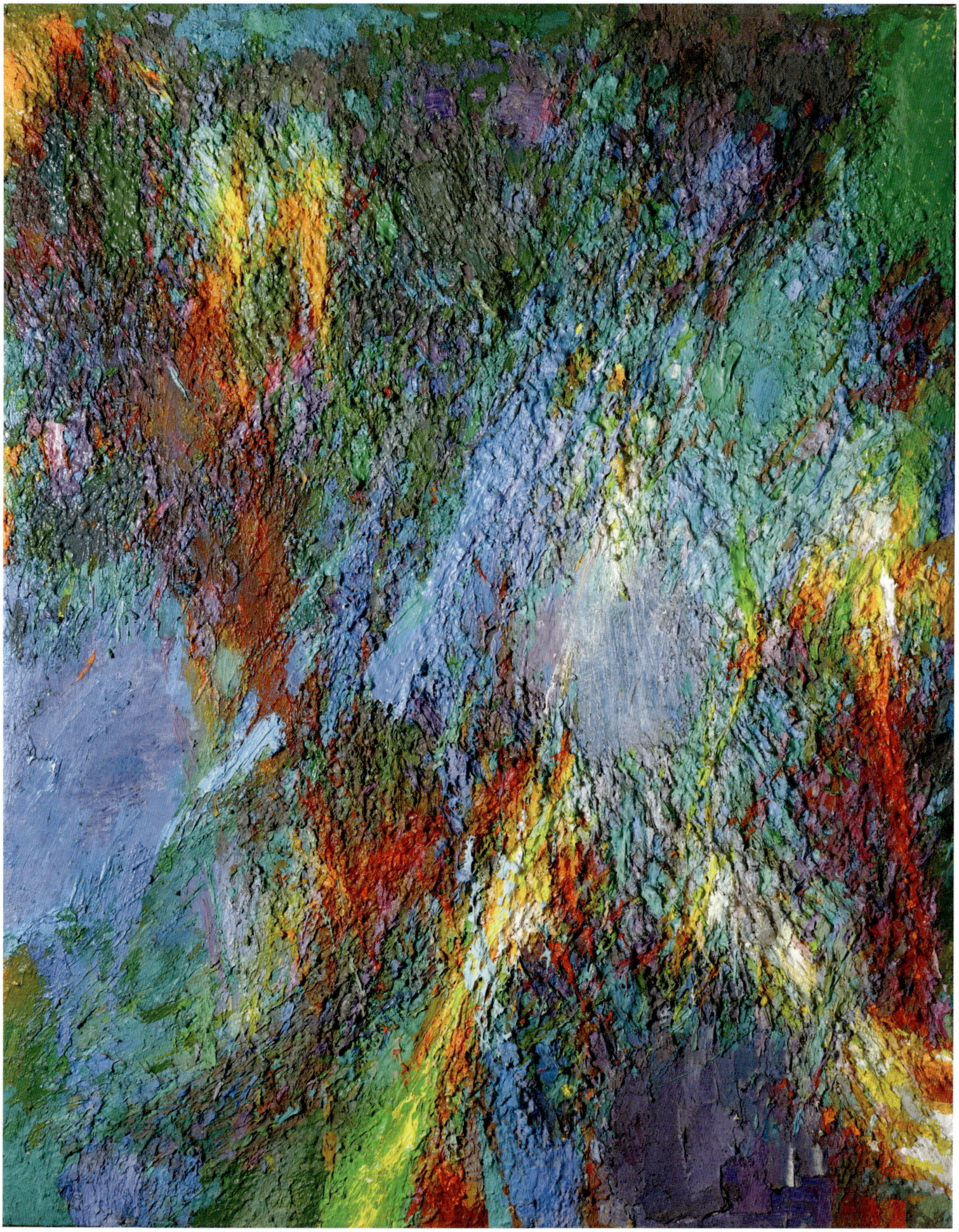

FIGURE 112. **Nightscape**, 1980s, by Sam Feinstein (Samuel L. Feinstein Trust) Photograph by Laszlo Bodo

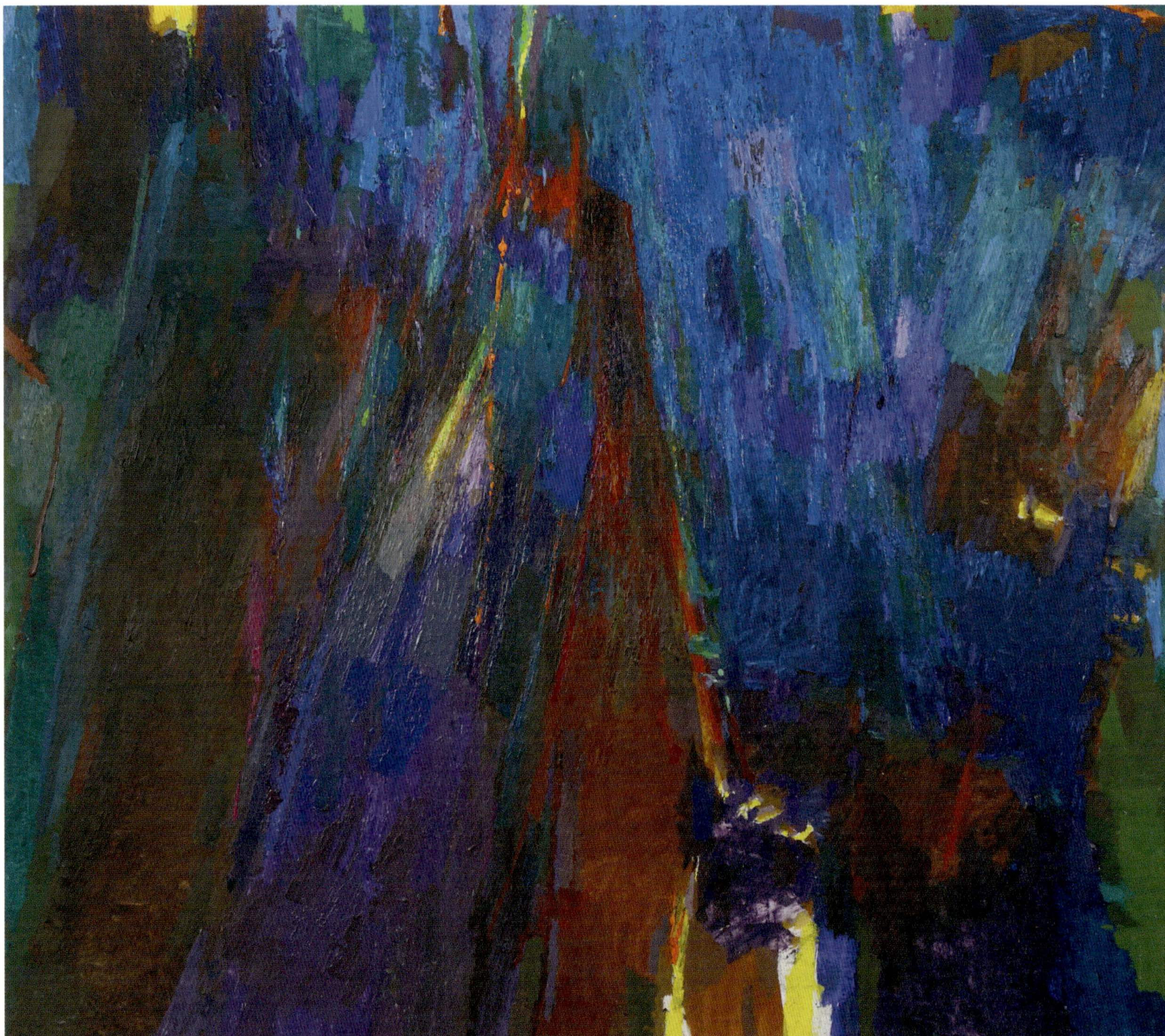

FIGURE 113. **Untitled**, 1996–2000, by Sam Feinstein (Samuel L. Feinstein Trust) Photograph by Laszlo Bodo

studio after his death (fig. 113). Is it "finished"? All we know is that he stopped when he stopped. Its grandeur and depth of color are set off, perhaps even challenged, by the lively area of brushwork at the bottom. In his teaching, Sam often encouraged the use of an opposite to "set off" a color or a theme.

Requiem (fig. 114) and *Untitled* (fig. 111) were both painted over a number of years late in Sam's life. Through the radiance of their color and the commanding gestures of their forms, they achieve the "intensity and density" that Sam sought in his work. These qualities were essential, he once explained. A painting must reach out to the viewer

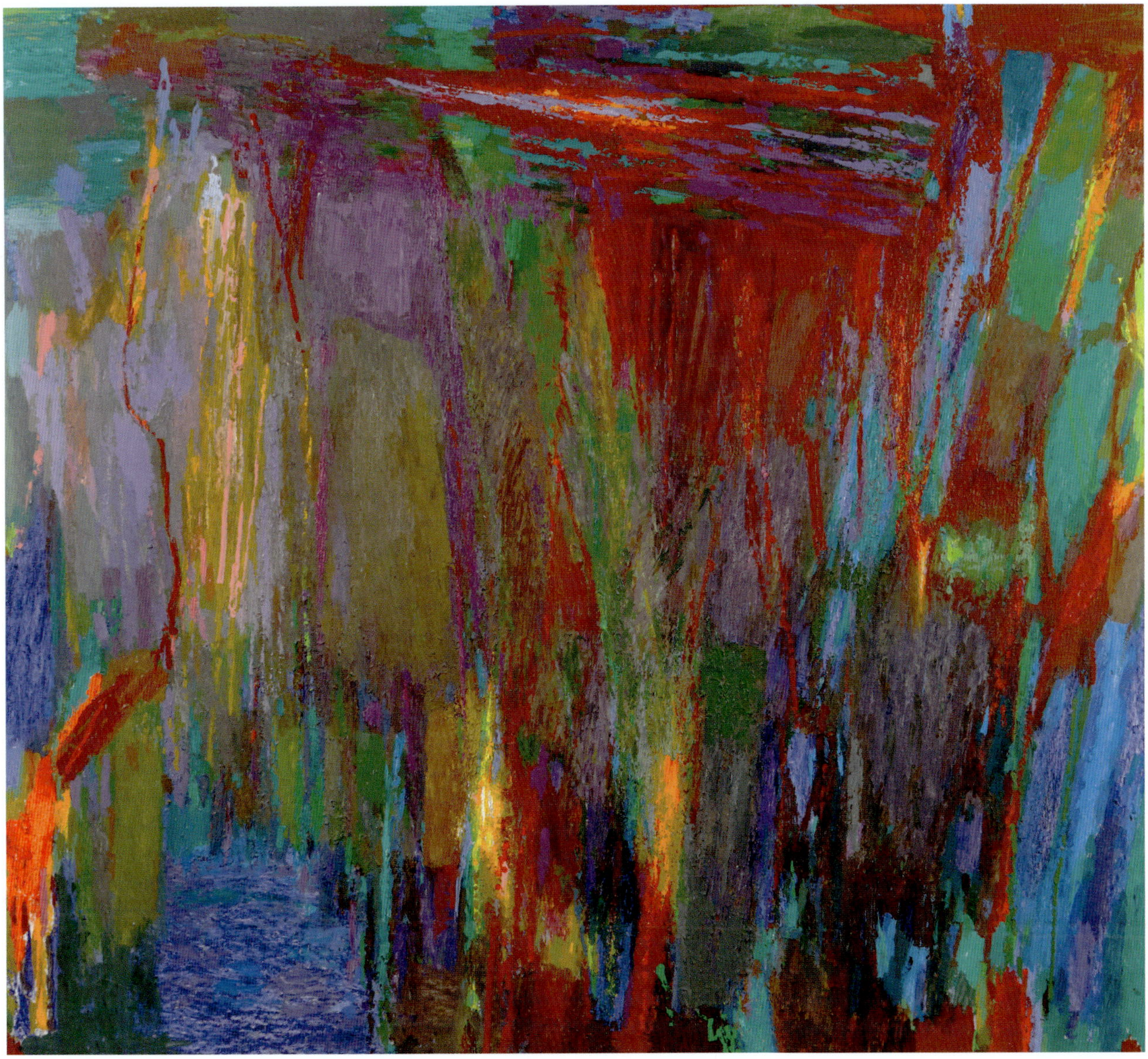

FIGURE 114. **Requiem**, 1990s, by Sam Feinstein (Samuel L. Feinstein Trust) Photograph by Laszlo Bodo

as "energy made visible as form." All the paintings in this exhibition, whether dynamic or meditative, immerse the viewer in realms that reveal themselves over time. In Sam's words: "These paintings are optical structures composed to touch human spirit, to turn a rectangle into an evocation."[25]

Teaching

Like painting, teaching was a continuity that ran through Sam's life. In the early 1960s, after years of public activity and exhibitions, Sam withdrew from the commercial art world to concentrate on creation and instruction. He was completely

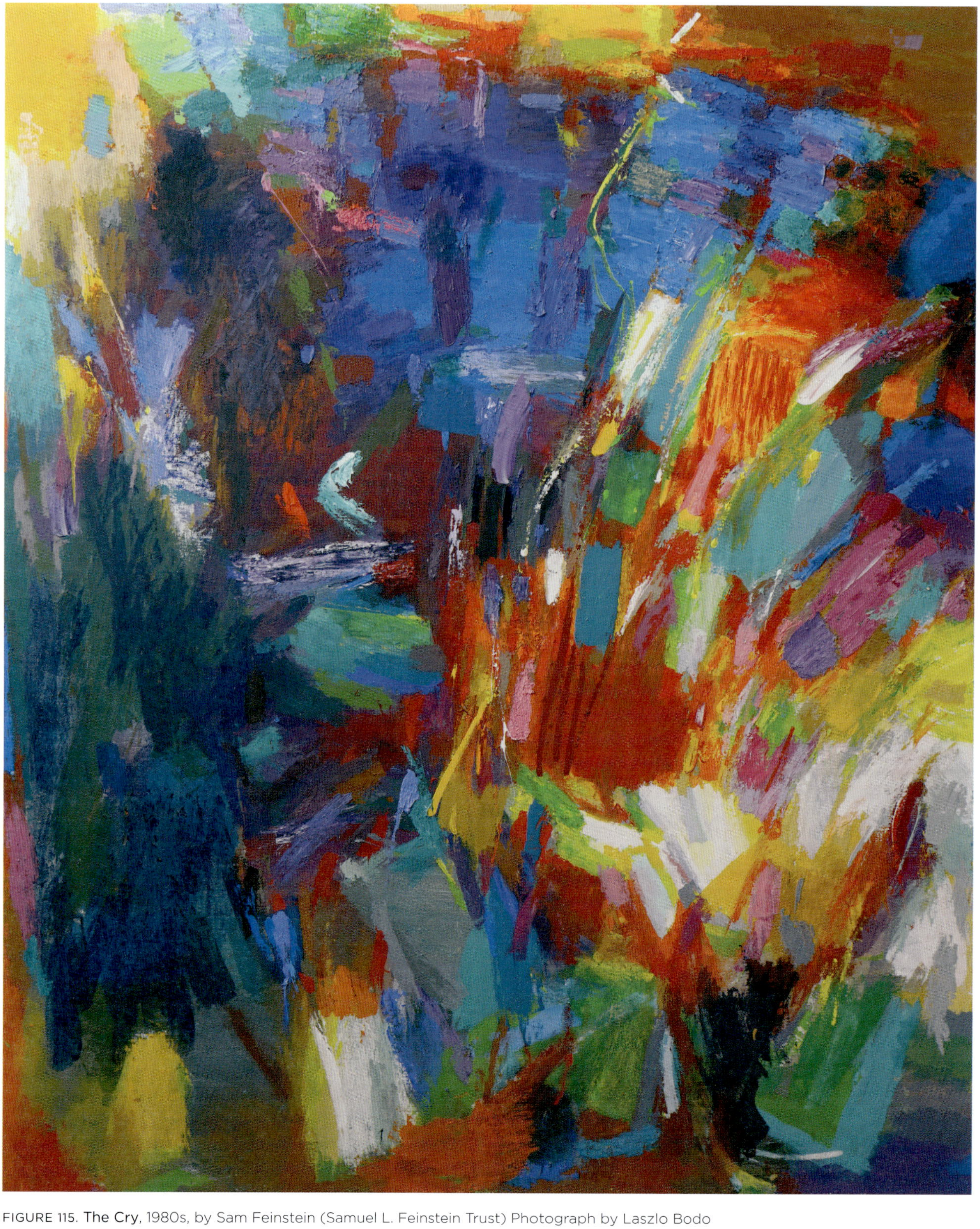

FIGURE 115. **The Cry**, 1980s, by Sam Feinstein (Samuel L. Feinstein Trust) Photograph by Laszlo Bodo

disillusioned with the gallery scene, where the artists' personalities had become more important than the art. He thought Pop art was a disaster that would eventually fall from its own lack of weight. He left Provincetown to settle in the quieter village of Dennis, near Cape Cod Bay, where he painted and taught each summer. In the winter he taught weekly classes in New York; Princeton, New Jersey; and Philadelphia, and for many years he held three-day painting workshops in Toronto.

Sam's teaching was serious, the judgments gentle and supportive or strong and directive, depending on the student. "You have to open yourself up to become a transmitter, a transformer, something more than you were originally. . . . The skills always come afterward," he explained. "All forms are quantum fluctuations that are constantly moving. . . .Look at the still life as a gathering of forces, not as a bunch of forms. . . .There are forces that go through everything and it is up to us to see them, to sense them and to convey that dance of energy and intelligence in our paintings." The principles he imparted to his students were the same as those he applied to his own work.

Sam could find merit in every attempt and respected everyone's work. In the "line-up" discussions that followed each painting session, he elicited insights from all the painters about their own work and that of others and then added his own in a way that buttressed our endeavors. We were all there to learn and grow, not to produce and impress. As Sam said: "You can manufacture a painting, but that's not art. . . . You must allow a painting to grow in a realm until you know what it wants to be." Sam enlightened each painter's efforts through his words or demonstrations. There was a logic to the way that visual elements coalesced to express meaning, and Sam taught us to understand this. Most importantly, he taught us to see. He taught us to look beyond outer surfaces to the inner structures and rhythmic drives within forms, whether the forms were realistic or abstract. Sam loved playing with words, and his talks in class entertained and informed as well as inspired. "Yellow ochre is the Switzerland of colors." "Aesthetic is just the opposite of anesthetic." His universal dictum was "Cover the white!" Sam conveyed a sense of connection to artists throughout history and to the history of science and culture, as well as a belief in the validity and nobility of painting.

I am one of many students who attended his classes for years, even decades, and who have continued to paint seriously, exhibit, and teach throughout our lives. Others painted as a form of meditation, a path to personal growth, and rarely showed their work. More than one has said to me, "I graduated from art school, but everything I know about art, I learned from Sam." His classes were never advertised. Sam was invited to teach, inherited students when Hofmann stopped teaching, and was coaxed into adding more classes. He organized exhibitions, gave gallery talks and slide lectures, planned gallery visits for his students, and led the forums that were an essential part of Group '55.

Conclusion

A great many changes took place in Sam's life beginning in 1958. After his marriage to Barbara came to an end, she stayed in Philadelphia while he went off to Provincetown, as usual. In the fall, back in a new loft he had rented in New York, Sam began teaching privately with over a dozen students from Hofmann's classes. Decades later Staffel would note

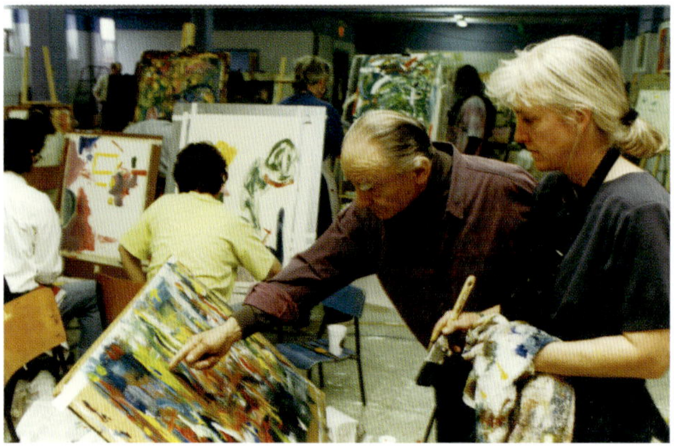

FIGURE 116. Sam Feinstein with student Diana Tabak in a painting workshop in Toronto, 1998 (Samuel L. Feinstein Trust)

what a loss it was to the Philadelphia art community when Sam moved to New York.[26] She never knew that his private classes continued on Chancellor Street for the rest of his life.

In 1962 Sam married Anita Askild, a fabric designer and painter who had also studied with Hofmann. Their son, Sascha, was born in 1963, but Anita tragically died in 1980, when Sascha was just seventeen years old. Throughout the years Sam continued to paint, an activity he has called prayer, and to teach, his routine schedule helping to sustain him.

During the early 1980s I began teaching at Riverdale Country School and painting in Sam's evening classes in New York. I had already audiotaped and transcribed many of the classes I had taken with Sam in Philadelphia years earlier. When he was asked to teach a painting workshop at a Gestalt conference center in the summer of 1983, he invited me to accompany him as his assistant. This was the first of eighteen annual workshops that became highlights of our lives. We were married in 1985 and woke up on New Year's Day 1986 on our honeymoon at Machu Picchu. Sam's painting of this magnificent and mysterious place was shown that summer at a small gallery on Cape Cod (fig. 118).[27]

Sam and I never talked about what would happen to the paintings he would leave behind. He certainly wouldn't have asked me to do all I have done. He told the story about El Greco, whose work was lost for centuries and then rediscovered by accident, and he added that it probably didn't matter to El Greco, wherever he had gone. But Sam and I both revered the paintings of El Greco and Rembrandt and Paul Cézanne and so many others. We visited countless museums to look at art, to nourish our souls, and to inspire our own creative endeavors. My goal is to have Sam's paintings shown in museums, where they belong, and to inspire others.

From a historical point of view, Sam might be called a second-generation Abstract Expressionist. Most of the first generation had reached a mature stage of their development by 1950, when Sam was just beginning to explore abstraction. Abstract Expressionism became associated with "action painting" through the writings of critic Harold Rosenberg, but this was not what Sam believed abstraction to be. As Hofmann said, "It's not what the artist does; it's what the painting does back."[28]

During the first half of the twentieth century there was a strong sense of optimism and idealism about art and its central role in culture and civilization. As the years passed, in the face of rising cynicism, commercialism, and materialism, Sam held onto this ideal. He wrote continually—sometimes on any scrap of paper he could find—refining over and over an as-yet-unpublished manuscript titled *Art for Life's Sake*.[29] Through all three phases of Sam's life—the early years of exploration, in which he called attention to social injustice and the horrors

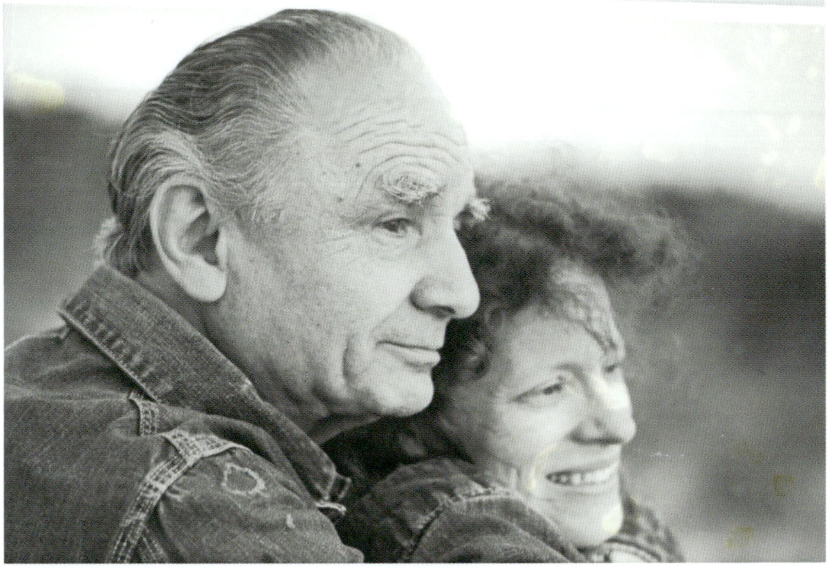

FIGURE 117. Sam Feinstein and Patricia Stark Feinstein, 1986 (Samuel L. Feinstein Trust)

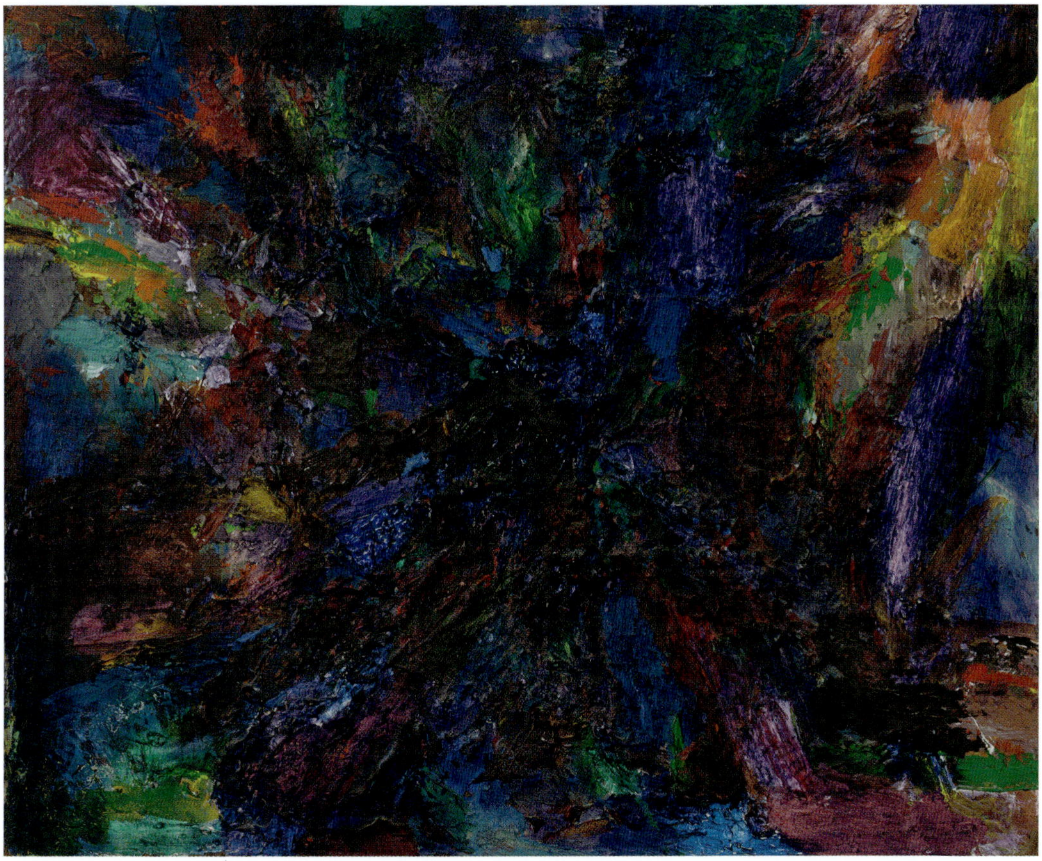

FIGURE 118. *Machu Picchu*, 1986, by Sam Feinstein (Patricia Stark Feinstein Collection)

of war with his art and began his teaching career; the 1950s, when he reached out to inform and uplift people through his writing, his filmmaking, and his leadership of Group '55; the later years, when he immersed himself in painting while continuing to nourish others through teaching—he remained devoted to principles of integrity, beauty, and truth. His insistence on the importance of art and his generosity of spirit influenced all who knew him. I was blessed to be part of his life as student, teaching assistant, and wife. I can still see him at age eighty-seven striding up the block in New York on his way to the subway, bus, and yet another bus, every Monday morning, to teach his class in Philadelphia—a class that had begun in 1952 and continued for fifty years.

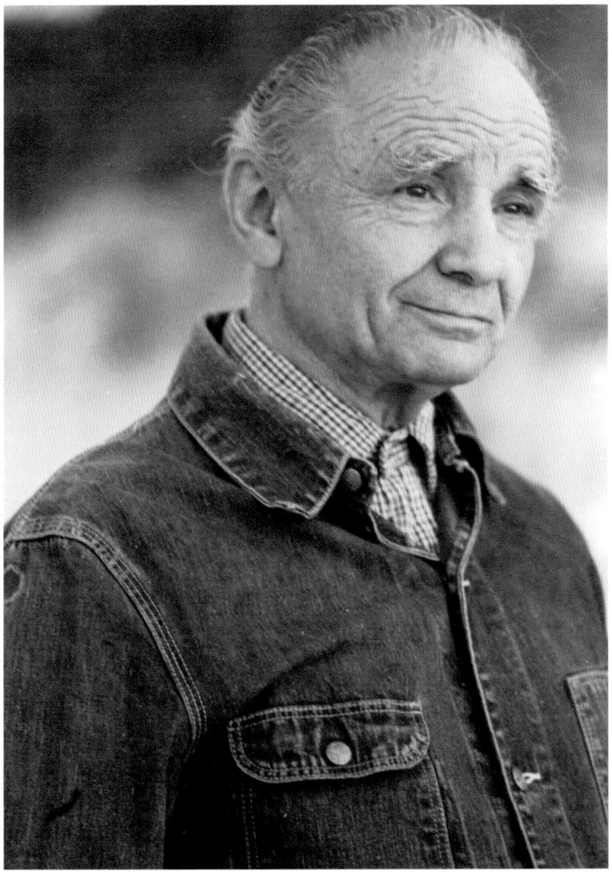

FIGURE 119. Sam Feinstein, 1986 (Samuel L. Feinstein Trust)

NOTES

1 Handwritten draft of a letter from Sam Feinstein to Ethel McConnell, October 1947, Samuel L. Feinstein Trust Archive. McConnell was an elderly woman whom Feinstein met through Barbara Crawford's mother, Anne Crawford. They corresponded for a decade, beginning in the mid-1940s. Unless otherwise noted, all quotes from Feinstein come from diverse sources in the Samuel L. Feinstein Trust Archive.

2 Patricia Stark Feinstein, *Sam Feinstein* (North Truro, MA: Fields Publishing, 2008).

3 Handwritten draft of a letter from Sam Feinstein to the United States draft board, undated but probably 1941–42, Samuel L. Feinstein Trust Archive. This letter was a follow-up to his formal request for conscientious objector status.

4 Handwritten draft of a letter from Sam Feinstein to Ralph M. Pearson, undated but probably 1945 or 1946, Samuel L. Feinstein Trust Archive.

5 *One World or None* was released in 1946 by the National Committee on Atomic Energy, with technical assistance by the Federation of American Scientists.

6 Sam Feinstein, *Art for Life's Sake*, unpublished manuscript, 1987, Samuel L. Feinstein Trust Archive.

7 Feinstein to McConnell, October 1947.

8 Sam Feinstein and Sascha Feinstein, *A Portrait of Hans Hofmann* (New York: Midmarch Arts Press, 2008), 8.

9 Hans Hofmann, *Search for the Real and Other Essays* (Andover, MA: Addison Gallery of American Art, 1948), 72.

10 Sam Feinstein, in *Hans Hofmann: The First Showing of Landscapes Created from 1936–1939*, exhibition brochure (New York: Kootz Gallery, 1953), 1.

11 *Franklin Watkins* (1948), film. Producer: Philadelphia Museum of Art. Director, writer, and narrator: E. M. Benson. Photographer and associate director: Sam Feinstein.

12 Handwritten draft of a letter from Sam Feinstein to Hans Hofmann, undated but probably 1950, Samuel L. Feinstein Trust Archive.

13 Letter from Hans Hofmann to Sam Feinstein, February 1, 1965, Samuel L. Feinstein Trust Archive.

14 Interview by the author, 2007.

15 Susanne K. Langer, *Feeling and Form: A Theory of Art* (New York: Charles Scribner's Sons, 1955).

16 Susanne K. Langer, *Problems of Art* (New York: Charles Scribner's Sons, 1957), 91.

17 Sam Feinstein, transcript of second Group '55 forum, March 16, 1956, timed at 09:45 minutes , Samuel L. Feinstein Trust Archive.

18 Sam Feinstein, transcript of first Group '55 forum, January 12, 1956, reel four, p. 10, Samuel L. Feinstein Trust Archive.

19 Sam Feinstein, transcript of first Group '55 forum, January 12, 1956, reel four, p. 10, Samuel L. Feinstein Trust Archive.

20 Taped interview by the author, 2007.

21 Sam Feinstein, transcript of first Group '55 forum, January 12, 1956, reel four, p. 1, Samuel L. Feinstein Trust Archive.

22 Handwritten draft from Samuel L. Feinstein Trust Archive.

23 Taped interview by the author, 2007.

24 *Sam's Show at Scargo* (1986), film. Producer: Paul Fitzgerald.

25 Sam Feinstein exhibition statement, *Sam Feinstein*, Scargo Stoneware Pottery Gallery, Dennis, Massachusetts, 1986.

26 Taped interview by the author, 2007.

27 *Sam Feinstein*, Scargo Stoneware Pottery Gallery, Dennis, Massachusetts, 1986. This sole one-man exhibition of Sam's paintings held between 1960 and 2003 took place at the urging of his friend, Harry Holl, potter and gallery owner.

28 Sam Feinstein, quoting Hans Hofmann.

29 Sam Feinstein, *Art for Life's Sake*, unpublished manuscript, 1987, Samuel L. Feinstein Trust Archive.

ACKNOWLEDGMENTS

I am enormously grateful to Woodmere Art Museum and Springside Chestnut Hill Academy for the opportunity to share Sam's legacy with the Philadelphia community. My thanks go to Woodmere director William R. Valerio, who guided this project to fruition with enthusiasm, wisdom, and insight, and to Woodmere curator Rachel Hruszkewycz for all her skillful help and thoughtful support. At Springside Chestnut Hill Academy, the art committee has spurred me along with their imagination and commitment to this part of the exhibition. To Ellen Fishman, Pia Druggan, and Melissa Maddonni Haims, I owe a great debt of gratitude. None of this would have come about without the extraordinary efforts of Barbara A. Wolanin and Victoria Schuh. They have my endless admiration and thanks. The enlightened editing of Gretchen Dykstra deserves special praise. I thank Sascha Feinstein for his photograph of Sam and me, and for one of Sam. I am endlessly grateful to Derek Nelson for his crucial technical expertise for this and many other projects.

MY FATHER'S LASTING LESSONS ON ART

SASCHA FEINSTEIN

As a child, I viewed my father with near-mythic reverence. There was, of course, our startling age difference (he was forty-eight when I was born) but, far more than that, I felt genuinely awed by his authoritative command of art, as both a painter and a teacher. I loved listening to him speak to his students—especially at the end of each class, when he'd discuss their work—because I valued the voice of brilliance, and it pleased me to witness so much adulation.

Beyond that, I realized early on that I was absorbing invaluable lessons about the nature of art—all arts, not just painting—and many of those lessons have shaped my own efforts to teach (in my case, creative writing). He worked tirelessly, for example, to have students embrace the canvas as an organic whole, not just a sum of inarticulate parts, and therefore to view a canvas holistically rather than concentrate on minor portions. This tends to be a pitfall in poetry workshops, at all levels, where students eagerly quibble over isolated words before first discussing the *nature* of the poem being discussed. Why does that happen? Because it's easier and, I suppose, comforting: one can be confident about a typo long before one can understand a work's emotional spirit. And so my father would frequently begin by asking a student, "Would you say this painting is more wintery or summery?" In doing so, the painter was forced to assess the essence of the painting before picking at smaller issues.

Of course, in order to achieve a united whole one must work at the problematic passages, and here, too, I learned a great deal about art in general from listening to my father teach painting. Sometimes, for example, he would say to a student, "Okay, let me show you something just to prove you're not perfect." (This inevitably provoked a humble chuckle.) Then he'd borrow the person's palette knife, add a bit of paint, and make a *small* addition to the edge of their canvas. He'd explain the importance of color touching the boundaries, the extra impact that had upon the eye, how you can stretch a gesture beyond the limitations of the canvas itself by energizing the framework. The effect upon a student's work was often astounding.

One can see this principle dramatically in play in all his work, including the acrylic on display titled *Rising* (fig. 121). Its seasonal identity is undeniably that of summer, and pushing against that sunniness are passages of green that, in their opposition, create both tension and movement. They surge from the lower left-hand corner and are then picked up by green on the right edge that then ascends until it is finally released in a sliver at the painting's peak. And the impact of this drama—the ascendency that inspired the work's title—is largely dependent upon the placement of that opposing color at the highlighted extremes.

This lesson in craft is by no means limited to the visual arts. If we consider the mechanics of poetry, the edges of a canvas might be compared to line and stanza breaks. A word at the end of a line inevitably has more impact upon the eye; a word at the end of a stanza resonates still more. Here, for example, is a passage from David Wojahn's "Satin Doll," where he's describing a pregnant aunt suffering through a divorce:

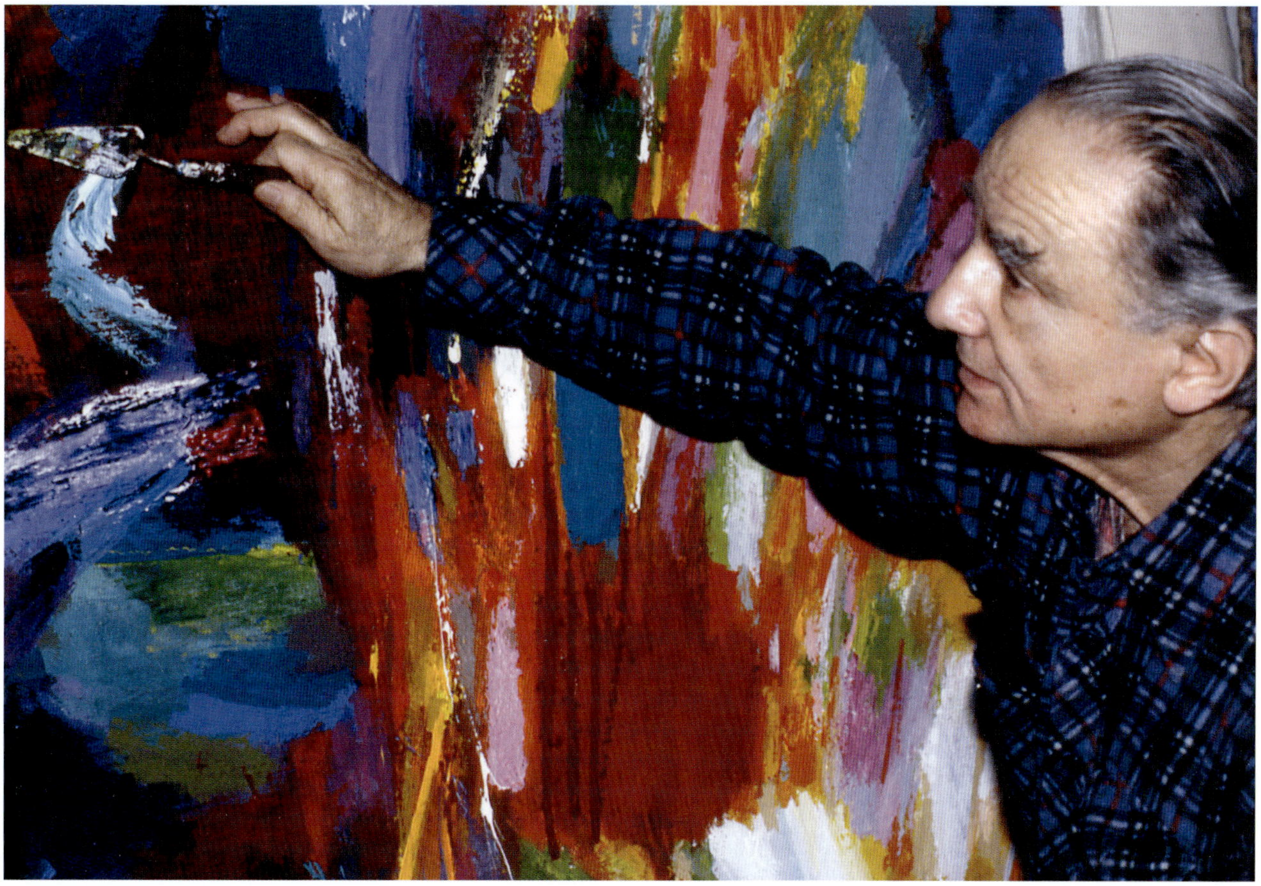

FIGURE 120. Sam Feinstein in action, early 1980s. Photograph by Sascha Feinstein

It's the year

she carries the novels and notebooks

into the backyard to burn them, and when she finishes

her dress and apron are covered with ashes, rising

in what she wants to call a pillar of fire

but it is only smoke on a damp day.

Because the stanza breaks on "rising," the word itself begins to rise, buoyed by all the white space surrounding it. Look at an alternative:

her dress and apron are covered with ashes,

rising in what she wants to call . . .

Placed below, the word no longer achieves the same mobility of smoke and ash.

Apart from listening to my father teach, I learned about art by watching him paint. During my lifetime, at least, the majority of his painting took place in the summer months on Cape Cod, where he'd retreat to his studio in the woods. Here he'd pin several large canvases onto Homasote boards and address them collectively; he also had much smaller sheets of paper on a low table and worked on those as well. His setup dismantled the clichéd image of the artist standing behind a solitary easel and provided instead a wise approach to avoiding creative stagnancy: if you're stuck on one project, move to another.

The last lesson about art that I learned came late in his life. It was summer. He would have been deep into his seventies. As usual, he had spent the entire morning in his studio and had returned to the house for lunch. But that day he radiated anger. I asked him what was wrong, and he spat out an inexact reply: "It *never* gets any easier!"

I didn't ask for clarification. (I had learned from childhood not to touch hot kettles.) But I imagine him in his studio, struggling to create cohesive statements and feeling temporarily stymied. What artist, in any field, does not experience such moments of frustration and doubt? Yet the memory will forever be fresh and engaging because I have known very few artists who share his confident, focused vision. This was Thor suddenly unable to throw his hammer, and I sometimes tell this story to students who, in their marvelous youth, think that struggle is somehow relegated to the inexperienced. I've come to consider my father's fury as being illuminating and inspiring.

That day he ate his lunch in silence. Then, when he rose from the table to return to his studio, I said, "I hope it goes better." He didn't reply. He didn't need to.

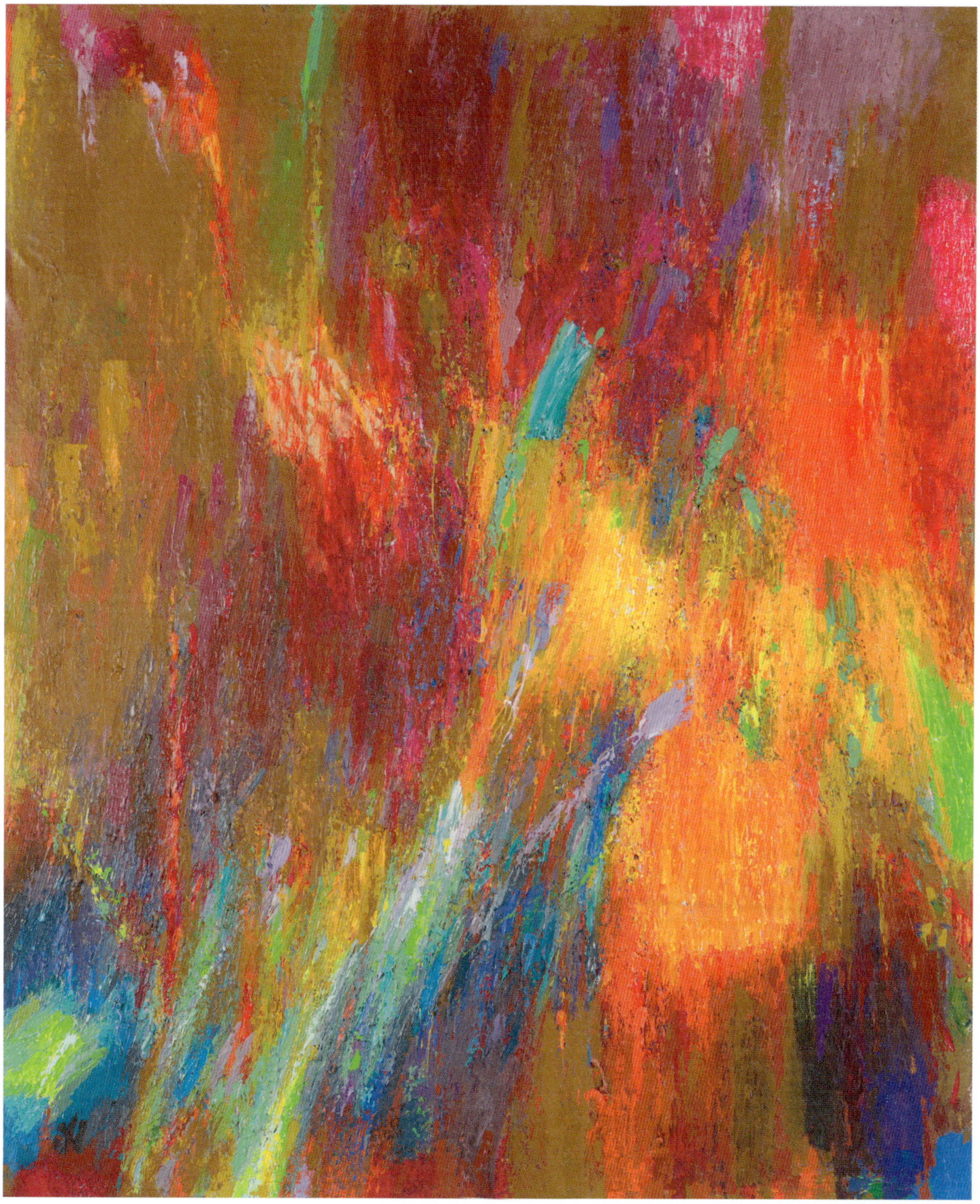

FIGURE 121. **Rising**, 1970s, by Sam Feinstein (Samuel L. Feinstein Trust)

Sascha Feinstein is a poet, essayist, and editor whose twelve books include Wreckage: My Father's Legacy of Art & Junk. *The founding editor of* Brilliant Corners: A Journal of Jazz & Literature, *he is the Robert L. & Charlene Shangraw Professor of English at Lycoming College, Williamsport, Pennsylvania. www.SaschaFeinstein.com.*

RECOLLECTIONS FROM STUDENTS OF SAM FEINSTEIN AND BARBARA CRAWFORD

In 1938, Sam Feinstein became head of the art department at Chestnut Hill Academy (CHA), where he gained a reputation as an innovative and insightful teacher. When he enlisted in the US Army at the start of World War II, his wife, artist Barbara Crawford, took over his teaching and leadership post; she would remain there for the next forty-eight years.[1] After the war, Feinstein returned to the classroom, teaching art history at Springside School for one year. The couple later divorced, but they remained friends and continued to paint together for the rest of their lives.

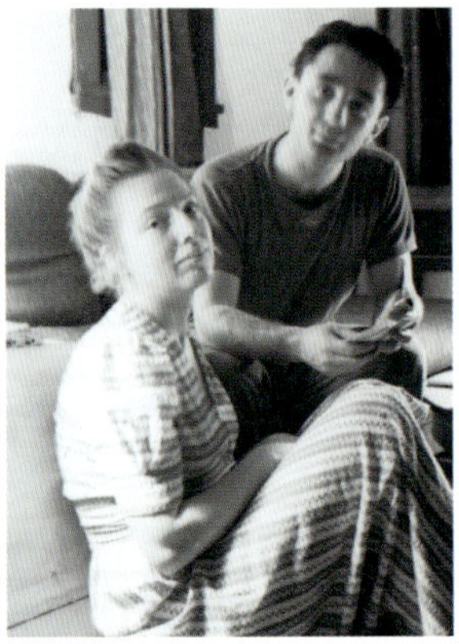

FIGURE 122. Sam Feinstein and Barbara Crawford, c. 1940s (Samuel L. Feinstein Trust)

BELOW FIGURE 123. "Darling, I am nuts about you. Waln't you be my Valentine?" Sam Feinstein used a print of his *Black Walnuts* (1950) to dedicate this loving note to Barbara Crawford. The original woodblock print is at the Philadelphia Museum of Art. (Courtesy of Springside Chestnut Hill Academy)

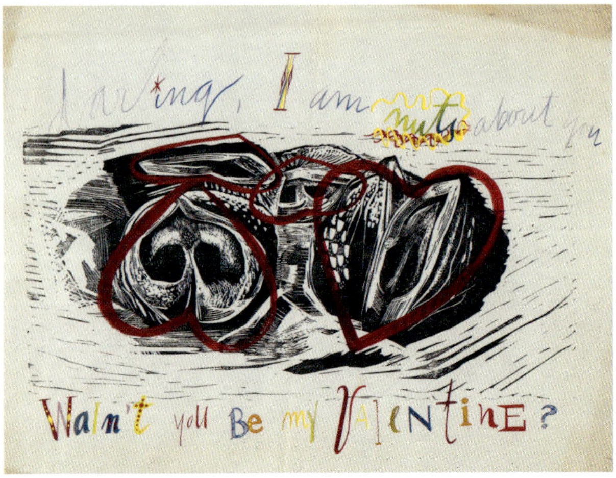

In 2010, the two schools were renamed Springside Chestnut Hill Academy, following their merger. Ellen Fishman, director of the arts and new media; Melissa Maddonni Haims, parent volunteer and curator; and Pia Druggan, art historian and assistant curator reached out to six of Feinstein's and Crawford's former students to share their recollections: John Wenzel, Thorpe Feidt, Theodore Clattenberg, Bonnie Warwick, Binney Meigs, and Lewis Tanner Moore. Some of the students called themselves the "Cellar Rats," as they spent whatever time they could in Crawford's art room, in the basement of the Wissahickon Inn. They shared their remembrances.

Sam Feinstein: The Early Years traces Feinstein's journey toward abstraction through his watercolors, oil paintings, and illustrations from the 1930s through the mid-1950s. The exhibition also includes a film Feinstein made about abstract painter Hans Hofmann and a selection of works by Crawford.

John Wenzel, Class of '41

Wenzel recalled Feinstein as a "really good teacher" who was progressive and engaging, and who interacted with his students outside the classroom. In the late 1940s or early 1950s, Wenzel ran into his former teacher near his Philadelphia studio. When Wenzel asked what he was doing, Feinstein said that he was working on a new style, a new outlook—that he would quit being a painter if he had to use the white-on-white or black-on-black style of the times. A few years later, Wenzel took a class at the Hans Hofmann School of Fine Arts in Provincetown, Massachusetts, where Feinstein was working as an assistant teacher. Wenzel noted how popular

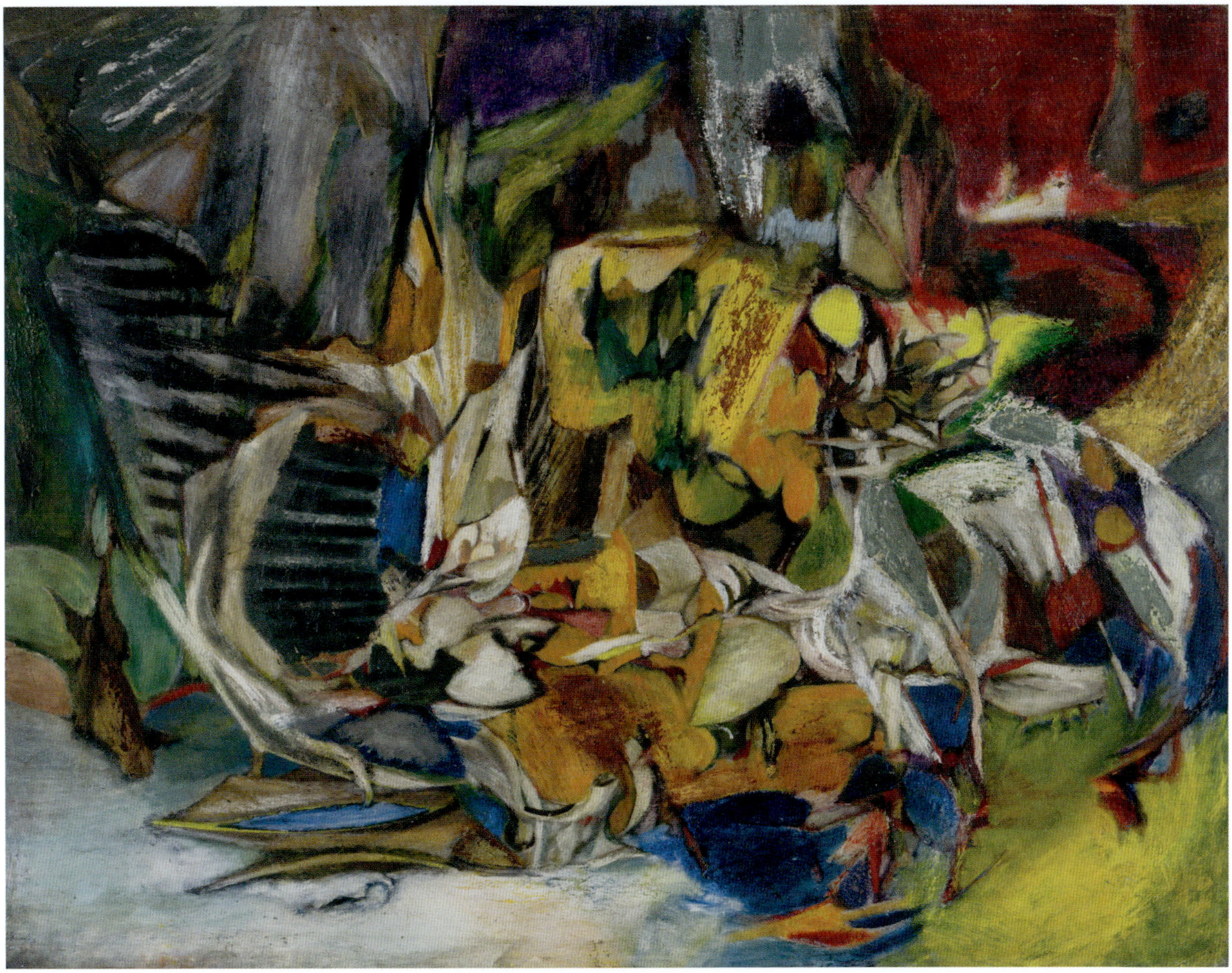

FIGURE 124. **Still Life**, late 1940s, by Sam Feinstein (Samuel L. Feinstein Trust)

Feinstein had become—studying with Hofmann and some of the great Abstract Expressionist artists, he was part of the Hofmann group, and the group was, in turn, a big part of his life. Wenzel also visited Feinstein's studio on the Upper West Side in New York: "It was fun to watch Sam operate; he was a very strong guy."[2]

Wenzel was a painter until the age of eighty-six.

Thorpe Feidt, Class of '59

I studied with Barbara at CHA straight through my senior year. After that, I studied for years privately with Sam. I'm indebted to Barbara and Sam far more than I can say; indeed, I cannot imagine my life without the instruction and sympathetic care they gave me. They taught me not only techniques but also—and most importantly—a creative

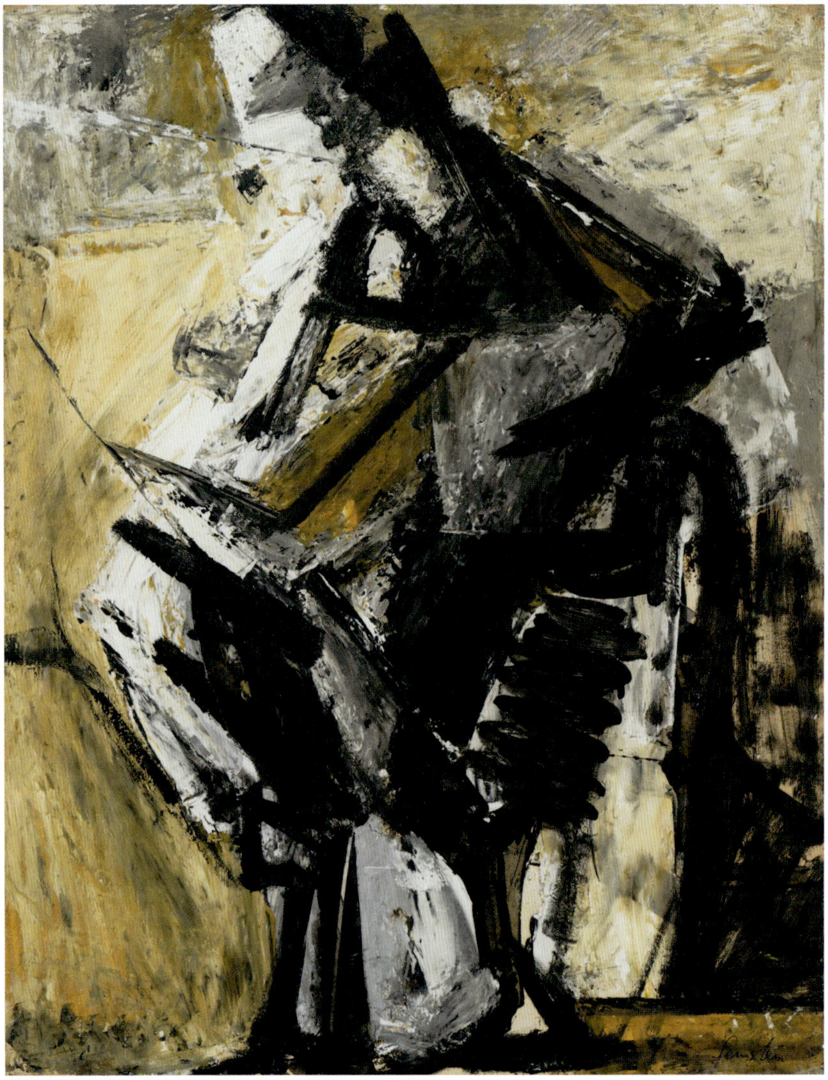

FIGURE 125.
Untitled, 1952,
by Sam Feinstein
(Samuel L.
Feinstein Trust)

attitude, without which nothing of value can be accomplished. Blessings on both Barbara and Sam![3]

Feidt received an MFA from Pratt Institute, in New York. Now retired, he taught at Pratt and at Montserrat College of Art, in Massachusetts.

Theodore Clattenberg, Class of '59

Clattenberg studied with Crawford at CHA from first through twelfth grade, and he remembers her as a nurturing and caring presence. As a young student, he used crayons to make simple forms and abstract cartoons. By the end of high school, he and the other Cellar Rats would escape during free periods or after school to Crawford's art sanctuary, where they talked with her about writing and music. It was a stimulating place to be for the young adults, an "oasis."

While he pursued a career as an attorney, Clattenberg painted with Feinstein each week at the artist's studio on Chancellor Street, seeking an escape from the pressures of the law. Clattenberg jokingly describes the space as a "spiritual gymnasium" where one was free to explore the nonverbal world by organizing forms and shapes on a canvas. Surrounded by a great

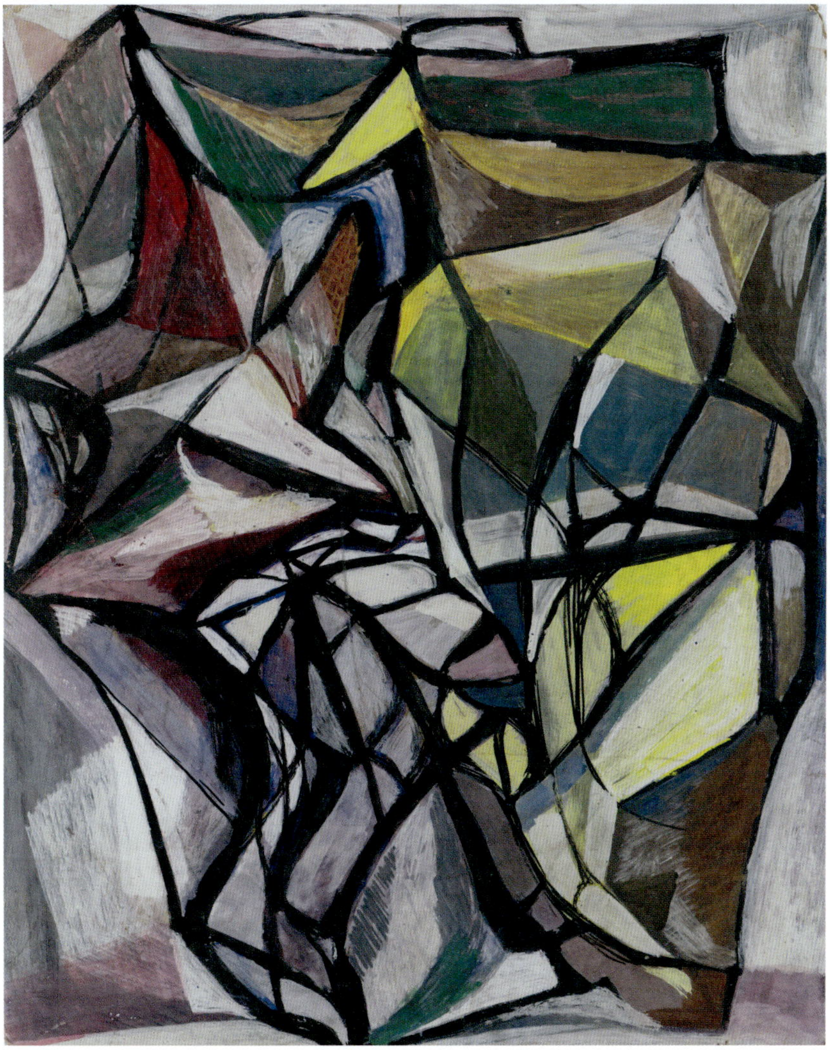

FIGURE 126.
Waterfall,
1949–50, by
Barbara Crawford
(Springside
Chestnut Hill
Academy)

group of students, he was able to connect with them through the making of art. Feinstein would start each class by sharing an article or looking at forms in a photograph. He would then invite his students to start painting by "covering the white." He encouraged them to let everything go, to avoid planning, to get away from conscious thought and reconnect with the spirit inside. Only through this process could one figure out where things should go, make consistent forms, that a triangle on its own did not appear with the curved forms. To Feinstein, color was the building block, the most important thing in a painting. It did not matter if you were painting a still life or an abstract piece, a sunny day or a rainy day: the principles of color use were the same. It was color that had the power to bring luminosity to a painting. Feinstein encouraged students to comment on one another's work, and when they left, he was known to dash the leftover paint on his own canvases, building up his boards.[4]

Clattenberg continued to paint and recently exhibited his work at the 2019 Springside Chestnut Hill Academy Alumni Art Show.

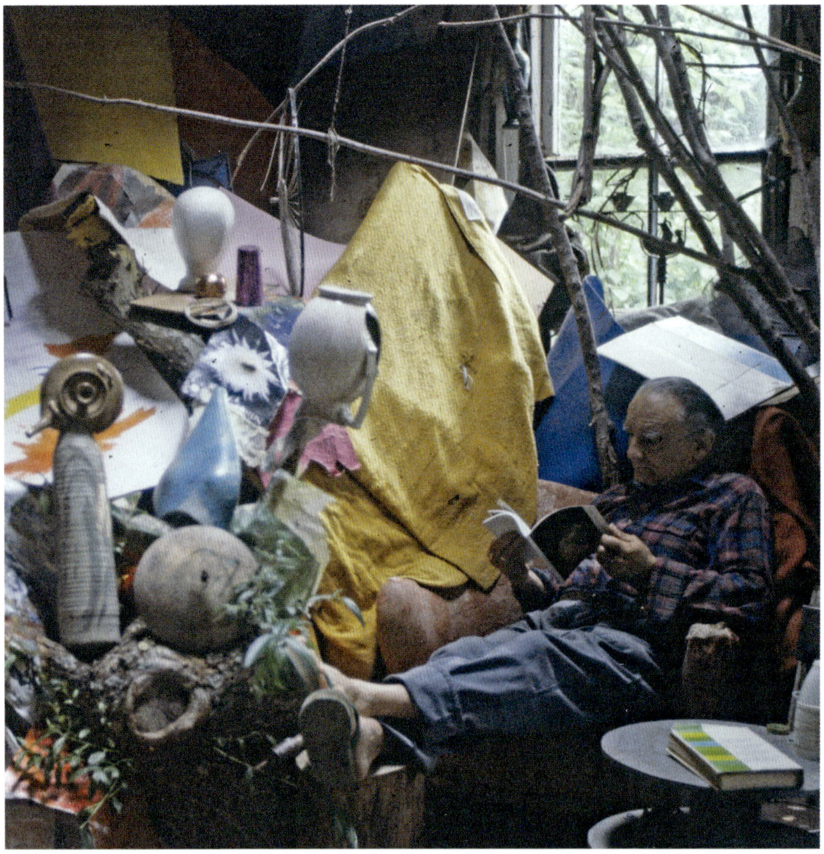

FIGURE 127. Sam Feinstein with still life arrangement at Cape Cod, c. 1995 (Courtesy of Sascha Feinstein)

Bonnie Warwick, Class of '61

When I think of Barbara, I see her first in her house on Chancellor Street, laughing with all of us younger friends, sometimes with her head thrown back and her hand on her throat. I hear her humming along with the jazz she always played—her favorite was "Satin Doll." I hear her extolling Kenneth Patchen's writing or rolling her eyes in mock horror at some escapade we had gotten into.

I got to know Barbara when I was in eleventh grade at Springside and attended the Summer in the Arts program she ran with Hank Putsch in the gym at the former location of Springside School, on Norwood Avenue. I remember sitting in the sun in the doorway, eating sandwiches, talking nonsense, and laughing with her, Thorpe Feidt, Dickie Broadhead, and Herbie Muschamp. Barbara was the best audience a kid could have, always responsive, always encouraging.

When I was sent home from college (for stupid misbehavior), Barbara was instrumental in arranging for me to be an aide to the junior schoolteachers. The next year I went to art school in Boston, but at the end of one year, I returned home, once again at loose ends. It was at this point that Barbara somehow pulled strings to have me hired as her assistant, teaching art to the little kids in the big room adjoining hers in the cellar.

I didn't realize at the time how much I learned about teaching from Barbara; I was just having fun. Barbara believed (as Sam did, and I do) that being creative was as basic a drive as eating, that everyone was or could be an artist. As she saw it, her job was to create a place where kids could enjoy finding out what they wanted to make and how to make it. In her sunny room, which looked out onto the kindergarten playground, she played music, drank tea, and laughed and chatted while everyone

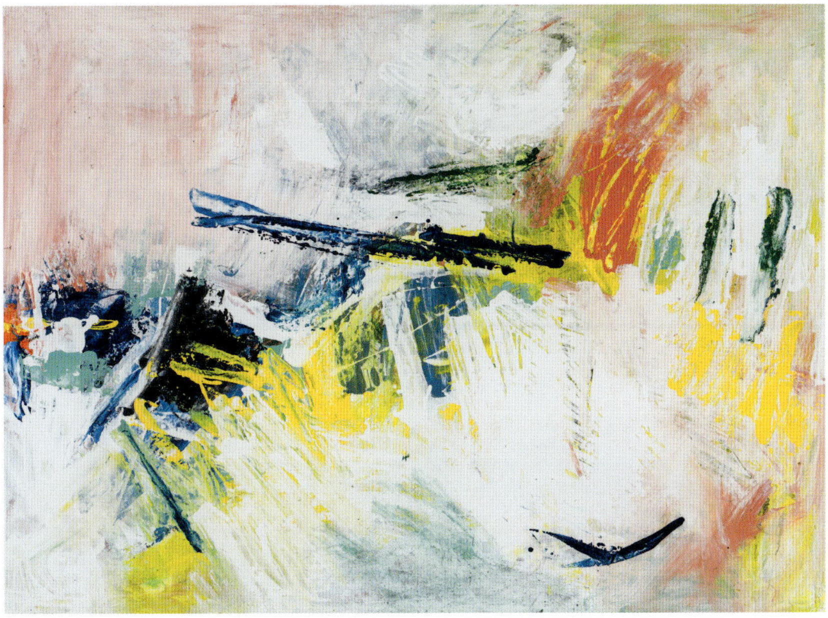

FIGURE 128. **Abstract 2**, 1957, by Barbara Crawford (Springside Chestnut Hill Academy)

worked; she made it all seem easy and pleasant. She had projects, of course, and, when it came up, she talked about the elements of art—color, gesture, volume, and so on—but mainly she was being a great audience, paying attention to each kid's needs and encouraging them. She was hostess to the kids who needed or wanted a safe place to hang out at school; these were the Cellar Rats, and they were proud of it.

I had an apartment on 18th Street, a few blocks from Chancellor Street, and I commuted on the train with Barbara most days. She loved walking across the fields from St. Martins Station. She often cooked suppers not just for me but for a lot of us younger people, one of whom was a great piano player, and we would make up and perform ridiculous operas. Barbara also hosted the monthly meetings of the Jungian Analytical Society of Philadelphia, so I got to hear marvelous discussions on fairy tales and archetypes and such, and I got to meet some of her friends, such as architects Louis Kahn and Anne Tyng and philosopher Lancelot Law Whyte. The most important person she introduced me to was, of course, her ex-husband, Sam, who would become my painting teacher, mentor, and friend. Barbara and Sam gave me the life I have lived ever since, and I am only one of many who count Barbara as a mother I took too much for granted and to whom I am forever grateful.

Much has been written about Sam and what a great painter and teacher he was, but when I think back on my years with him, I think first of his charm. Sam had many flaws, like all human beings, but he was warm and caring about people in general, and he was sensitive to what they needed.

Barbara had me go to one of Sam's classes on Chancellor Street in early 1963. I arrived at the cellar and Sam greeted me, looked me in the eye, smiled, and kissed me on both cheeks. Coming from what was then a WASP ghetto, where, no matter how much they loved you, no one ever touched each other or said "I love you," I was amazed—though of course I didn't let it show.

I started painting in my usual rather tight, timid way. Sam came over, gently took away my brushes, and told me simply to cover as many papers or canvases as I had, with my hands or with a rag. I did,

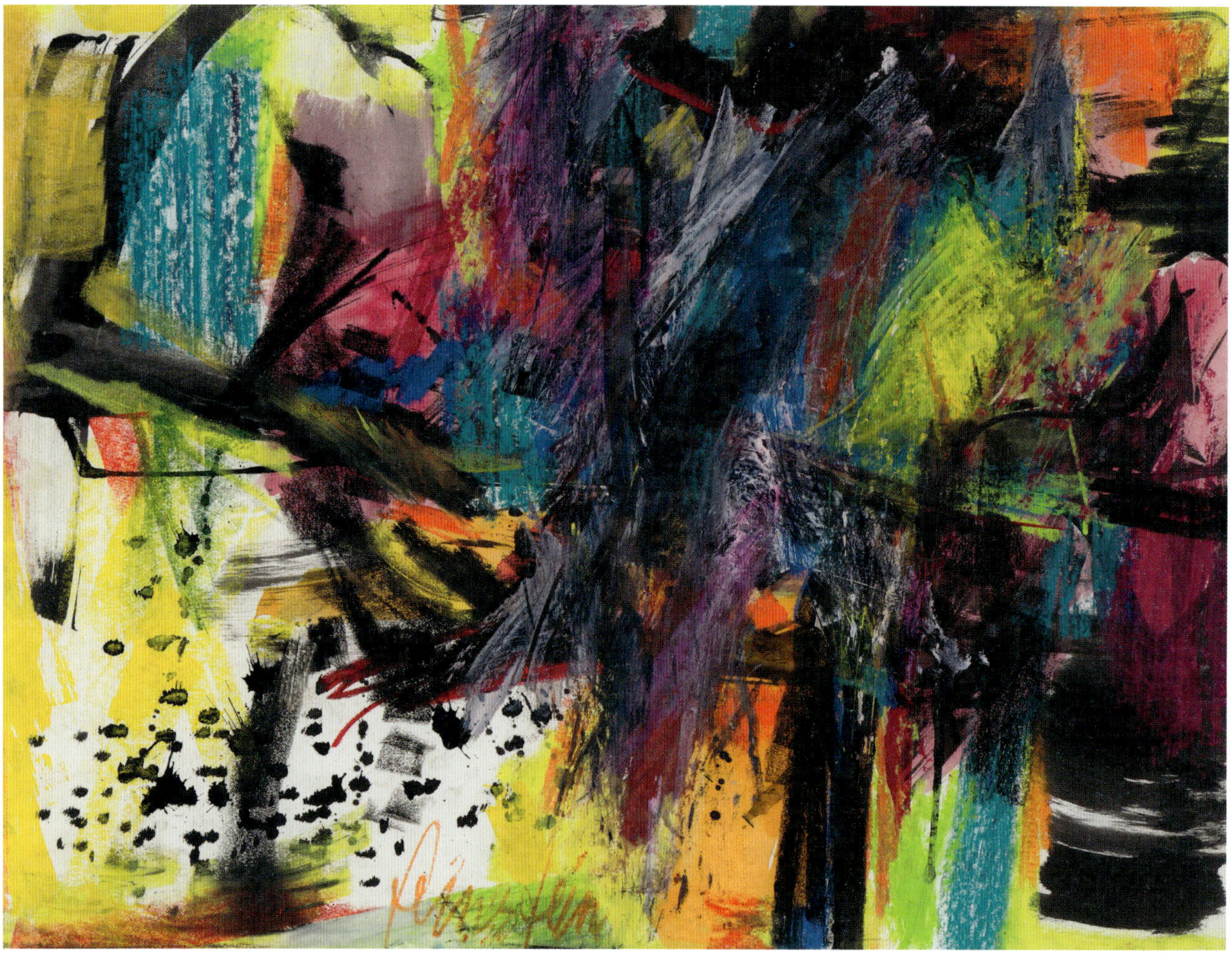

FIGURE 129. **Untitled**, mid-1950s, by Sam Feinstein (Samuel L. Feinstein Trust)

and it felt good. He continued to have me do this for months, encouraging me, chatting and joking with me, but saying very little about my work. Only slowly did he begin to talk to me about what I was actually painting. Eventually he told me I had been so overcharged that it was clear that I needed to just let go and throw the paint around for a while, until I was calm enough to actually make a painting. That was Sam. He saw very quickly what his various students needed, how much and how fast they could be pushed, and what kind of tone would work with them. With some he was very gentle; with others, more teasing or challenging. He was very intuitive—he had good instincts about people as well as about painting.

In Philadelphia and New York, we painted in the cellar; in Dennis, Massachusetts, we painted in a barn as dark and full of junk as the cellars. Sam was king of the pack rats—he saw possibilities in every bit of wood or metal or other piece of trash and felt the need to save it for some great project. It drove his wives crazy, and yet some of the things he made were exquisitely beautiful: for example, the candelabra made from a wrought-iron chair at Chancellor Street, or the stairwell made from tree branches on 90th Street. But the studios were full of junk; you squeezed in wherever you could and looked at whatever still life Sam had created out of torn paper or metal, broken crockery, chipped plaster busts, driftwood, whatever. If you were really looking, you could see the rhythms of color and form without being distracted by what the objects really were.

Before you worked on your own still life, if that was what you wanted to do, you were supposed to do a few wild ones to stretch, relax, and see what was up with yourself—always, the wild ones. While you worked, Sam might read to you from a newspaper or from books (I remember he read the whole of Truman Capote's *In Cold Blood* to the Philadelphia class), or he might talk about painters, or he might just chat and banter. Toward the end of class we would have a line-up. One at a time we would put up our paintings, and he would talk about them, always encouraging the newer and shyer students, always pushing the old-timers. He would talk about in-betweens, colors that linked the various parts of the whole, or about tonality versus hue, effects made from dark and light as opposed to the better effects made from the actual hue of a color. He would talk about how a painting had to present itself as a whole, like a tree does, or a person. It had to breathe; it had to be radiant and alive. Subject did not matter—in fact, it often got in the way, as it would conjure viewers' past associations and therefore cause them to miss what was being presented in the moment.

Sam was priestlike in his seriousness about creation, but those of us who knew him well would give him a hard time just for the fun of it. Line-ups were never without yelps of pain and screams of laughter. We would tease him and imitate him because he allowed it, because he knew how much we loved him.[5]

For Warwick, painting is a way of life, and it keeps her going, taught her that it is the process that matters, not the product. Sometimes in the winter, when it is too cold to leave the kitchen, Warwick switches from painting to making collages, but she always spends her days making something. Especially now, she says, when the news is generally bad or frightening, art saves! It always has, and it always will.

Binney Meigs, Class of '72

Attending CHA from kindergarten through twelfth grade, and studying art with Barbara starting in about the third grade, I slowly realized the significance of her pedagogy. I found myself drawn to the art room because the music was good and the students were allowed to talk as long as they were quiet. Around ninth grade Barbara permitted me to use the school's only potter's wheel, which had been damaged and abandoned. Having studied the basics at a summer craft school, I was asked to teach other students clamoring to "try" the wheel. It was then that she and I began a lasting friendship.

One day Barbara insisted that I get off the wheel and try painting. Initially reluctant, I struggled with my first still life, attempting to somehow duplicate nature's radiance. Though crude, the effort was deemed a success. Before long, an "extra" class developed among other interested students, which Barbara delegated to Steve Rawls, a CHA graduate who swiftly added English literature to his graphic teaching. A universe of possibility began to emerge for me.

Barbara lost no time announcing the fundamentals of her artistic philosophy: The limitless creative capacities of all humanity are never defined by talent alone. Close observation of nature balanced with intuitive release is the key. Realism and abstraction exert their power through the same graphic necessity of spatial dynamism. Perceived lack of ability and self-criticism have to take a back seat and provide no excuse for inaction. She was teaching what she had learned from Sam, who had absorbed it from Hans Hofmann. When the "extra" class was deemed sufficiently seasoned, Barbara announced that it would now be held in Sam's studio, in the carriage house the divorced couple shared off Rittenhouse Square. Her long interest in Jungian studies, symbolism, and dream analysis seamlessly entered the curriculum.

Their studio and living quarters presented an enchanting world of found and homemade furniture, handcrafted light fixtures, and woodwork. The downstairs studio was a wonderland of objects collected on trash days, piled high into disjointed, garish protrusions awaiting still life study by Sam's students. As in Barbara's classes at school, Sam's students were encouraged to abandon themselves to their instincts while simultaneously taking stock of a picture's demands for wholeness of form. Using the still life as nature's example, Sam strove to enlighten his students about the energy-connecting dynamism that artists must embrace—not to copy it but to transcend it in their own graphic voices. Class would end with tea and molasses crisps while students received individual critiques of their work. No student's effort was ever found to be without some forward progress and possibility. All were encouraged to accept their paintings' potential at that time and to build on it during their next effort.[6]

Meigs later continued his study with Feinstein in New York. Today he carves large-scale granite sculptures in the Massachusetts Berkshires, and he exhibited two works in the 2019 Springside Chestnut Hill Academy Alumni Art Show.

Lewis Tanner Moore, Class of '71

Barbara lived a life marked by generosity, informed by empathy, and filled with artistic exploration. It was a life of the mind or, more accurately, the spirit. She provided for me and for many others a gateway to a world where creativity and ideas were the real currency. She was quietly committed to investigating expression through her art and examining the sources of that creative impulse, the mind, and what Carl Jung called the "collective unconscious" and "archetypes." Her commitment was not to the "art world" of galleries, self-promotion, and exhibitions. She was drawn to the process of turning pigment into form. She was a maker, and what she sought was more elusive. On rare occasions, it existed in the space between the artist and the canvas.

By the mid-1960s, when I met her, she was well settled into a routine that allowed her to wear many hats. She was the driving force for the C. G. Jung Center of Philadelphia, creating a space where Jung's ideas and theories could be explored and inviting guest speakers to address the forum. At her home/studio, she hosted weekly painting classes taught by her former husband and fellow artist, Sam. She was painting—exploring color, line, and form—and finding new ways to render her essence on the canvas. She was also writing plays as yet another outlet for her need to express herself. It was a need that was always simmering, about to boil over.

Barbara was the head of the art department at CHA. I first encountered her in the basement classrooms that were her domain. Her role as a teacher was built on her mastery of her craft and enhanced by her knack for supporting those

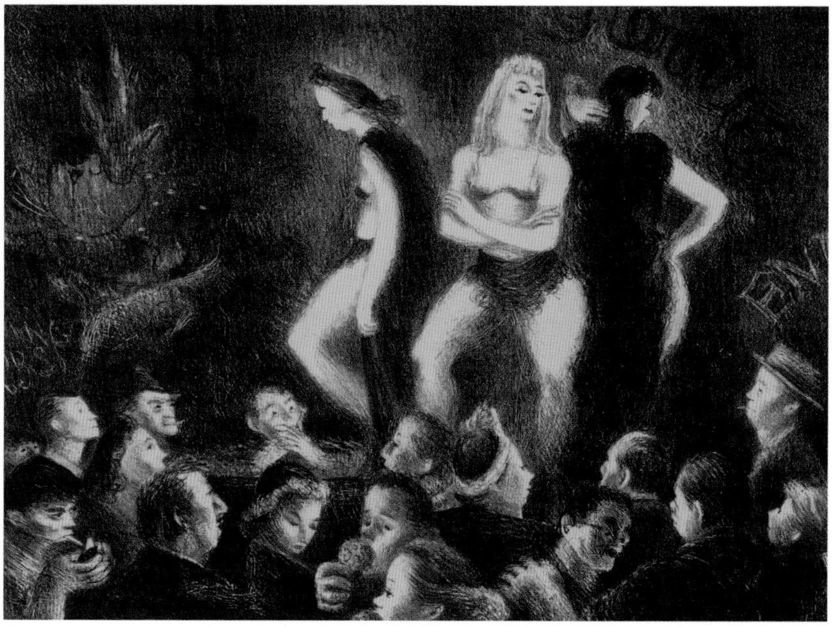

FIGURE 130. **They Amuse Themselves, They Do Not Sing, They Do Not Dance**, 1939, by Barbara Crawford (Courtesy of Lewis Tanner Moore)

students who, in one way or another, did not fit in—a group referred to as the Cellar Rats. She gradually became a protector and a mentor for me during much of my time at CHA, a place where I generally felt like an unwelcome guest. She introduced me to a world of sounds, ideas, and possibilities that continue to enrich my life more than half a century later.

Barbara was a painter, a printmaker, and an illustrator. Over the years, the depth of her talent and the scope and range of her art have revealed themselves slowly. Her work has largely been hidden from view, though I recently learned that as early as 1952, one of her woodcuts was collected by the Philadelphia Museum of Art. The trove she left behind includes a lifetime of compositions that built the foundation for her rich, nuanced late abstractions. The latter pieces have a quiet energy; on her way, she created a body of work that can be considered a primer of twentieth-century art.

The 1939 print *They Amuse Themselves—They Do Not Sing, They Do Not Dance* not only reveals her skill, but also shows us something of her approach to the world. She did not seek the spotlight of the marketplace or critical approval. She painted because, at her core, she was a painter.[7]

NOTES

1 The Springside Chestnut Hill Academy exhibition *Sam Feinstein: The Early Years* includes seven Crawford paintings to show how her style was influenced throughout her life by Feinstein.

2 Phone interview by Stephen Druggan, November 1, 2019.

3 Email to Jennifer McHugh, January 21, 2020.

4 Interview by Pia and Stephen Druggan, January 30, 2020.

5 Email interviews by Pia Druggan, March 2020.

6 Interview by Pia and Stephen Druggan, November 6, 2019.

7 Email to Pia Druggan, August 2020.

More About Group '55

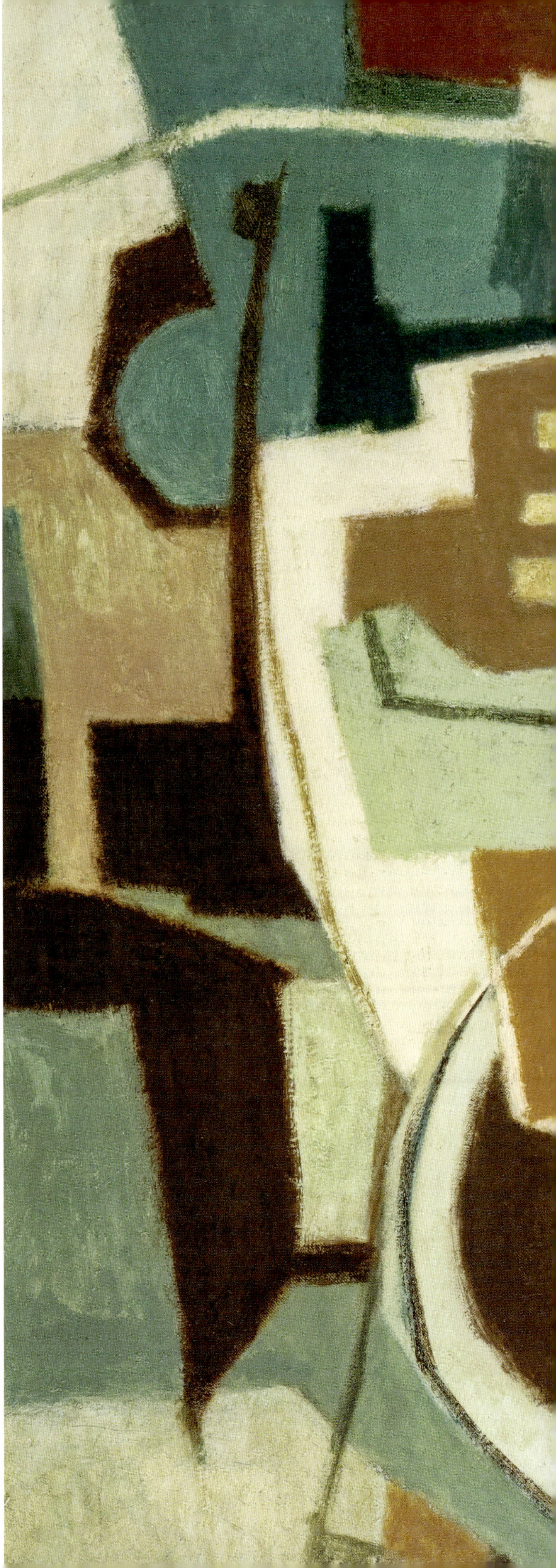

FIGURE 131. Untitled (detail of Fig. 54), 1957–59, by C. Ronald Bechtle (Woodmere Art Museum: Gift of Reid and Dorothy Bechtle, 2020)

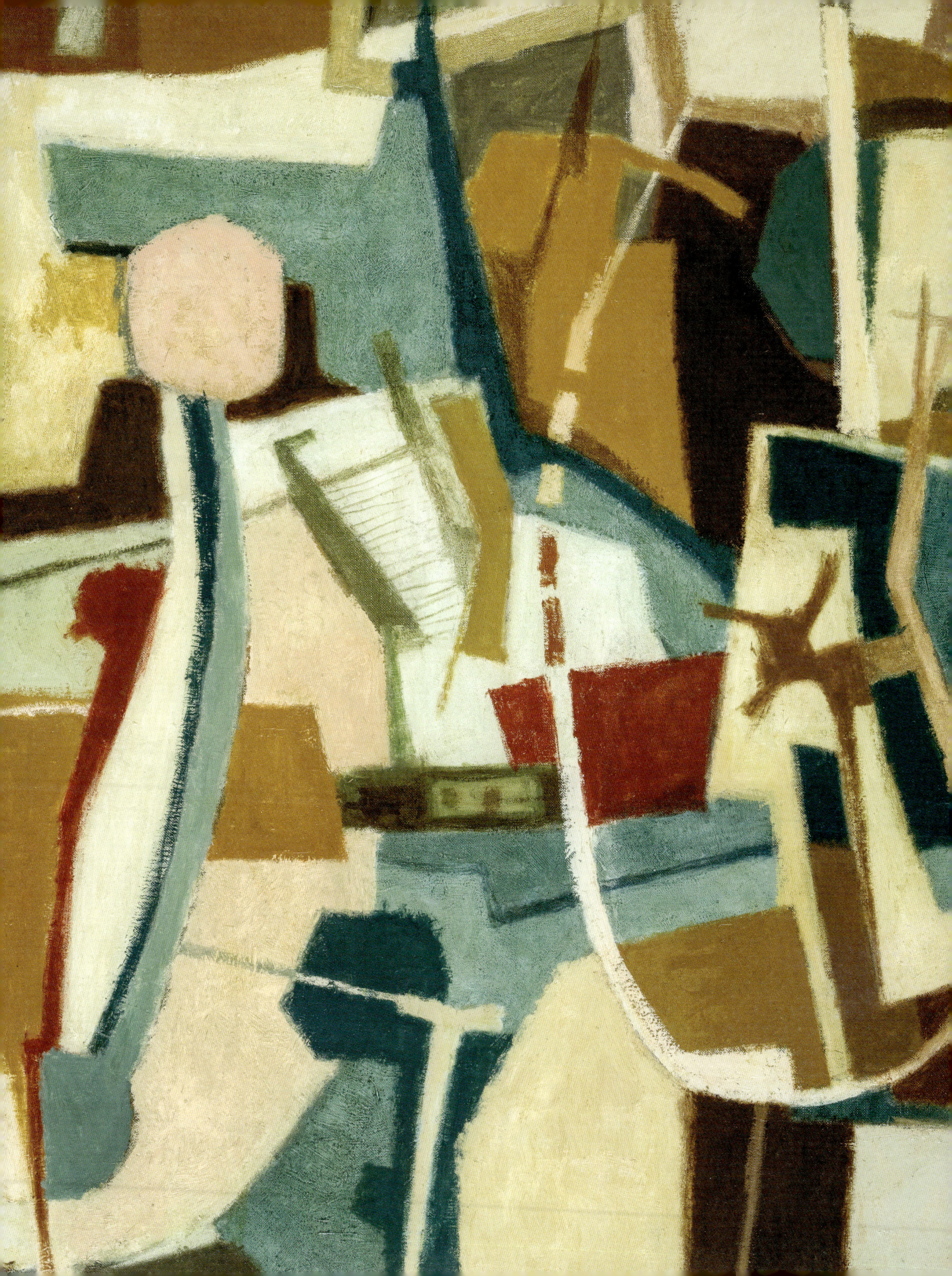

SELECTIONS FROM THE GROUP '55 FORUM TRANSCRIPTS

The following excerpts are taken from the transcript of the forum "Changing Forms in Art," held on January 12, 1956. Paragraphs are excerpted from many different parts of the forum transcripts.

Art and Empathy: "Communication but without the Specific Involved"

LOUIS KAHN: Somehow I feel that art is a matter of expression; it is the active part of our life. If, when we walk, when we talk, when we write, when we draw, it is near the realm of art, not necessarily doing works of art but we are in the realm of art. We are choosing and we are personalizing, we are deriving things, deriving forms of expression; we are struggling with the forms of expression. A work of art, however, is something which emerges out of this field of art into a kind of imagery, a kind of thing which you can describe, a kind of thing you can possibly see, a kind of thing you can feel; it doesn't have to be necessarily tangible. But it has a power of imagery—it has a power, in other words, of memory. You can remember it, you can talk about it, you can redraw it, you can do things with it. A work of art has that wonderful quality.[1]

SAM FEINSTEIN: The artist today, especially the painter, it seems to me, is in a strange position. On the one hand, I think those contemporary painters who are working earnestly today feel that painting has made tremendous strides in the last century. At the same time, they are being accused of having taken many steps backward. The one thing, one of the many accusations against them, is that they are not communicating to people, that their work has become dehumanized, merely decorative. And it is a problem they must face.

[Quoting from Robert Oppenheimer's book *The Open Mind*] "Often the artist has an aching sense of great loneliness, for the community to which he addresses himself is largely not there, the traditions and culture and the symbols and the history. The myths and common experience which is his function to illuminate, to harmonize and to portray, have been dissolved in a changing world."

Now the painter of today faces that problem. He can face it by attempting to be merely an illustrator. He can face it by drawing pictures of the things we already know and, therefore, avoid facing the problem entirely, because there are means today that we have in our civilization which the painters of the past never had. We have movies today, which Rembrandt simply could not conceive of in his spiritual quest. We have television. We have a spread of literature which is simply phenomenal compared to that almost nonexistence of it during the Renaissance.[2]

SAM FEINSTEIN: There are at least two kinds of communication I can think of. One is on a documentary level, in which you describe something, and the other is on an esthetic level, in which you are made to feel something through the relationships existing in a work of art, as something which holds

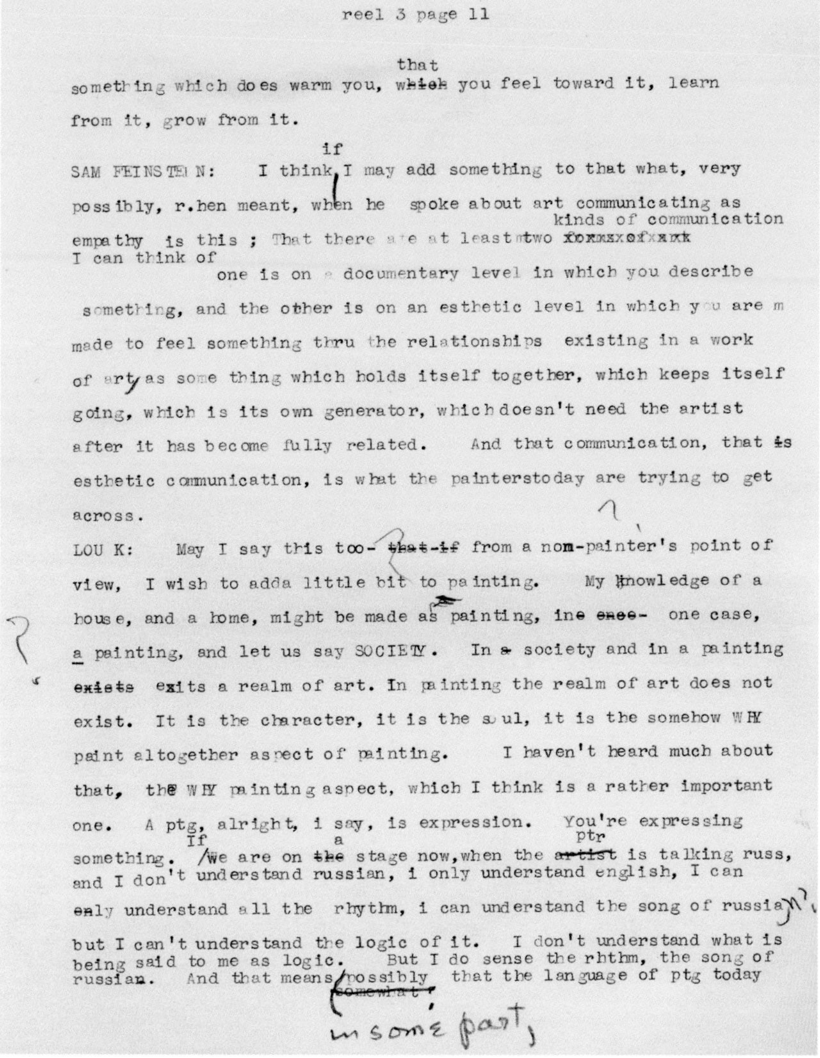

reel 3 page 11

something which does warm you, that ~~which~~ you feel toward it, learn from it, grow from it.

SAM FEINSTEIN: I think, if I may add something to that what, very possibly, r.hen meant, when he spoke about art communicating as empathy is this ; That there are at least two kinds of communication ~~formsxofxart~~ I can think of one is on a documentary level in which you describe something, and the other is on an esthetic level in which you are m made to feel something thru the relationships existing in a work of art, as some thing which holds itself together, which keeps itself going, which is its own generator, which doesn't need the artist after it has become fully related. And that communication, that ~~is~~ esthetic communication, is what the painterstoday are trying to get across.

LOU K: May I say this too- ~~that-if~~ from a non-painter's point of view, I wish to adda little bit to painting. My knowledge of a house, and a home, might be made as painting, ine ~~onee-~~ one case, a painting, and let us say SOCIETY. In a society and in a painting ~~exists~~ exits a realm of art. In painting the realm of art does not exist. It is the character, it is the soul, it is the somehow WHY paint altogether aspect of painting. I haven't heard much about that, the WHY painting aspect, which I think is a rather important one. A ptg, alright, i say, is expression. You're expressing something. If we are on a stage now, when the ~~artist~~ ptr is talking russ, and I don't understand russian, i only understand english, I can ~~only~~ understand all the rhythm, i can understand the song of russian, but I can't understand the logic of it. I don't understand what is being said to me as logic. But I do sense the rhthm, the song of russian. And that means possibly ~~somewhat~~, in some part, that the language of ptg today

FIGURE 132. Excerpt from 1956 transcription of Forum 1 reel-to-reel recording (Samuel L. Feinstein Trust)

itself together, which keeps itself going, which is its own generator, which doesn't need the artist after it has become fully related. And that communication, that an esthetic communication, is what the painters today are trying to get across.[3]

SAM FEINSTEIN: I think we've come across a problem here that faces the audience and that is the difference between the anatomy of the object that one is working from and the anatomy of the canvas that he's working on. The two are radically different. . . .the artist comes to a canvas which is two-dimensional, which in most cases in not shaped like the object or even a collection of given objects. It's flat. It's rectangular. It's white. It's his job not to simply impose upon it those semblances of an object which makes you recognize what the outside of that object looks like. His idea, or in another case her idea, would be to make an object in itself. The canvas is a nature in itself. It is not simply merely an echo of nature—there's no point to it. If you really want a record of something, you'd be silly not to take a photograph of it.[4]

DORIS STAFFEL: As I look around at the paintings, I am aware of the means of painting. I am aware of the canvas, the paint, and I am aware of the processes of painting. In a way, I think there is an

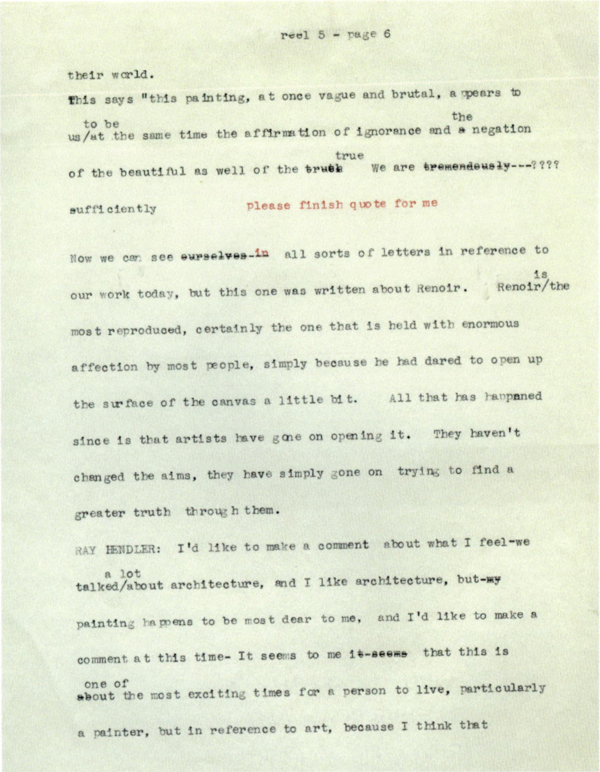

reel 5 - page 6

their world.

This says "this painting, at once vague and brutal, appears to

to be
us/at the same time the affirmation of ignorance and a negation

true
of the beautiful as well of the truth We are tremendously---????

sufficiently please finish quote for me

Now we can see ourselves-in all sorts of letters in reference to

is
our work today, but this one was written about Renoir. Renoir/the

most reproduced, certainly the one that is held with enormous

affection by most people, simply because he had dared to open up

the surface of the canvas a little bit. All that has happened

since is that artists have gone on opening it. They haven't

changed the aims, they have simply gone on trying to find a

greater truth through them.

RAY HENDLER: I'd like to make a comment about what I feel-we

a lot
talked/about architecture, and I like architecture, but-my

painting happens to be most dear to me, and I'd like to make a

comment at this time- It seems to me it-seems that this is

one of
about the most exciting times for a person to live, particularly

a painter, but in reference to art, because I think that

FIGURE 133. Excerpt from 1956 transcription of Forum 1 reel-to-reel recording (Samuel L. Feinstein Trust)

equality of means that seems evident. The paint and the painter have come to terms with each other, and I feel too that the process, the findings, and I say "findings" rather than "searchings," full of the subject, the image, the emotions are there for you to see. Sometimes, I think that painters are very brave people. I think they permitted themselves to identify with internal aspects and external influences, and that in these processes of findings they stand very courageously—what shall we say, they stand, they stand willing to be seen as they are.[5]

I feel that there is a directness, and that is the word I was looking for before, that there is a directness in the painter's findings today. He doesn't erase—he deletes areas, he subtracts, he adds, but all the processes are there for you, the spectator, to find, to see and to feel. I think that there is, shall I say, infinity and affinity that the painter has to deal with. There is paint, canvas, shall we say, [a] thirty-six by thirty-six inch surface plane, and there's an infinity of tragedy, humor, and tranquility. And I think there's not such a thing as the structure and the flesh of a painting. The structure is the flesh of a painting. I think that painting today is more a part of nature than it's ever been because the painter finds patterns within patterns. In a way, almost empathically, he's associated with the movement, the tension, the new concept of space, and the many levels that we're becoming aware of.[6]

They say that many of our senses, because we don't use them, become atrophied. And very often I feel that when we respond to paintings, it isn't a sense, but the ability to identify with the reality of the painting—with the movement, the struggle, the changes, the patterns within patterns, is so poor that we are used to seeing paintings that look like, oh, impressionist paintings, cubist paintings, or we can go further back to maybe even the brown sauce period, so that we have no final records and we don't trust ourselves when we come to look at the paintings today. Have you ever watched anyone who is approaching a very low doorway and without being aware of it, they pull their whole body down, they duck because they know that their stature is more than the doorway will permit? Their height is more than the height of the doorway. Well, very often I feel that people cannot react nervously, muscularly, associatively, however you want to put it, to paintings in this way. And that the painter, in the process of painting, works this way, or very many of us do. It's very important.[7]

SAM FREID: When you don't completely understand a work of art, it is a good thing, if the artist is around, to ask him about it. And, of course, that is the function of a forum like this. And I have a habit of asking painters, [whether] I enjoy their work or don't, "What motivated your painting?"

One day, liking Sam Feinstein's painting over there, I asked him casually what motivated it. He hesitated, of course, and then said that up at Gloucester, during the summer, the waves and the rocks, and the seemingly irresistible waves and rocks and the waves washing over them constantly changing the forms of the rocks. Now there isn't anything in Sam's painting that indicates there are rocks or waves there. And the time is night, according to Sam. He gives you that in his color.

Now there have been seascapes painted in the past. You all are acquainted with Courbet's work. He did a lot of them, rocks and water, and all that kind of thing. But this has a new dimension to it. It makes me think of a couple of lines in James Joyce's *Finnegans Wake*. In talking about the river drifting as it flows through Dublin, he says this: "Night, night, tell me tale of stem or stone—by the rivering waters of—hithering, thithering waters of—Night." Now he takes these two words, "hither" and "thither," and he evokes the feeling in the person that reads of a water in motion. And without any water being visible in this picture, you do have a picture of those forms by the way they plunge around. It's that kind of thing that also makes me think of the great French poet Rimbaud when he spoke of a poetry that would have perfumes, sounds, and colors. These are the dimensions in which painters and poets deal today. They are seemingly intangible things, but that is what the poet-painter has in mind a great deal of the time.[8]

RAYMOND HENDLER: I personally feel, and I back this with fact, I believe, from art history, that painting no longer needs to communicate. That's a pretty tough statement, a pretty dogmatic statement. However, a little further explanation on it might make you get back into my camp if I just chased you out. And that is that communication in the accepted sense of the way it's used by most people means that you're going to tell something about something. You're going to tell a story; you're going to preach, or you're going to teach, or something like that, and I believe very firmly that a painting no longer has to do that for the very reasons that Sam mentioned, that today there are other means, or other medium or media that do this better, or at least as good, and today we have the opportunity of doing it more creatively, more directly, than any of our painting medium would today.

I do believe, however, and this is a big "however," I do believe that painting has to have empathy. . . . communication, but without the specific involved—a very fine but important difference. And painting today, I believe, in its very radical change from art history, no longer communicates but has empathy.[9]

My work, as far as I'm concerned, never has a specific meaning. Never. It may have for an individual a specific meaning, and as long as they realize that the painting is not that, it's valid as far as I'm concerned, but at one time it may mean one thing to one person, and to the same person mean another thing, and to me this is valid.[10]

It seems to me that this is one of the most exciting times for a person to live, particularly a painter, but in reference to art, because I think that we're

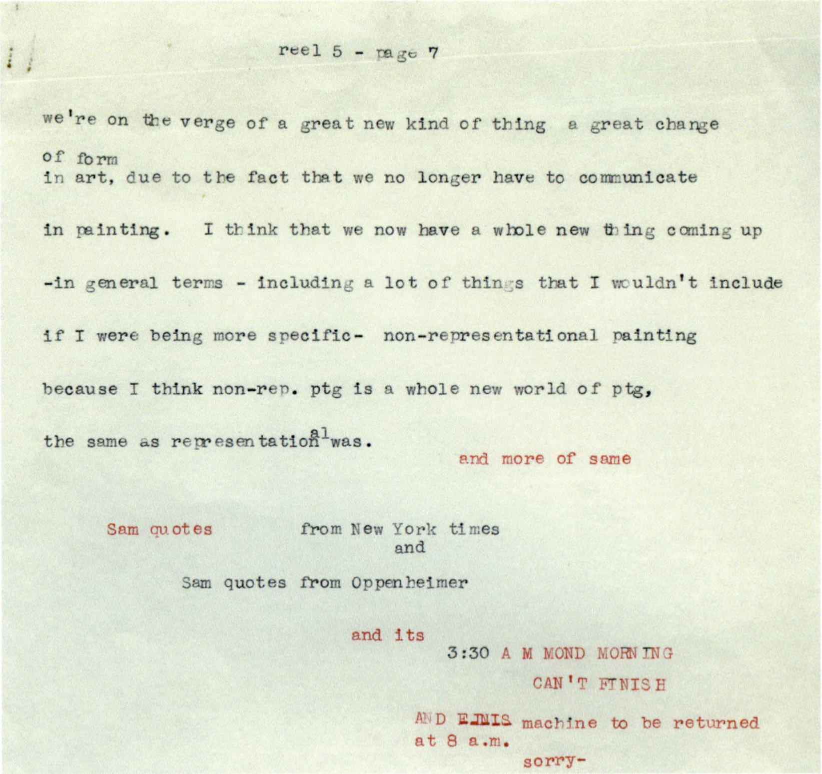

reel 5 - page 7

we're on the verge of a great new kind of thing a great change of form
in art, due to the fact that we no longer have to communicate
in painting. I think that we now have a whole new thing coming up
-in general terms - including a lot of things that I wouldn't include
if I were being more specific- non-representational painting
because I think non-rep. ptg is a whole new world of ptg,
the same as representational was.

and more of same

Sam quotes from New York times
and
Sam quotes from Oppenheimer

and its
3:30 A M MOND MORNING
CAN'T FINISH

AND FINIS machine to be returned
at 8 a.m.
sorry-

FIGURE 134. Excerpt from 1956 transcription of Forum 1 reel-to-reel recording (Samuel L. Feinstein Trust)

on the verge of a great new kind of thing, a great change of form in art due to the fact that we no longer have to communicate in painting. . . . I think nonrepresentational painting is a whole new world of painting, the same as representational was.[11]

Space: "The Look of the World Is Really Changing"

LOUIS KAHN: Space is something you either visualize or walk into. The clearer space is space you can see the beginning and end of—it's never a space which is divided—you don't sense it because by dividing a space you've got to see how it's made—therefore, you don't sense that space anymore. If you had a dome-like space and put a partition in the middle of it, you don't have the same space—you can't divide space. Therefore, one must speak in terms of order as the order of spaces, spaces which are doing one thing and spaces which are doing another. You might say that there are servant spaces and there are actual spaces—spaces you come to; let us say a living room is a space that needs closets, toilets. Stairways and all kinds of things. These are the servants of the living room space. Should you try to clutter—force—those things into the space, spaces are lost by it. Architecture essentially is a matter of designing spaces.[12]

SAM FEINSTEIN: Lou, it seems to me that our analogy between painting today and architecture today, in relation to a statement you made where you said that space in architecture is not divided—it isn't just an area—that's one of the prime considerations of a contemporary painter. If he has given up the outside forms of things, he is concerned very much with space as an active, vital factor in terms of making the pictorial transformation as a parallel to what his experience has been in nature—whether he begins by working directly from nature or whether he works as a result of an accumulation of memory images is not really the important thing. The important thing to him is that the space is not simply dead areas, is not simply that which surrounds a form which you can easily recognize—[it is] that the space, and you use the words "servant of spaces," every space in a canvas, all the spaces are servants of each other.[13]

DORIS STAFFEL: I keep thinking about what Lou said in regard to space, and I think it's terribly important, because he speaks so eloquently for architectural space, and I think we might talk just a little more about the painter's space.

The absolute, confined, encircled object is very seldom found in paintings today. The painter, just as other creative individuals in our time, [has] taken the skin away so that we know what's under the skin. For some of us this table is silver and so many feet by so many feet, but for the scientist I wonder if he doesn't see the table as a collection of neutrons or a collection of electrons which form certain patterns, and the type of pattern determines, I suppose you might say, the recalcitrant surface that we all know so well. In other words, the thing that is touchable, that resists you.

Well the painter is very sensitive whether he knows it or he doesn't, whether he can verbalize about it or not, to his environment. And he is very aware of the fact that we have many more points of view than we had before. We travel faster than we've ever traveled. We have the microscope; we have the telescope and many other instruments that we've never had before so that the look of the world is really changing. You might also say that our reality is changing. And the reality of the painter is the flat canvas and his paint.

Now how does space come into it? Just as soon as the paint touches the surface of the canvas, it activates the surface. And there is a relationship, and this is a very important word, between this area of paint and the rest of the white canvas. Now for me, and I speak very personally, at this point "space" means the area which the painter chooses to include in his canvas, its route, its tensions, its movement, interval to interval, if you will, from facet to facet, very seldom from volume to volume. And it's the sense of tension going from the flat surface, and sometimes where a painting's very thick, it comes out of the surface. This is a new dimension for painters, and a very important one. But it's the movement through the canvas, the way the eye and the muscles and the nerves are moved by color, by pattern, by directional line, or however you word it—this traveling through the space that the painting itself creates, that to me is the space of painting.[14]

"The moderator for the first forum, "Changing Forms in Art," was Sam Feinstein, president of Group '55. The panelists included architect Louis Kahn, composer George Rochberg, and painters Raymond Hendler, Sam Freid, and Doris Staffel. Feinstein arranged to have the discussions audio-taped on a reel-to-reel recorder. Five reels were transcribed shortly thereafter using a typewriter, probably by Barbara Crawford, for a total of 82 pages. Fragments of audiotape from other forums were found and transcribed at a later date. The selections presented here were compiled by Patricia Stark Feinstein.

NOTES

1 Reel 1 transcript, 20–21, Samuel L. Feinstein Trust Archive (SLFTA).
2 Reel 2 transcript, 8–9, SLFTA.
3 Reel 3 transcript, 11, SLFTA.
4 Reel 3 transcript, 8, SLFTA
5 Reel 2 transcript, 16, SLFTA.
6 Reel 2 transcript, 17–18, SLFTA.
7 Reel 4 transcript, 9, SLFTA.
8 Reel 3 transcript, 13, SLFTA.
9 Reel 2 transcript, 20–21, SLFTA.
10 Reel 3 transcript, 17, SLFTA.
11 Reel 5 transcript, 6–7, SLFTA.
12 Reel 1 transcript, 17–18, SLFTA.
13 Reel 4 transcript, 12–13, SLFTA.
14 Reel 5 transcript, 1–3, SLFTA.

SELECTED CHRONOLOGY

Exhibition dates and titles are provided when known; this information was not always included in the *Art in Focus* publication. Exhibitions were usually on view for about one month. Names of Group '55 and Philadelphia Abstract Artists exhibitors are given when known from publicity or reviews. Gallery addresses are given for the first exhibition at that venue or when there was a change of location. Only significant membership meetings are included. Events with extant recordings and/or transcripts are indicated with an asterisk. All events and exhibitions took place in Philadelphia unless otherwise noted.

1949

October

Exhibition: *Abstract Watercolors, Ruth Wollman [Zion]*, Dubin Galleries, 312 South 16th Street.

November

Exhibition: *Bernice Anderson Oils*, Philadelphia Art Alliance, 251 South 18th Street.

December

Exhibition: *Husband and Wife Duo* (oils, gouaches, and drawings by Sam Freid; crayon and gouache sketches, metal and wood jewelry by Hilda Berger Freid), Dubin Galleries.

1950

September 30–October 22

Exhibition: *Oils by Clayton Whitehill*, Dubin Galleries, now located at 2046 Locust Street.

November

Exhibition: *Gouaches by Samuel L. Feinstein*, Chestnut Hill Academy, 500 West Willow Street.

1951

Closes October 14

Exhibition: *Paintings by Ray Hendler*, Dubin Galleries.

December

Exhibition: *Watercolors by Samuel Freid, Oils by Doris Staffel*, Dubin Galleries.

1952

February 16

Program: "Today's Trends in the Arts," Ellen Donovan Gallery, 1716 Rittenhouse Square.

Panelists: Sam Feinstein, a professor of American civilization, an interior designer, and an architect.

Opens October 25

Exhibition: Group show, Hendler Galleries, 1429 Spruce Street.

Exhibitors: Willem de Kooning, Sam Francis, Sanford Greenberg, Robert Keyser, Franz Kline, George McNeil, Jackson Pollock, and Jean-Paul Riopelle.

December

Exhibition: *Creative Parallels*, Dubin Galleries.

Exhibitors: Barbara Crawford, Feinstein, Leonard Nelson, Melville Price, Doris Staffel, Rudolf Staffel, Whitehill, and Zion.

1953

February 1

Article: Feinstein publishes his first reviews in *Art Digest*; listed as Philadelphia correspondent as of March (and a contributing editor as of October 15, 1954).

November 4–28

Exhibition: Group show, Hendler Galleries.

Exhibitors: Feinstein, Philip Guston, Hendler, Shirley Jaffe, Kline, McNeil, Price, Riopelle, and Jack Tworkov.

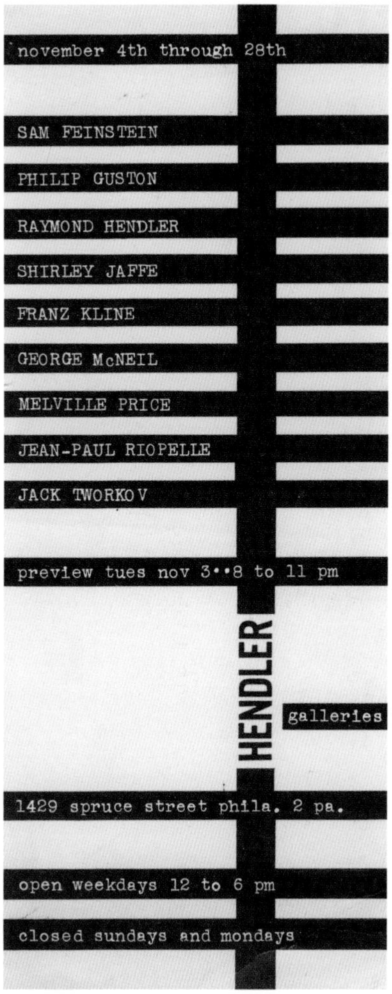

FIGURE 135. Invitation to group show, Hendler Galleries, November 4–28, 1953 (Samuel L. Feinstein Trust)

1954

January

Exhibition: *Paintings by Raymond Hendler*, Hendler Galleries.

March

Exhibition: *Paintings by Jane Piper*, Dubin Galleries.

Exhibition: *Paintings, Drawings by Sam Freid; Jewelry, Wire Sculpture by Hilda Freid*, Beryl Lush Gallery, 2007 Walnut Street.

December

Exhibition: *Paintings, Prints by Itzhak Sankowsky*, Beryl Lush Gallery.

1955

January 5–22

Exhibition: *Paintings by Barbara Crawford and Drawings by Sam Feinstein*, Dubin Galleries.

Closes January 20

Exhibition: *Frances Lachman and Leroy Smith*, Beryl Lush Gallery.

February 15

Article: Feinstein, "The State of Criticism," *Art Digest*. C. Ronald Bechtle and Margaret Milliken write letters of support, published the next month.

May 20

Meeting: First meeting of abstract artists invited to discuss "aims, activities, and a name for the group," Dubin Galleries.

July 1

Article: Last review by Feinstein in *Art Digest*.

August 3

Incorporation of Dubin-Lush Galleries, 2016 Locust Street.

September 30

Meeting: Decision to name selves "Group '55." Election of officers: Feinstein, president; Sam Freid, vice president; and Quita Brodhead, secretary.

Closes November 7

Exhibition: *Paintings Sanford Greenberg*, Dubin-Lush Galleries.

November 18

Meeting: Decision to hold meetings once a month, on third Fridays.

December 16

Meeting: Decision to hold exhibitions and forums at Dubin-Lush Galleries. Planning for exhibition, store windows, and first forum.

1956

January 4–23

Exhibition: *Group '55*, Dubin-Lush Galleries.

Exhibitors: Allman, Bernice Anderson, Brodhead, Crawford, Patricia Evans Mangione, Feinstein, Dorothy Felbin, Eugene Feldman, Freid, Jack Gerber, Esther Gould, Greenberg, Abraham P. Hankins, Hendler, Francis Jennings, Lachman, Jack Mayerson, Milliken, Piper, Sankowsky, Doris Staffel, Mitchel G. Wagman, Dorcas Weidner, Whitehill, and Zion.

January 12

Forum: "Changing Forms in Art," Dubin-Lush Galleries. Moderator: Feinstein.

Panelists: Freid, Hendler, architect Louis Kahn, composer George Rochberg, and Staffel. Two hundred people are turned away.*

March 16

Forum: "The Artist's Vision and the Public's Views," Lecture Hall, Free Library of Philadelphia, 1901 Vine Street. Moderator: Staffel.

Panelists: Feinstein, pediatrician Dr. Joseph Lachman, and art historian Robert M. Walker. Paintings by Crawford, Feinstein, Hendler, Jennings, Piper, Sankowsky, and Wagman on view. One hundred people attend, despite blizzard.*

March 20–April 19

Exhibition: *C. Ronald Bechtle Oil Paintings*, Red Door Gallery, 7944 Thouron Avenue (first solo show).

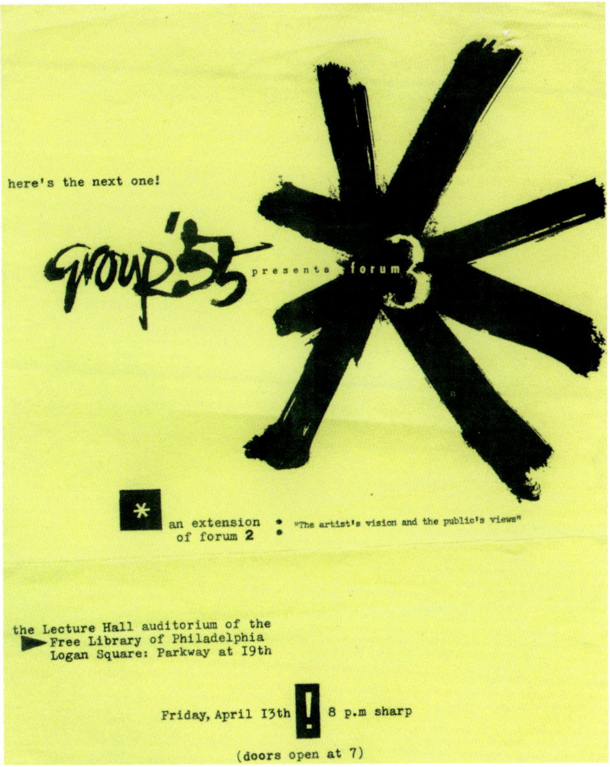

FIGURE 136. Poster for third Group '55 forum, April 13, 1956 (Samuel L. Feinstein Trust)

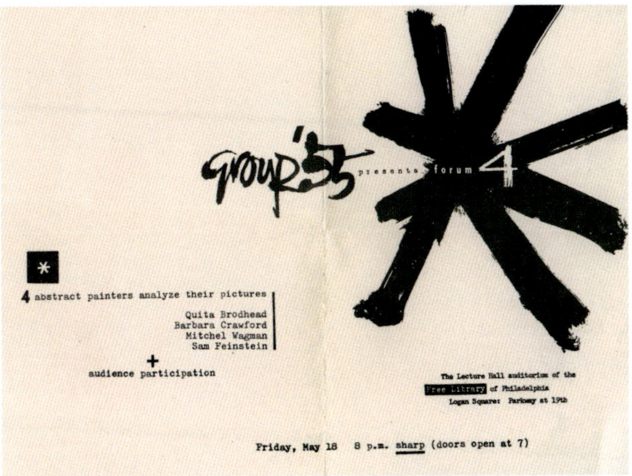

FIGURE 137. Poster for fourth Group '55 forum, May 18, 1956 (Samuel L. Feinstein Trust)

Closes April 2

Exhibition: *Clarence Laughlin Photographs*, Dubin-Lush Galleries.

Closes April 3

Exhibition: *Ruth Wollman [Zion] Paintings*, Dubin-Lush Galleries.

April 13

Forum: "The Artist's Vision and the Public's Views," Free Library of Philadelphia.

Panelists: Same as previous forum.

April 21

Meeting: Critique of forum. Discussion of relationship with the Little Symphony of Philadelphia. Decision to hold meetings twice a month.

May 6

Radio forum: "Modern Art—Is It Art?," Station WFIL studio, 46th and Market Streets. Moderator: Attorney Stanley P. Stern.

Panelists: Feinstein and Kurt Loeb of Carriage House Studios, Germantown.

May 18

Forum: "Four Abstract Painters Analyze Their Pictures," Free Library of Philadelphia.

Panelists: Brodhead, Crawford, Feinstein, and Wagman. Audience participation.

May 25

Meeting: Election of officers and new board of governors for the second year: Feinstein, president; Freid, vice president; and Frances Lachman, secretary.

September 26–October 16

Exhibition: *Paintings by Mitchel G. Wagman*, Dubin Galleries (first solo show).

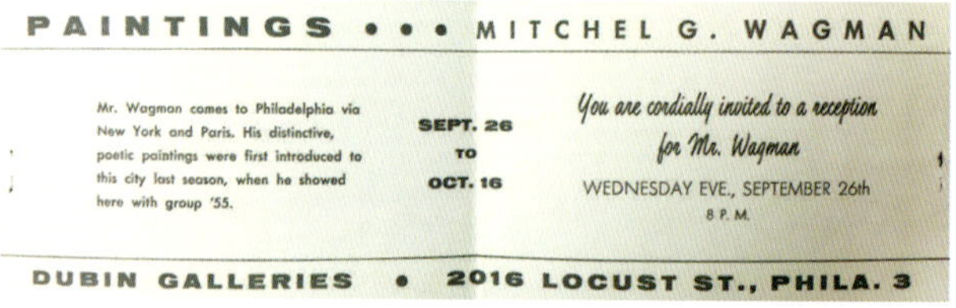

FIGURE 138. Invitation for *Paintings by Mitchel G. Wagman* (Estate of Mitchel G. Wagman)

September 28

Meeting: Recommendations for new rules by board of governors. Discussion of who is considered "professional." Majority vote to continue forums.

October 19

Meeting: Meeting announcement postcard states that memberships of those who do not attend without written notice are considered terminated. This includes three board members. Discussion of how to readmit members.

November

Exhibition: *In the Abstract*, Dubin-Lush Galleries.

Exhibitors: Jennings, Mayerson, and possibly others.

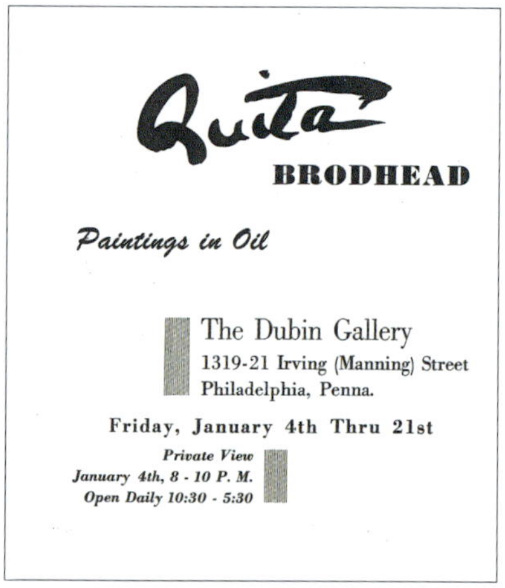

FIGURE 139. Invitation for *Paintings by Quita Brodhead* , January 4–21, 1957 (Estate of Quita Brodhead)

November 30

Program: "What Do Abstract Forms Communicate?," Free Library of Philadelphia.

Panelists: Bechtle (slide talk), Feinstein, Freid, and Wagman.

December

Exhibition: *Work by Leonard Nelson*, Dubin Galleries.

December 14

Meeting: Discussion of the hanging of the upcoming Wallingford Community Arts Center show. Approval of Dubin Galleries in new location, 1319–21 Irving Street, as the home for Group '55.

1957

January 4–21

Exhibition: *Paintings by Quita Brodhead*, Dubin Gallery, 1319–21 Irving Street.

Exhibition: *Work by Members of Group '55*, Gallery '55, 1319–21 Irving Street.

Exhibitors: Anderson, Crawford, Feinstein, Laura Goodman, Lachman, Mayerson, and Milliken.

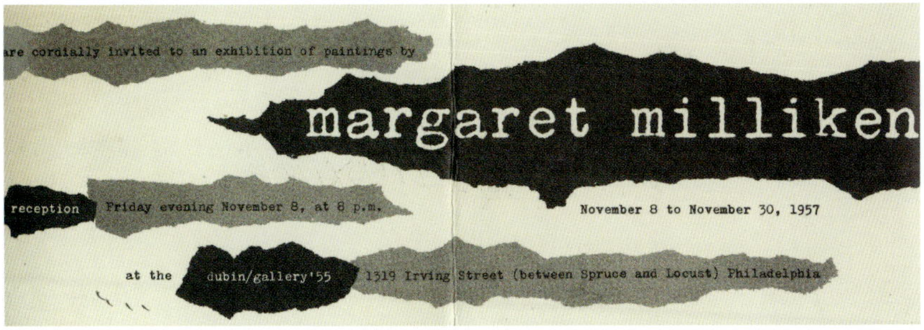

FIGURE 140. Invitation for Paintings by Margaret Milliken, November 8–30, 1957 (Samuel L. Feinstein Trust)

Opens January 6

Exhibition: *Group '55 Exhibition*, Community Arts Center, 414 Plush Mill Road, Wallingford, Pennsylvania. Opening reception with illustrated talk, "Abstract Painting," by Feinstein.

Exhibitors: Anderson, Bechtle, Michael Ciliberti, Crawford, Feinstein, Felbin, Feldman, Freid, Goodman, Greenberg, Lachman, Mayerson, Milliken, and Wagman.

January 18

Meeting: Feinstein resigns as president. Bechtle elected as new president.

February 1

Letter: Bechtle, Ciliberti, Freid, Greenberg, and Wagman resign from Group '55.

February 2

Letter: Bechtle, Ciliberti, Freid, Greenberg, and Wagman invite Group '55 members to join a new group.

Closes February 12

Exhibition: *Peter Paone*, Dubin/Gallery '55, 1319–21 Irving Street.

February 15

Meeting: Artists invited to form a new group meet at the Print Club and submit preferences for goals and activities. Bechtle takes role as director.

Attendees: Bechtle, Brodhead, Ciliberti, Freid, Greenberg, Hankins, Jennings, Staffel, Wagman, and Whitehill.

Opens February 15

Exhibition: *Abstract Expressionist-Impressionist Paintings by Artists Showing in New York Galleries*, Dubin/Gallery '55. Opening reception with discussion and analysis by Feinstein.

Exhibitors: Janice Biala, Ernest Briggs, James Brooks, Nicolas Carone, Herman Cherry, Robert De Niro Sr., Richard Diebenkorn, Edward Dugmore, Michael Goldberg, Hans Hofmann, Kline, McNeil, Joan Mitchell, Al Newbill, Stephen Pace, Milton Resnick, Syd Solomon, and Joseph Stefanelli. Lenders: Kootz, Stable, and Poindexter Galleries.

Exhibition: *Work by Members of Group '55*, Gallery '55.

Exhibitors: Feinstein, Lachman, Milliken, and others.

March 24

Program: Harp and horn recital by Marcella DeCray and Leonard Hale, Dubin/Gallery '55.

Discussion: Music director Joseph Castaldo and Feinstein compare related problems in contemporary music and painting. Audience participation.*

April

Exhibition: *New Work by Members of Group '55*, Dubin/Gallery '55.

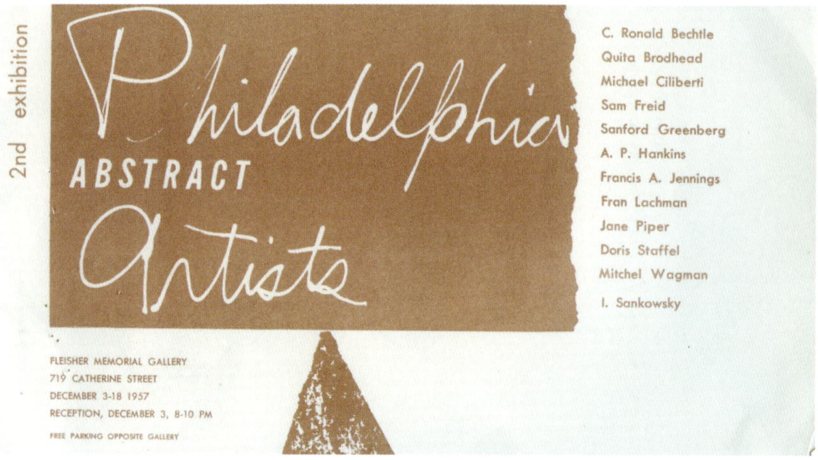

FIGURE 141. Announcement for *Philadelphia Abstract Artists Second Exhibition*, December 3–18, 1957 (Estate of Mitchel G. Wagman)

May 22

Program: Contemporary music for the piano by Natalie Hinderas, Dubin/Gallery '55.

Discussion: Castaldo and Feinstein consider "the new artist-audience relationship in America." Audience participation.

October 4–31

Exhibition: *Philadelphia Abstract Artists First Exhibition*, Carlen Galleries, 323 South 16th Street.

Exhibitors (all former members of Group '55): Bechtle, Brodhead, Ciliberti, Freid, Greenberg, Hankins, Jennings, Lachman, Piper, Staffel, and Wagman.

Opens October 5

Exhibition: *Group '55,* Dubin/Gallery '55.

November 8–30

Exhibition: *Paintings by Margaret Milliken*, Dubin/Gallery '55.

December

Exhibition: *Abstractionists: Group '55*, Dubin/Gallery '55.

December 3–18

Exhibition: *Philadelphia Abstract Artists Second Exhibition*, Samuel S. Fleisher Art Memorial, 715–19 Catharine Street.

Exhibitors (all former members of Group '55): Bechtle, Brodhead, Ciliberti, Freid, Greenberg, Hankins, Jennings, Lachman, Piper, Sankowsky, Staffel, and Wagman.

1958

February 7–28

Exhibition: *Oil Paintings and Mixed Media by Samuel Feinstein*, Dubin/Gallery '55.

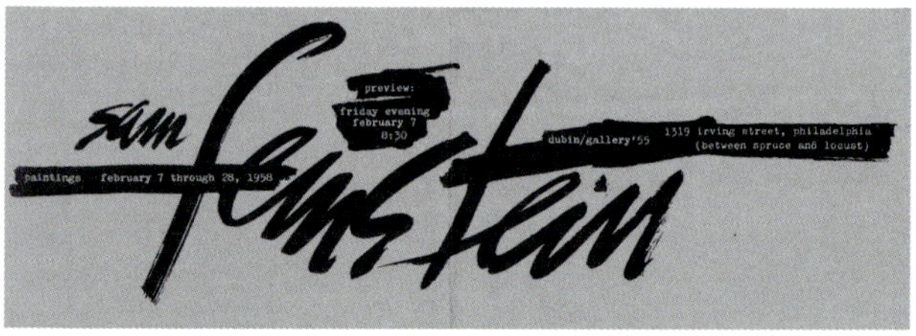

FIGURE 142. "Invitation for Feinstein solo exhibition (Samuel L Feinstein Trust)

February 14

Forum: "Contemporary Creative Problems," Dubin/Gallery '55.

Panelists: Feinstein, Kahn, composer Vincent Persichetti, and dancer Malvena Fried Taiz.

March 7–28

Exhibition: *Paintings of Bernice Anderson*, Dubin/Gallery '55.

March 14

Forum: "Dramatic Aspects of Dance," Dubin/Gallery '55.

Performance by Taiz and Company.

March 29–April 15

Exhibition: *Arthur B. Carles*, Dubin/Gallery '55.

April 11

Forum: "The New Dimensions of Man," Dubin/Gallery '55.

Panelists: Physicist Leonard Eisenbud, Jungian analyst David Hart, minister Jean P. Jordan, and astronomer Peter van de Kamp.

Closes May 7

Exhibition: *Paintings by Constance Contry and Robert Kristler Allen*, Dubin/Gallery '55.

May 9

Forum: "Expressive Uses of Space," Dubin/Gallery '55.

Panelists: Castaldo, Feinstein, Kahn, and Taiz.

June

Exhibition: *Group Show*, Dubin/Gallery '55. (Last known Group '55 show.)

October 1–18

Exhibition: *Paintings by the Philadelphia Abstract Artists*, Parma Gallery, 1111 Lexington Avenue, New York.

Exhibitors (all former members of Group '55): Bechtle, Brodhead, Ciliberti, Greenberg, Lachman, Piper, Sankowsky, Staffel, and Wagman.

November 3

Group '55 officers Anderson, Feinstein, and Milliken approve payment to Castaldo from group account; last evidence of Group '55 activity.

1959

March 15–April 30

Exhibition: *Philadelphia Abstract Artists*, T'ien Hsia Gallery, 1319 Irving Street (location of former Dubin/Gallery '55).

Exhibitors: Bechtle, Ciliberti, Lachman, Harold Mesibov, and possibly others.

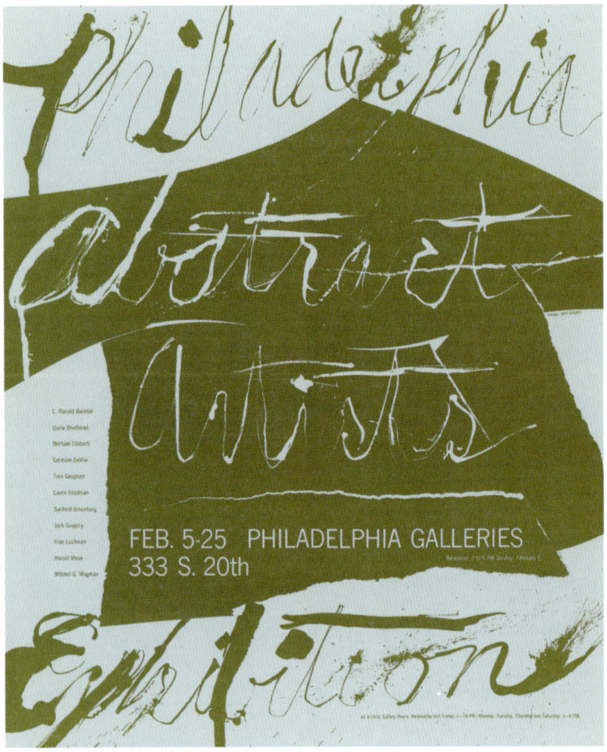

FIGURE 143. Announcement for *Philadelphia Abstract Artists*, February 5–25, 1961 (Charles Ronald Bechtle Jr. Papers, 1951–1998, Archives of American Art, Smithsonian Institution)

1960

February 23–March 11

Exhibition: *Exhibition by the Philadelphia Abstract Artists*, Samuel S. Fleisher Art Memorial.

Exhibitors: Bechtle, Ciliberti, Freid, Greenberg, Hankins, Lachman, Mesibov, and Wagman, with additional members Adolph Dioda, Thomas Gaughan, Jack Gregory, Mildred Hurwitz, Samuel Maitin, Nelson, and Walter Redding.

1961

February 5–25

Exhibition: *Philadelphia Abstract Artists*, Philadelphia Galleries, 333 South 20th Street.

Exhibitors: Bechtle, Brodhead, Ciliberti, Carmine De Vivi, Gaughan, Goodman, Greenberg, Gregory, Lachman, Mesibov, and Wagman.

March 4

Bechtle invites a group of Philadelphia Abstract Artists to Gaughan's home to discuss the formation of another new group.

1962

January 17–February 14

Exhibition: *Abstract Artists of Philadelphia,* Penn Center Galleries, 1725 Chestnut Street. (Last official Philadelphia Abstract Artists show).

Exhibitors: Bechtle, Ciliberti, Freid, Gaughan, Greenberg, Hankins, and Lachman.

Closes February 10

Exhibition: Group show of New York and Philadelphia artists, Philadelphia Galleries.

Exhibitors: Bechtle, De Vivi, Gaughan, Greenberg, Hankins, and Lachman, as well as A. Migliore, Milliken, Rose Naftulin, Nelson, Newbill, A. Plowhoski, Howard Weinstone, and P. Zhurow.

March 22

Forum: "Creative Achievement in the Arts and Its Relationship to Contemporary Man," Bryn Mawr Art Center, Bryn Mawr. Organized by Freid and others. First of six forums on the topic, ending June 14. Castaldo and Taiz were participants.

1963

April

Exhibition: *Paintings by Mitchel Wagman*, Philadelphia Gallery, now located at 1911 Walnut Street.

1965

Opens December 7

Exhibition: *Tradition in Evolution: Abstract Expressionist Paintings*, Princeton Art Association, McCarter Theatre Center, 91 University Place, Princeton, New Jersey. Organized by Feinstein, then teaching privately in Princeton.

1967

April 11–May 1

Exhibition: *Eight Artists*, Samuel S. Fleisher Art Memorial.

Exhibitors (including five former members of Philadelphia Abstract Artists): Bechtle, Freid, Gaughan, Greenberg, and Lachman, as well as Thomas Chimes, Al Hirshman, and Henry W. Peacock.

1968

March 5–26

Exhibition: *An Exhibition of Painting and Sculpture*, Samuel S. Fleisher Art Memorial.

Exhibitors (all former members of Philadelphia Abstract Artists): Dioda, Freid, Gaughan, Greenberg, and Lachman.

1969

February 4–27

Exhibition: *8 Artists*, Samuel S. Fleisher Art Memorial.

Exhibitors (including six former members of Group '55 and one former member of Philadelphia Abstract Artists): Bechtle, Ciliberti, Freid, Gaughan, Greenberg, Hankins, and Lachman, plus Hirshman.

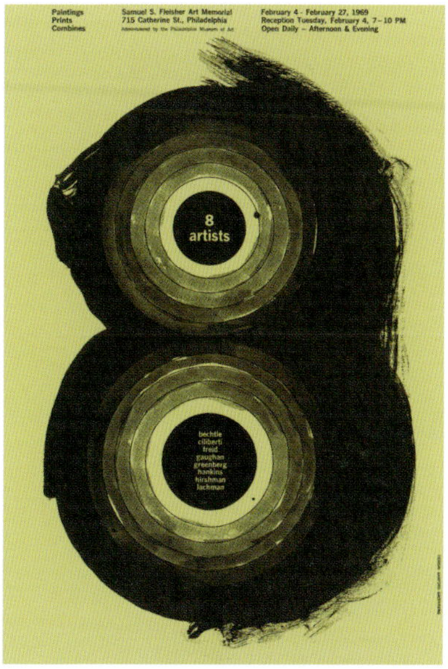

FIGURE 144. Announcement for *8 Artists*, February 4–27, 1969 (Charles Ronald Bechtle Jr. Papers, 1951–1998, Archives of American Art, Smithsonian Institution)

Group '55 and Philadelphia Abstract Artists

This list includes only exhibitions for which artists are known, which is not the case for many Group '55 group shows.

ARTIST	KNOWN PARTICIPATION
Margo Allman (born 1933)	First Group '55 exhibition
Bernice Anderson (1914–2002)	Secretary, three group exhibitions, and one solo exhibition with Group '55
C. Ronald Bechtle (1924–2014)	One exhibition and one forum with Group '55; director and seven exhibitions with Philadelphia Abstract Artists (PAA)
Quita Brodhead (1901–2002)	Secretary, one group exhibition, one solo exhibition, and one forum with Group '55; four PAA exhibitions
Michael Ciliberti (1925–2020)	One Group '55 exhibition; seven PAA exhibitions
Barbara Crawford (1914–2003)	Three exhibitions and one forum with Group '55
Carmine De Vivi (1929–2017)	Two PAA exhibitions
Adolph Dioda (1915–1991)	One PAA exhibition
Henry (Hank) P. Dubin (1903–1987)	Gallery owner and member of Group '55
Sam Feinstein (1915–2003)	President, six exhibitions, and all forums and programs with Group '55
Dorothy Felbin (dates unknown)	Two Group '55 exhibitions
Eugene Feldman (1921–1975)	Two Group '55 exhibitions
Sam Freid (1908–1983)	Vice president and, two exhibitions with Group '55; four PAA exhibitions
Thomas Gaughan (1925–2007)	Three PAA exhibitions
Jack Gerber (born 1927)	First Group '55 exhibition
Laura Goodman (1910–2004)	Two Group '55 exhibitions; one PAA exhibition
Esther Gould (born 1928)	First Group '55 exhibition
Sanford Greenberg (1926–2011)	Two Group '55 exhibitions; seven PAA exhibitions

ARTIST	KNOWN PARTICIPATION
Paul A. Greenwood (1921–1985)	First Group '55 exhibition
Jack Gregory (1930–2014)	Two PAA exhibitions
Abraham P. Hankins (1903–1963)	First Group '55 exhibition; seven PAA exhibitions
Jean Harris (dates unknown)	Group '55 member, no known exhibitions
Raymond Hendler (1923–1998)	First exhibition and one forum with Group '55
Mildred Hurwitz (1922–2012)	One Group '55 exhibition; one PAA exhibition
Francis Jennings (dates unknown)	Two Group '55 exhibitions; two PAA exhibitions
Frances Lachman (1913–1994)	Secretary and four exhibitions with Group '55; seven PAA exhibitions
Samuel Maitin (1928–2004)	One PAA exhibition
Patricia Evans Mangione (1915–2002)	First Group '55 exhibition
Jack Mayerson (1908–1985)	Three Group '55 exhibitions
Harold Mesibov (1928–2012)	One Group '55 exhibition; three PAA exhibitions
Margaret Milliken (1913–1968)	Treasurer and five exhibitions with Group '55
Leonard Nelson (1912–1993)	One solo exhibition at Dubin Gallery; one PAA exhibition
Jane Piper (1916–1991)	Two Group '55 exhibitions; three PAA exhibitions
Walter Redding (1902–1972)	One PAA exhibition
Itzhak Sankowsky (1908–1994)	First Group '55 exhibition; two PAA exhibitions
Doris Staffel (1921–2013)	First exhibition and two forums with Group '55; two PAA exhibitions
Mitchel G. Wagman (1923–2002)	Two group exhibitions and one solo exhibition with Group '55; all seven PAA exhibitions
Dorcas Weidner (1910–2000)	First Group '55 exhibition
Clayton Whitehill (1898–1963)	First Group '55 exhibition
Ruth Zion (1923–2010)	First group exhibition and one solo exhibition with Group '55

ARTIST BIOGRAPHIES

MARGO ALLMAN
American, born 1933

Painter and printmaker Margo Allman was a member of Group '55 in its first year.

Allman was attending Smith College, Northampton, Massachusetts, when she encountered a book on Joan Miró that inspired her to pursue a career in the arts. She went on to study at Philadelphia's Moore College of Art and Design with Leonard Nelson, who encouraged her to enroll at the Hans Hofmann School of Fine Arts, Provincetown, Massachusetts, in the summer of 1953. It was there that she met Sam Feinstein, with whom she studied after the summer was over. Newly married and living in Newark, Delaware, Allman commuted by train to Feinstein's classes and to participate in Group '55 meetings and events.

Allman's work has been shown in numerous solo and group exhibitions in the United States and abroad, including, most recently, in a two-person retrospective (with Helen Mason) at the Delaware Art Museum, Wilmington. In 2019, the Delaware Contemporary and the Delaware College of Art and Design, also in Wilmington, collaborated to create the Allman Gallery Fellowship supporting the professional development of future museum curators. Allman's work is in the collections of the Delaware Art Museum, Philadelphia Museum of Art, and West Chester University, Pennsylvania.

EDNA ANDRADE
American, 1917–2008

Abstract artist Edna Andrade occasionally exhibited with members of Group '55 and the Philadelphia Abstract Artists, though she was not a member of either group. Andrade studied at the Barnes Foundation, the University of Pennsylvania, and the Pennsylvania Academy of the Fine Arts (PAFA), all in Philadelphia. Her early watercolor collages and ink drawings of abstracted landscapes evolved into abstract geometric paintings in the 1950s, influenced by the Bauhaus and works of European modernism she had encountered as a student through travel scholarships. She taught at the University of the Arts, Philadelphia, for more than twenty years.

Andrade had more than twenty solo exhibitions, and her work is held in the collections of numerous museums and galleries, including the Addison Gallery of American Art, Andover, Massachusetts; Dallas Museum of Art; Museum of Fine Arts, Houston; PAFA; Philadelphia Museum of Art; Virginia Museum of Fine Arts, Richmond; Woodmere Art Museum; and Yale University Art Gallery, New Haven.

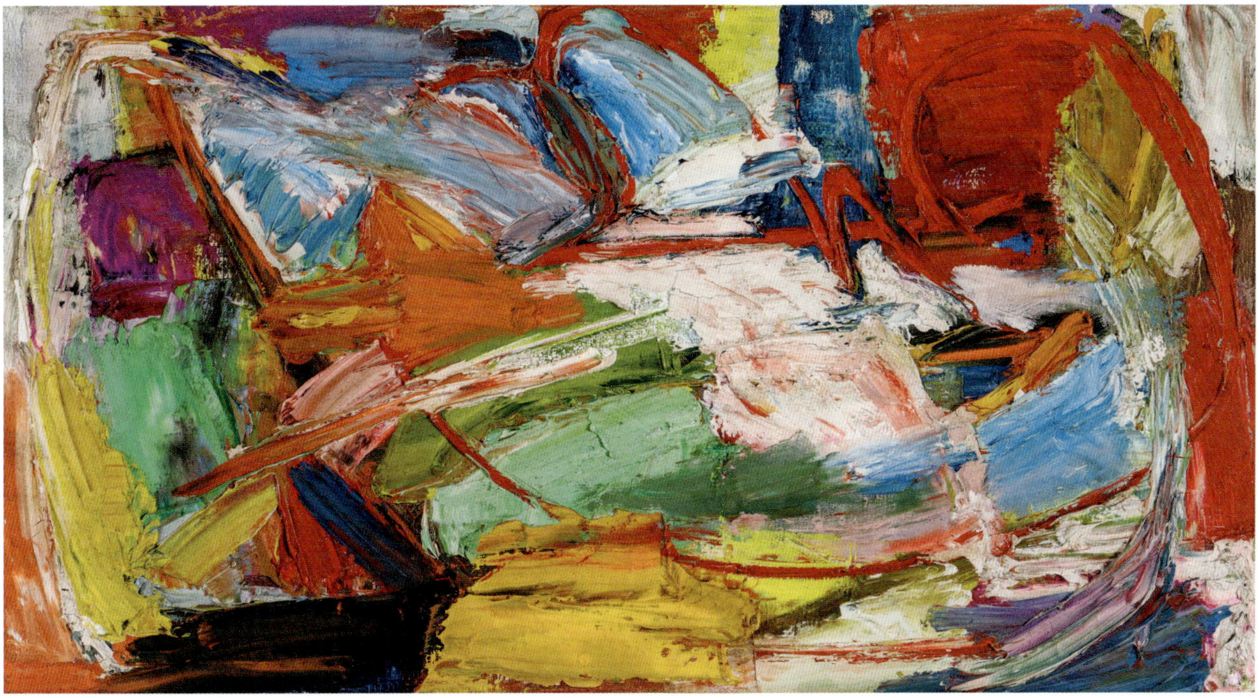

FIGURE 145. **Untitled**, c. 1955–56, by Jack Mayerson (Woodmere Art Museum: Gift of Patricia Stark Feinstein, 2020)

C. RONALD BECHTLE

American, 1924–2014

C. Ronald Bechtle joined Group '55 in 1956, participating in one exhibition and one forum. Disagreements with some members motivated him to organize the Philadelphia Abstract Artists, which focused on internal discussions and exhibiting. He was director of the group from 1957 to 1962 and participated in all its exhibitions.

After serving in the Army, Bechtle studied painting briefly at Eastern Tennessee University, Johnson City, and then in Philadelphia at Temple University's Stella Elkins Tyler School of Fine Arts (now the Tyler School of Art and Architecture), the Samuel S. Fleisher Art Memorial, and the Philadelphia Museum of School of Industrial Art (now the University of the Arts), as well as with Benton Spruance. Though he worked as an industrial engineer, cost estimator, and design consultant for the Philco Corporation, he devoted hours every day to art, moving from dark, figurative early paintings to abstract compositions around 1950. His first solo show was in 1956 at Red Door Gallery, Philadelphia; Dorothy Grafly described his work as "precisely organized." In the 1960s he began focusing on watercolor, exploring materials and chance effects. He was also constantly sketching.

Bechtle's work is in the collections of a number of universities and museums, among them the Akron Art Museum; Amherst College, Massachusetts; Bowdoin College, Brunswick, Maine; Brandeis University, Waltham, Massachusetts; Butler Institute of American Art, Youngstown, Ohio; Denver Art Museum; Santa Barbara Museum of Art, California; and Smithsonian American Art Museum, Washington, DC. ; and Woodmere Art Museum

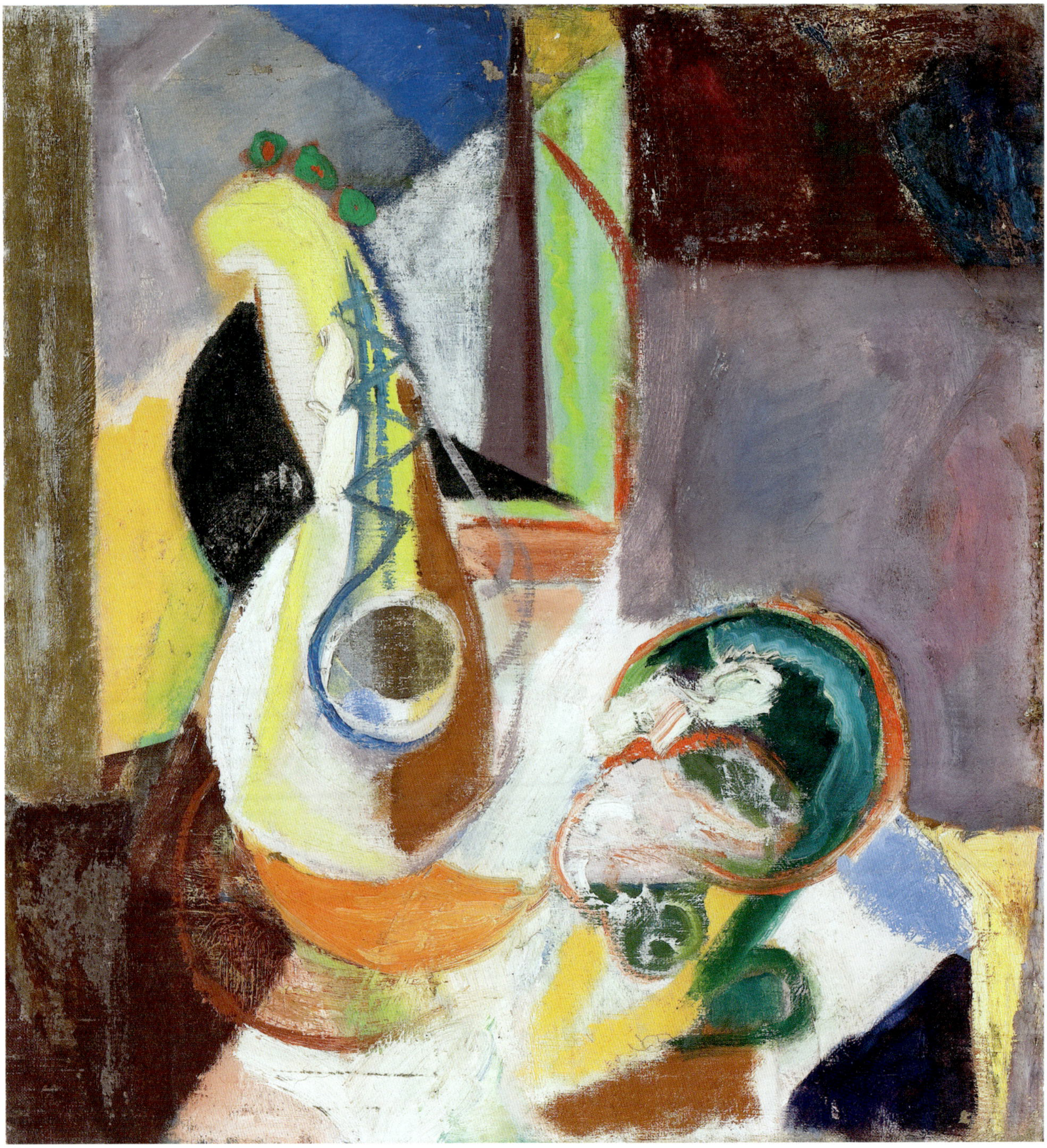

FIGURE 146. **Still Life with Mandolin**, c. 1940–42, by Quita Brodhead (Woodmere Art Museum: Gift of Bill Scott, 2011)
Photograph by Rick Echelmeyer

BENJAMIN BRITT
American, 1923–1996

Although not a member of Group '55 or Philadelphia Abstract Artists, Benjamin Britt exhibited his work in Philadelphia for almost fifty years. He first studied commercial art, then attended the Philadelphia Museum School of Industrial Art (now the University of the Arts) and the Art Students League in New York. He explored Cubism and abstraction in the 1950s, then later moved into Surrealism. He painted a wide variety of subjects, including African themes, landscapes, and portraits. Britt taught at the Wharton Center, the YMCA, and St. John's Family Center. His work is in the collection of Woodmere Art Museum.

QUITA BRODHEAD
American, 1901–2002

Quita Brodhead was a founding and active member of Group '55, serving as secretary the first year, speaking on one panel, and having one solo exhibition. She later showed in all the Philadelphia Abstract Artists exhibitions except those held in the years when she was living in Europe.

Nicknamed Quita by her father, Marie Waggaman Berl was born in Wilmington, Delaware. She attended the Pennsylvania Academy of the Fine Arts (PAFA), Philadelphia, where she was in Arthur B. Carles's sketch class. She also studied in Paris and took private lessons with Carles. After her marriage to Truxtun Brodhead, in 1927, she relocated to Wayne, Pennsylvania. She had her first solo exhibition in 1934, and she began having well-reviewed solo shows in New York galleries starting in 1938. She won a gold medal from PAFA in 1943. By 1950 she was working abstractly, using color as her primary element. She continued exploring and evolving new forms in her paintings and actively exhibiting for the next fifty years. The 2001 exhibition at Hollis Taggart Galleries, New York, celebrating her hundredth birthday was her thirty-fifth solo show.

Brodhead's paintings are in the collections of more than twenty museums, including the Delaware Art Museum, Wilmington; Munson-Williams-Proctor Arts Institute, Utica, New York; Museo Municipal de Bellas Artes, Santa Cruz de Tenerife, Spain; New Jersey State Museum, Trenton; PAFA; Philadelphia Museum of Art; State Museum of Pennsylvania, Harrisburg; and Woodmere Art Museum.

ARTHUR B. CARLES
American, 1882–1952

The paintings of Arthur B. Carles were admired by Group '55 and Philadelphia Abstract Artists members, several of whom had been his students.

Carles was born in Philadelphia and studied at the Pennsylvania Academy of the Fine Arts (PAFA), where he learned to admire French Impressionism and Post-Impressionism from his teachers William Merritt Chase, Cecilia Beaux, Hugh Henry Breckenridge, and Henry McCarter. Living in Paris, he was drawn to the work of Paul Cézanne and Henri Matisse and connected with other American modernists. Carles's paintings were exhibited at Alfred Stieglitz's 291 Gallery and in the seminal 1913 Armory Show. In 1920 and 1921, he helped organized exhibitions at PAFA to bring European and American modernists to Philadelphia. In 1923 Carles and McCarter persuaded Albert C. Barnes to exhibit his recently acquired paintings at PAFA, which horrified critics and the public. He taught at PAFA from 1917 to 1925. Beloved by many students, Carles continued to teach privately until 1942, influencing artists including Quita Brodhead and Jane Piper. His late work was prophetic of Abstract Expressionism and was admired by many artists including Sam Feinstein and Hans Hofmann.

Carles's work is in the collections of numerous museums across the country, including, the Hirshhorn Museum and Sculpture Garden, Washington, DC; the Museum of Modern Art, New York; PAFA; Philadelphia Museum of Art; and Woodmere Art Museum.

MICHAEL CILIBERTI
American, 1925–2020

Michael Ciliberti was an early member of Group '55, drawn to the opportunity to explore abstraction and to interact with great creative minds in many disciplines. When Mitchel G. Wagman invited Ciliberti to join, he was the display manager for the Blum Store at 13th and Chestnut Streets in Philadelphia, where he had freedom to create imaginative settings for fashion and evoke celebrated artistic styles. He brought attention to the new group and its first exhibition by incorporating the Group '55 logo and paintings in all four windows. He continued to support its events even after he helped found the Philadelphia Abstract Artists (PAA), in 1957. He showed in all the PAA shows and in exhibitions featuring artists associated with both groups.

Ciliberti grew up in South Philadelphia. He studied commercial art and then fine art at the Samuel S. Fleisher Art Memorial, the Barnes Foundation, and the Pennsylvania Academy of the Fine Arts, all in his hometown. He made many trips to Europe, especially Italy, for the art and the landscape. Over time he moved from fully abstract work to impressionistic scenes of nature, primarily depictions of Maine, Philadelphia parks, and Cape May, New Jersey.

Ciliberti's work is included in the collections of Bates College, Lewiston, Maine, and Woodmere Art Museum, as well as in many private collections.

BARBARA CRAWFORD
American, 1914–2003

Painter, printmaker, writer, and teacher Barbara Crawford was an active member of Group '55. She often hosted jazz-filled soirees for members and panelists at the carriage house she shared with her husband, Sam Feinstein.

Crawford was a graduate of the Philadelphia Museum School of Industrial Art (now the University of the Arts). In 1940, the US Treasury Department's Section of Fine Arts commissioned her mural *Slate Belt People*. She painted immigrants who worked in the largest slate-producing area in the world on slate panels for the post office in Bangor, Pennsylvania. When Feinstein joined the Army, in 1942, Crawford took over his teaching position at Chestnut Hill Academy, Philadelphia. She taught there for nearly fifty years, influencing hundreds of students with her passion for teaching and for art. She opened her home for meetings of the C. G. Jung Center of Philadelphia, with which she remained involved for thirty-two years.

Crawford exhibited her paintings and prints frequently from 1950 to 1957 in Philadelphia. Her work is in the collections of the Philadelphia Museum of Art Springside Chestnut Hill Academy, and Tate, London.

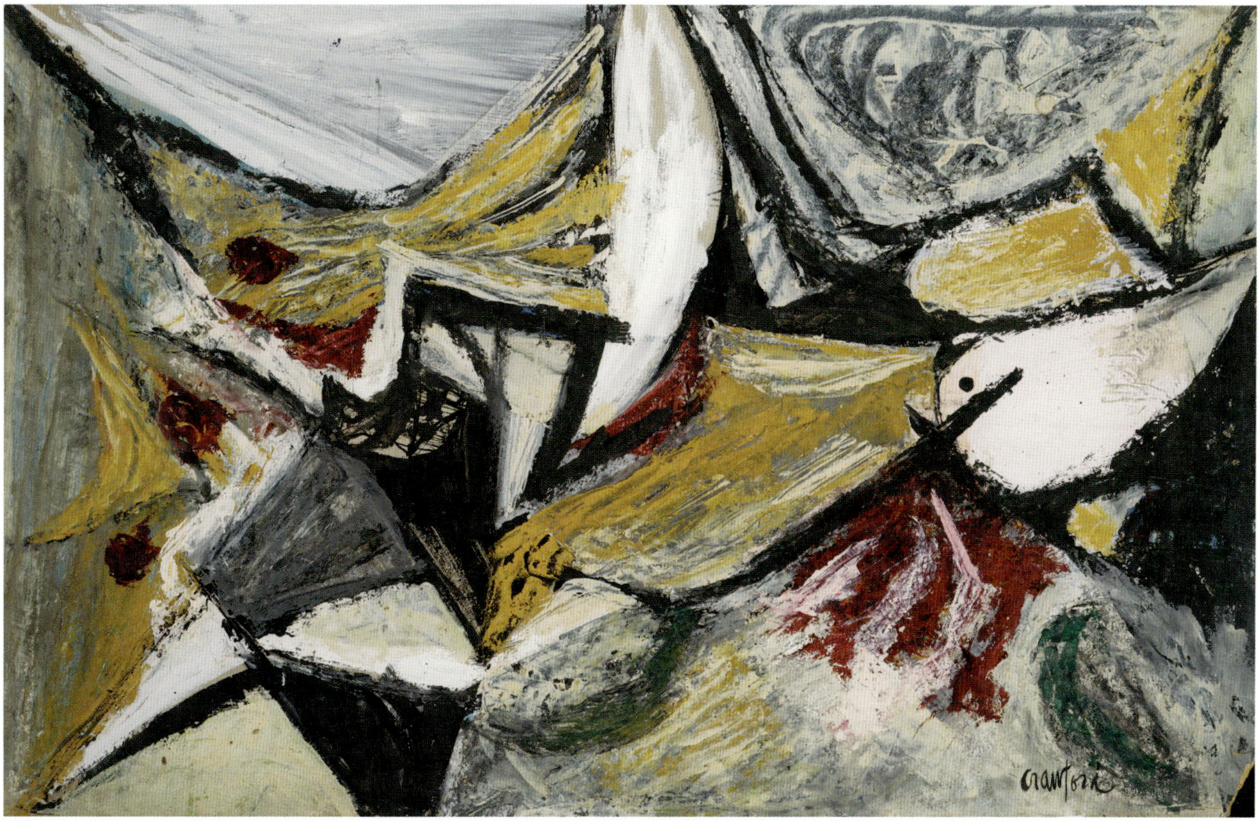

FIGURE 147. **Untitled**, date unknown, by Barbara Crawford (Springside Chestnut Hill Academy)

LARRY DAY
American, 1921–1998

Larry Day showed with Group '55 members on numerous occasions and taught with several of them at the Philadelphia College of Art (now the University of the Arts). Though he was invited to join the Philadelphia Abstract Artists, he did not become a member of either group.

Born Lorenzo del Giorno in Philadelphia, Day served in the Army, graduated from Temple University's Tyler School of Art, Philadelphia, and earned a second degree in education. Though he practiced abstraction in the 1950s, he later specialized in figuration and became known for his fine draftsmanship. From 1953 to 1988 he taught painting at the Philadelphia College of Art and at the University of Pennsylvania, Philadelphia. Day was known as the "dean of Philadelphia artists."

Day's work is in the collections of numerous museums, including the Art Institute of Chicago; British Museum, London; Metropolitan Museum of Art, New York; National Gallery of Art, Washington, DC; Pennsylvania Academy of the Fine Arts, Philadelphia; Philadelphia Museum of Art; Rhode Island School of Design Museum, Providence; and Woodmere Art Museum.

SAM FEINSTEIN

American, born Russia, 1915–2003

Sam Feinstein was a founder and president of Group '55. He served as a panelist or participant in all but one of its forums and programs, and he became codirector of Dubin/Gallery '55, Philadelphia, in 1957. He continued to serve as a leader in Group '55 until the group disbanded, in 1958.

A graduate of the Philadelphia Museum School of Industrial Art (now the University of the Arts), Feinstein studied with Hans Hofmann from 1949 through 1952. Though he was primarily known as a painter, he was also a printmaker and filmmaker through the 1940s, and he created an important film with Hofmann. His painting evolved from realism through expressionism to Abstract Expressionism, and he frequently exhibited in Philadelphia, New York, and Provincetown, Massachusetts, until 1960—when, disillusioned by commercialism, he stopped showing his work but continued to paint.

Passionate, culturally enlightened, idealistic, and articulate, Feinstein shared his strong beliefs about art through lectures and teaching. He was an instructor at Chestnut Hill Academy, Philadelphia; the Philadelphia Museum of Art; and Pratt Institute, New York, in addition to teaching private classes and painting workshops for more than forty years. He was also a respected writer, serving as Philadelphia correspondent and contributing editor for *Art Digest* from 1953 through 1955.

Feinstein's art is in the collections of the Cape Ann Museum, Gloucester, Massachusetts; Cape Cod Museum of Art, Dennis, Massachusetts; Metropolitan Museum of Art, New York; New Britain Museum of American Art, Connecticut; Philadelphia Museum of Art; Provincetown Art Association and Museum; and Woodmere Art Museum.

EUGENE FELDMAN

American, 1921–1975

Graphic artist, teacher, and commercial printer Eugene Feldman was one of the original members of Group '55. He is believed to have printed its distinctive promotional materials, designed by Sam Feinstein.

Feldman started a printing business at age thirteen that paid for his studies at the Philadelphia Museum School of Industrial Art (now the University of the Arts). He returned to the school as director of typography after serving in the Army. Innovative in his use of offset lithography as a fine art, he won a Guggenheim Fellowship to support his exploration of the medium, and in 1948 he founded Falcon Press, Philadelphia, one of few fine small presses in the United States in the mid- to late twentieth century. Feldman published eight books. In 1954 he published a single-issue journal with artist Ed Colker, *Re-Art: A Reflection of Current Ideas on the Arts*, which notes the antagonisms that "arise from the opposing premises held by artists and laymen," a subject explored in multiple Group '55 panels. It features essays by Barbara Crawford and the composer George Rochberg. He also published *The Notebooks and Drawings of Louis I. Kahn*, a collaboration with Richard Saul Wurman, in 1962.

Feldman's prints were shown widely and are in the collections of the Library of Congress, Washington, DC; Museum of Modern Art, New York; Philadelphia Museum of Art; and Stedelijk Museum, Amsterdam; and Woodmere Art Museum.

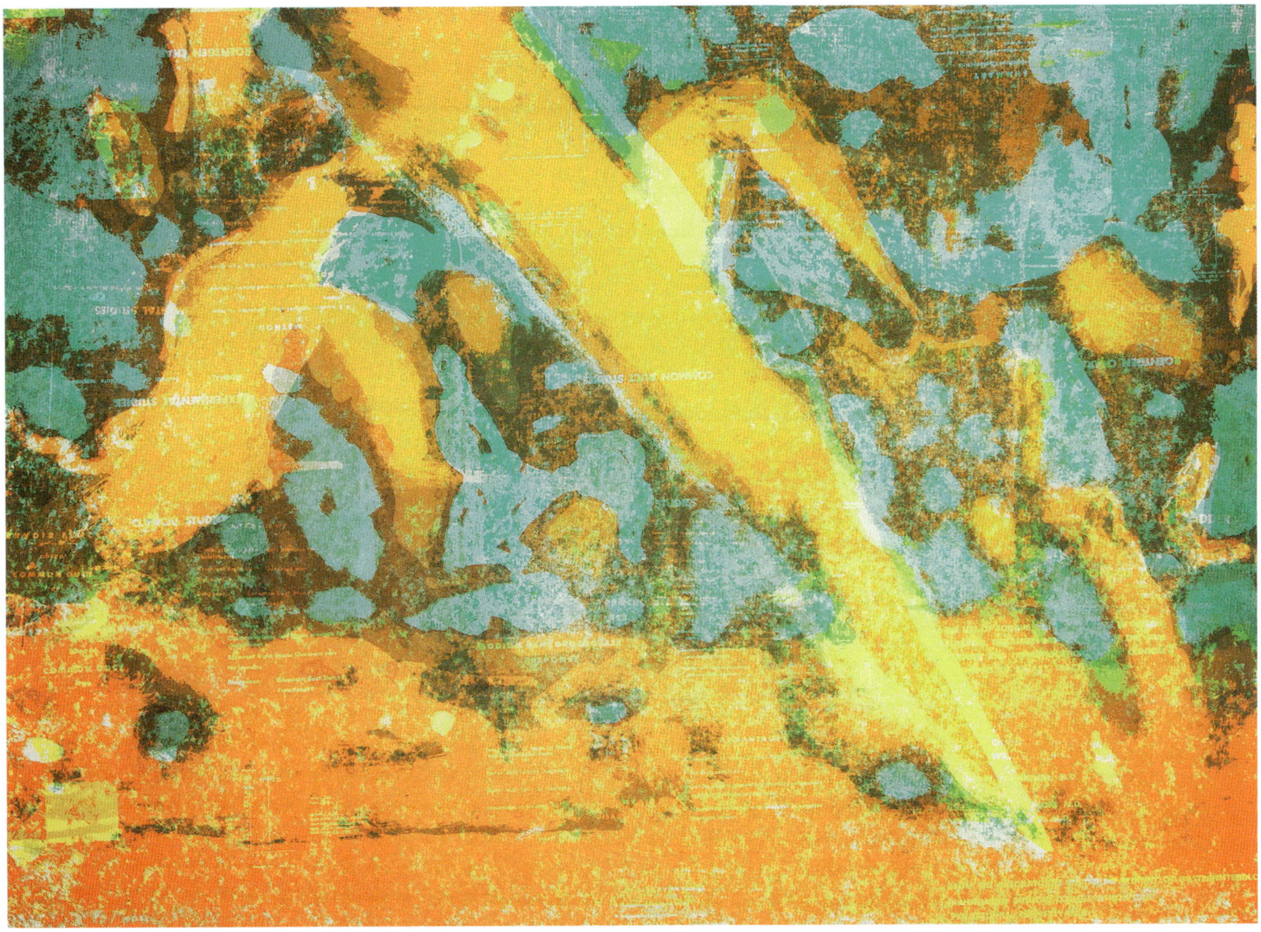

FIGURE 148. **Printer's Cornfield**, 1956, by Eugene Feldman (Woodmere Art Museum: Gift of Rosina Feldman, 2008)
Photograph by Rick Echelmeyer

SAM FREID
American, 1908–1983

Sam Freid was an original member of Group '55, serving as a vice president and a forum panelist. He helped found the Philadelphia Abstract Artists in 1957 and exhibited in four of its shows.

Born in the coal country of Pennsylvania, Freid studied at the Pennsylvania Academy of the Fine Arts, Philadelphia. His early black-and-white drawings and oil paintings focus on coal miners and their families. Working with his wife, Hilda Berger Freid, as he often did, he created an innovative film titled *The Barbarianism of Nazis*, in which War Department footage is interspersed with his pastel drawings depicting the brutalities of World War II.. By the late 1940s his canvases were brightly colored scenes of city life, and by the early 1950s he was showing abstract oils and gouaches. Freid was also a skillful writer, knowledgeable about poetry and music as well as art history. In 1962 he organized and served as a panelist for six art forums at Bryn Mawr College, Pennsylvania, and he taught drawing and painting at the Samuel S. Fleisher Art Memorial, Philadelphia, for many years.

Freid exhibited regularly beginning in the 1930s, with solo shows in Philadelphia and New York over the course of his career. His work is in the collection of Woodmere Art Museum.

THOMAS GAUGHAN
American, born England, 1925–2007

Thomas Gaughan participated in three exhibitions with the Philadelphia Abstract Artists, beginning in 1960. He also showed with many of its members in other exhibitions.

Gaughan was born in England and studied at the Pennsylvania Academy of the Fine Arts (PAFA), Philadelphia. He taught at the Samuel S. Fleisher Art Memorial, Philadelphia, and had a solo exhibition there in 1961.

Gaughan's paintings are in the collections of the Philadelphia Museum of Art and Woodmere Art Museum.

SANFORD GREENBERG
American, 1926–2011

Sanford Greenberg was a founding member of Group '55, showing in two of its exhibitions, and of the Philadelphia Abstract Artists, showing in all its exhibitions.

Greenberg was born in Philadelphia; his father was from Russia, as were his mother's parents. He studied at the Philadelphia Museum School of Industrial Art (later the Philadelphia College of Art, now the University of the Arts). After serving in the military during the war, he lived in Paris from 1947 to 1949. He exhibited work there at Galerie Huit, at the Salon de l'Art Libre, and with the Atelier Fernand Léger. He continued to paint and exhibit after he returned to Philadelphia, where he lived for the rest of his life. To support his family he took freelance work in advertising, served as art director for the television station WHYY, and taught at the Philadelphia College of Art, the Philadelphia Museum of Art, and the Samuel S. Fleisher Art Memorial.

In 1952 Greenberg showed at the Hendler Galleries, Philadelphia, with Franz Kline, Willem de Kooning, Jackson Pollock, and others. In his solo exhibition at Hendler the next year he showed work made in Paris. Sam Feinstein wrote in his review: "There are no specifics in these paintings: they evoke rather than

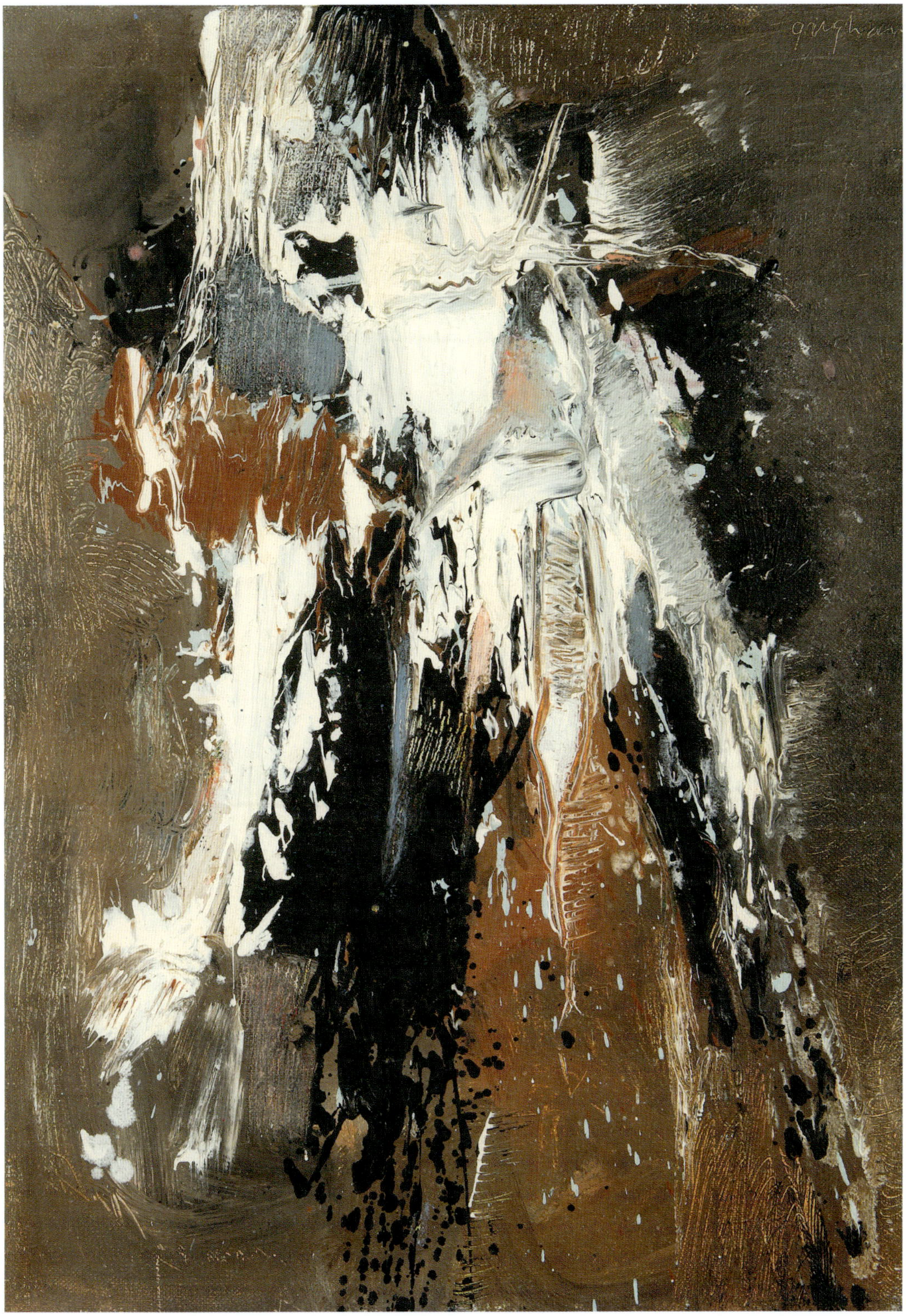

FIGURE 149.
Cascade, date unknown, by Thomas Gaughan (Woodmere Art Museum: Gift of Harvey S. Shipley Miller in memory of Betty E. Miller, 2015) Photograph by Rick Echelmeyer

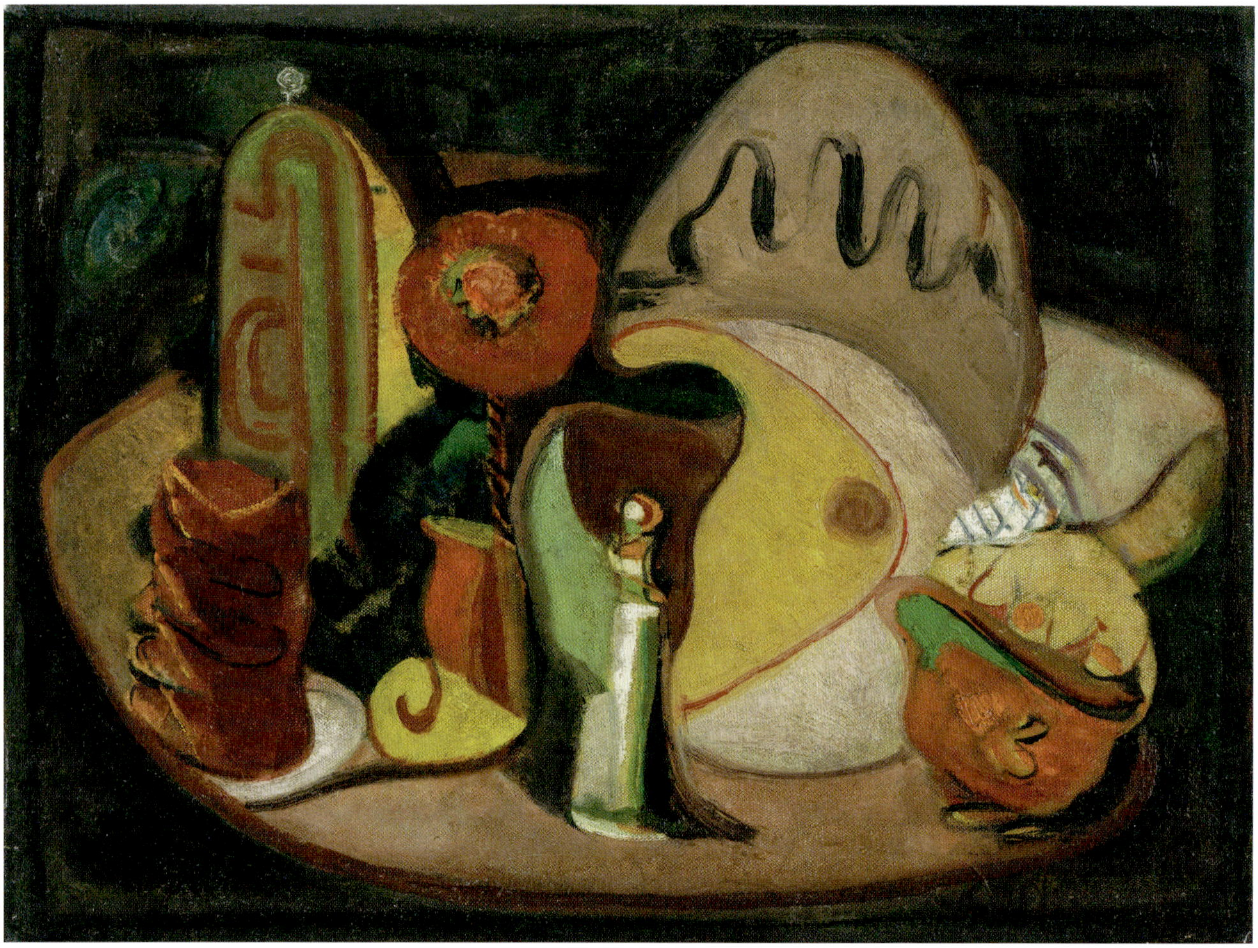

FIGURE 150. **Still Life**, c. 1950, by Abraham P. Hankins (Woodmere Art Museum: Museum purchase, 2019)

define." Greenberg had a sold-out solo exhibition at Dubin-Lush Galleries, Philadelphia, in 1955. His work is in the collection of Woodmere Art Museum.

ABRAHAM P. HANKINS

American, born Russia, 1903–1963

Painter, printmaker, and sculptor Abraham P. Hankins was an original member of Group '55 and later exhibited with the Philadelphia Abstract Artists.

Hankins emigrated from Russia to the United States as a child. He studied at the Académie Julian, in Paris, and at the Pennsylvania Academy of the Fine Arts (PAFA), in Philadelphia. By the early 1950s he had shifted from realism to abstraction; his work would be recognized for its subtle color, its elemental nature, and, later, its calligraphic vitality. A 1951 *Art in Focus* review stated, "Hankins is best when he is completely himself, using a rich, yet sensitive color range with olive green, rust, blue, and yellow." In addition to his paintings, Hankins's color monoprints, woodblock prints, and lithographs were exhibited extensively in solo and group shows in Philadelphia and New York and won many awards. His work was also selected for multiple exhibitions organized by Traveling Art Inc., which sent the best of Philadelphia art to universities and museums elsewhere in order to educate and promote goodwill.

Hankins's work is in the collections of the Barnes Foundation, Philadelphia; Samuel S. Fleisher Art Memorial, Philadelphia; National Gallery of Art, Washington, DC; PAFA; Philadelphia Museum of Art; and Woodmere Art Museum.

RAYMOND HENDLER

American, 1923–1998

Raymond Hendler helped launch Group '55, participating in its first exhibition and forum.

Hendler studied at the Philadelphia College of Art (now the University of the Arts) before serving in the Army. He later attended the Pennsylvania Academy of the Fine Arts (PAFA) and Temple University's Tyler School of Art (now Tyler School of Art and Architecture), both in Philadelphia, and painted in Paris under the GI Bill. There he developed an Abstract Expressionist style and helped found Galerie Huit, a cooperative that promoted the exchange of ideas between European and American artists.

Returning to the United States, Hendler became the youngest voting member of the Eighth Street Club in New York. He then moved to Philadelphia and opened the Hendler Galleries, the city's first strictly avant-garde gallery, showing work by leading Abstract Expressionists between 1954 and 1957. In 1958 he became head of the painting department at the Minneapolis School of Art (now the Minneapolis College of Art and Design).

In the 1960s Hendler's Abstract Expressionist style evolved into calligraphic, hard-edge abstraction, and he exhibited widely in group and solo shows. After teaching in New York, he moved to the University of Minnesota, Minneapolis, where he retired as a full professor in 1984. Hendler's work is in the collections of the Birla Academy of Art and Culture, Calcutta; Grey Art Gallery, New York University; Minneapolis Institute of Art; PAFA; Philadelphia Museum of Art; University of New Mexico Art Museum, Albuquerque; Walker Art Center, Minneapolis; and Woodmere Art Museum.

BEN HERR
American, 1935–2019

Ben Herr, although not a Group '55 member, was an Abstract Expressionist painter and sculptor from Lancaster, Pennsylvania, who studied and worked in Philadelphia in the mid-1950s. He attended the Philadelphia Museum School of Industrial Art (now the University of the Arts) and studied with Melville Price, Franz Kline, and Larry Day. Herr included a variety of collage elements into his work, even using a blowtorch to create new textures. His sculptures incorporated metal, stone, cement, wood, and other discarded materials from Philadelphia's Society Hill neighborhood.

Herr's work was in numerous exhibitions, including the first Philadelphia Art Festival, in 1955; the Philadelphia Art Alliance's *Regional Prints and Drawing Exhibition,* in 1956; and Roland de Aenlle Gallery's *4 Philadelphia Painters,* in New York in 1960. Herr returned to Lancaster in 1960, and he continued to paint there for the rest his life. He had retrospective exhibitions at Susquehanna Art Museum, Harrisburg, Pennsylvania in 2009; McCormick Gallery, Chicago, in 2014; and Demuth Museum, Lancaster Museum of Art, and West Chester University, both in Pennsylvania in 2015.

PAUL F. KEENE JR.
American, 1920–2009

Paul F. Keene Jr. was invited to join the Philadelphia Abstract Artists in 1957, although he did not become a member. He studied at the Philadelphia Museum School of Industrial Art (now University of the Arts); Temple University's Tyler School of Art (now Tyler School of Art and Architecture), Philadelphia; and the Académie Julian, Paris. While in Paris, he co-founded Galerie Huit with Raymond Hendler and became a good friend of Sanford Greenberg. His sense of vibrant color was inspired by European modernism and by years living in Haiti. He taught at the Philadelphia College of Art from 1954 to 1968 and established a new art department at Bucks County Community College, Newtown, Pennsylvania.

Keene's work is in the collections of the James A. Michener Art Museum, Doylestown, Pennsylvania; Pennsylvania Academy of the Fine Arts; Philadelphia Museum of Art; and Woodmere Art Museum.

FRANCES LACHMAN
American, 1913–1994

Frances Lachman was an active member and secretary of Group '55. She was also a member of the Philadelphia Abstract Artists, showing in all its exhibitions. Her pediatrician husband, Joseph Lachman, was a panelist in at least one Group '55 forum.

Lachman attended Moore College of Art and Design and the Pennsylvania Academy of the Fine Arts, both in Philadelphia, in addition to studying painting privately with Sam Feinstein for many years. Known for her mastery of drawing and her sensuous use of color, Lachman depicted nudes, dancers, still lifes, and landscapes before moving on to poetic abstractions. She taught at the Community Arts Center, Wallingford, Pennsylvania, and at the Samuel S. Fleisher Art Memorial, Philadelphia, and continued to paint throughout her life.

Lachman exhibited frequently in group and solo shows in Philadelphia and had solo exhibitions in Miami and Washington, DC. Her work is in the collections of CoreStates First Pennsylvania Bank; Drexel University, Philadelphia; Reading Public Museum, Pennsylvania; and Woodmere Art Museum.

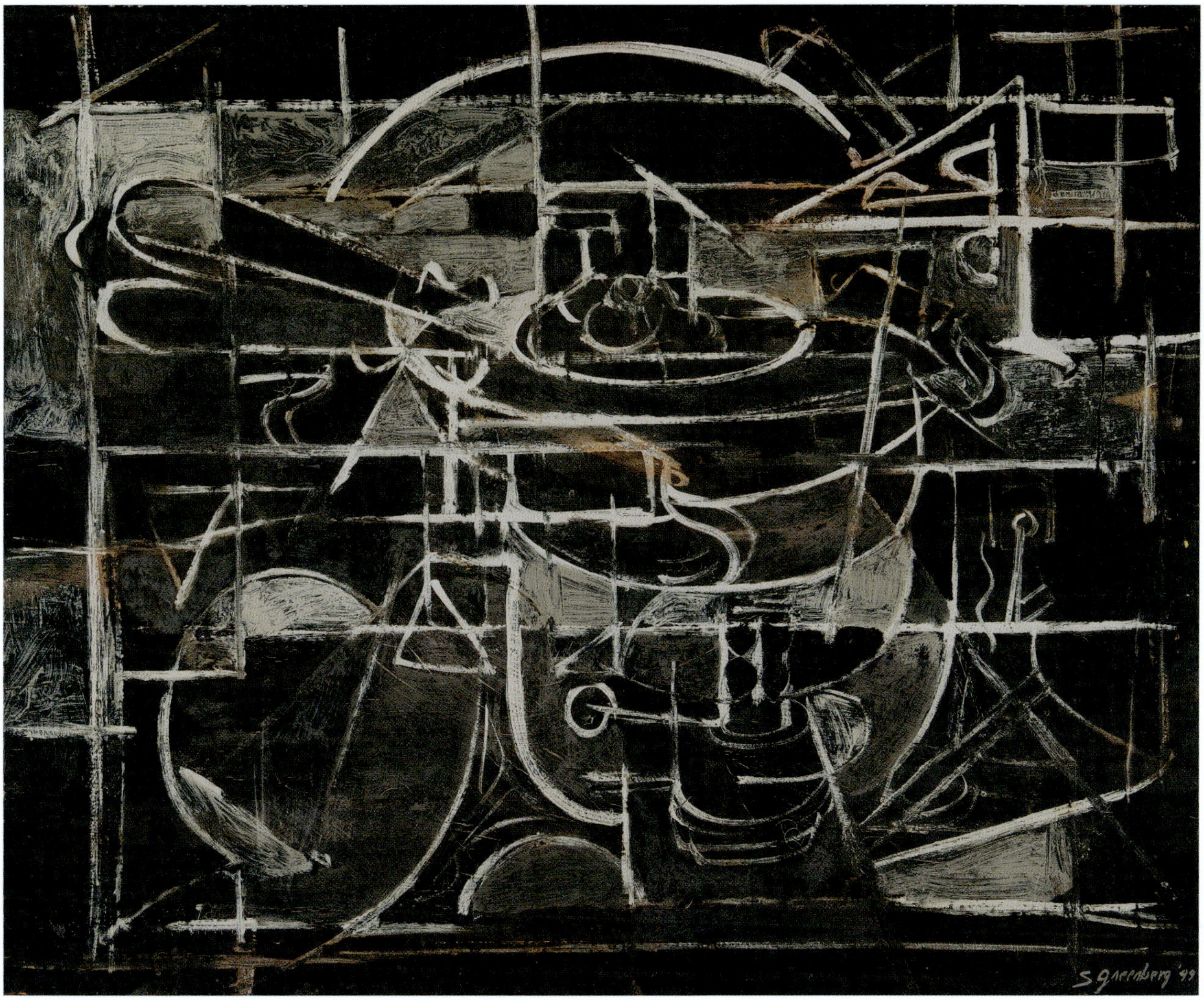

FIGURE 151. **Untitled (Abstract)**, 1949, by Sanford Greenberg (Woodmere Art Museum: Museum purchase, 2014)
Photograph by Rick Echelmeyer

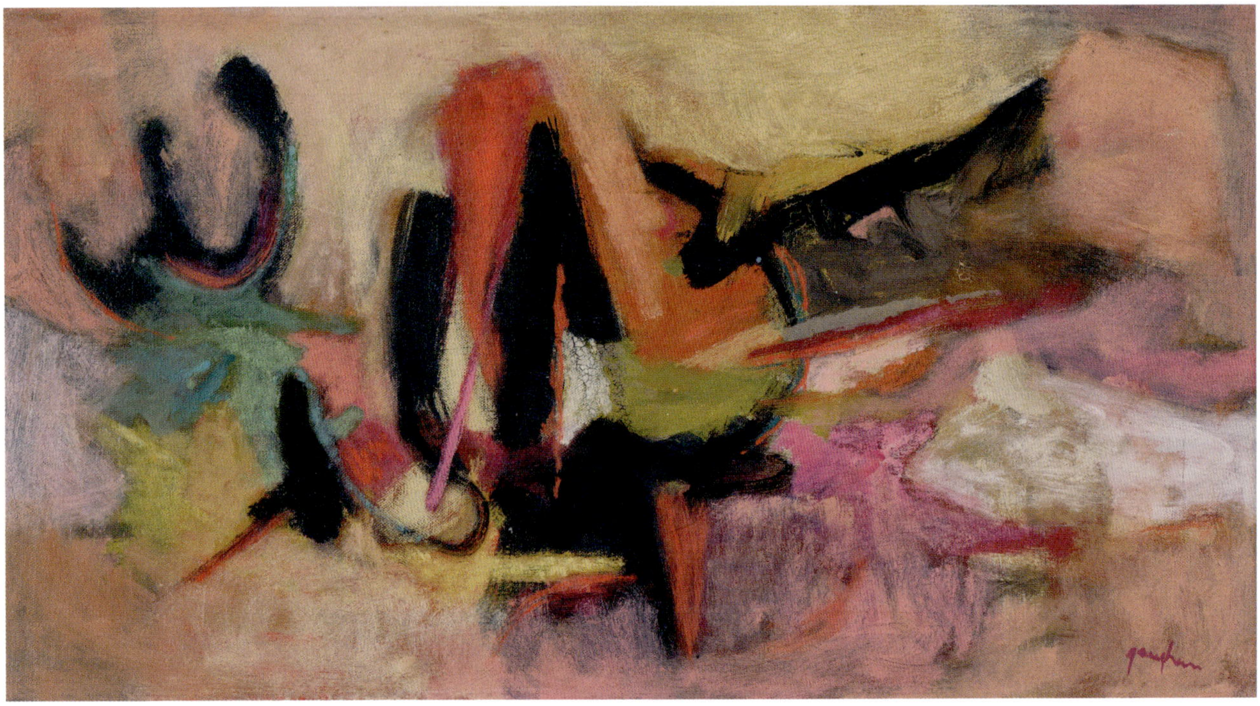

FIGURE 152. **Morning**, date unknown, by Thomas Gaughan (Courtesy of Esther and Stephen Hrabrick)

SAMUEL MAITIN

American, 1928–2004

Samuel Maitin exhibited only once with the Philadelphia Abstract Artists, but he participated in many other shows throughout the city with its members.

Maitin studied at the Philadelphia Museum School of Industrial Art (now the University of the Arts) and became a painter, printmaker, graphic designer, and sculptor. He was so active in the cultural life of Philadelphia that he was known as the city's "mayor of the arts": He served on Woodmere Art Museum's board of trustees; he designed posters and invitations and created mosaics and murals for hospitals and universities; and he directed the Visual Graphics Communication Laboratory at the University of Pennsylvania's Annenberg School for Communication from 1965 to 1972.

Maitin's work is in the collections of numerous museums, including the Museum of Modern Art, New York; National Gallery of Art, Washington, DC; Pennsylvania Academy of the Fine Arts; Philadelphia Museum of Art; Tate, London; and Woodmere Art Museum.

PATRICIA EVANS MANGIONE
American, 1915–2002

Patricia Mangione, who then painted as Patricia Evans, participated in the first Group '55 exhibition. She is not known to have exhibited with Group '55 or the Philadelphia Abstract Artists thereafter, but her work was often shown in Philadelphia while they were active.

Born in Seattle, Mangione trained at the Samuel S. Fleisher Art Memorial and the Barnes Foundation, both in Philadelphia, as well as in Europe. She developed her painting over the course of a series of residencies at the MacDowell Colony, Peterborough, New Hampshire, and at Yaddo, Saratoga Springs, New York. Though her work was initially landscape-inspired, she eventually moved into figurative abstraction, with color her primary interest. She taught at the Fleisher Art Memorial for many years and received the Artists Equity Award for artistic contribution to the cultural spirit of Philadelphia, recognition for outstanding teaching, and first-prize medals from the Philadelphia Sketch Club; the Smithsonian Institution, Washington, DC; and the Saratoga Springs Art Fair.

Mangione's work has been shown extensively in solo and group shows in the United States and abroad, including at the American Academy in Rome; Le Piol, Saint-Paul-de-Vence, France; Museum of Modern Art, New York; Pennsylvania Academy of the Fine Arts, Philadelphia; Philadelphia Museum of Art; and USIS Gallery, Palermo, Italy. Her work is in the collection of Woodmere Art Museum.

JACK MAYERSON
American, 1908–1985

Jack Mayerson was an original member of Group '55 and participated in three of its exhibitions: *In the Abstract,* in 1956, at Dubin-Lush Galleries, which featured Mayerson's work alongside that of Francis Jennings and Hans Hofmann; and two group shows in 1957, one at Gallery '55, the other at the Community Arts Center, Wallingford, Pennsylvania. There is no evidence of further activity with Group '55 or in other Philadelphia exhibitions.

Mayerson painted with bold strokes of bright color that invigorated his entire compositions. Little is known about his art training except that he was a student of Sam Feinstein, who taught principles conveyed by Hofmann. His work is in the collection of Woodmere Art Museum.

HAROLD MESIBOV
American, 1928–2012

Harold Mesibov was a member of Group '55, exhibiting once with its artists and three times with the Philadelphia Abstract Artists.

Mesibov studied in Philadelphia at the Samuel S. Fleisher Art Memorial, the Tyler School of Art (now the Tyler School of Art and Architecture) at Temple University, and the Barnes Foundation. He worked in various styles throughout his career—sometimes under the name "Mesa" to distinguish his work from that of his artist brother, Hugh Mesibov—but he primarily considered himself an abstract figure painter, likening his canvases to musical compositions.

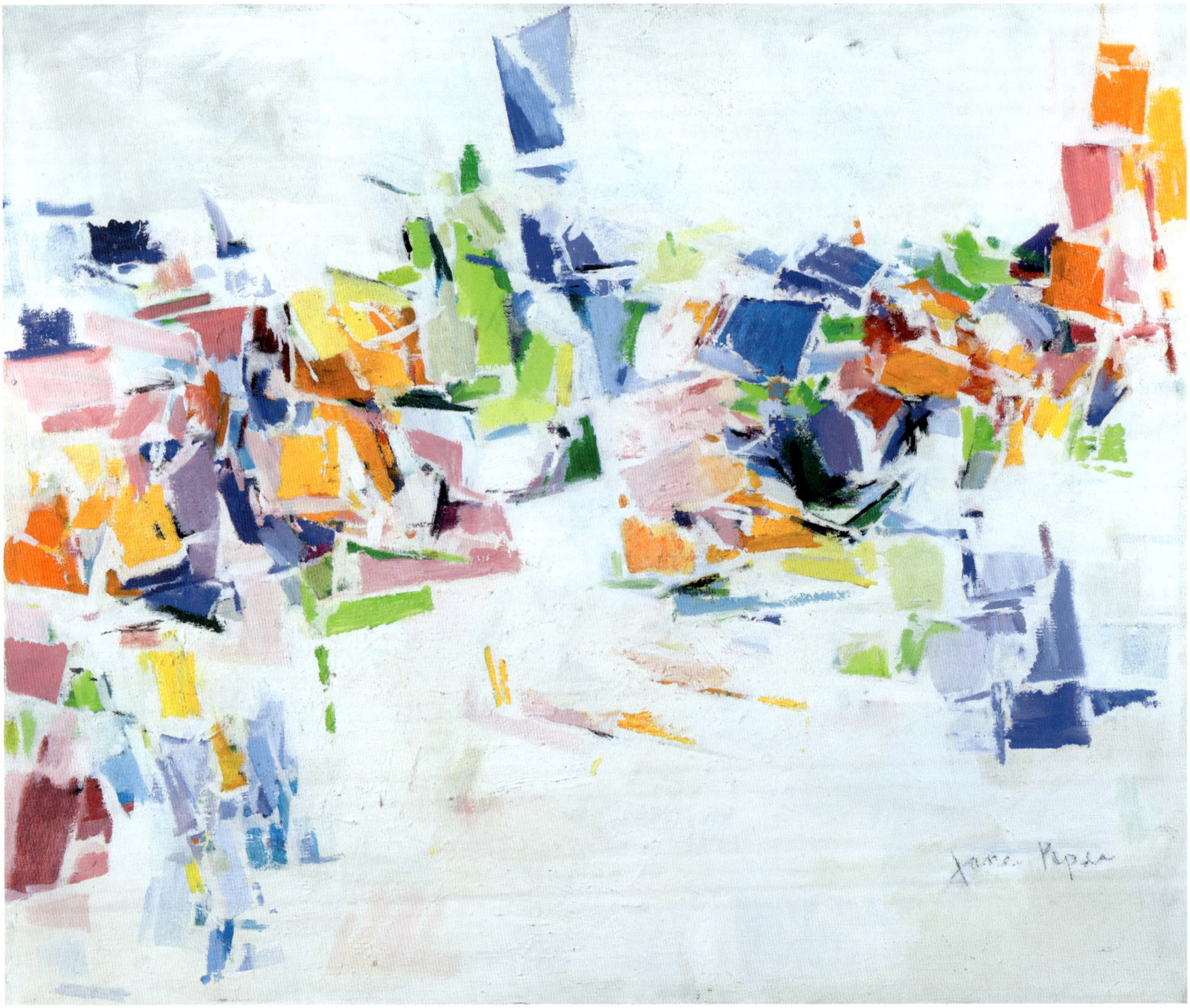

FIGURE 153. **Trade Winds 2**, 1958, by Jane Piper (Woodmere Art Museum: Gift of Karen Segal, 2017) Photograph by Rick Echelmeyer

Mesibov had solo exhibitions in New York and Philadelphia, in addition to participating in many group shows. His works are in the collection of the Boston Art Club and in many private collections.

LEONARD NELSON

American, 1912–1993

Leonard Nelson had a solo exhibition at Dubin Galleries in 1956 and later became a member of the Philadelphia Abstract Artists. He only showed with the group once, but he exhibited with many of its members over the years.

Born in New Jersey, Nelson studied in Philadelphia at the Pennsylvania Academy of the Fine Arts and the Barnes Foundation. He designed murals for a hospital while serving in the ArmyBy the mid 1940s, Nelson made two important contacts who would assure his ascendancy in the nascent New York School: the art dealers Peggy Guggenheim and Betty Parsons. He began to exhibit in the New York galleries, in particular Parsons' gallery, and his work reflected the Abstract Expressionist style made famous by this school. He eventually developed a signature style that was not accepted in New York, but his work was frequently shown in Philadelphia. His work is in the collections of the Philadelphia Museum of Art and Woodmere Art Museum.

PETER PAONE

American, born 1936

Peter Paone was a student when Group '55 was formed and did not exhibit with them. He grew up in a first-generation Italian-American home where the only art on the walls was religious in nature. In the 1950s, Paone attended the Philadelphia Museum School of Industrial Art (now the University of the Arts) and received a bachelor of fine arts degree in art education. His instructors included Benton Spruance and other great narrative artists and illustrators.

Paone has been enthusiastically involved in the Philadelphia arts community as an artist, collector, and teacher for over five decades. In 1980 he established the printmaking department at the Pennsylvania Academy of the Fine Arts (PAFA), where he taught from 1978 to 2009, and served as the department's first chair. He was also the vice president of the Print Club (now the Print Center) for six years, and he currently serves on Woodmere's collection management committee.

Paone's work has been exhibited at institutions across the United States and across the globe, and he has held senior teaching positions at PAFA and at Pratt Institute, New York. His work is in numerous public and private collections including Woodmere Art Museum, PAFA, and the Philadelphia Museum of Art.

JANE PIPER
American, 1916–1991

Jane Piper was an original member of Group '55; she participated in two shows, and her paintings were displayed and discussed at two forums. She later joined the Philadelphia Abstract Artists and participated in three of its exhibitions.

Discouraged by having to draw from plaster casts at the Pennsylvania Academy of the Fine Arts (PAFA), Philadelphia, Piper studied at the nearby Barnes Foundation and with Earl Horter, Arthur B. Carles, and Hans Hofmann. Color was always her focus. Her paintings were fully abstract by the early 1960s, but she later returned to her origins with complex still lifes, developing signature compositions unified by her use of white as a color rather than a value. Piper was also an inspiring teacher for three decades at the Philadelphia Museum School of Industrial Art (now the University of the Arts).

Piper participated in dozens of group shows over the course of her career. She also had more than two dozen solo exhibitions at the Carlen Galleries, Philadelphia, beginning in 1943; one at the Dubin Galleries, Philadelphia, in 1954; and more at institutions such as PAFA and Woodmere Art Museum. She showed with the Gross McCleaf Gallery in Philadelphia for many years, and her paintings are in the collections of the Allentown Art Museum, Pennsylvania; Carnegie Institute of Art, Pittsburgh; Museum of Modern Art, New York; PAFA; Philadelphia Museum of Art; and Woodmere Art Museum.

MELVILLE PRICE
American, 1920–1970

Melville Price was invited to join Group '55 but did not become a member. Price studied at the Art Students League and painted in the Works Progress Administration. He became friends with future Abstract Expressionist painters in New York and participated in the famous *Ninth Street Show* in Greenwich Village in 1951. He taught at the Philadelphia Museum School of Industrial Art (now University of the Arts) and the Samuel S. Fleisher Art Memorial before leaving Philadelphia in 1958 for a position at the University of Alabama.

Price's work is in the collections of the American University Museum, Washington, DC; Art Institute of Chicago; Baltimore Museum of Art; Birmingham Museum of Art; Los Angeles County Museum of Art; Milwaukee Art Museum; Pennsylvania Academy of the Fine Arts; Philadelphia Museum of Art; Smithsonian American Art Museum, Washington, DC; and Woodmere Art Museum.

ITZHAK SANKOWSKY
American, born Romania, 1908–1994

Artist and teacher Itzhak Sankowsky was an original member of Group '55. He showed with its artists and later with the Philadelphia Abstract Artists.

Sankowsky studied at the University of Florence, Italy; the Academy of Fine Arts, Florence; the University of Pennsylvania, Philadelphia; and privately with Arthur B. Carles. He was a prolific and experimental artist who explored a wide range of materials and techniques in painting, printmaking, and sculpture. In *Art Digest* Sam Feinstein described the "feeling for movement and delicate color perception" in

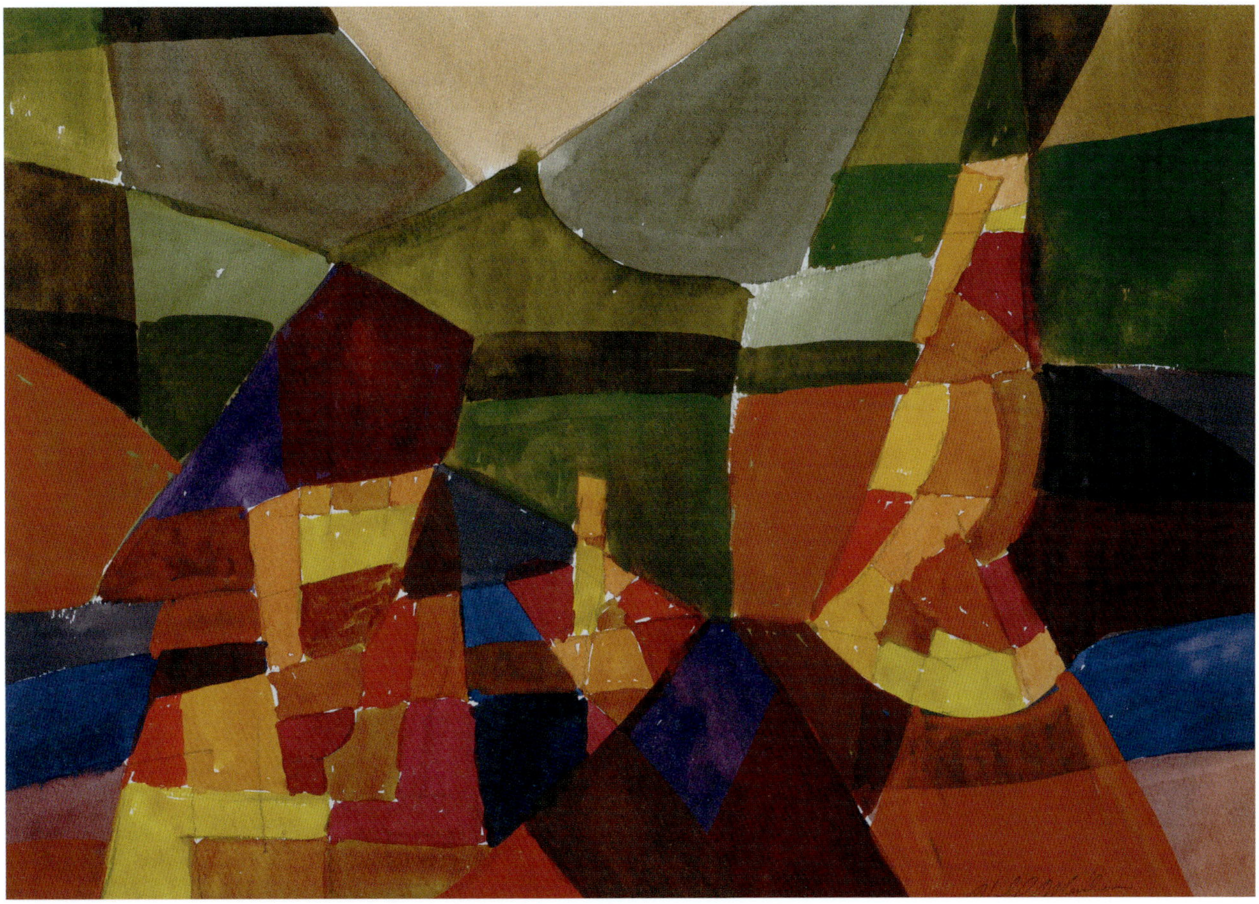

FIGURE 154. **Untitled**, 1950s, by Harold Mesibov (Private Collection)

Sankowsky's 1953 solo show at Beryl Lush Gallery, Philadelphia. He noted: "Sankowsky is working in sensitive, almost pastel-toned pigments . . . and has an admirable command of pictorial space, which he organizes with variety and flow. . . . The two-dimensionality of his canvas surface is strongly established; depth is not confused with naturalistic distance." Sankowsky also taught for many years at the Philadelphia Museum of Art; Gratz College, Melrose Park, Pennsylvania; Har Zion Temple, Penn Valley, Pennsylvania; and Main Line Art Center, Haverford, Pennsylvania. He belonged to the Philadelphia Art Alliance, Philadelphia Print Club, and Artists Equity Association.

In addition to seventeen solo exhibitions throughout Philadelphia, Sankowsky had one-person shows at the AGRA Gallery, Washington, DC; Burr Galleries, New York and Franklin and Marshall College, Lancaster, Pennsylvania, among other venues. He also participated in the International Watercolor Show in Chicago. His work is in the collections of the Philadelphia Museum of Art and Woodmere Art Museum.

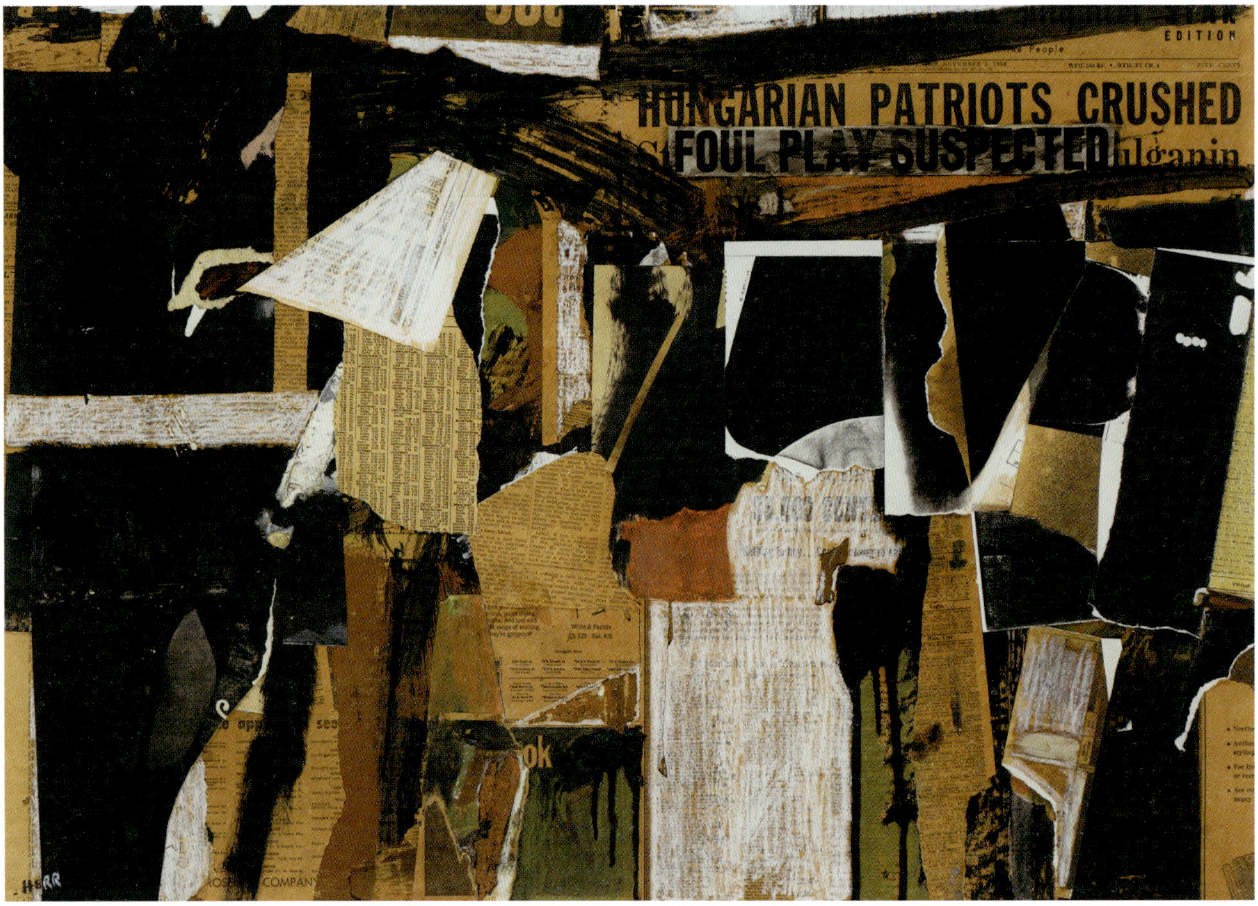

FIGURE 155. **For the Hungarian Revolution**, 1956, by Ben Herr (Collection of Andrea Herr-Turoff)

DORIS STAFFEL

American, 1921–2013

Doris Staffel was a founding member of Group '55 and a participant in several forums. Her involvement ceased in fall 1956; she joined the Philadelphia Abstract Artists and exhibited with them from 1957 through 1962.

After painting in elementary school with her teacher Mark Rothko, Staffel graduated from Temple University's Tyler School of Art (now Tyler School of Art and Architecture), Philadelphia, where she was greatly influenced by her instructor Franklin C. Watkins. She earned a master's degree at the University of Iowa, Iowa City, under Philip Guston, and attended Hans Hofmann's classes in New York. Staffel's paintings and drawings focus on essence and flux rather than outward appearance. After 1968 she frequently worked in series that reflected her Buddhist beliefs. "They are open to enter, rather than to observe from the outside. They contain undisclosed mysteries and resist interpretation," observed her former student Ron Rumford. Staffel taught at the Philadelphia College of Art (now the University of the Arts) from

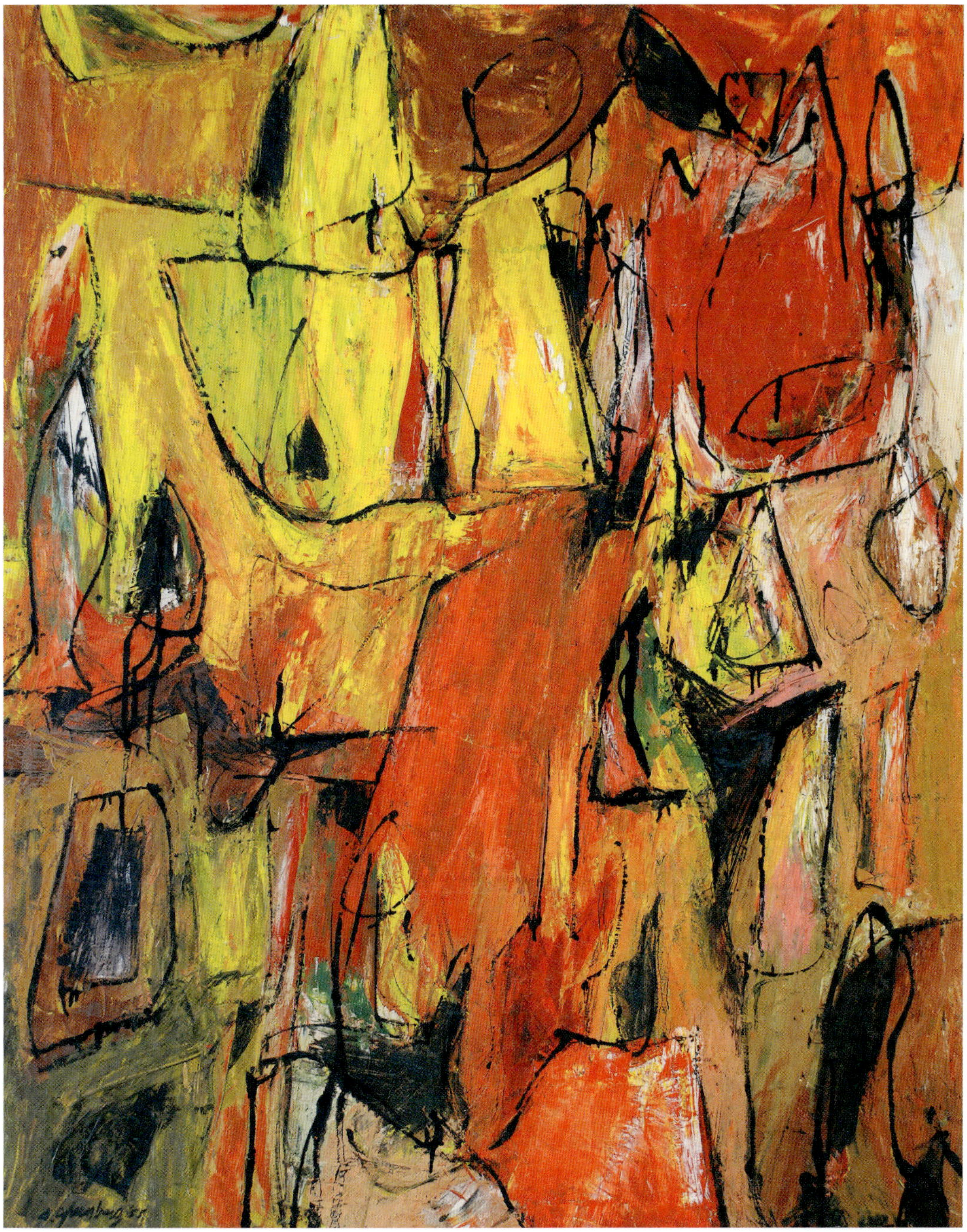

FIGURE 156. No. 4, 1955, by Sanford Greenberg (Sanford Greenberg Estate) Photograph by Rick Echelmeyer

1968 to 1990, influencing a generation of artists, many of whom also became teachers.

Married to ceramicist Rudolf Staffel and a lifelong resident of Philadelphia, Doris Staffel exhibited in solo and group shows continually for sixty years, including a 2012 retrospective at Woodmere Art Museum. Her work is in the collections of the Asheville Art Museum, North Carolina; Bryn Mawr College, Pennsylvania; Butler Institute of American Art, Youngstown, Ohio; New Jersey State Museum, Trenton; Philadelphia Museum of Art; State Museum of Pennsylvania, Harrisburg; and Woodmere Art Museum.

MITCHEL G. WAGMAN
American, 1923–2002

Mitchel G. Wagman was a founding member of Group '55 and a member of the board of governors. He was also a founder of the Philadelphia Abstract Artists, participating in all seven of its exhibitions, hosting one at his Philadelphia Galleries, and including work by its members in other shows he organized.

Wagman grew up in New York, where he studied at the Art Students League and Pratt Institute. After serving in the Army, he studied art in Paris at the Atelier Fernand Léger, moved to Philadelphia, and studied with Hans Hofmann in New York. He had a solo exhibition of his "distinctive, poetic paintings" at Dubin Galleries, Philadelphia, in 1956. In the 1950s, he opened Philadelphia Galleries (later Philadelphia Gallery) at 333 South 20th Street, where he offered framing services in addition to hosting exhibitions of work by Abstract Expressionist artists from Philadelphia and New York, including his own. He also showed and advocated for African American artists. By 1963 he moved the Philadelphia Gallery to 1911 Walnut Street, where he ran art classes and remained in operation until 1974. He retired to California in 1982.

Wagman's work is in a number of private and public collections, including the La Salle University Art Museum, Philadelphia; and the University of the Arts, Philadelphia.

RUTH ZION
American, born 1923–2010

Ruth Zion was an original member of Group '55; she painted under the name Ruth Wollman in the 1950s and later as Ruth Bressler and Ruth Harley. An Abstract Expressionist and art teacher, she is credited with encouraging artists across creative disciplines—painters, writers, musicians—to become engaged with Group '55. She was represented in several of the group's exhibitions and taught at the Allens Lane Art Center, Philadelphia, along with Doris Staffel and Itzhak Sankowsky.

In October 1956, Zion married and moved to Ventnor, New Jersey, where she became art supervisor for the city's public schools. She established the Ruth Bressler Art Award (presented annually until 1995) and painted portraits on commission. She furthered her interest in interdisciplinary collaboration through her work with a photographer to create photosensitized canvas collages. She also developed a clothing line from materials found during her travels in India, Indonesia, and Bali. Upon moving to Florida in 1995, she again brought artists together across disciplines to collaborate through the Melrose Bay Art Gallery and annual Melrose Open Air Arts event.

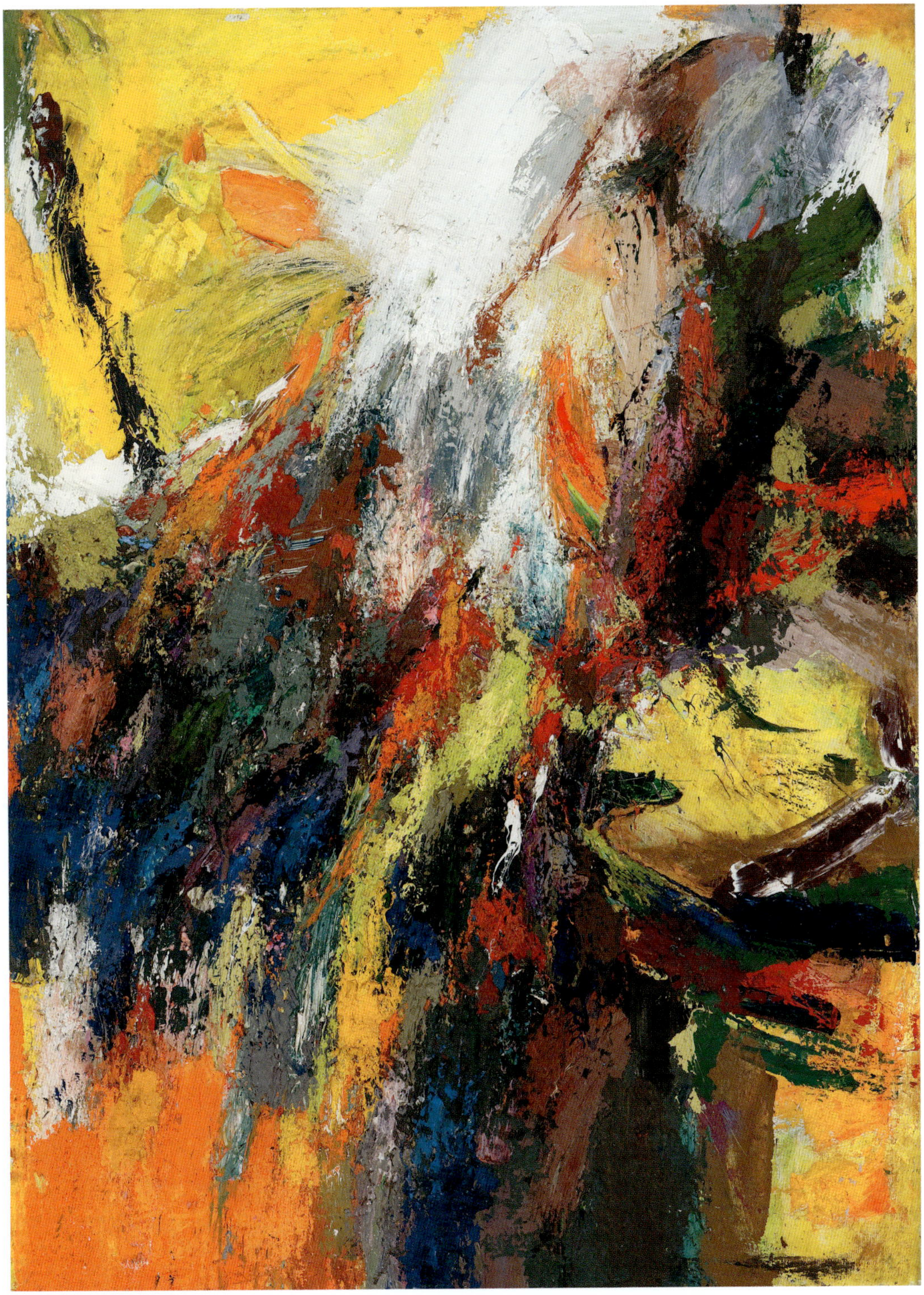

FIGURE 157. **Untitled**, 1950s, by Sam Feinstein (Woodmere Art Museum: Gift of the Samuel L. Feinstein Trust, 2011)
Photograph by Rick Echelmeyer

Exhibition Checklists

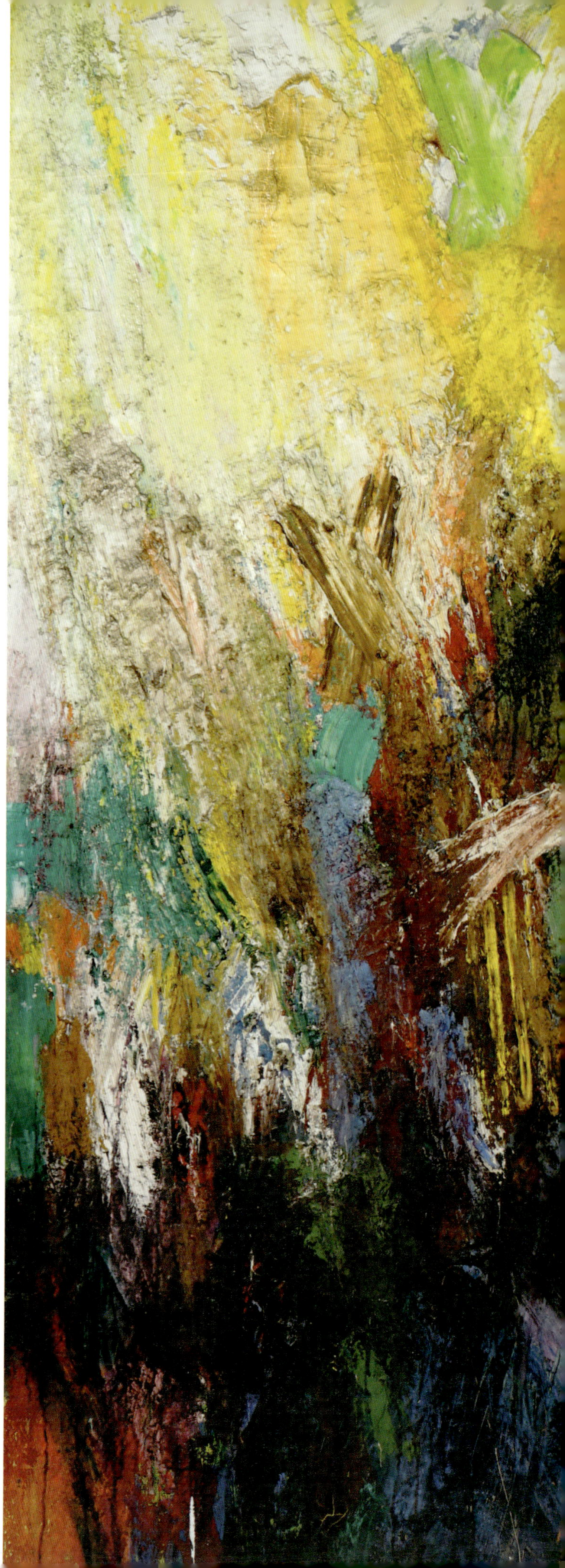

FIGURE 158. Untitled (detail of Fig. 169), 1960, by Sam Feinstein (Samuel L. Feinstein Trust) Photograph by Laszlo Bodo

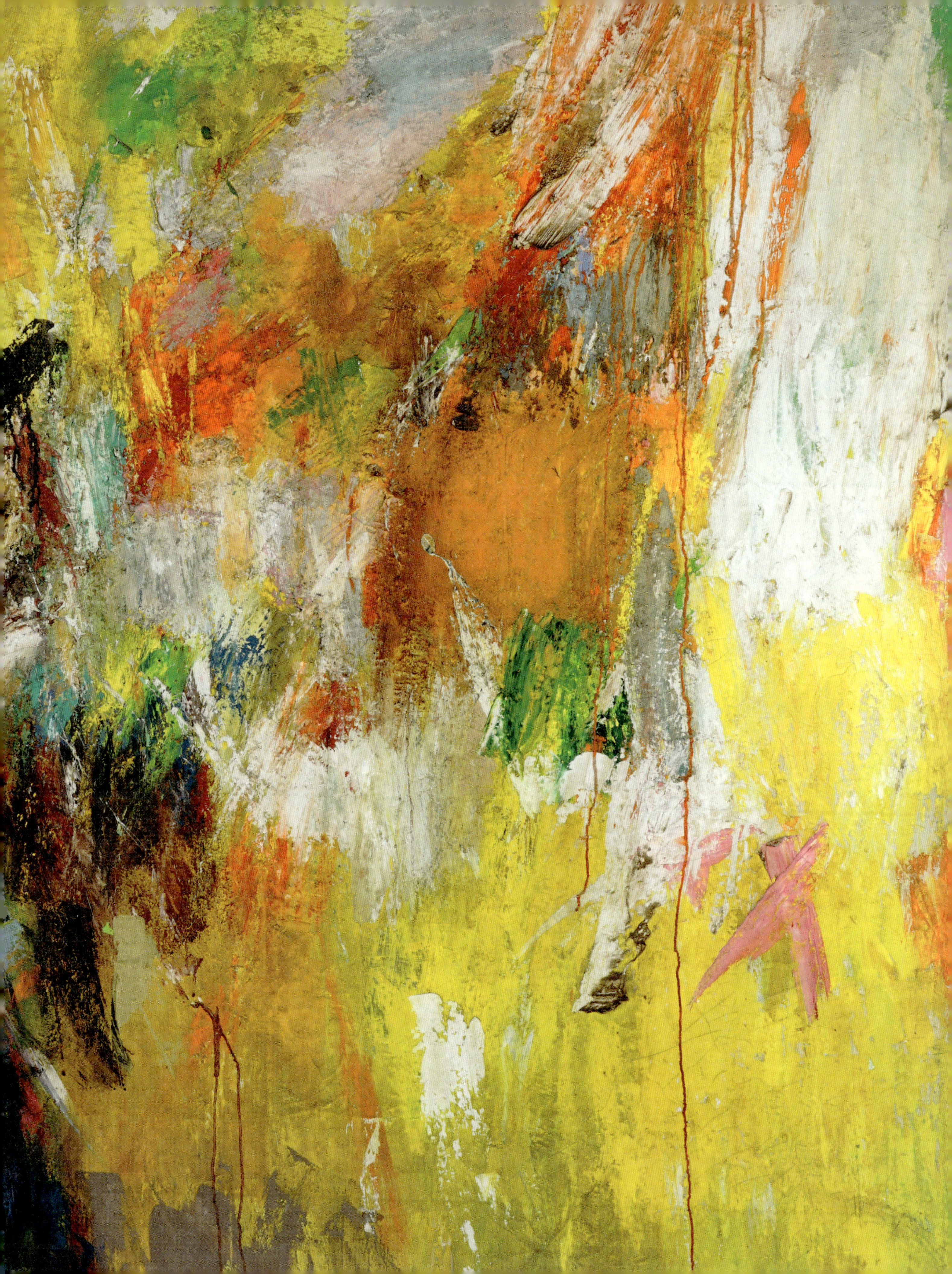

Sam Feinstein: The Early Years

September 26, 2020–January 24, 2021
Barbara Crawford Art Gallery, Springside Chestnut Hill Academy

WORKS IN THE EXHIBITION

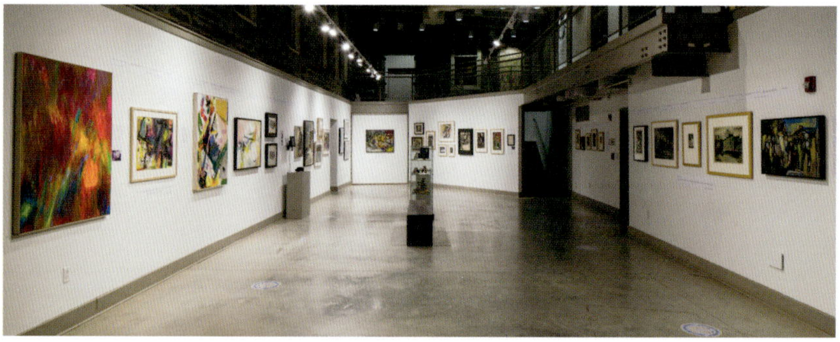

FIGURE 159. Installation view of *Sam Feinstein: The Early Years*

SAM FEINSTEIN
American born Russia, 1915–2003

Self-Portrait, 1932
Pen and ink on paper, 7 x 5 in.
Samuel L. Feinstein Trust
FIGURE 96

Factories, 1930s
Watercolor on paper, 17 1/2 x 23 in.
Samuel L. Feinstein Trust
FIGURE 98

Immigrants, 1930s
Oil on canvasboard, 20 x 30 in.
Samuel L. Feinstein Trust
FIGURE 95

Market AM, 1930s
Watercolor on paper, 14 1/2 x 20 in.
Samuel L. Feinstein Trust
FIGURE 4

Young Woman in Blue, 1930s
Oil on canvas, 25 x 18 in.
Samuel L. Feinstein Trust
FIGURE 163

Aladdin and His Magic Lamp, c. 1934
Watercolor on paper, 11 1/2 x 8 in.
Samuel L. Feinstein Trust

Little Red Riding Hood, c. 1934
Casein on paper, 4 3/4 x 3 3/4 in.
Samuel L. Feinstein Trust

Don Quixote, 1935
Casein on paper, 10 3/4 x 8 1/2 in.
Samuel L. Feinstein Trust
FIGURE 97

Railroad Bridge at Girard Avenue, 1936
Pen and ink on paper, 10 x 6 1/4 in.
Samuel L. Feinstein Trust
FIGURE 162

Worry, 1940
Casein on paper, 20 1/2 x 14 in.
Samuel L. Feinstein Trust

After the Party, 1940s
Linoleum print, 12 x 15 in.
Samuel L. Feinstein Trust

The Threat of War, c. 1941
Charcoal on paper, 18 x 12 in.
Samuel L. Feinstein Trust
FIGURE 99

Untitled, c. 1943
Charcoal on paper, 20 x 16 in.
Samuel L. Feinstein Trust

Loading Ambulance, 1943
Casein on paper, 7 1/2 x 10 in.
Samuel L. Feinstein Trust
FIGURE 100

Rest in Pieces, 1945
Reproduction of the cover of the V-E Day edition of *The Medical Soldier*, 16 1/2 x 11 in.
Samuel L. Feinstein Trust
FIGURE 101

Still Life, late 1940s
Oil on plywood, 30 x 38 in.
Samuel L. Feinstein Trust
FIGURE 124

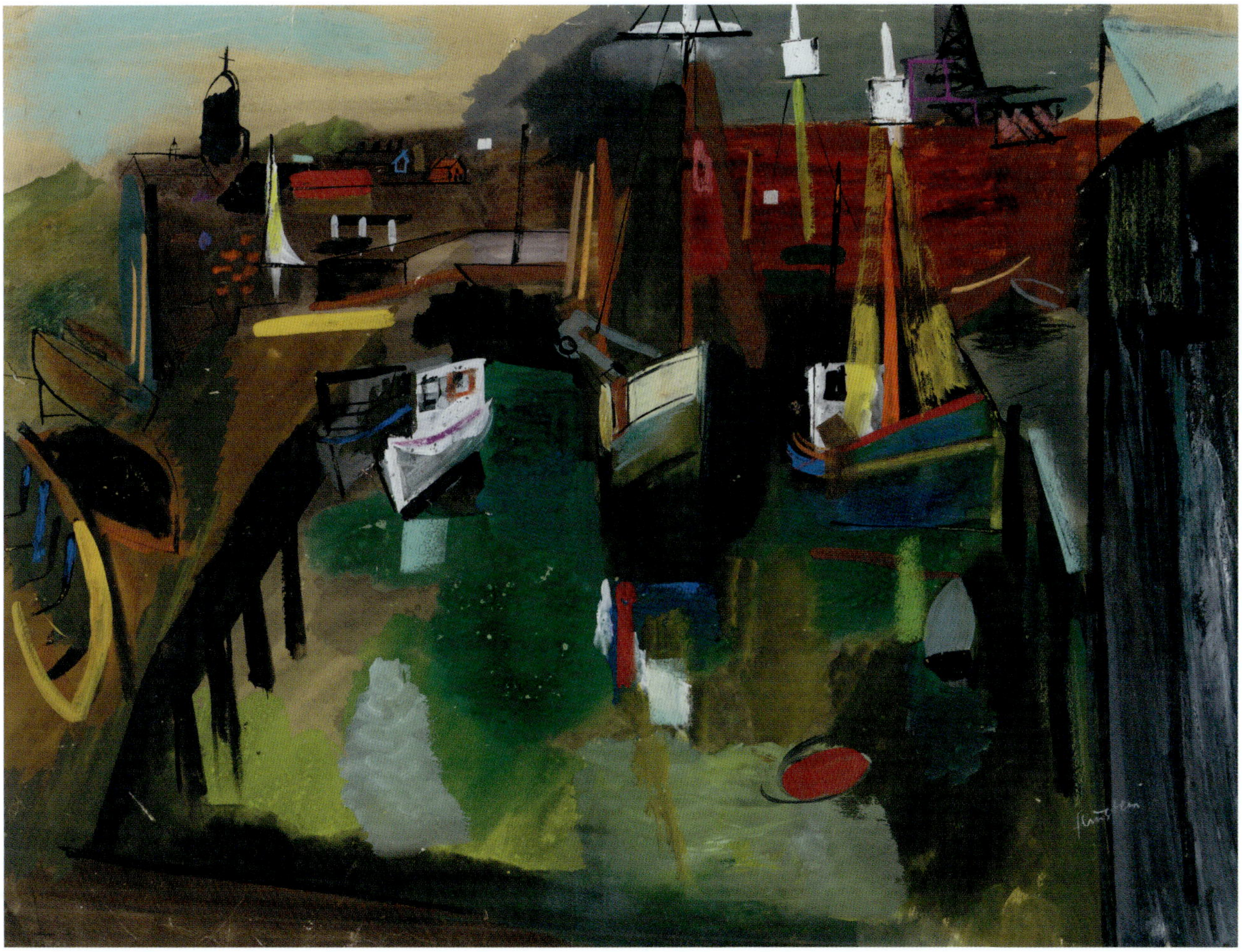

FIGURE 160. **Harbor**, 1947, by Sam Feinstein (Private Collection)

Harbor, 1947
Casein and pastel on paper, 18 x 24 in.
Private Collection
FIGURE 160

Harbor, 1947
Casein and pastel on paper, 20 x 26 in.
Samuel L. Feinstein Trust
FIGURE 102

Untitled, c. 1949
Reproduction of original oil pastel, crayon, and casein on paper, 18 x 24 in.
Samuel L. Feinstein Trust
FIGURE 103

Black Walnuts, 1950
Woodblock print with red ink, 12 x 18 in.
Springside Chestnut Hill Academy
FIGURE 123

Black Walnuts, 1950
Woodblock print, 12 x 18 in.
Samuel L. Feinstein Trust

Untitled, c. 1952
Oil on canvas, 48 x 36 in.
Samuel L. Feinstein Trust
FIGURE 104 AND 88

Untitled, 1952
Oil on Bristol board, 26 x 20 in.
Samuel L. Feinstein Trust
FIGURE 125

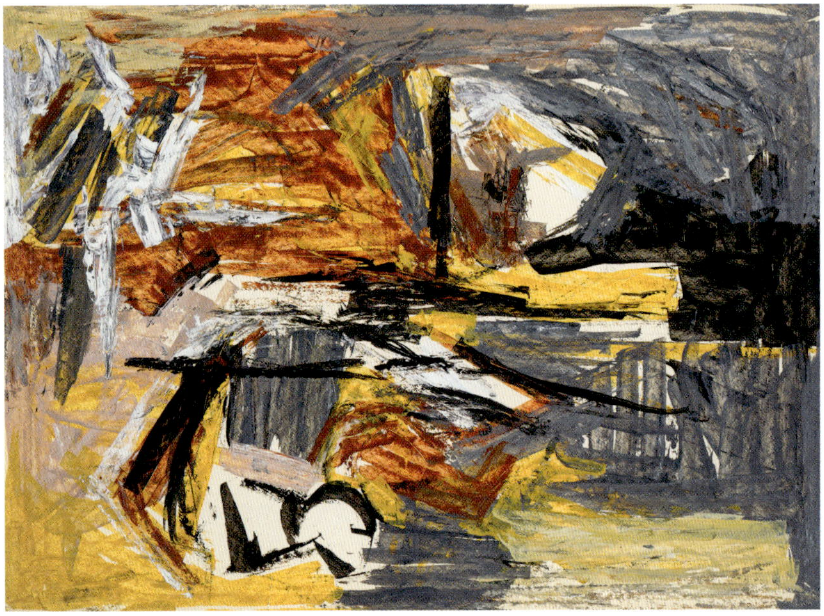

FIGURE 161. **Untitled**, date unknown, by Barbara Crawford (Springside Chestnut Hill Academy)

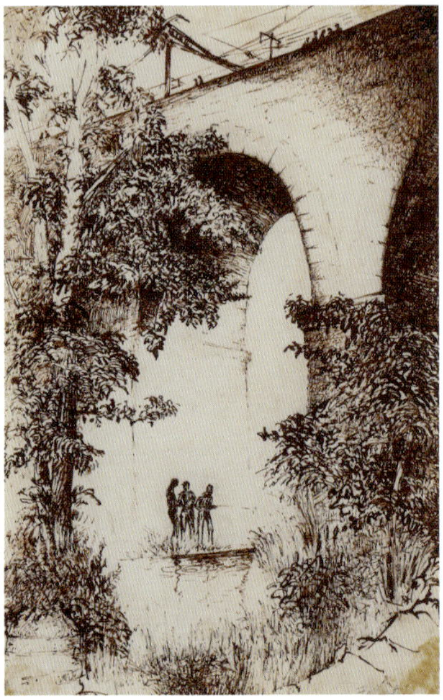

FIGURE 162. **Railroad Bridge at Girard Avenue**, 1936, by Sam Feinstein (Samuel L. Feinstein Trust)

Untitled, mid-1950s
Casein and pastel on paper, 22 x 28 in.
Samuel L. Feinstein Trust
FIGURE 129

Rising, 1970s
Acrylic on canvas, 51 x 41 in.
Samuel L. Feinstein Trust
FIGURE 121

BARBARA CRAWFORD
American, 1914–2003

Market, 1930
Lithograph, 10 3/4 x 17 in.
Springside Chestnut Hill Academy

Sleeping Beauty, 1935
Watercolor, pen, and ink on illustration board, 10 1/2 x 15 in.
Springside Chestnut Hill Academy
FIGURE 3

They Amuse Themselves, They Do Not Sing, They Do Not Dance, 1939
Print, 9 x 12 in.
Courtesy of Lewis Tanner Moore
FIGURE 130

Boats, 1947
Gouache on paper, 10 1/4 x 13 1/2 in.
Springside Chestnut Hill Academy

Waterfall, 1949–50
Oil pastel on board, 22 x 28 in.
Springside Chestnut Hill Academy
FIGURE 126

Untitled, 1950s
Oil on board, 38 x 42 in.
Springside Chestnut Hill Academy

Gold Abstract 1, 1952
Paint on paper, 29 1/2 x 39 1/2 in.
Springside Chestnut Hill Academy

Abstract 2, 1957
Paint on board, 30 x 40 in.
Springside Chestnut Hill Academy
FIGURE 128

Abstract 3, 1972
Oil on canvas, 46 1/2 x 68 in.
Springside Chestnut Hill Academy

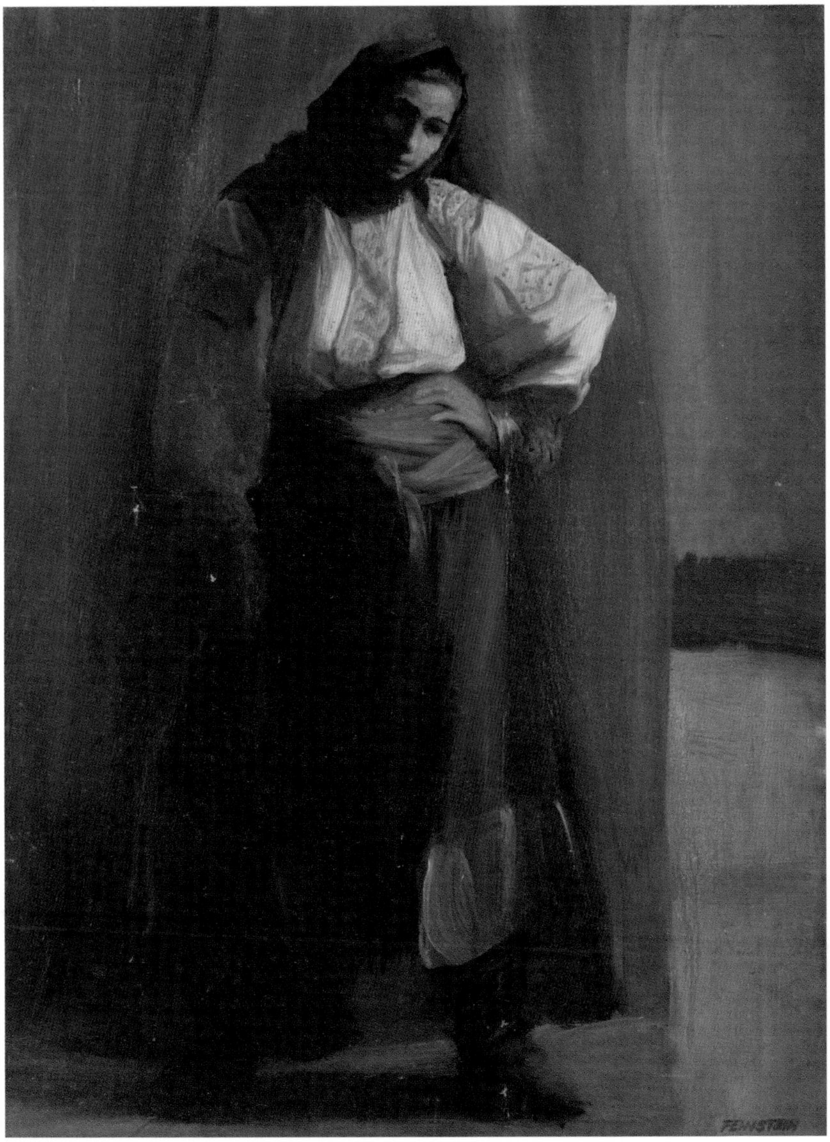

FIGURE 163. Young Woman in Blue, 1930s, by Sam Feinstein (Samuel L. Feinstein Trust)

PHOTOGRAPHS

Barbara Crawford and Sam Feinstein
Samuel L. Feinstein Trust

Hans Hofmann in his studio, 1951; photograph by Sam Feinstein
Samuel L. Feinstein Trust

The Feinstein family in Bucharest
Samuel L. Feinstein Trust

Sam Feinstein analyzing a painting in class, late 1950s
Samuel L. Feinstein Trust

Sam Feinstein painting on-site
Samuel L. Feinstein Trust

Sam Feinstein with *Still Life*, c. 1995
Courtesy of Sascha Feinstein

Sam Feinstein working as a commercial artist
Samuel L. Feinstein Trust

FILM

Hans Hofmann, 1950; documentary film by Sam Feinstein, with narration by Hofmann and Feinstein
Samuel L. Feinstein Trust

Group '55 and Midcentury Abstraction in Philadelphia

September 26, 2020–January 24, 2021
Catherine M. Kuch Gallery, Woodmere Art Museum

WORKS IN THE EXHIBITION

MARGO ALLMAN
American, born 1933

Nicht Wahr Hans Hofmann, 1955
Oil on canvas, 25 1/2 x 20 1/2 in.
Courtesy of the artist
FIGURE 30

EDNA ANDRADE
American, 1917–2008

Untitled, 1960s
Ink on paper, 24 x 32 in.
Courtesy of Elizabeth Osborne
FIGURE 166

C. RONALD BECHTLE
American, 1924–2014

Untitled, 1957–59
Oil on canvas, 32 x 36 in.
Woodmere Art Museum: Gift of Reid and Dorothy Bechtle, 2020
FIGURE 54 AND 131

Man with a Guitar, 1958
Oil on canvas, 28 x 21 in.
Courtesy of Reid and Dorothy Bechtle
FIGURE 167

Untitled, 1958–59
Oil on canvas, 30 x 36 in.
Woodmere Art Museum: Gift of Reid and Dorothy Bechtle, 2020
FIGURE 50

BENJAMIN BRITT
American, 1923–1996

Untitled (Abstract), c. 1950s
Oil on paper on board, 20 x 16 in.
Woodmere Art Museum: Museum purchase, 2015
FIGURE 34

QUITA BRODHEAD
American, 1901–2002

Still Life with Mandolin, c. 1940–42
Oil on canvas, 24 x 21 3/4 in.
Woodmere Art Museum: Gift of Bill Scott, 2011
FIGURE 146

From a Peach Orchard, 1954
Oil on board, 20 x 24 in.
Woodmere Art Museum: Gift of Bill Scott, 2011
FIGURE 28

Abstract #1, c. 1955
Oil on canvas, 64 x 45 in.
Woodmere Art Museum: Gift of the Brodhead Family, 2013
FIGURE 49

ARTHUR B. CARLES
American, 1882–1952

Abstract Bouquet, 1939
Oil on canvas, 33 1/2 x 39 1/2 in.
Woodmere Art Museum: Partial museum purchase and partial gift of Fredrica and Howard Wagman, 2011
FIGURE 12

MICHAEL CILIBERTI
American, 1925–2020

Group 55, c. 1956
Oil on canvas, 39 3/4 x 25 in.
Collection of Valerie Ciliberti
FIGURE 8

Untitled, 1960
Gouache on paper, 20 1/2 x 27 3/8 in.
Woodmere Art Museum: Gift of the artist, 2016
FIGURE 2

BARBARA CRAWFORD
American, 1914–2003

Untitled, date unknown
Acrylic on paper, 20 x 30 in.
Springside Chestnut Hill Academy
FIGURE 147

LARRY DAY
American, 1921–1998

Various Asides, c. 1958
Oil on canvas, 29 x 23 in.
Woodmere Art Museum: Gift of Gregory and Candace Wilkin, 2017
FIGURE 19

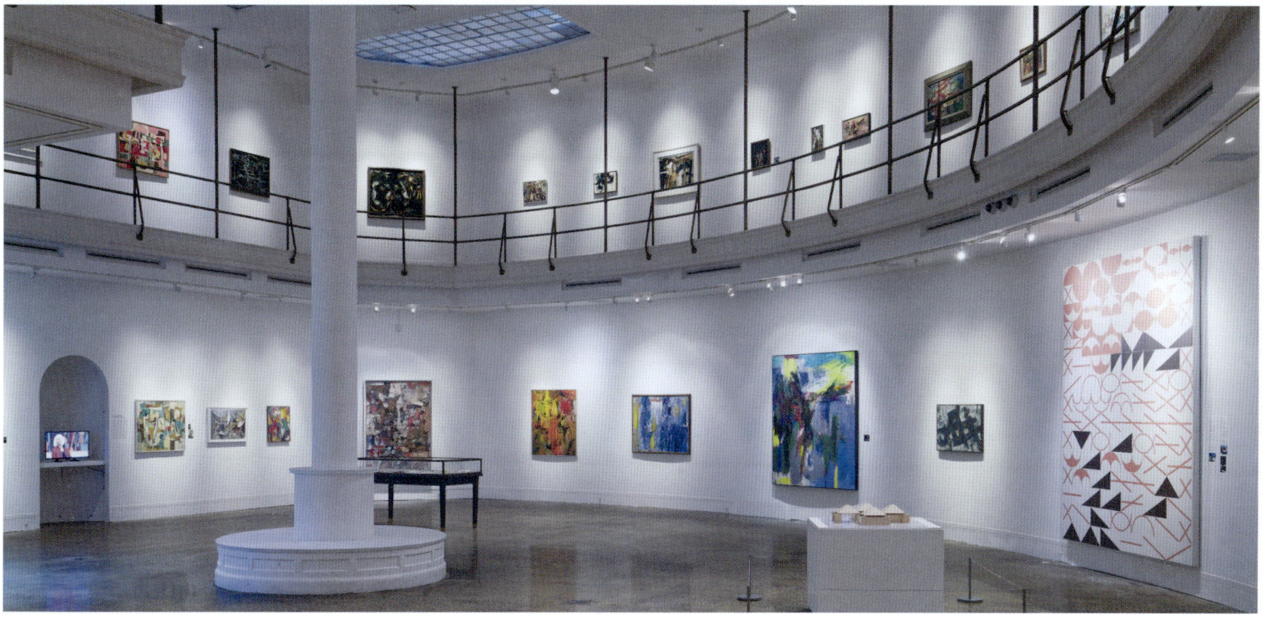

FIGURE 164. Installation view of *Group '55 and Midcentury Abstraction in Philadelphia*

SAM FEINSTEIN
American born Russia, 1915–2003

Untitled, 1955
Watercolor and pastel, 19 x 24 in.
Samuel L. Feinstein Trust
FIGURE 59

Pieta I, 1956
Oil on canvas, 48 x 36 in.
Samuel L. Feinstein Trust
FIGURE 6, DETAIL ON COVER

Pieta II, 1957
Oil on canvas, 48 x 36 in.
Samuel L. Feinstein Trust
FIGURE 24

Untitled, 1958
Oil on canvas, 47 1/2 x 34 in.
Samuel L. Feinstein Trust
FIGURE 109

Untitled, 1959
Oil on canvas, 82 x 72 in.
Samuel L. Feinstein Trust
FIGURE 1

EUGENE FELDMAN
American, 1921–1975

Drip Print, 1956
Offset lithograph, 20 x 26 in.
Woodmere Art Museum: Gift of Rosina Feldman, 2008
FIGURE 36

Printer's Cornfield, 1956
Offset lithograph, 22 1/2 x 35 1/8 in.
Woodmere Art Museum: Gift of Rosina Feldman, 2008
FIGURE 148

SAM FREID
American, 1908–1983

Hawks over Appomattox, June 24, 1955
Pastel on paper, 18 x 24 in.
Woodmere Art Museum: Museum purchase with funds generously provided by Patricia Stark Feinstein, 2019
FIGURE 27

THOMAS GAUGHAN
American, born England, 1925–2007

Cascade, date unknown
Oil on canvas, 16 x 10 3/4 in.
Woodmere Art Museum: Gift of Harvey S. Shipley Miller in memory of Betty E. Miller, 2015
FIGURE 149

Morning, date unknown
Oil on canvas, 12 x 22 in.
Courtesy of Esther and Stephen Hrabrick
FIGURE 152

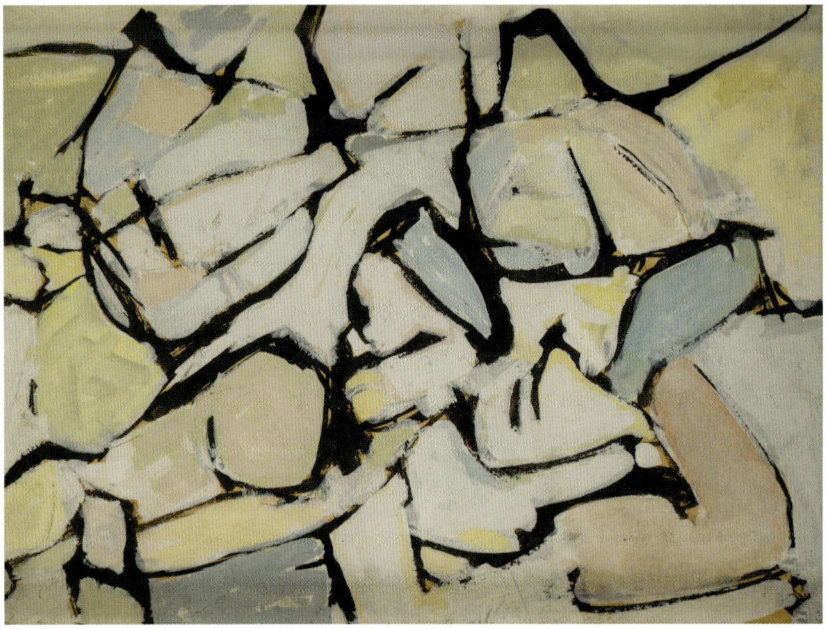

FIGURE 165. **Untitled**, 1950–52, from the *Maze* series, by Melville Price (Collection of Andrea Herr-Turoff)

Winter Landscape, 1958
Oil on canvas, 40 x 48 in.
Courtesy of Esther and Stephen Hrabrick
FIGURE 63

SANFORD GREENBERG
American, 1926–2011

Untitled (Abstract), 1949
Oil on canvas, 28 x 34 in.
Woodmere Art Museum: Museum purchase, 2014
FIGURE 151

No. 4, 1955
Oil on canvas, 49 x 39 1/4 in.
Sanford Greenberg Estate
FIGURE 156

No. 24, 1955
Oil on canvas, 14 1/4 x 20 in.
Woodmere Art Museum: Museum purchase, 2014
FIGURE 57

Untitled, 1955
Oil on canvas, 42 x 51 in.
Private Collection
FIGURE 64

ABRAHAM P. HANKINS
American, born Russia, 1903–1963

Still Life, c. 1950
Oil on board, 12 x 16 in.
Woodmere Art Museum: Museum purchase, 2019
FIGURE 150

Halibut Point, 1951
Serigraph, 11 7/8 x 9 7/8 in.
Woodmere Art Museum: Museum purchase, 2018
FIGURE 37

RAYMOND HENDLER
American, 1923–1998

(No. 9), 1952
Oil on canvas, 70 x 20 in.
Woodmere Art Museum: Gift of the Estate of Raymond Hendler, 2020
FIGURE 26

Grand Marais (No. 3), 1955
Oil on canvas, 16 x 22 in.
Woodmere Art Museum: Gift of the Estate of Raymond Hendler, 2020
FIGURE 42

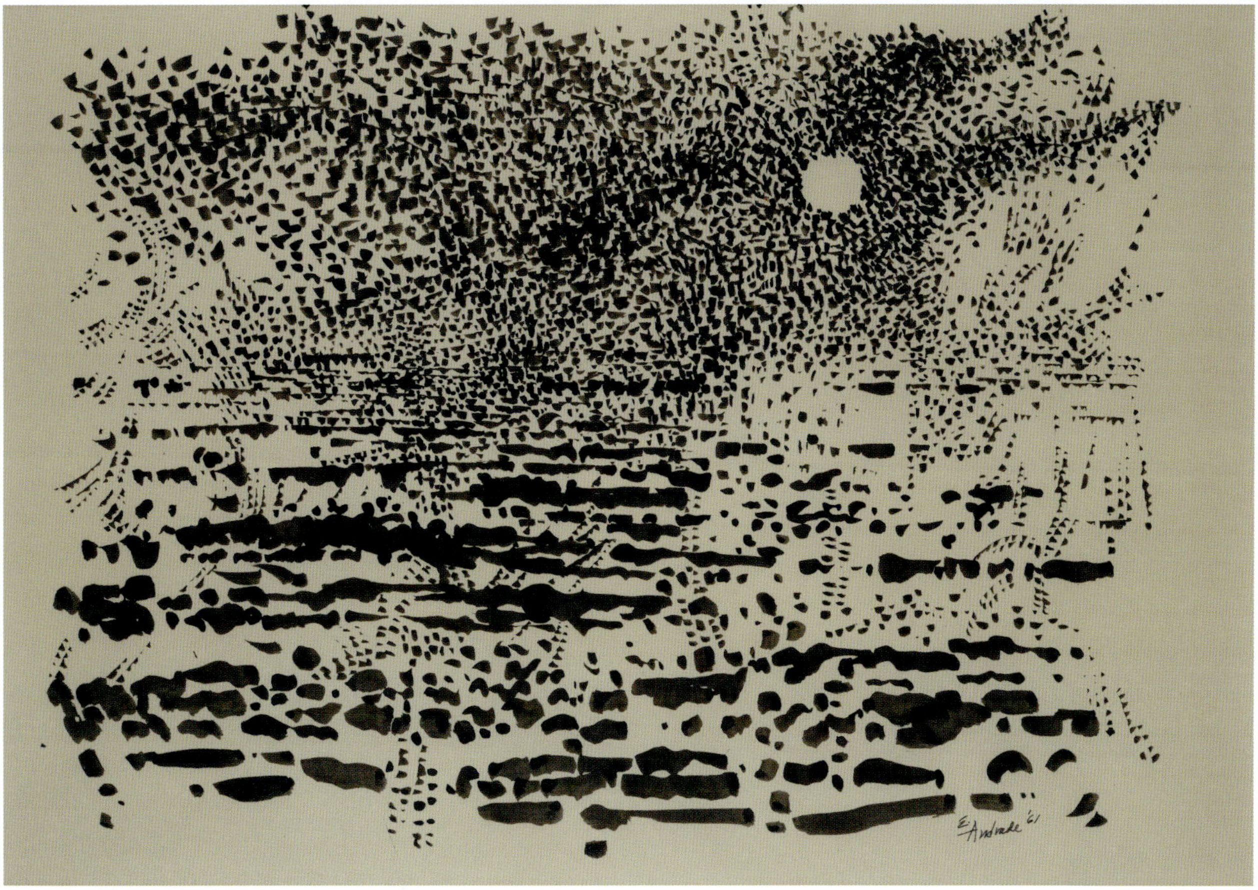

FIGURE 166. **Untitled**, 1960s, by Edna Andrade (Courtesy of Elizabeth Osborne)

BEN HERR
American, 1935–2019

Gettysburg, 1955
Oil and enamel with mixed media on Upson board, 72 x 48 in.
Collection of Andrea Herr-Turoff
FIGURE 14

For the Hungarian Revolution, 1956
Collage elements with paint, 23 x 31 in.
Collection of Andrea Herr-Turoff
FIGURE 155

LOUIS KAHN
American, 1901–1974

ANNE TYNG
American, 1920–2011

Model of the Trenton Bathhouse, 1991
Wood, acrylic, and metal, 6 1/2 x 32 x 32 in.
Fabricated by Bill Christensen, Linda Brenner, and Laurie Kass
Architectural Archives, University of Pennsylvania, by gift of the Museum of Contemporary Art, Los Angeles
FIGURES 72 AND 73

LOUIS KAHN
American, 1901–1974

MARIE KUO
Life dates unknown

Replica of Trenton Mural, 2012
Acrylic on cotton canvas, 11 ft x 8 ft x 2 1/2 in.
Fabricated by Canning Studios
Architectural Archives, University of Pennsylvania, by gift of the Vitra Design Museum
FIGURES 70

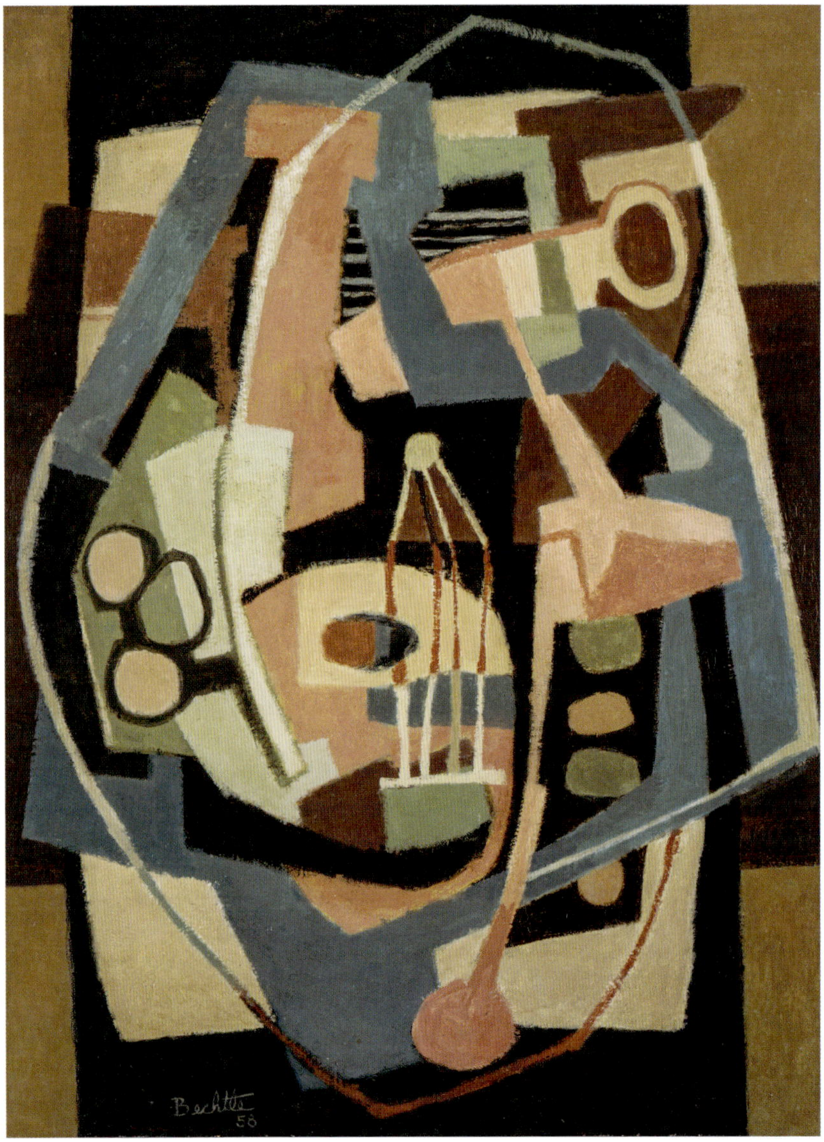

FIGURE 167. **Man with a Guitar**, 1958, by C. Ronald Bechtle (Courtesy of Reid & Dorothy Bechtle)

PAUL F. KEENE JR.
American, 1920–2009

Blues Singer, 1958
Mixed media on Strathmore laid paper, 18 x 24 in.
Courtesy of Terenchin Gallery
FIGURE 33

FRANCES LACHMAN
American, 1913–1994

September, 1957
Oil on linen, 28 x 26 in.
Woodmere Art Museum: Gift of the Lachman Family, 2020
FIGURE 29

SAMUEL MAITIN
American, 1928–2004

Figure of a Woman, 1956–57
Woodcut, 23 x 10 3/4 in.
Woodmere Art Museum: Gift of Ronald Rumford, 2002
FIGURE 62

PATRICIA EVANS MANGIONE
American, 1915–2002

Garden Gate, c. 1955
Oil on canvas, 20 x 30 in.
Woodmere Art Museum: Museum purchase, 2019
FIGURE 20

JACK MAYERSON
American, 1908–1985

Untitled, c. 1955–56
Oil on canvas, 12 x 22 in.
Woodmere Art Museum: Gift of Patricia Stark Feinstein, 2020
FIGURE 145

HAROLD MESIBOV
American, 1928–2012

Untitled, 1950s
Watercolor, 18 x 24 in.
Private Collection
FIGURE 154

LEONARD NELSON
American, 1912–1993

Woman and Birds, 1952
Oil on canvas, 36 x 40 in.
Woodmere Art Museum: Museum purchase, 2019
FIGURE 52

PETER PAONE
American, born 1936

Untitled, 1957
Oil on canvas, 40 x 35 1/2 in.
Woodmere Art Museum: Museum purchase, 2019
FIGURE 11

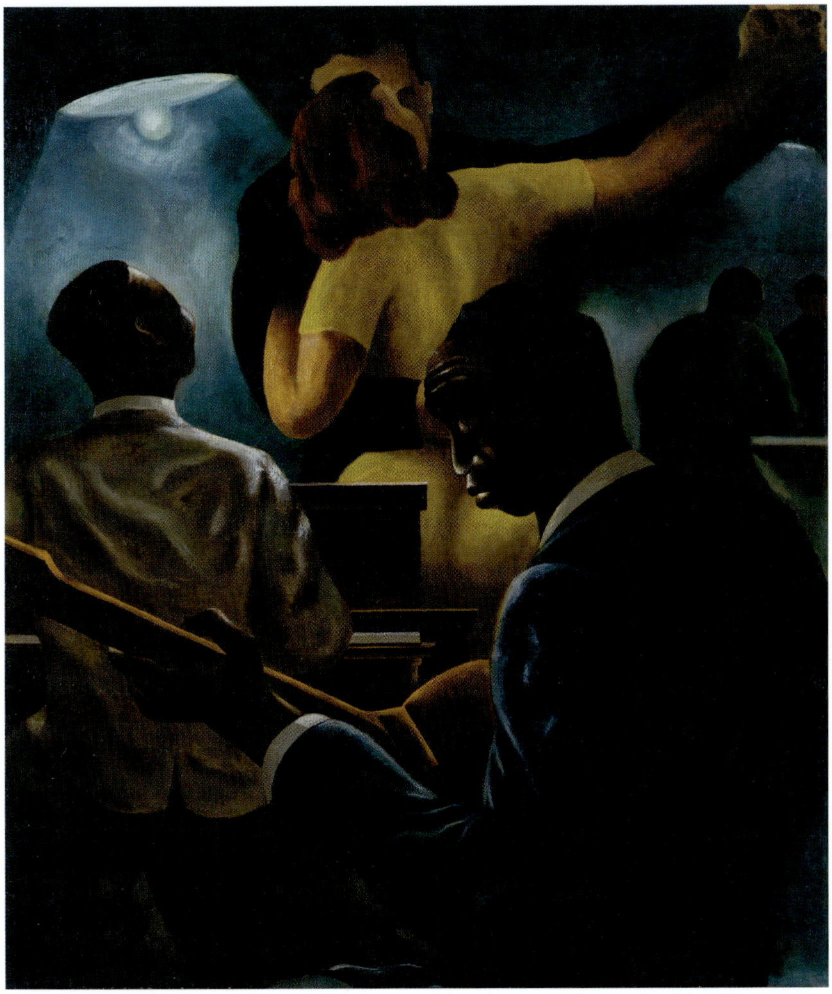

FIGURE 168. **7th Street Cellar**, c. 1951, by C. Ronald Bechtle (Woodmere Art Museum: Gift of Reid and Dorothy Bechtle, 2020)

ITZHAK SANKOWSKY
American, born Romania, 1908–1994

Self-Portrait, 1953
Woodblock print with hand-coloring, 22 x 17 1/2 in.
Woodmere Art Museum: Gift of Roslyn Silverman Hahn, 2013
FIGURE 35

DORIS STAFFEL
American, 1921–2013

Untitled, c. 1950
Oil on canvas, 24 x 24 in.
Woodmere Art Museum: Gift of the artist, 2011
FIGURE 43

MITCHEL G. WAGMAN
American, 1923–2002

Time #4, 1955
Oil on canvas, 53 x 51 in.
Collection of Laurie Wagman
FIGURE 55

Untitled, 1960
From *Zen Series 2*
Oil on canvas, 15 1/2 x 14 in.
Estate of Mitchel G. Wagman
FIGURE 46

RUTH ZION
American, 1923–2010

Abstract, 1959
Oil on French linen, gesso, 50 x 51 in.
Private Collection
FIGURE 32

JANE PIPER
American, 1916–1991

Trade Winds 2, 1958
Oil on canvas, 30 1/2 x 36 in.
Woodmere Art Museum: Gift of Karen Segal, 2017
FIGURES 5 AND 153

Landscape towards Abstraction (Torremolinos), 1958–59
Oil on canvas, 19 3/4 x 24 1/8 in.
Woodmere Art Museum: Gift of Karen Segal, 2017
FIGURE 45

MELVILLE PRICE
American, 1920–1970

Untitled, 1950–52
From the *Maze Series*
Gouache and ink on board, 14 3/8 x 10 7/8 in.
Collection of Andrea Herr-Turoff
FIGURE 165

The Tornado, 1954
Oil on canvas, 24 x 36 in.
Woodmere Art Museum: Gift of Barbara Gillette Price, 2020
FIGURE 40

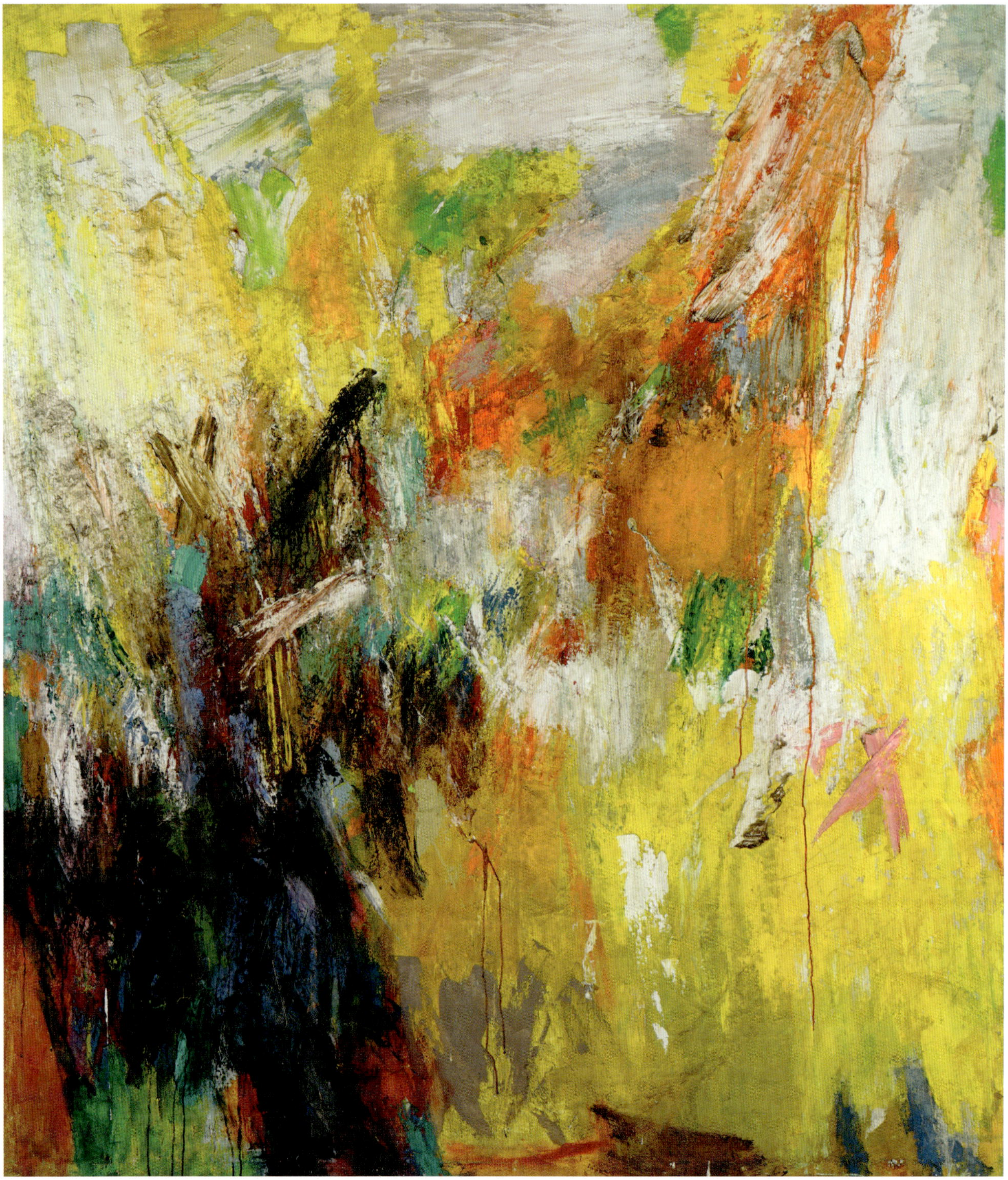

FIGURE 169. **Untitled**, 1960, by Sam Feinstein (Samuel L. Feinstein Trust) Photograph by Laszlo Bodo

Sam Feinstein: Immersive Abstraction

July 24, 2020–January 24, 2021
Ethel M. Schnader Gallery, Woodmere Art Museum

WORKS IN THE EXHIBITION

All works are by Sam Feinstein, American, born Russia, 1915–2003. All works are in the collection of the Samuel L. Feinstein Trust.

Untitled, 1960
Oil on canvas, 82 x 72 in.
FIGURES 158 AND 169

Nightscape, 1980s
Acrylic on canvas, 52 x 40 in.
FIGURE 112

The Cry, 1980s
Acrylic on canvas, 79 1/4 x 65 in.
FIGURE 115

Untitled, 1988–2002
Acrylic on canvas, 55 x 65 in.
FIGURE 111

Requiem, 1990s
Acrylic on canvas, 77 x 84 in.
FIGURE 114

Untitled, 1996–2000
Acrylic on canvas, 83 x 94 1/2 in.
FIGURE 113

"These paintings are optical structures composed to touch human spirit, to turn a rectangle into an evocation."
—Sam Feinstein, 1986

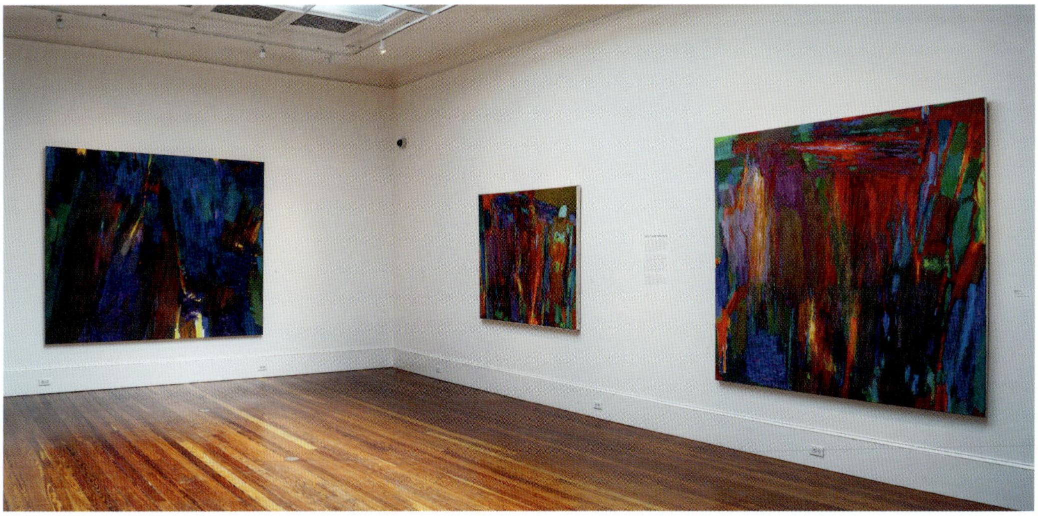

FIGURE 170. Installation view of *Sam Feinstein: Immersive Abstraction.* Photograph by Laszlo Bodo